THE FUTURE OF MEDICAL DEVICE REGULATION

Regulators have been more permissive for medical devices compared to their drug and biologic counterparts. While innovative products can thereby reach consumers more quickly, this approach raises serious public health and safety concerns. Additionally, the nature of medical devices is rapidly changing, as software has become as important as hardware. Regulation must keep pace with the current developments and controversies of this technology. This volume provides a multidisciplinary evaluation of the ethical, legal, and regulatory concerns surrounding medical devices in the United States and European Union. For medical providers, policymakers, and other stakeholders, the book offers a framework for the opportunities and challenges on the horizon for medical device regulation. Readers will gain a nuanced overview of the latest developments in patient privacy and safety, innovation, and new regulatory laws. This book is also available as Open Access on Cambridge Core.

I. Glenn Cohen is James A. Attwood and Leslie Williams Professor of Law, Deputy Dean, and Faculty Director at the Petrie-Flom Center for Health Law Policy, Biotechnology, and Bioethics at Harvard Law School.

Timo Minssen is Professor of Law and Director of the Center for Advanced Studies in Biomedical Innovation Law (CeBIL) at the Faculty of Law, University of Copenhagen, Denmark.

W. Nicholson Price II is Professor of Law at the University of Michigan School of Law.

Christopher Robertson is Professor and N. Neal Pike Scholar in Health & Disability Law at the School of Law, Boston University.

Carmel Shachar is Executive Director of the Petrie-Flom Center for Health Law Policy, Biotechnology, and Bioethics at Harvard Law School.

The Future of Medical Device Regulation

INNOVATION AND PROTECTION

Edited by

I. GLENN COHEN

Harvard Law School

TIMO MINSSEN

University of Copenhagen

W. NICHOLSON PRICE II

University of Michigan

CHRISTOPHER ROBERTSON

Boston University

CARMEL SHACHAR

Harvard Law School

CAMBRIDGE
UNIVERSITY PRESS

CAMBRIDGE
UNIVERSITY PRESS

Shaftesbury Road, Cambridge CB2 8EA, United Kingdom

One Liberty Plaza, 20th Floor, New York, NY 10006, USA

477 Williamstown Road, Port Melbourne, VIC 3207, Australia

314–321, 3rd Floor, Plot 3, Splendor Forum, Jasola District Centre, New Delhi – 110025, India

103 Penang Road, #05–06/07, Visioncrest Commercial, Singapore 238467

Cambridge University Press is part of Cambridge University Press & Assessment, a department of the University of Cambridge.

We share the University's mission to contribute to society through the pursuit of education, learning, and research at the highest international levels of excellence.

www.cambridge.org
Information on this title: www.cambridge.org/9781108838634
DOI: 10.1017/9781108975452

First published 2022

A catalogue record for this publication is available from the British Library.

ISBN 978-1-108-83863-4 Hardback
ISBN 978-1-108-97205-5 Paperback

Glenn Cohen:
For Peter Barton Hutt, who taught me everything I know about FDA and much more.

Timo Minssen:
For my family, Effie and friends who helped me to "hang in there"!

W. Nicholson Price II:
For Ana Bracic, who makes life better, and Suzanne Wilsey, who first taught me to edit.

Christopher Robertson:
For my family.

Carmel Shachar:
For my mother, although Consumer Genetics would have been a more apt fit.

Contents

Figures

Tables

Contributors

Mateo Aboy, University of Cambridge

Adeyemi Adediran, J.D. 2021, Harvard Law School

Barbara Andraka-Christou, University of Central Florida

Elisabetta Biasin, KU Leuven Centre for IT & IP Law

Mark G. Bloom, TechNomos, Inc.

I. Glenn Cohen, Harvard Law School

Marcelo Corrales Compagnucci, University of Copenhagen

Nathan Cortez, SMU Dedman School of Law

Jonathan J. Darrow, Harvard Medical School

Sanket S. Dhruva, University of California, San Francisco

Lori Ann Eldridge, Indiana University

Wendy Netter Epstein, DePaul University College of Law

Barbara J. Evans, University of Florida

Joseph J. Fins, Weill Cornell Medical College

Sara Gerke, Penn State Law

Matthew Herder, Schulich School of Law, Dalhousie University

Thomas J. Hwang, Brigham and Women's Hospital; Harvard Medical School

Erik Kamenjasevic, KU Leuven Centre for IT & IP Law

Aaron S. Kesselheim, Brigham and Women's Hospital; Harvard Medical School

Craig Konnoth, University of Colorado Law School

Daniel B. Kramer, Beth Israel Deaconess Medical Center; Harvard Medical School

Katherine L. Kraschel, Yale Law School

Jody Lyneé Madeira, Maurer School of Law, Indiana University

Preeti Mehrotra, Beth Israel Deaconess Medical Center; Harvard Medical School

Janos Meszaros, KU Leuven Centre for IT & IP Law

Timo Minssen, University of Copenhagen

Efthimios Parasidis, The Ohio State University

Frank Pasquale, Brooklyn Law School

W. Nicholson Price II, University of Michigan School of Law

Rita F. Redberg, University of California, San Francisco

Barak D. Richman, Duke University School of Law

Christopher Robertson, Boston University School of Law

David Rosenberg, Harvard Law School

Ameet Sarpatwari, Brigham and Women's Hospital; Harvard Medical School

Carmel Shachar, Harvard Law School

Jacob S. Sherkow, University of Illinois College of Law

Ross D. Silverman, Indiana University

Barry Solaiman, Hamad Bin Khalifa University

Hannah van Kolfschooten, University of Amsterdam

Kerstin N. Vokinger, University of Zurich

David J. Weber, University of Maryland School of Medicine

Anthony P. Weiss, Beth Israel Deaconess Medical Center; Harvard Medical School

Megan S. Wright, Penn State Law

Helen Yu, University of Copenhagen

Acknowledgments

A book like this is the result of the hard work of many. We thank our student line editors for their meticulous work.[1] We are grateful to Cristine Hutchison-Jones and Chloe Reichel for their administrative support in organizing the conference that gave rise to this book as well as nimbly translating it into a podcast series when disrupted by COVID-19. We are also grateful for Laura Chong's hard work shepherding all the many pieces of this manuscript.

This book was made possible in part by the generosity and leadership of the Center for Advanced Studies in Biomedical Innovation Law (CeBIL) at the University of Copenhagen and the support of the Novo Nordisk Foundation through a grant for a Collaborative Research Programme (grant agreement number NNF17SA0027784). We thankfully acknowledge the Petrie-Flom Center for Health Law Policy, Biotechnology, and Bioethics at Harvard Law School, with support from the Oswald DeN. Cammann Fund, for conference sponsorship. Finally, of course, we thank the contributors for their thoughtful and important scholarly contributions.

[1] Melyssa Eigen, Brian Brooks, and Nathan Rabb.

Volume Introduction

I. Glenn Cohen, Timo Minssen, W. Nicholson Price II, Christopher Robertson, and Carmel Shachar

Medical devices have historically been less regulated than their drug and biologic counterparts. A benefit of this less demanding regulatory regime is facilitating innovation by making new devices available to consumers in a timely fashion. Nevertheless, there is increasing concern that this approach raises serious public health and safety concerns. The Institute of Medicine in 2011 published a critique of the American pathway allowing moderate-risk devices to be brought to the market through the less-rigorous 501(k) pathway,[1] flagging a need for increased postmarket review and surveillance. High-profile recalls of medical devices, such as vaginal mesh products, along with reports globally of nearly two million injuries and more than 80,000 deaths linked to faulty medical devices,[2] have raised public health critiques regarding the oversight of these products. Should we follow the recommendation of the Institute of Medicine to reduce the use of the 510(k) pathway, and, if so, what should replace it? What would an ideal regulatory pathway, reflecting the twin goals of innovation and patient protection, look like in the twenty-first century? These questions are complicated by new tools and mechanisms that can be used to achieve our goals. For example, in an era of big data, where we have the capabilities to better follow postmarket incidents, what should postmarket review look like?

Speaking of new tools, there is a digital revolution happening in the field of medical devices. Devices have traditionally been hardware, but are now increasingly hybrids of hardware and software, or even software as a medical device (SaMD). Of course, software is revised much more frequently than hardware, especially when it involves machine learning. To address the challenges of overseeing SaMDs, the Food and Drug Administration (FDA) launched the software precertification program in 2017. The FDA proposed a new framework to review ongoing artificial

[1] Medical Devices and the Public's Health: FDA 510(k) Clearance Process at 35 Years, 13150 (2011), http://www.nap.edu/catalog/13150.

[2] The Implant Files: a Global Investigation into Medical Devices, ICIJ, http://www.icij.org/investigations/implant-files/.

intelligence algorithm changes for device software,[3] using a total product lifecycle approach to regulate these algorithms, and recently began to implement this framework.[4] What does a robust regulatory regime for medical device software look like in the coming years?

Across the Atlantic, the European Union adopted new medical device regulations[5] that have been somewhat delayed by the COVID-19 pandemic but will be implemented in the coming years. These regulations are meant to address safety and effectiveness concerns, including increasing postmarket surveillance and establishing an EU database on medical devices, as well as a response to some of the innovations that have occurred in the medical device field. These new regulations, coupled with the experiences of the FDA in the United States, suggest that medical device regulation overall faces some global challenges, including the correct balance between patient protection and avoiding stifling business and innovation, the changing nature of medical devices that are increasingly software-based, and the difficulties of postmarket surveillance. How might these concerns be expressed and successfully addressed in a variety of countries, each with a different medical device market?

This edited volume provides an overview of the challenges facing medical device regulation in the twenty-first century. The volume will explore the tension between facilitating innovation and access to devices while protecting patient safety. At times the volume will pay specific attention to key developments, such as the rise of software and data as medical devices, the need to modernize regulation to accommodate these new products, and the differences between the American and European approaches to medical device regulations. The reader will gain a sense of the current state of medical device regulation, but also a framework for developments, opportunities, and challenges on the horizon.

This book is divided into five parts. Part I, *AI and Data as Medical Devices*, introduced by W. Nicholson Price II, focuses on what is perhaps the most exciting and cutting-edge topic currently in medical device regulation. These chapters explore the digital health revolution, and the struggle of regulators to keep up with the changing landscape of medical products. Certainly, algorithms and data sets used in medical treatment can be thought of as medical products that can impact patient outcomes and lives just as significantly as physical devices and pharmaceuticals. But how should we regulate these less-tangible products?

Kerstin Vokinger, Thomas Hwang, and Aaron Kesselheim, in their chapter, "Lifecycle Regulation and Evaluation of Artificial Intelligence and Machine

[3] US Food & Drug Admin., Proposed Regulatory Framework for Modifications to Artificial Intelligence/Machine Learning (AI/ML)-based Software as a Medical Device (SaMD) (2019), https://www.fda.gov/media/122535/download.

[4] US Food & Drug Admin., Artificial Intelligence/Machine Learning (AI/ML)-Based Software as a Medical Device Action Plan (2021), https://www.fda.gov/media/145022/download.

[5] European Parliament and the Council of the European Union, Regulation (EU) 2017/745 on Medical Devices (2017), https://eur-lex.europa.eu/legal-content/EN/TXT/PDF/?uri=CELEX:32017R0745.

Learning-Based Medical Devices," introduce the reader to the most significant difference between regulating classic devices and software: the challenge of plasticity in attempting to regulate constantly updating products. Virtually all AI-powered software will include updates, meaning that the product on the market may differ significantly from what regulators evaluated during the approval process. The authors first consider the approaches already taken by the FDA as well as European regulators. They then argue that regulators must pursue a complex strategy based on the lifecycle of AI-powered software. This strategy would ideally incorporate significant evidence for safety and effectiveness prior to market entry, preapproved "safe harbor" updates and changes that would require minimal regulatory oversight to implement, and a high level of transparency to empower patients and providers using these products.

Barbara Evans and Frank Pasquale, in their chapter, "Product Liability Suits for FDA-Regulated AI/ML Software," consider the interplay between the American regulatory and litigation systems when it comes to AI-powered software. They illustrate to the reader that choices made by regulators may shape how these products are treated in liability suits. By the very act of regulating at least some software as a medical device and therefore a product, the FDA essentially resolves the light wave-particle duality of whether these algorithms are products or services. This is an important development because it opens the door to potential product liability and shapes how tort law may govern AI-powered software systems in the future. This chapter demonstrates to the reader that there are multiple paths to consumer protection when it comes to medical devices, and that these paths do not exist entirely independent of each other.

Craig Konnoth closes this section with his contribution, "Are Electronic Health Records Medical Devices?," which focuses more specifically on electronic health records (EHR) rather than AI-powered software. Konnoth articulates why EHR systems are poorly suited for FDA regulation, focusing particularly on their wide-ranging use that connects a variety of different stakeholders in the health care system. As a result, he argues, the FDA should not serve as the sole regulatory agency to govern EHR systems. Instead, other agencies, such as the Office of the National Coordinator for Health Information Technology, could better guide the development, implementation, and marketing of these products. Konnoth's chapter is interesting to read directly after the work by Evans and Pasquale, because in a way they reach the same conclusion: with novel technologies there are multiple ways to regulate that could and should be implemented.

Part II, *The European Regulation of Medical Devices*, introduced by Timo Minssen, takes the reader from the United States to the European Union. Beyond the obvious geographical shift in focus, this part introduces the reader to a regulatory regime that involves significant change in its approach to governing medical devices. In 2017, EU Regulation 2017/745 and EU Regulation 2017/746 significantly changed the regulatory framework for medical devices and in vitro diagnostic medical devices. While the COVID-19 pandemic has delayed the implementation of these new regulations, stakeholders in the European Union are facing significant changes in the governance of medical devices in the next few years, including incorporating new laws, guidance documents, policy papers, and other sub-regulatory materials. The authors of the chapters in Part II explore the choices made by EU regulators, which parallel at times but also diverge at times from the decisions made by their US counterparts. These chapters all focus on some aspect of digital health, making Part II very much the European counterpart to Part I. This focus should indicate to the reader the importance of incorporating digital health products into the medical device regulatory framework, as well as the complexities of doing so.

Elisabetta Biasin and Erik Kamenjasevic open Part II with their chapter, "Cybersecurity of Medical Devices: Regulatory Challenges in the European Union." Biasin and Kamenjasevic build upon the contributions from Part I to explore EU cybersecurity policy objectives. Their chapter also bears some similarity to Aboy and Sherkow's as well as Gerke's, in that they explore the intersection of two regulatory frameworks: in this case, the medical devices legal framework with cybersecurity regulations. Biasin and Kamenjasevic ultimately conclude that the cybersecurity needs of digital hospital systems and medical devices have not been met and urge EU regulators to take concrete action to address regulatory gaps in this area.

Hannah van Kolfschooten considers a different aspect of digital health in her chapter, "The mHealth Power Paradox: Improving Data Protection in Health Apps through Self-Regulation in the European Union," namely the rise of mobile health and health-focused apps. van Kolfschooten introduces the reader to the General Data Protection Regulation (GDPR) that governs much of European data privacy and security. She concludes that the GDPR, coupled with industry self-regulation in app stores such as Google's Google Play, does not provide sufficient protection for consumers. Similar to Biasin and Kamenjasevic, van Kolfschooten proposes several policy suggestions to better protect stakeholders, although she focuses her recommendations on the self-regulation practiced by app stores. This chapter flags for the reader that regulation is practiced not just by governmental agencies, but also by other stakeholders such as industry and manufacturers.

Janos Meszaros, Marcelo Corrales Compagnucci, and Timo Minssen also examine the application of the GDPR on digital health product regulations in their contribution, "The Interaction of the Medical Device Regulation and the GDPR: Do European Rules on Privacy and Scientific Research Impair the Safety and Performance of AI Medical Devices?" The three authors attempt to harmonize the new EU Medical Device Regulations with the GDPR's requirements relating to deidentification and scientific research. Ultimately, they are concerned that the interaction of these regulatory regimes "might result in obstacles" for the development and implementation of medical devices relying on data. Again, the reader is reminded that multiple regulatory regimes govern the design, implementation, and marketing of medical devices and often their interactions create inadvertent problems. Here, the authors suggest that harmonization, with an eye to individual's rights and patient safety, can help resolve their concerns.

Barry Solaiman and Mark Bloom turn the focus of Part II to a specific type of digital health product, wearables that utilize AI, in their contribution, "AI, Explainability, and Safeguarding Patient Safety in Europe: Towards a Science-Focused Regulatory Model." Solaiman and Bloom unpack for the reader the difficulties in ensuring that AI-generated predictions are understood and explainable to stakeholders, including policymakers, medical providers, and patients. The authors emphasize that explainability is necessary for informed decision making. In this chapter the reader is asked to consider the relationship between technology and regulations in Solaiman and Bloom's argument for a regulatory model that will "level-up" as the underlying technology improves.

Part II closes with Helen Yu's chapter, "Regulation of Digital Health Technologies in the European Union: Intended versus Actual Use." Yu's chapter demonstrates for the reader that devices, including digital health products, are often used in ways that go beyond their initial purpose. Therefore, we need mechanisms to govern the actual use of medical devices. Unfortunately, both courts and regulators have been inconsistent in their treatment of manufacturers who encourage a gap between intended and actual uses of their products. Yu suggests that a framework is needed to regulate digital health products based on their actual use by consumers, and not just the intended use declared by manufacturers during the regulatory approval process. Yu's chapter serves as a good transition to the latter half of the volume, which is concerned with the postapproval uses of medical devices.

Part III, *Designing Medical Device Regulations*, explores how regulation can shape the design and construction of medical devices. Introduced by I. Glenn Cohen, these chapters document how FDA choices in areas as divergent as patents, digital home health, and drug efficacy evaluations influence the products eventually available to consumers.

Mateo Aboy and Jacob Sherkow open this section with their chapter, "IP and FDA Regulation of De Novo Medical Devices." Aboy and Sherkow explore the fairly recent policy change that allows for a De Novo device to serve as a "predicate" for a follow-on device application under the 510(k) pathway. This change has some significant implications for anticompetitiveness when the predicate device is patented because the holders of that patent can use the patent in question to prevent follow-on device applications from competitors. Striking a balance between promoting innovation, protecting the hard work of device creators, and ensuring patient safety can be very difficult, as Aboy and Sherkow demonstrate.

Matthew Herder and Nathan Cortez follow with their chapter, "A 'DESI' for Devices? Can a Pharmaceutical Program from the 1960s Improve FDA Oversight of Medical Devices?" They provide a historical examination of the "Drug Efficacy Study Implementation" (DESI) program from the mid-twentieth century. The

DESI program resulted in the reevaluation of more than 3,000 drugs for efficacy, using real-world evidence. Herder and Cortez argue that the time is ripe for a DESI 2.0 to focus on medical devices. This chapter introduces the reader to a theme found throughout the book: the challenge of understanding the performance of post-approval medical devices and appropriately monitoring their availability to consumers.

Part III closes with a consideration of the intersection of public health emergency regulations and medical device regulations in Sara Gerke's chapter, "Digital Home Health During the COVID-19 Pandemic: Challenges to Safety, Liability, and Informed Consent, and the Way to Move Forward." Gerke uses the COVID-19 pandemic to explore the application of Emergency Use Authorization (EUA) regulations governed by the PREP Act to medical devices, specifically digital home health products. As further explored in Part III of this volume, our regulatory system struggles to delineate when digital health products should be regulated as medical devices. Some digital home health products do not require FDA review as medical devices, meaning that they also do not require EUA approval. While this may be a benefit to the manufacturer, who can bring these products to market quicker, it can also be problematic in that the manufacturer does not qualify for the immunity protections offered under the PREP Act through EUA status. Unfortunately, this means that the liability outcomes for these products is unclear, which can ultimately leave users unprotected. Gerke's chapter is similar to Aboy and Sherkow's, in that she again illustrates to the reader that disparate regulatory frameworks can have a significant impact on the development, marketing, and access to medical devices for consumers.

Part IV, *The Impact of Medical Device Regulation on Patients and Markets*, introduced by Christopher Robertson, marks the shift of the volume's focus to the effects, both intended and inadvertent, that postapproval medical devices have on their users and other stakeholders. The chapters in Part IV are concerned with the challenge of demonstrating safety and efficacy once a product has gone through the relatively controlled regulatory approval process and are released onto the market. Here the tension becomes evident between innovation – we want to encourage the release of cutting-edge devices and novel uses that will hopefully improve lives – and protection – we struggle to monitor devices once they are released to a broad audience. Much of Part IV is devoted to instances in which the FDA has failed to act sufficiently to protect consumer interests. What regulatory changes would we need to implement to better advocate for the ultimate users of medical devices, the patients? Are these changes feasible in our current system?

Jody Lyneé Madeira, Barbara Andraka-Christou, Lori Ann Eldridge, and Ross Silverman open Part IV with "Clouded Judgement: Preventing Conflicts of Interest in Problem-Solving Courts," a chapter that explores the relationship between the FDA, drug and device manufacturers, and drug courts. The authors focus on a neurostimulation device, "the Bridge," that was originally intended for chronic and acute pain management but was then also approved for managing opioid withdrawal symptoms. The safety and efficacy of the Bridge for opioid withdrawal symptoms is still in doubt, despite the FDA's approval. The authors document the strategy of the Bridge's manufacturers to groom judges and other key drug court personnel in order to promote its use in these programs. The reader should consider the case study of the Bridge as illustrative of the limited ability of the FDA, and other regulatory authorities, to protect patient interests in the face of sophisticated marketing. How can our regulatory systems be improved to require stronger evidence and avoid ethically dubious marketing strategies once products are approved?

We then turn to Wendy Netter Epstein's chapter, "Disrupting the Market for Ineffective Medical Devices." Epstein's contribution is a thoughtful exploration of the value and importance of innovation when it comes to medical devices. Not all innovation is worth the tradeoffs it may pose. Epstein focuses on the incentives in our current system to ensure that innovative products are effective and argues that the FDA and tort system do not promote efficacy successfully. Instead, she argues that payors are uniquely well positioned to incentivize the development of efficacy because they have access to performance data and can refuse reimbursement for ineffective medical devices. Epstein's chapter contrasts with the other chapters in Part IV, which have focused on how the FDA has arguably failed to protect the interests of consumers when faced with unique challenges in addressing substance use, reproduction, and infection control. Epstein instead reminds the reader that there are other stakeholders who can act to promote the key goals of safety and efficacy.

Preeti Mehrotra, David Weber, and Ameet Sarpatwari then direct our attention to the challenge of dirty devices in their chapter, "Preventing Medical Device-Borne Outbreaks: The Case of High-Level Disinfection Policy for Duodenoscopes." Duodenoscopes are tubes that are snaked through the digestive system to the top of the small intestine to diagnose and treat problems in the pancreas and bile ducts. Because they are very complex with many small working parts, they can be very difficult to thoroughly clean and disinfect. To better understand the connection between multi-drug resistant bacterial infections and duodenoscope use, the FDA required several manufacturers to conduct postmarket surveillance studies. Using the duodenoscope example, the authors argue that our medical device regulatory approval process is too "binary." Devices can be safe and effective, they argue, but also pose some serious risks to patients because of downstream use. Unfortunately, the interaction between devices and downstream use is governed by a fragmented and uncoordinated rainbow of entities, including hospital policymakers, medical associations, and other stakeholders. The authors argue that we need to restructure our approval system to better reflect that devices will not always be used perfectly, and that there may be a gap between the safety and efficacy profile of a device as initially presented to regulators and how it is used "in the real world."

We close Part IV by turning to assisted reproductive technology (ART) devices with Katherine Kraschel's chapter, "Regulating Devices that Create Life." The FDA has struggled to define the boundaries of its jurisdiction when it comes to ART, because while it has the power to regulate products "used in" or "intended to affect . . . man or other animals," pre-embryos, embryos, and fetuses do not fall under that definition. At the same time, these organisms are not generally considered people or animals under US law, creating a regulatory gap. The FDA's silence when it comes to ART means that ART patients are often left unprotected. For example, without FDA requirements for manufacturers to demonstrate proof of safety and efficacy, very little reliable evidence of either is generated. If the Bridge is a story about the FDA not going far enough to protect consumers' interests, then the story that Kraschel tells is about what happens when the FDA never chooses to be involved. This chapter justifies for the reader the value of our regulatory agencies, even with their limitations.

Part V, *Medical and Legal Oversight of Medical Devices*, introduced by Carmel Shachar, builds on Part IV to continue our exploration of the ethical, regulatory, and legal complexities of governing postapproval medical devices. If Part IV concerned itself with how to balance innovation and protection in the postapproval context, Part V focuses on the who, what, and how. Who should ensure safety and efficacy of postapproval products? What are the tools available to oversee postapproval medical devices? How should we incorporate these products, and their postapproval regulatory oversight, into the medical system? Part V asks the reader to envision alternative postapproval realities, in which different regulatory or legal choices are made to better achieve various goals, be they patient safety, establishment of efficacy, or innovation.

Sanket Dhruva, Jonathon Darrow, Aaron Kesselheim, and Rita Redberg open Part V with their contribution, "Ensuring Patient Safety and Benefit in Use of Medical Devices Granted Expedited Approval." The authors focus on the pathways designed to accelerate patient access to novel medical devices, flagging that the products approved through these pathways may not always meet the statutory standards for safety and efficacy. They then suggest that conditional approval can be an effective regulatory tool for ensuring that these breakthrough products meet these important goals. Tying conditional approval to postmarket studies and data demonstrating that the threshold of reasonable assurance of safety and effectiveness has been met can incentivize manufacturers to generate important postapproval data. Dhruva et al. note that conditional approval is rarely used but does have precedent in the approach that the FDA has taken to pharmaceuticals.

Efthimios Parasidis and Daniel Kramer consider a different postapproval regulatory tool in their chapter, "Compulsory Medical Device Registries: Legal and Regulatory Issues." Parasidis and Kramer argue that postmarket registries can be a useful regulatory tool for monitoring high-risk medical devices. Agencies such as the FDA and CDC can encourage the development of registries by tying approval or reimbursement to their establishment. Unfortunately, these registries have been underdeveloped from an ethical and regulatory perspective, with significant questions regarding health privacy laws and ethical standards for human subjects research. This chapter, continuing a theme of the book, emphasizes that there are a host of regulatory approaches to achieving the ultimate goal of patient access to safe and effective devices. Some of the tools in the regulatory toolbox appear to be underdeveloped and require further thought to achieve maximum impact.

Anthony Weiss and Barak Richman turn the focus of Part V from humans regulating medical devices to medical devices regulating humans in their chapter, "Professional Self-Regulation in Medicine: Will the Rise of Intelligent Tools Mean the End of Peer Review?" Physicians have largely kept oversight of their profession within their own ranks, arguing that only other physicians have the necessary expertise to evaluate medical decision making. With the rise of medical decision-making algorithms, that argument is increasingly being undercut. In some ways, this chapter is the logical outgrowth of the concepts discussed in Part I, *AI and Data as Medical Devices.* Once these "software as devices" products are released into broader use, what are the best ways to incorporate them into our current medical system? Weiss and Richman consider the benefits of incorporating artificial intelligence into physician review, as well as the challenges of interfacing humans and machines. While we should not ignore potentially useful tools, they argue, we also need to preserve space for a human approach to medical practice.

The next chapter, "Regulating Posttrial Access to In-Dwelling Class III Neural Devices," by Megan Wright and Joseph Fins, considers devices that fail to go to market, specifically those implanted in the brain. Since these devices may remain implanted in research subjects, what duties are owed to these individuals? What are the posttrial obligations of study sponsors and investigators to maintain or even replace these devices for their former research subjects? Wright and Fins note that transparency about posttrial access is, at minimum, necessary as part of the informed consent process. This chapter illustrates to the reader that not all devices developed and evaluated by the regulatory system will come to market. How should that be reflected in the approval process?

The closing chapter of Part V, "Strengthening the Power of Health Care Insurers to Regulate Medical Device Risks," by David Rosenberg and Adeyemi Adediran, reemphasizes that regulatory agencies are not the only actors that can provide and enforce postapproval consumer protections. Rosenberg and Adediran draw the reader's attention to the interplay between FDA action and state negligence actions as two alternative approaches to ensuring optimal levels of safety for consumers using medical devices. They propose a system of strict liability, in which first-party insurers would be required to investigate and report to the FDA any potential causal connections between patient injury and a particular medical device. The FDA would work to verify such a connection and then work with the Department of Justice Civil Division for a federal strict liability action against the device's manufacturer. Rosenberg and Adediran suggest that the manufacturer should bear liability in full, with no reduction for the risk contributed by the patient and pay the damages to the federal government. This chapter asks the reader to consider the importance of patient safety and how best to prioritize it. Rosenberg and Adediran have presented a system that could optimize for patient safety, but how should it be balanced with the interest of encouraging the development of innovative new products?

CONCLUSIONS

Compared to drugs, the regulation of medical devices has received relatively little attention. Medical devices, nevertheless, can have significant positive and negative impacts on patients that use them. Navigating between the needs to provide patient access to innovative medical devices, to ensure that these devices are effective, and ultimately to preserve patient safety as much as possible is challenging. One of the major themes highlighted in this volume is that there is significant ferment at this moment when it comes to medical device regulation. Regulators in the European Union are working to implement significant changes to their medical device regulations in the midst of a global pandemic. Furthermore, with the explosion of digital health, including software as a medical device, there is a strong need to revisit the regulatory framework that governs medical devices. Our authors explore these changes and developments with an eye to articulating what a twenty-first century medical device regulation system should look like. Another significant theme is complex interplay between regulators, device designers, manufacturers, physicians, and patients. Different authors throughout the volume explore the roles of key stakeholders, highlight underutilized regulatory tools, or flag how different mechanisms could be used to promote innovation and/or protection. The regulation of medical devices is as complex as the products it governs.

PART I

AI and Data as Medical Devices

Introduction

W. Nicholson Price II

It may seem counterintuitive to open a book on medical devices with chapters on software and data, but these are the frontiers of new medical device regulation and law. Physical devices are still crucial to medicine, but they – and medical practice as a whole – are embedded in and permeated by networks of software and caches of data. Those software systems are often mindbogglingly complex and largely inscrutable, involving artificial intelligence and machine learning. Ensuring that such software works effectively and safely remains a substantial challenge for regulators and policymakers. Each of the three chapters in this part examines different aspects of how best to meet this challenge, focusing on review by drug regulators and, crucially, what aspects of oversight fall outside that purview.

Kerstin Vokinger, Thomas Hwang, and Aaron Kesselheim tackle the question of how food and drug regulators should oversee AI head-on in "Lifecycle Regulation and Evaluation of Artificial Intelligence and Machine Learning-Based Medical Devices." A crucial difference between AI-powered software systems and classic devices, including software devices, is that AI-powered systems are frequently plastic: that is, they change more regularly (or at least can), given new data and new information about the world in which they are deployed. Vokinger and colleagues highlight how American and European regulators are fitting such plastic AI approaches into existing frameworks and suggest that accomplishing the regulatory task requires a combination of strong prospective evidence, ongoing oversight after approval, and transparency to agencies and others.

It is to those others that Barbara Evans and Frank Pasquale turn in "Product Liability Suits for FDA-Regulated AI/ML Software." Regulators are only one part of the oversight picture; tort law lurks in the background to pick up the slack where products result in injury. The relationship between the FDA and tort suits for injuries caused by medical technology is complex, and mostly focused on preemption – when can plaintiffs sue in state court where the products involved are FDA-approved?[1] Evans and Pasquale focus on another aspect of the relationship: the very fact of FDA

[1] See, e.g., Charlotte A. Tschider, Medical Device Artificial Intelligence: The New Tort Frontier, 46 BYU L. Rev. 1551 (2021).

regulation for at least some clinical decision support software helps define the involved software as a "product" – neatly resolving the product/service distinction that has bedeviled tort liability for software more generally. Opening the door to product liability suits generates new possibilities for tort law to enforce requirements on AI-powered software systems. Evans and Pasquale explore the potential for novel tort suits brought on this basis, notably to address questions of explainability and the adequacy of training datasets. Here, too, the analysis highlights the boundary-crossing nature of AI-powered software, as these issues could be tackled by tort law, regulators, or both.

Finally, Craig Konnoth broadens the regulatory oversight focus beyond just artificial intelligence in "Are Electronic Health Records Medical Devices,?" considering the appropriate regulation of electronic health records (EHRs) more generally. Konnoth asks about the EHRs into which clinical decision support and other software are embedded, and which connect different parts of the health system (sometimes with greater success than others). Such interstitial technologies are a persistently challenging target for agency oversight, where different actors have the differing expertise and jurisdiction. Konnoth argues that here, too, the oversight role of the FDA may fruitfully be complemented by another: in this case, the Office of the National Coordinator for Health Information Technology, which could oversee the networking-focused aspects of electronic health records.

Collectively, these chapters demonstrate the challenge of regulating and overseeing the AI- and data-powered software which increasingly shapes medical practice, both behind the scenes and within the examining room. These technologies bring immense potential along with real risk, but present new regulatory challenges due to their opacity, their plasticity, and the speed with which they are being incorporated into the health system. Ensuring the right sort of oversight so that medical devices centered on AI and big data are safe, effective, and deployed in such a way as to actually help the health system demands concerted action from stakeholders across the board.

1

Lifecycle Regulation and Evaluation of Artificial Intelligence and Machine Learning-Based Medical Devices

Kerstin N. Vokinger, Thomas J. Hwang, and Aaron S. Kesselheim

1.1 INTRODUCTION

Artificial intelligence- and machine learning (AI/ML)-based technologies aim to improve patient care by uncovering new insights from the vast amount of data generated by an individual patient, and by the collective experience of many patients.[1]

Though there is no unified definition of AI,[2] a good working definition is that it is a branch of computer science devoted to the performance of tasks that normally require human intelligence.[3] A major subbranch of this field is ML, in which, based on the US Food and Drug Administration's (FDA) definition, techniques are applied to design and train software algorithms to learn from and act on data.[4] When intended to diagnose, treat, or prevent a disease or other conditions, AI/ML-based software is a medical device under the Food, Drug, and Cosmetic Act in the United States as well as the Council Directive 93/42/EEC and Therapeutic Products Act in the European Union and Switzerland, respectively.[5] Examples of AI/ML-based medical devices include an imaging system that uses algorithms to give diagnostic information for skin cancer or a smart electrocardiogram device that estimates the probability of a heart attack.[6]

1 T.J. Hwang et al., Lifecycle Regulation of Artificial Intelligence and Machine Learning-Based Software Devices in Medicine, 322 JAMA 2285 (2019); M.E. Matheny et al., Artificial Intelligence in Health Care: A Report from the National Academy of Medicine, 323 JAMA 507 (2020).

2 M. Hutson, AI Glossary: Artificial Intelligence, in So Many Words, 357 Science 19 (2017).

3 A.S. Adamson & H.G. Welch, Machine Learning and the Cancer-Diagnosis Problem – No Gold Standard, 381 N. Engl. J. Med. 2285, 2285–7 (2019).

4 Id.; see US Food & Drug Admin., Proposed Regulatory Framework for Modifications to Artificial Intelligence/Machine Learning (AI/ML)-Based Software as a Medical Device (SaMD) (Apr. 2, 2019), www.fda.gov/media/122535/download; G. Hinton, Deep Learning – A Technology with the Potential to Transform Health Care, 320 JAMA 1101 (2018).

5 US Food & Drug Admin., Proposed Regulatory Framework, supra note 4.

6 US Food & Drug Admin., Artificial Intelligence and Machine Learning in Software as a Medical Device, www.fda.gov/medical-devices/software-medical-device-samd/artificial-intelligence-and-machine-learning-software-medical-device.

Medical devices that are AI/ML-based exist on a spectrum from locked to continuously learning. "Locked" algorithms provide the same result each time the same input is provided.[7] Such algorithms need manual processes for updates and validation. By contrast, adaptive or continuously learning algorithms change their behavior using defined learning processes. These changes are typically implemented and validated through a well-defined and possibly fully automated process that aims at improving performance based on analysis of new or additional data.[8]

While AI/ML-based technologies hold promise, they also raise questions about how to ensure their safety and effectiveness.[9] In April 2019, the FDA published a discussion paper and announced that it was reviewing its regulation of AI/ML-based medical devices.[10] The distinctive characteristics of AI/ML-based software require a regulatory approach that spans the lifecycle of AI/ML-based technologies, allowing necessary steps to improve treatment while assuring safety outcomes.

In this chapter, we analyze the regulation of the clearance and certification of AI/ML-based software products in the United States and Europe. Due to the distinctive characteristics of AI/ML-based software, we believe that a regulatory approach is required that spans the lifecycle of these technologies, allowing indicated steps to improve treatment and ensure safety.[11] We conclude by reviewing the regulatory implications of this approach.

1.2 CLEARANCE OF AI/ML-BASED MEDICAL DEVICES IN THE UNITED STATES

There is no separate regulatory pathway for AI/ML-based medical devices. Rather, in the United States, the FDA reviews medical devices based on the risks of the devices primarily through the 1) premarket approval pathway (most stringent review for high-risk devices), 2) the 510(k) pathway, or 3) de novo premarket review (for low- and moderate-risk devices).[12] Additionally, the humanitarian device exemption can apply to medical devices intended to benefit patients in the treatment or diagnosis of diseases or conditions that affect fewer than 8,000 individuals in the United States per year.[13]

Premarket approval (PMA) is the most likely FDA pathway for new Class III medical devices. Class III devices are those that support or sustain human life, are of

[7] US Food & Drug Admin., Proposed Regulatory Framework, supra note 4.

[8] US Food & Drug Admin., Proposed Regulatory Framework, supra note 4; Hwang et al., supra note 1.

[9] W.N. Price, Regulating Black-Box Medicine, 116 Mich. L. Rev. 421 (2017).

[10] US Food & Drug Admin., Proposed Regulatory Framework, supra note 4.

[11] Hwang et al., supra note 1.

[12] Hwang et al., supra note 1; US Food & Drug Admin., Premarket Notification 510(k), www.fda.gov/medical-devices/premarket-submissions/premarket-notification-510k; US Food & Drug Admin., Premarket Approval (PMA), www.fda.gov/medical-devices/premarket-submissions/premarket-approval-pma.

[13] US Food & Drug Admin., Humanitarian Device Exception, www.fda.gov/medical-devices/premarket-submissions/humanitarian-device-exemption.

substantial importance in preventing impairment of human health, or which present a potential unreasonable risk of illness or injury. The FDA determined that general and special controls alone are insufficient to guarantee safety and effectiveness of such devices. Thus, such devices require a PMA application to obtain marketing approval. Premarket approval requires the demonstration of "reasonable assurance" that the medical device is safe and effective and generally includes at least one prospective trial.[14] Clearance through the 510(k) pathway is intended for devices for which a PMA is not required (Class I, II, and III devices). In contrast to the PMA, the 510(k) pathway only requires "substantial equivalence" to an already marketed device.[15] The de novo pathway is an alternate pathway to classify novel medical devices that had automatically been placed in Class III after receiving a "not substantially equivalent" (NSE) determination in response to a 510(k) submission. There are two options for de novo classification for novel devices of low to moderate risk. In the first option, any sponsor that receives an NSE determination may submit a de novo request to make a risk-based evaluation for classification of the device into Class I or II. In option 2, any sponsor that determines that there is no legally marketed device upon which to base a determination of substantial equivalence may submit a de novo request for the FDA to make a risk-based classification of the device into Class I or II, without first submitting a 510(k) and receiving an NSE determination.[16] The de novo pathway allows new devices to serve as references or predicates for future 510(k) submissions.[17]

A majority of AI/ML-based medical devices are cleared through the 510(k) pathway.[18] However, the 510(k) pathway has been criticized for not sufficiently guaranteeing safety and effectiveness. The 510(k) clearance can lead to chains of medical devices that claim substantial equivalence to each other, but over years or even decades, may diverge substantially from the original device.[19] For example, certain metal-on-metal hip implants were cleared without clinical studies and based on predicate medical devices that did not demonstrate safety and effectiveness or were discontinued.[20] Indeed, past clearance of AI/ML-based medical devices can be traced back to other devices that do not have an AI/ML component. For example, the AI/ML-based medical device, Arterys Oncology DL, cleared in 2018, which is

14 US Food & Drug Admin., Premarket Approval (PMA), supra note 12.

15 US Food & Drug Admin., The 510(k) Program: Evaluating Substantial Equivalence in Premarket Notifications [510(k)] (Feb. 5, 2018), www.fda.gov/regulatory-information/search-fda-guidance-documents/510k-program-evaluating-substantial-equivalence-premarket-notifications-510k.

16 US Food & Drug Admin., Evaluation of Automatic Class III Designation (De Novo) Summaries (Oct. 27, 2020), www.fda.gov/about-fda/cdrh-transparency/evaluation-automatic-class-iii-designation-de-novo-summaries.

17 Hwang et al., supra note 1.

18 Id.; U.J. Muehlematter et al., Artificial Intelligence and Machine Learning Based Medical Devices in the US and Europe (2015–2020) – A Comparative Analysis (accepted at The Lancet Digital Health).

19 Hwang et al., supra note 1.

20 B.M. Ardaugh et al., The 510(k) Ancestry of a Metal-on-Metal Hip Implant, 368 N. Engl. J. Med 97, 97–100 (2013).

indicated to assist with liver and lung cancer diagnosis, can be traced back to cardiac imaging software cleared in 1998, which was considered as substantially equivalent to devices marketed prior to 1976.[21] The clearance decision does not provide any information regarding clinical validation, and such testing may not have been done.[22]

Changes or modifications after marketing of a device requires additional FDA notification and possibly review, either as a supplement to the premarket approval or as a new 510(k) submission.[23] Of course, this is a further challenge for AI/ML devices, since adaptive algorithms that enable continuous learning from clinical application and experience may result in outputs that differ from what has initially been reviewed prior to regulatory approval.[24]

The FDA publishes summaries of the cleared medical devices' safety and effectiveness as well as statements. However, only rarely does the device description state whether the medical device contains an AI/ML component.[25] One example in which this was indicated was BriefCase, a radiological computer-aided triage and notification software that was 510(k) cleared in 2018 and indicated for use in the analysis of nonenhanced head CT images. According to the FDA's summary, BriefCase uses an artificial intelligence algorithm to analyze images and highlight cases with detected intracranial hemorrhage on a standalone desktop application in parallel to the ongoing standard of care image interpretation. The user is presented with notifications for cases with suspected intracranial hemorrhage findings.[26] Another example is AiCE (Advanced Intelligent Clear-IQ Engine), an AI/ML-based medical device that was 510(k) cleared in 2020. AiCE is a noise-reduction algorithm that improves image quality and reduces image noise by employing deep convolutional neural network methods for abdomen, pelvis, lung, cardiac, extremities, head, and inner ear applications.[27] However, the FDA's summaries and statements do not reveal whether a cleared AI/ML-based medical device contains locked or adaptive algorithms.[28] For example, Illumeo System, an image management system software used with general purpose computing hardware to acquire, store, distribute, process, and display images and associated data throughout the

21 Hwang et al., supra note 1; Letter from Robert Ochs, Director, US Food & Drug Admin., to John Axerio-Cilies, Chief Operating Officer, Arterys, Inc. (Jan. 25, 2018), www.accessdata.fda.gov/cdrh_docs/pdf17/K173542.pdf.

22 See Ochs, supra note 21.

23 Hwang et al., supra note 1.

24 Id.

25 Muehlematter et al., supra note 18.

26 Letter from Robert Ochs, Director, US Food & Drug Admin., to John J. Smith, Partner, Hogan Lovells US LLP (Aug. 1, 2018), www.accessdata.fda.gov/cdrh_docs/pdf18/K180647.pdf.

27 Letter from Robert Ochs, Director, US Food & Drug Admin., to Orlando Tadeo Jr., Senior Manager, Canon Medical Systems USA (Feb. 21, 2020), www.accessdata.fda.gov/cdrh_docs/pdf19/K192832.pdf.

28 Muehlematter et al., supra note 18.

clinical environment, is promoted as "adaptive" on the manufacturer's website, but this is not explicitly mentioned in the FDA's summary.[29]

1.3 CE MARKING OF AI/ML-BASED MEDICAL DEVICES IN EUROPE

In Europe, there is also no specific regulatory pathway for AI/ML-based medical devices.[30] In contrast to the United States, medical products are not approved by a centralized agency. Apart from the lowest-risk medical devices (Class I) that can be carried out under the sole responsibility of the manufacturer, initial review of medical devices of higher-risk Classes (IIa, IIb, and III) are handled by private so-called notified bodies.[31] In Vitro Medical Devices (IVD) are, based on their risks, either marketed on the basis of the sole responsibility of the manufacturer or handled by notified bodies.[32] The EU Member States, EFTA States (Liechtenstein, Iceland, Norway, and Switzerland), and Turkey concluded treaties with regard to the mutual recognition of conformity assessments for medical devices.[33] For simplicity, we use "Europe" to refer to these countries, unless otherwise denoted. Each of these European countries recognize certificates ("Conformité Européenne" [CE] marks) issued by accredited private notified bodies in the other European countries, meaning that after a manufacturer obtains a CE mark in one European country, direct distribution is possible across Europe. Country-specific requirements remain valid, such as mandatory notification for new medical devices, requirements regarding the languages in which the product information must be provided, provisions regarding the prescription and professional use, advertising, reimbursement by social insurances, surveillance.[34]

Studies show that medical devices are often certified in Europe prior to approval in the United States.[35] However, faster access in Europe brings with it important risks that have been well documented. Recent changes to the current European device regulatory system are intended to better safeguard

29 Compare Royal Philips, Philips Illumeo with adaptive intelligence has been selected by University of Utah Health radiologists, Philips News Center (Nov. 26, 2018), www.philips.com/a-w/about/news/archive/standard/news/press/2018/20181126-philips-illumeo-with-adaptive-intelligence-has-been-selected-by-university-of-utah-health-radiologists.html, with Letter from Robert Ochs, Director, US Food & Drug Admin., to Yoram Levy, QA/RA Consultant, Philips Medical Systems Technologies Ltd. (Jan. 12, 2018), www.accessdata.fda.gov/cdrh_docs/pdf17/K173588.pdf.

30 K.N. Vokinger et al., Artificial Intelligence und Machine Learning in der Medizin, Jusletter (Aug. 28, 2017), www.zora.uzh.ch/id/eprint/142601/.

31 Id.

32 Swissmedic, Guide to the Regulation of Medical Devices, www.swissmedic.ch/swissmedic/en/home/medical-devices/regulation-of-medical-devices/medical-device-regulation_online-guide.html.

33 Id.

34 Id.

35 Muehlematter et al., supra note 18; T.J. Hwang et al., Comparison of Rates of Safety Issues and Reporting of Trial Outcomes for Medical Devices Approved in the European Union and United States: Cohort Study, 353 BMJ 3323 (2016).

patient safety.[36] For example, the revised laws (Regulation 2017/745 on Medical Devices [MDR] and Regulation 2017/46 on in vitro diagnostic medical devices [IVDR]) raised the certification threshold for medical products. However, these new laws still do not address AI/ML-based medical devices specifically. Due to the COVID-19 pandemic, the date of implementation of these laws by Member States has been postponed by one year to May 2021 for the MDR and May 2022 for the IVDR.[37]

In contrast to the United States, Europe does not have a publicly accessible, comprehensive database for certified medical devices and summaries of the regulatory decisions. The EC database on medical devices (Eudamed) is a repository for information on market surveillance exchanged between national competent authorities and the Commission. However, its use is restricted to national competent authorities, the country-specific device regulatory authorities for medical devices, such as Swissmedic in Switzerland.[38] In some European countries, for example, Germany, the United Kingdom, or France,[39] such authorities have publicly accessible databases for registered medical devices in their country. However, such databases only reflect a fraction of the medical devices CE marked in Europe.

1.4 IMPLICATIONS FOR LIFECYCLE REGULATION OF AI/ML-BASED MEDICAL DEVICES

The traditional paradigm of medical device regulation in both the United States and Europe was not designed for (adaptive) AI/ML technologies, which have the potential to adapt and optimize device performance in real time. The iterative and autonomous nature of such AI/ML-based medical devices require a new lifecycle-based framework with the goal of facilitating a rapid cycle of product improvement and to allow such devices to continuously improve while providing patients' safety.[40]

First, we believe it is important to address the currently limited evidence for safety and effectiveness available at the time of market entry for such products. Both in the

36 Id.; A.G. Fraser et al., Commentary: International Collaboration Needed on Device Clinical Standards, 342 BMJ 2952 (2011); N. Williams, The Scandal of Device Regulation in the UK, 379 Lancet 1789–90 (2012); D. Cohen, Patient Groups Accuse European Parliament of Putting Economic Interests Ahead of Safety on Medical Devices, 347 BMJ 6446 (2013); D.B. Kramer et al., Regulation of Medical Devices in the United States and European Union, 366 N. Engl. J. Med. 848–55 (2012).

37 European Comm'n, Medical Devices – EUDAMED, https://ec.europa.eu/growth/sectors/medical-devices/new-regulations/eudamed_en.

38 Id.

39 BAM, Recherche in öffentlichen Medizinprodukte Datenbanken, www.dimdi.de/dynamic/de/medizinprodukte/datenbankrecherche/; MHRA, Medical Device Manufacturers by Name, http://aic.mhra.gov.uk/era/pdr.nsf/name?openpage&start=2001&count=1000; ANSM, Mise sur le marché des dispositifs médicaux et dispositifs médicaux de diagnostic in vitro (DM/DMIA/DMDIV), www.ansm.sante.fr/Activites/Mise-sur-le-marche-des-dispositifs-medicaux-et-dispositifs-medicaux-de-diagnostic-in-vitro-DM-DMIA-DMDIV/DM-classe-I-DM-sur-mesure-assemblage-Declaration/(offset)/5.

40 US Food & Drug Admin., Proposed Regulatory Framework, supra note 4.

United States and in Europe, a majority of the cleared and CE-marked AI/ML-based medical devices have not required new clinical testing.[41] This can deprive patients and clinicians of important information needed to make informed diagnostic and therapeutic decisions. Ideally, AI/ML-based medical devices that aim to predict, diagnose, or treat, should be evaluated in prospective clinical trials using meaningful patient-centered endpoints.[42] More rigorous premarket assessment of the performance of AI/ML-based medical devices could also facilitate trustworthiness and thus broader and faster access to these new technologies.[43] Implementation of AI/ML-based medical devices in clinical care will need to meet particularly high standards to satisfy clinicians and patients. Mistakes based on the reliance of an AI/ML-based medical device will drive negative perceptions that could reduce overall enthusiasm for the field and slow innovation. This can be seen with another AI-fueled innovation, autonomous and semi-autonomous vehicles. Even though such vehicles may be, on average, safer than human drivers, a pedestrian death due to such a vehicle error caused great alarm.[44] As pointed out in a prior study, it is also crucial to ensure that new regulations help contribute to an environment in which innovation in the development of new AI/ML-based medical devices can flourish.[45] Thus, the prerequisites for clinical testing must be aligned with the risks of AI/ML-based medical devices.

Second, to address the postapproval period ("surveillance"), manufacturers and the agencies (FDA in the United States, national authorities in Europe) should work together to generate a list of allowable changes and modifications that AI/ML-based medical devices can use to adapt in real time to new data that would be subject to "safe harbors" and thus not necessarily require premarket review. This is especially crucial for devices with adaptive algorithms. Such a "safe harbor" could, for example, apply to modifications in performance, with no change to the intended use or new input type, provided that the manufacturer agrees that such changes would not cause safety risks to patients.[46] These modifications should be documented in the manufacturer's change history and other appropriate records. However, modifications to the AI/ML-based medical device's intended use (e.g., from an "aid in diagnosis" to a "definitive diagnosis") could be deemed to fall out of the "safe harbor" scope and require submission of a new review.[47] Depending on the modification, it may be reasonable that a focus of the review lies on the underlying algorithm changes for a particular AI/ML-based medical device.

41 Hwang et al., supra note 1; Muehlematter et al., supra note 18.
42 T.M. Maddox et al., Questions for Artificial Intelligence in Health Care, 321 JAMA 31, 31 (2019); W. W. Stead, Clinical Implications of Artificial Intelligence and Deep Learning, 320 JAMA 1107, 1107 (2018).
43 Hwang et al., supra note 1.
44 Maddox et al., supra note 42.
45 Price, supra note 9.
46 Hwang et al., supra note 1.
47 US Food & Drug Admin., Proposed Regulatory Framework, supra note 4.

Since even anticipated changes may accumulate over time to generate an unanticipated divergence in the AI/ML-based software's eventual performance, there should be appropriate guardrails as software evolves after its initial regulatory approval. One possibility would be to develop built-in audits for regular intervals using data from ongoing implementation and assessing outcomes prespecified at the time of approval.[48] Another example would be to implement an automatic sunset after a specific amount of years, such as five years.[49] This would allow the regulatory agencies to periodically review accumulated modifications and postapproval performance to ensure that the risk-benefit profile for the device remains acceptable.[50] A stronger focus on the postapproval period is also in line with the FDA's discussion paper that proposes, among other things, that manufacturers provide periodic reporting to the FDA on updates to their software.[51]

Lastly, transparency has the potential to improve the usefulness, safety, and quality of clinical research by allowing agencies, regulators, researchers, and companies to learn from successes and failures of products.[52] It also fosters trust.[53] Function and modifications of AI/ML-based medical devices are key aspects of their safety, especially for adaptive software, and should therefore be made publicly accessible. Since modifications to AI/ML-based medical devices may be supported by the collection and monitoring of real-world data, manufacturers should also provide information about the data being collected in an annual report. A further approach to enhance transparency and trustworthiness could be that manufacturers actively update the FDA and European agencies, as well as the public (clinicians, patients, general users) with regard to modifications in algorithms, change in inputs, or the updated performance of the AI/ML-based medical devices.[54]

A stronger focus on transparency should also be pursued by the FDA and European agencies. For example, medical devices that contain an AI/ML component should be indicated as such in the FDA's summaries. The FDA should also clarify in the summaries whether such AI/ML-based medical devices include locked or adaptive algorithms. In Europe, the public does not have access to reviews or summaries of notified bodies or national authorities. National authorities in Europe should adopt the FDA's approach.

48 Hwang et al., supra note 1.

49 Id.; R.B. Barikh et al., Regulation of Predictive Analytics in Medicine, 363 Science 810, 810–12 (2019).

50 Hwang et al., supra note 1.

51 US Food & Drug Admin., Proposed Regulatory Framework, supra note 4; T. Minssen et al., Regulatory Responses to Medical Machine Learning, 7 J. Law & Biosciences 1 (2020).

52 T.J. Hwang et al., Evaluating New Rules on Transparency in Cancer Research and Drug Development, 5 JAMA Oncol. 461 (2019).

53 Id.

54 US Food & Drug Admin., Proposed Regulatory Framework, supra note 4.

Medical devices that are AI/ML-based pose new chances and challenges. Current regulations in the United States and in Europe are not designed specifically for AI/ML-based medical devices, and do not fit well with adaptive technologies. We recommend a regulatory approach that spans the lifecycle of these technologies.

2

Product Liability Suits for FDA-Regulated AI/ML Software

Barbara J. Evans and Frank Pasquale

The 21st Century Cures Act confirmed the FDA's authority to regulate certain categories of software that, increasingly, incorporate artificial intelligence/machine-learning (AI/ML) techniques. The agency's September 27, 2019 draft guidance on Clinical Decision Support Software proposed an approach for regulating CDS software and sheds light on plans for regulating genomic bioinformatics software (whether or not it constitutes CDS software). No matter how the FDA's regulatory approach ultimately evolves, the agency's involvement in this sphere has an important – and underexamined – implication: FDA-regulated software seemingly has the status of a medical product (as opposed to an informational service), which opens the door to product liability for defects causing patient injury. When a diagnostic or treatment decision relies on FDA-regulated CDS software, will mistakes invite strict liability, as opposed to being judged by the professional or general negligence standards of care that traditionally governed diagnostic and therapeutic errors? This chapter explores the policy rationales for product liability suits and asks whether such suits may have a helpful rôle to play as an adjunct to FDA oversight in promoting safety, effectiveness, and transparency of CDS software as it moves into wider use in clinical health care settings.

2.1 INTRODUCTION

The term "clinical decision support" (CDS) software includes various tools for enhancing clinical decision making and patient care. Examples include systems that provide alerts and reminders to health care providers and patients, or algorithms that offer recommendations about the best diagnosis or treatment for a patient.[1] The US Food and Drug Administration (FDA) conceives CDS software as data processing systems that combine patient-specific information (such as a patient's test results or clinical history) with generally applicable medical knowledge (such as clinical practice guidelines, information from drug labeling, or insights gleaned from outcomes observed in

[1] See, e.g., Clinical Decision Support, HealthIT.gov (Apr. 10, 2018), www.healthit.gov/policy-researchers-implementers/clinical-decision-support-cds [https://perma.cc/JWV8-YUGQ].

other patients) to provide a health care professional with patient-specific recommendations about how to diagnose, treat, or prevent disease in clinical health care settings.[2]

Congress defines an FDA-regulable medical device as an "instrument, apparatus, implement, machine, contrivance ... " or "any component, part, or accessory" thereof which is "intended for use in the diagnosis of disease or other conditions, or in the cure, mitigation, treatment, or prevention of disease."[3] Despite its physical intangibility, CDS software arguably meets this definition. For many years, the FDA has regulated "software in a medical device"[4] – software embedded in traditional hardware devices like x-ray machines, where the software affects the safety and effectiveness of the device as a whole.[5] In 2013, as CDS software was growing more common in clinical health care, the FDA worked with medical product regulators in other countries to develop the concept of "software as a medical device" (SaMD): standalone medical software, designed to run on diverse platforms such as smartphones, laptops, or in the cloud, that constitutes a medical device in its own right.[6] The notion was that when software is intended for use in diagnosing, treating, or preventing disease, then the software is itself a medical device, and its status as a device does not hinge on being incorporated into specific hardware.

Concerned that the FDA might be contemplating broad regulation of standalone medical software, the software industry pressed Congress for clarification. In December 2016, Congress responded in Section 3060 of the 21st Century Cures Act (the "Cures Act").[7] Section 3060 includes some (but not all) CDS software in the definition of a device that the FDA can regulate and provides a jurisdictional rule distinguishing which software is – and which is not – a medical device.[8] In two subsequent draft guidance documents,[9] the FDA has attempted to clarify this distinction, but key uncertainties remain unresolved for CDS software that incorporates AI/ML techniques.

Whether a piece of software is subject to FDA oversight has important legal impacts apart from the immediate burden and delay of having to comply with the FDA's regulations. This chapter explains why the FDA's regulation of medical

2 See US Food & Drug Admin., Clinical Decision Support Software: Draft Guidance for Industry and Food and Drug Administration Staff (Sept. 2019), www.fda.gov/regulatory-information/search-fda-guidance-documents/clinical-decision-support-software; see also US Food & Drug Admin., Clinical and Patient Decision Support Software: Draft Guidance for Industry and Food and Drug Administration Staff (Dec. 2017) (providing earlier draft guidance replaced in Sept. 2019).

3 21 U.S.C. § 321(h).

4 See Int'l Medical Device Regulator's Forum, Software as a Medical Device (SaMD): Key Definitions (Dec. 9, 2013), www.imdrf.org/docs/imdrf/final/technical/imdrf-tech-131209-samd-key-definitions-140901.pdf.

5 Id.; see also, US Food & Drug Admin., What Are Examples of Software as a Medical Device? (updated Dec. 6, 2017), www.fda.gov/medicaldevices/digitalhealth/softwareasamedicaldevice/ucm587924.htm.

6 See Int'l Medical Device Regulator's Forum, supra note 4.

7 21st Century Cures Act, Pub. L. No. 114–255, § 3060(a), 130 Stat. 1033 (2016).

8 21 U.S.C. § 360j(o)(1)(E).

9 See US Food & Drug Admin., supra note 2.

software could increase the likelihood that state courts would view it as a product that is subject to strict product liability tort regimes. Software liability has long been a contested topic. Courts have shown reluctance to apply product liability to software, whether because its intangible nature seems at odds with the notion of a product, or because software seems better characterized as a service.[10] If classified as a service, professional malpractice or ordinary negligence regimes would apply to software vendors. If classified as a product, they could face product liability (which encompasses both negligence and strict liability claims). The fact that product vendors face product liability does not prevent plaintiffs from also bringing malpractice suits against physicians and other health care professionals who ordered, prescribed, or used a defective product in the course of treating the patient. Product liability and malpractice coexist in the medical setting, and a single injury can generate both types of suit.

This chapter briefly explains the jurisdictional rule Congress set out in Section 3060 of the Cures Act and identifies key uncertainties after the FDA's two recent attempts at clarification. The chapter next summarizes some of the policy rationales for product liability and their applicability to CDS software. The chapter then explores two intriguing types of product liability suits that could emerge in connection with FDA-regulated AI/ML CDS software.

2.2 THE FDA'S AUTHORITY TO REGULATE CDS SOFTWARE

The very fact that the FDA regulates a piece of software militates in favor of its classification as a product, as opposed to an informational or professional service, potentially subjecting it to product liability suits. This proposition may strike readers as nonobvious, but it is an artifact of how the FDA's jurisdiction is defined under the Food, Drug, and Cosmetic Act (FDCA).

A key divide in health law is between FDA regulation of medical products versus state-level licensure directed at health care services such as the practice of medicine. "The scope of FDA's power is defined almost entirely by the list of product categories over which it has jurisdiction."[11] The major exception is that the FDA shares broad powers with the Centers for Disease Control and Prevention to manage the spread of communicable diseases, but those powers arise under a different statute.[12] Under the FDCA, the FDA's ability to regulate persons or entities rests on whether they are developing, manufacturing, shipping, storing, importing, or selling an item that fits within one of the product categories that Congress authorizes the FDA to regulate: drugs, devices, biological products, food,

[10] See Joseph L. Reutiman, Defective Information: Should Information Be a Product Subject to Products Liability Claims, 22 Cornell J. L. and Pub. Pol'y 194–6 (2012) (discussing cases that have treated software as a service).

[11] Peter Barton Hutt et al., Food and Drug Law 77 (4th ed. 2014).

[12] See id. (discussing the FDA's jurisdiction under the Public Health Service Act).

animal drugs, et cetera.[13] The FDA's regulatory authority under the FDCA extends to products rather than services.[14] Medical devices, as FDA-regulated products, are routinely subject to product liability suits.[15]

When the FDA asserts that it has jurisdiction to regulate something, the agency is making a determination that that thing fits into one of these congressionally defined product categories, and therefore is not a service. Once the FDA determines that something is a product, it is conceivable that a state court hearing a tort lawsuit might disagree, but this is unlikely. Doing so would amount to a state court finding that the FDA regulated outside of its lawful jurisdiction. Suits challenging the FDA's jurisdiction pose federal questions to be heard in federal court, not state court. Moreover, the FDA is making scientific/technical determinations when it classifies something as a medical product, and courts (both state and federal) tend to give "super deference" to such decisions.[16] If the FDA determines that software fits within Congress's definition of a medical device, and therefore is a product, state courts seem likely to defer.

The jurisdictional rule for CDS software under the Cures Act carefully respects the line between products and services, as has all FDA-related legislation dating back to the 1930s when the scope of the FDA's power to regulate medical practice was hotly debated before Congress passed the FDCA.[17] Congress denied intent for FDA regulation of medical products to encompass regulation of health care services, a traditional province of the states.[18] As a policy matter, the FDA seeks to avoid regulating physicians' activities, even though courts have never found constitutional limits on the FDA's power to do so.[19] "There is little doubt under modern law that Congress has ample power to regulate the manufacture, distribution, and *use* of drugs and medical devices."[20] Regulating use is tantamount to regulating health care

13 See 21 U.S.C. § 321 (defining these and other product categories that trigger FDA jurisdiction).

14 US Food & Drug Admin., What Does FDA Regulate? (2018), www.fda.gov/about-fda/fda-basics/what-does-fda-regulate.

15 Elizabeth O. Tomlinson, Proof of Defective Design of Medical Device in Products Liability Action, 149 Am. Jur. Proof of Facts 407 (2015); See also Barbara J. Evans & Ellen Wright Clayton, Deadly Delay: The FDA's Role in America's COVID-Testing Debacle, 130 Yale Law Journal Forum 78–100 (2020), www.yalelawjournal.org/forum/deadly-delay-the-fdas-role-in-americas-covid-testing-debacle (discussing the product/service distinction in FDA regulation of diagnostics).

16 Emily Hammond Meazell, Super Deference, the Science Obsession, and Judicial Review as Translation of Agency Science, 109 Mich. L. Rev. 733 (2010–11).

17 See Joel E. Hoffman, Administrative Procedures of the Food and Drug Administration, in 2 Fundamentals of Law and Regulation: An In-Depth Look at Therapeutic Products 13, 17–24 (David G. Adams et al. eds., 1999) [hereinafter Fundamentals of Law and Regulation].

18 See Legal Status of Approved Labeling of Prescription Drugs; Prescribing for Uses Unapproved by the Food and Drug Administration, 37 Fed. Reg. 16,503 (Aug. 15, 1972) (discussing Congress's legislative intent).

19 Id.; see also David G. Adams, The Food and Drug Administration's Regulation of Health Care Professionals, in 2 Fundamentals of Law and Regulation, supra note 17, at 423–5.

20 Richard A. Epstein, Why the FDA Must Preempt Tort Litigation: A Critique of Chevron Deference and a Response to Richard Nagareda, 1 J. Tort L. 7 (2006), www.bepress.com/jtl/vol1/iss1/art5 (emphasis added).

services when, for many types of devices used in health care facilities, the provider rather than the patient is the user.[21] Tension is seen in the 1976 Medical Device Amendments, which authorize the FDA to approve medical devices subject to restrictions on their use,[22] but expressly forbid the FDA to interfere with physicians' discretion to use those devices however they see fit in the context of practitioner–patient relationships.[23]

The product/service distinction grows even more strained when the device is CDS software, which by its very design is intended to influence the practice of medicine. The Cures Act traces a line between CDS software that performs device-like functions (which the FDA appropriately can regulate) versus CDS software whose functions resemble medical practice (which the FDA should not regulate).[24] The baseline assumption is that CDS software performs a practice-related function and should be excluded from the FDA's oversight. Congress recognizes two situations, however, where FDA oversight is appropriate. These are portrayed in Figure 2.1.

At the far left, the FDA can regulate CDS software when its "function is intended to acquire, process, or analyze a medical image or a signal from an

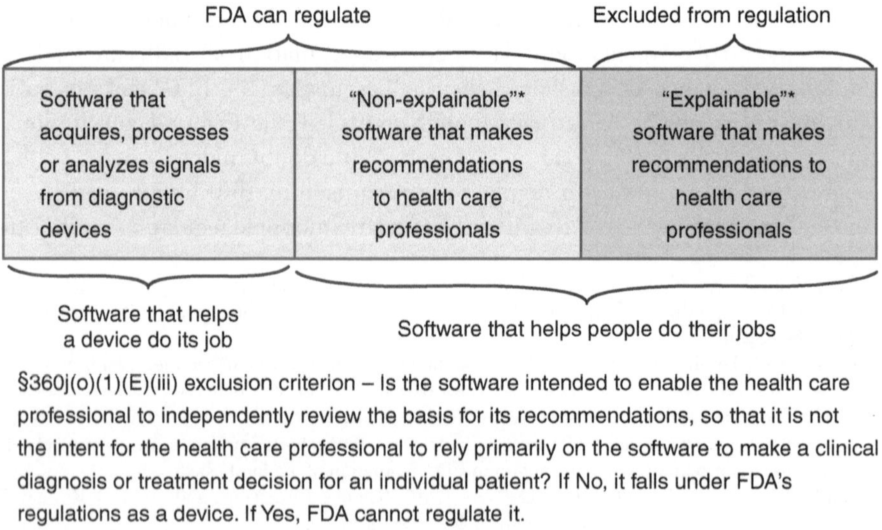

FIGURE 2.1: The FDA's jurisdiction to regulate CDS software under the Cures Act

21 See Patricia J. Zettler, Toward Coherent Federal Oversight of Medicine, 52 San Diego L. Rev. 427 (2015) (exploring de facto FDA regulation of medical practice).

22 Medical Device Amendments of 1976, Pub. L. No. 94–295, § 2, 90 Stat. 539, 565 (adding Section 520(e) of the Food, Drug, and Cosmetic Act) (codified as amended at 21 U.S.C. § 360j(e) (2006)).

23 21 U.S.C. § 396.

24 21 U.S.C. § 360j(o)(1)(E).

in vitro diagnostic device or a pattern or signal from a signal acquisition system."[25] The FDA has, for many years, regulated this type of software which includes, for example, software that enhances mammogram images to highlight areas suspicious for disease.[26] In one sense, this is CDS software because it helps a human actor – the radiologist – make a diagnosis. Still, another way to view it is that the software is helping a device (the imaging machine) do its job better by transforming outputs into a user-friendly format. By leaving such software under the FDA's oversight, the Cures Act treats it as mainly enhancing the performance of the device rather than the human using the device. The software is, in effect, a device accessory, and an accessory to a device is itself a device that the FDA can regulate.[27]

The FDA can regulate some, but not all, of the remaining CDS software which more directly aims to bolster human performance. The Cures Act allows the FDA to regulate CDS software if it is not intended to enable the "health care professional to independently review the basis for such recommendations that such software presents" so that there is an intent that the "health care professional rely primarily on any of such recommendations to make a clinical diagnosis or treatment decision regarding an individual patient."[28] This murky language expresses a rather simple concept: the FDA can regulate CDS software if the developer intends for it to operate as a "black box," to use Nicholson Price's phrase.[29] To use engineering parlance, the FDA can regulate AI/ML CDS software if it is not intended to function as explainable artificial intelligence (XAI).[30] CDS software that makes recommendations falls under the FDA's regulatory jurisdiction if those recommendations are not intended to be transparent to the health care professionals using the software. On the other hand, if CDS software is transparent enough that a health care professional would be able to understand its recommendations and challenge them – that is, when it is not a black box – then Congress excludes it from FDA regulatory oversight.

The Cures Act parses the product/practice regulatory distinction as follows: Congress sees it as a medical practice issue (instead of a product regulatory issue) to make sure health care professionals safely apply CDS software recommendations that are amenable to independent professional review. In that situation, safe and effective use of CDS software is best left to clinicians and to their state practice regulators, institutional policies, and the medical

25 Id.

26 Bradley Merrill Thompson, Learning from Experience: FDA's Treatment of Machine Learning, Mobile Health News (Aug. 23, 2017), www.mobihealthnews.com/content/learning-experience-fda%E2%80%99s-treatment-machine-learning; [https://perma.cc/Q95C-9R22].

27 21 U.S.C. § 321(h).

28 21 U.S.C. § 360j(o)(1)(E)(iii).

29 W. Nicholson Price II, Regulating Black-Box Medicine, 116 Mich. L. Rev. 421–74 (2017).

30 Enrico Tjoa & Cuntai Guan, A Survey on Explainable Artificial Intelligence (XAI): Towards Medical XAI, https://arxiv.org/pdf/1907.07374.pdf.

profession. When CDS software is not intended to be independently reviewable by the health care provider at the point of care, there is no way for these bodies to police appropriate clinical use of the software. In that situation, the Cures Act tasks the FDA with overseeing its safety and effectiveness. Doing so has the side effect of exposing CDS software developers to a risk of product liability suits. Product liability regimes may provide a useful legal framing for some of the problems CDS software presents.

2.3 WHY THERE MAY BE A ROLE FOR PRODUCT LIABILITY

An emerging literature on the limits of AI and big data analytics has raised serious concerns about the safety of these technologies, including in their CDS software applications. Lack of reproducibility may occur because of nonrepresentative datasets, or because vendors and developers refuse to permit others to scrutinize their wares. As Rebecca Robbins reported in 2020, "Some of these AI models are fraught with bias, and even those that have been demonstrated to be accurate largely haven't yet been shown to improve patient outcomes. Some hospitals don't share data on how well the systems work."[31] Narrow validity undermines some models' applicability in certain health care settings, but overblown claims of accuracy or assistance can lead physicians not to mention that the software is in use, much less to seek patients' informed consent to it.[32] Data opacity also creates situations where even those who might be concerned about CDS software cannot adequately complete due diligence or otherwise explore its limits. Dr. Eric Topol summarized many examples of these problems (lack of reproducibility, narrow validity, overblown claims, and nontransparent or hidden data).[33]

There is also concern that the data involved may not merely lack representativeness generally but may be biased in particularly troubling ways. Datasets may inadequately reflect all groups in society,[34] or may underinclude women[35] and

[31] Rebecca Robbins, An Invisible Hand: Patients Aren't Being Told about the AI Systems Advising Their Care, Stat News (July 15, 2020), www.statnews.com/2020/07/15/artificial-intelligence-patient-consent-hospitals/.

[32] See W. Nicholson Price II, Medical AI and Contextual Bias, 33 Harv. J. L. & Tech. 66 (2019) (discussing narrow validity of AI systems developed in resource-rich contexts when implemented in lower-resource settings).

[33] Eric Topol, Deep Medicine: How Artificial Intelligence Can Make Healthcare Human Again (Basic Books ed., 2019); See also Matthew Zook et al., 10 Simple Rules for Responsible Big Data Research, 13 PLoS Computational Biology (2017) (identifying similar limits); Danah Boyd & Kate Crawford, Critical Questions for Big Data, 15 J. Info., Commc'n and Soc'y 662–79 (2012).

[34] Ziad Obermeyer et al., Dissecting Racial Bias in an Algorithm Used to Manage the Health of Populations, 366 Science 447–53 (2019); Ruha Benjamin, Assessing Risk, Automating Racism, 366 Science 421–2 (2019). But see Frank Pasquale & Danielle Keats Citron, Promoting Innovation While Preventing Discrimination: Policy Goals for the Scored Society, 89 Wash. L. Rev. 1413–24 (2014) (discussing ways to address biases).

[35] Carolyn Criado Perez, Invisible Women: Data Bias in a World Designed for Men (Abrams ed., 2019).

overrepresent persons of European ancestry,[36] causing the software to provide unreliable or unsafe recommendations for the underrepresented groups.[37]

Some observers hope that the FDA or National Institute of Standards and Technology will gradually nudge CDS software vendors toward better practices. However, the current path of development of medical software casts doubt on whether FDA oversight can fulfil this role. The agency's Digital Innovation Action Plan[38] and its Digital Health Software Precertification (Pre-Cert) Program[39] acknowledge these concerns:

> FDA's traditional approach to moderate and higher risk hardware-based medical devices is not well suited for the faster iterative design, development, and type of validation used for software-based medical technologies. Traditional implementation of the premarket requirements may impede or delay patient access to critical evolutions of software technology.[40]

In response, the FDA is "reimagining its approach to digital health medical devices,"[41] but the agency's policies are still a work in progress. Roiled by long-term trends toward underfunding, politically motivated attacks on its expertise, and flagging public confidence in the wake of the US COVID-19 debacle, the FDA faces a difficult path ahead and may be particularly challenged when it comes to regulating the safety and effectiveness of AI/ML CDS software.[42] The agency's priorities may justifiably be elsewhere, and its ability to recruit experts at government salary scales is suspect when AI/ML experts command significantly more than current public compensation levels.

When diagnostic AI ignores problems with inclusivity and bias yet still manages to deliver better results than unaided human observation for many or most patients, the patients who do suffer an injury may not have a tort remedy under a negligence standard – particularly if the standard of care is unaided human observation. Even if standard-setting bodies enunciate standards for database inclusion, many states continue to base negligence liability on customary standards of care.[43] The next

36 Alice B. Popejoy et al., The Clinical Imperative for Inclusivity: Race, Ethnicity, and Ancestry (REA) in Genomics, 39 Human Mutation 1713–20 (2018).

37 Adewole S. Adamson & Avery Smith, Machine Learning and Health Care Disparities in Dermatology, 154 JAMA Dermatology 1247 (2018).

38 US Food & Drug Admin., Digital Health Innovation Action Plan (2017), www.fda.gov/downloads/MedicalDevices/DigitalHealth/UCM568735.pdf.

39 US Food & Drug Admin., Digital Health Software Precertification (Pre-Cert) Program, www.fda.gov/medical-devices/digital-health-center-excellence/digital-health-software-precertification-pre-cert-program.

40 US Food & Drug Admin., supra note 38, at 2.

41 Id. at 5.

42 On the history of challenges to the FDA, see Frank Pasquale, Grand Bargains for Big Data: The Emerging Law of Health Information, 72 Md. L. Rev. 682 (2013); Efthimios Parasidis, Patients over Politics: Addressing Legislative Failure in the Regulation of Medical Products, 5 Wis. L. Rev. 929 (2011).

43 Frank Pasquale, Data Informed Duties, 119 Colum. L. Rev. 1917–39 (2019).

section explores whether failures to use more representative databases might be deemed actionable in strict product liability.

The FDA's announced approaches for regulating Software as a Medical Device (SaMD) seemingly would not preempt state product liability suits under doctrines announced in prior medical device cases like *Medtronic v. Lohr*[44] and *Riegel v. Medtronic.*[45] This opens the door for product liability suits to help fill the regulatory gaps and help incentivize quality improvement, accountability, and responsibility that an overburdened FDA may be incapable of ensuring.[46]

Other factors suggesting a need for product liability include medical software contract practices that blunt the impact of negligence suits against software developers. It is common for developers to shield themselves from negligence through license terms that shift liability to (or require indemnification from) health care providers that use their software.[47] Such terms are seen, for example, in vendor contracts for electronic health record (EHR) systems, which may also include alternative dispute resolution procedures and gag clauses that stifle public disclosure of safety problems.[48] Patients hurt by defective medical software might attempt to sue their health care provider but would face challenges establishing negligence of the software developer. The provider, who might possess facts bearing on the developer's negligence, cannot pursue claims under terms of the licensing agreement. The result is to channel negligence claims toward providers while the software developer goes unscathed. In contrast, product liability widens opportunities for patients to sue any party in the chain of commerce that resulted in their injuries. Private contracts between software developers and health care providers can foreclose suits between those two signatories but cannot waive the rights of patients to sue developers whose defective software causes medical injuries.

The next section explores two possible product liability causes of action that offer promise for this gap-filling role. The first is manufacturing defect suits for lack of explainability, when software fails to live up to developers' claims that the algorithm is transparent to physicians tasked with using it. The second is design defect suits when software uses training or operational datasets that are too small, inaccurate, biased, or otherwise inappropriate for the actual patients for whom the software renders recommendations.

44 518 U.S.C. § 470 (1996).

45 552 U.S.C. § 312 (2008); See also Barbara J. Evans, The Streetlight Effect: Regulating Genomics Where the Light Is, 48 J. L., Med. Ethics Supp: LawSeq 105 (2020) (discussing why the FDA's proposed approaches do not appear to preempt failure-to-warn suits).

46 There is not complete harmony between tort and regulation here; some preemption issues may arise, for example, if high-risk software were regulated as a Class III medical device. See, e.g., Charlotte Tschider, Medical Device Artificial Intelligence: The New Tort Frontier, 46 BYU L. Rev. 1551, 1573–86 (2021), https://papers.ssrn.com/sol3/papers.cfm?abstract_id=3443987.

47 Liis Vihul, The Liability of Software Manufacturers for Defective Products, Tallinn Paper No. 2 (Cooperative Cyber Defense Center of Excellence ed., 2014).

48 See Jim Hawkins et al., Nontransparency in Electronic Health Record Systems, in Transparency in Health and Health Care in the United States 273–85 (Holly F. Lynch et al. eds., 2019).

2.4 CAN MANUFACTURING DEFECT SUITS PROMOTE EXPLAINABILITY OF AI/ML CDS SOFTWARE?

In its 2017 and 2019 draft guidance documents on CDS software,[49] the FDA failed to clarify the central jurisdictional enigma in the Cures Act: How will the agency determine whether AI/ML CDS software is intended to enable the health care professional to independently review the basis for the software's recommendations? This section describes the problem and explores whether product liability suits might help.

The FDA has a clear process for assessing device manufacturers' intent,[50] but needs to explain how this process applies to developers of AI/ML software: How, exactly, will the FDA assess whether a software developer intends for its software to be explainable? The agency could, for example, describe algorithmic features that support an inference that CDS software is medical XAI. Alternatively, the agency could prescribe a clinical testing process (such as having physicians use the software and surveying whether they understand the basis for its decisions). The FDA has done neither.

The draft guidance documents both view simple, rule-based CDS systems – those that merely apply existing knowledge that is "publicly available (e.g., clinical practice guidelines, published literature)"[51] – as meeting the § 360j(o)(1)(E)(iii) "explainability" standard, thus escaping FDA regulation. The 2017 draft guidance did not directly discuss AI/ML systems that derive and apply new insights from real-world evidence. It seemed to presume that all such systems would be subject to FDA regulation – an overly expansive view of the FDA's authority that ignored the jurisdictional rule in the Cures Act. The 2019 draft guidance acknowledges that the explainability of AI/ML software is a key jurisdictional issue but failed to provide any standards or processes for judging whether software is intended to be explainable.

This default has serious consequences. If the FDA deems all but the simplest CDS systems to be unexplainable, this could have detrimental impacts on innovation and on patients. What incentive will software developers have to invest in making AI/ML medical software more explainable to physicians, if the FDA deems all such software to be unexplainable no matter what they do? Simple, rule-based CDS software would escape FDA oversight. Promising AI/ML software to enable a learning health care system informed by real clinical evidence might face long regulatory delays.

The FDA's failure to set standards – or at least a process – for assessing software explainability leaves the agency with no basis to rebut developers' claims that their software is intended to be explainable and to allow independent review by

[49] See US Food & Drug Admin., supra note 2.

[50] See 21 C.F.R. § 801.4.

[51] See US Food & Drug Admin 2017 Draft Guidance, supra note 2, at 8.

physicians. Developers seemingly could escape FDA regulation by simply asserting that they intend for software to be explainable (whether or not it actually is) and by labeling the software as "not intended for use without independent review by a healthcare professional" and "not intended to serve as the primary basis for making a clinical diagnosis or treatment decision regarding an individual patient."[52] Developers have strong incentives to pursue this strategy. They might escape FDA regulation under the Cures Act's jurisdictional rule. This in turn would let them argue that their software is a service, rather than an FDA-regulated product subject to product liability. Any physician that relies on the software's recommendations as the main basis for decision making would be using it off-label, and negligence liability for off-label use rests with the physician, rather than the software developer. Why would a rational software developer not try this strategy?

Strict product liability might provide an answer. Under the Third Restatement of Torts, a plaintiff establishes a manufacturing defect by showing that a product "departs from its intended design even though all possible care was exercised in the preparation and marketing of the product."[53] The plaintiff merely needs to show that the product deviated from the intended design when it left the developer's possession.[54] If an AI/ML CDS software developer states that it intended for its software to allow independent review by physicians, and perhaps even escaped FDA oversight by making that claim, then that proves that the software was intended to be explainable. If the software later lacks explainability, hindering independent physician review, then the software clearly departs from its intended design and has a manufacturing defect. Plaintiffs seemingly face low evidentiary hurdles to establish the defect: they could call their physician to the witness stand and ask the physician to explain to the jury how the AI/ML software reached its recommendations that affected patient care. If the physician cannot do so, the plaintiff would have proved the defect. In light of the FDA's ongoing failure to enunciate standards for AI/ML software explainability, manufacturing defect suits are a promising tool to incentivize investment in improved explainability (and frank disclosures when explainability is lacking).

2.5 CAN DESIGN DEFECTS PROMOTE THE USE OF APPROPRIATE TRAINING DATASETS?

The FDA's 2017 draft guidance on CDS software suggested that the Cures Act explainability standard cannot be met unless physician users have access to the data underlying a software product's recommendations.[55] The agency backed away from this position in its 2019 draft guidance, possibly reflecting the reality that

52 See 21 U.S.C. § 360j(o)(1)(E)(iii).
53 Restatement (Third) of Torts: Products Liability § 2(a).
54 Id.
55 21 U.S.C. § 360j(o)(1)(E)(iii).

software developers are deeply opposed to sharing their proprietary training datasets with anyone – neither users nor regulators. At most, developers express willingness to share summary statistics, such as the kinds of health conditions, demographics, and number of patients included in the training dataset. The FDA's oversight of AI/ML training datasets thus seems destined to be cursory.

There have been calls for software developers to have legal duties relating to the accuracy and appropriateness (representativeness) of training datasets, as well as the integrity of all data inputs and the transparency of outputs.[56] Prospective regulation by the FDA is proving an uncertain legal vehicle for establishing such duties. Can design defect suits address this deficiency?

"Strict" product liability/design defect suits allege that a product is unreasonably dangerous even though it may conform to its intended design. Complex products like CDS software are unsuitable for a consumer expectations test, which applies only if jurors would be able to understand a product's risks without the aid of expert witnesses. Courts likely would apply a risk-utility test, which usually involves requiring the plaintiff to show that a reasonable alternative design (RAD) existed at the time of sale and distribution. This reliance on reasonability concepts causes strict liability suits for design defects to bear a considerable resemblance to negligence suits, which is why this paragraph put "strict" between quotation marks.

Selection of the training dataset is a central design decision when developing AI/ML software. If the training dataset is too small, inappropriate, inaccurate, or biased and nonrepresentative of patients the software later will analyze, then the software – by its design – cannot provide accurate recommendations for their care. An alternative design seemingly always exists: that is, train the software on a larger, more appropriate, more accurate, less biased dataset that better reflects the intended patient population. However, the "R" in RAD stands for "reasonable," and it would be left for the trier of fact to decide whether it would have been reasonable for the software developer to have used that alternative, better dataset, in view of the cost, delay, availability, and accessibility of additional data.

Framing the problem as a design defect of the AI/ML software (which in most cases will be an FDA-regulated product) may avert some of the difficulties seen in prior product liability suits alleging defects in information itself. Because information is intangible, some courts struggle with treating it as a product and applying strict liability.[57] Suits for defective graphic presentation of information occasionally succeed, as in *Aetna Casualty and Surety v. Jeppeson & Co.*,[58] involving a deadly air crash after the pilot relied on a Jeppeson instrument approach chart – a product consisting almost entirely of the graphic presentation of information, which the

56 Pasquale, supra note 43.

57 Reutiman, supra note 10, at 183.

58 642 F.2d 339 (9th Cir. 1981); see also Brocklesby v. United States, 767 F.2d 1288, 1294–5 (9th Cir. 1985), and discussion in Oren Bracha & Frank Pasquale, Federal Search Commission? Access, Fairness, and Accountability in the Law of Search, 93 Cornell L. Rev. 1149, 1194 (2008).

district court found defective. That case is considered anomalous, however, and many courts hesitate to allow design defect suits over deadly information, whether on First Amendment grounds or reluctance to hinder free flows of information in our society.[59] Suits for defective information seem most likely to fail when the information in question resembles expressive content,[60] which might not be an issue for AI/ML training datasets, which are not expressive. Still, courts have a well-known reluctance to treat information as a "product" that was "defective." The approach proposed here avoids this problem. The alleged defect is not in the information itself, but in the design of the software product that relied on the information. The information in an AI/ML training dataset is best conceived as a design feature of the software rather than a product in its own right.

2.6 CONCLUSION

Some commentators express concern that applying product liability to software could have adverse impacts on innovation and might delay diffusion of software.[61] We agree that these are valid concerns that courts will need to weigh carefully when considering claims by patients injured during the use of AI/ML CDS software. At the same time, however, a vast and growing literature on algorithmic accountability and critical algorithm studies has painstakingly documented that AI/ML software, even if it provides useful results for most people, can harm members of groups that were underrepresented in the datasets on which the software relies.[62] Such injuries are predictable and need remedies when they do occur. Product liability should not be ruled out. Slowing the diffusion of software might well be justified if the software injures people or entrenches historical disparities in access to high-quality health care.

Other commentators question applying product liability to AI/ML continuous-learning software which can evolve independently of the manufacturer.[63] To date, the FDA has only cleared or approved software that is "locked" – that is, stops evolving – prior to the FDA's review, which removes this concern. As continuously learning software does reach the market, the possibility of software evolution

59 See Reutiman, supra note 10, at 188–9.

60 See, e.g., Winter v. G.P. Putnam's Sons, 938 F.28 1033 (9th Cir. 1991) (no liability for dangerous misinformation in a book); Wilson v. Midway Games, Inc., 198 F. Supp 2d 167 (D. Conn. 2002) (rejecting claim that a video game was dangerously defective for stimulating violent behavior in users, noting similarities to expressive media like movies and television).

61 See, e.g., Bryan H. Choi, Crashworthy Code, 94 Wash. L. Rev. 39 (Mar. 2019); Jamil Ammar, Defective Computer-Aided Design Software Liability in 3d Bioprinted Human Organ Equivalents, 35 Santa Clara High Tech. L. J. 58 (2019); Karni A. Chagal-Feferkorn, Am I an Algorithm or a Product? When Products Liability Should Apply to Algorithmic Decision-Makers, 30 Stan. L. & Pol'y Rev. 82 (2019).

62 Frank Pasquale, The Black Box Society (Harvard University Press ed., 2015); Frank Pasquale, New Laws of Robotics (Harvard University Press ed., 2020).

63 Jacob Turner, Robot Rules: Regulating Artificial Intelligence 94–100 (Palgrave Macmillan ed., 2018).

underscores the need to program in restraints and checks against problematic forms of evolution.[64] The FDA has not explained how it will (or whether it can) ensure such restraints. Product liability has long served alongside the FDA's oversight to promote patient safety.

Some commentators endorse product liability in the CDS context, pointing to the need for courts to recognize and counteract automation bias, which can arise when often overworked professionals seek tools to ease their workload.[65] More stringent product liability standards are a way of promoting a lower risk level in the health care industry and can ease the difficulties injured patients will face establishing negligence, given the extraordinarily complex and even trade-secret protected methods used to develop CDS software.[66]

The time may be right to reconsider product liability for medical software. The FDA's foray into this regulatory sphere bestows "product" status on medical software that courts often have tended to view as information services. By doing so, the agency's regulation of CDS software opens the door to product liability suits. This chapter has suggested two examples that merit further study. Such suits could help nudge software developers to improve the explainability of their software and ensure appropriate training datasets and could promote greater industry transparency about CDS software on which patients' lives may depend.

64 Stuart J. Russell, Human Compatible: Artificial Intelligence and the Problem of Control (New York: Penguin Random House ed., 2019).

65 Efthimios Parasidis, Clinical Decision Support: Elements of a Sensible Legal Framework, 20 J. Healthcare L. & Pol'y (2018); see also Nicholas Carr, The Glass Cage: How Our Computers Are Changing Us (W.W. Norton ed., 2015); see also, Kevin R. Pinkney, Putting Blame where Blame Is Due: Software Manufacturer and Customer Liability for Security-Related Software Failure, 13 Albany L. J. Sci. & Tech. (2002) (focusing on security defects); Michael D. Scott, Tort Liability for Vendors of Insecure Software: Has the Time Finally Come?, 67 Md. L. Rev. 469–70 (2017) (same).

66 Frances E. Zollers et al., No More Soft Landings for Software: Liability for Defects in an Industry That Has Come of Age, 21 Santa Clara Computer & High Tech. L. J. 777 (2005).

3

Are Electronic Health Records Medical Devices?

Craig Konnoth

Are Electronic Health Records (EHRs) medical devices? Answering this question is important. It will determine, in part, which agency will regulate EHRs, and under what paradigms. Either the Food and Drug Administration (FDA) will regulate EHRs as medical devices, or the Office of the National Coordinator of Health Information Technology (ONC), another subagency within HHS that focuses on health data regulation, will provide the framework. This chapter argues that the task should be divided between the two agencies in a way that reflects their respective expertise to produce an optimum outcome. The criterion should be the extent to which the particular function being regulated involves networking with other systems and users. To the degree that it does, the ONC should hold primacy. But for more patient-facing functions that do not involve networking, the FDA should run point. Thus, the ONC should control data-format standardization in EHRs; the FDA might lead clinical decision support (CDS) efforts.

At the outset, some may argue that the question I raise is moot, and my solution is impossible. Section 520(o)(1)(C) of the Food Drug and Cosmetic Act (FDCA), inserted by the 21st Century Cures Act of 2016 (Cures Act), seems to shift the balance of power toward the ONC. It provides that EHRs are not medical devices if they were "created, stored, transferred, or reviewed by health care professionals," "are part of health information technology that is certified" by the ONC, and "such function is not intended to interpret or analyze patient records."[1] But at the same time, the HHS Secretary has the authority to undo the exclusion, admittedly subject to notice and comment rulemaking, and a finding that a particular "software function would be reasonably likely to have serious adverse health consequences."[2] If the exclusion of EHRs from FDA jurisdiction does not make sense, then, the Secretary could likely take steps to undo or modify the statutory mandate.

The question then is, should they? And the statute provides no answer to that question. On one hand, the statute does exclude EHRs as medical devices. But at the

[1] 21 U.S.C. § 360j(o)(1)(C).
[2] 21 U.S.C. § 360j(o)(3)(A)–(B).

same time, by negative implication, Section 520(o)(1)(C) suggests that but for its exclusion, EHRs would be medical devices – after all, why bother to say a product was not a device, if that product would not have, anyway, been covered in the definition of device?[3] While the statute quite clearly excludes EHRs as medical devices, neither the statute, nor the legislative history, is clear on the reasons for doing so. Thus, there is little guidance in the statute as to how the Secretary can and should exercise discretion.

I argue that the key aspect of EHRs that render them foreign to the FDA's jurisdiction is their systemwide interconnectedness; they affect and are affected, both directly and indirectly, by third parties. First, a patient's EHR affects others. The EHRs must work in a certain way, not just for the safety of the patient, but for the integrity of the system as a whole. The data from EHRs is used for both clinical and quality management research, for example. On the other hand, the safety of EHRs involves greater systematic, upstream regulation – of third-party networks, data formats, and other issues that present collective action problems. This goes far beyond the mandate of the FDA that fails to consider such issues and lacks jurisdiction over many necessary third parties.[4]

While I therefore endorse some aspects of the FDA's historic reasoning with respect to EHRs, which I describe below, I argue that it should be allowed to regulate only those functions that have a direct and primary effect on the particular patient – such as the quality of a particular algorithm that renders CDS. However, it should not be allowed to regulate aspects of EHRs such as data format and interoperability that present these third-party and systematic considerations.

3.1 EXISTING REASONS AGAINST REGULATING EHRS AND THEIR SHORTCOMINGS

The Food, Drug, and Cosmetic Act of 1938 was amended in 1976 to include medical devices within the FDA's ambit. A device is:

> [A]n instrument, apparatus, implement, machine, contrivance, implant, in vitro reagent, or other similar or related article, including any component, part, or accessory, which is ... intended for use in the diagnosis of disease or other conditions, or in the cure, mitigation, treatment, or prevention of disease.[5]

Devices are categorized as Class I through III, depending on the extent to which they support or sustain human life, or present a risk of injury. Class I devices do not

[3] Cf. Metro. Life Ins. Co. v. Massachusetts, 471 U.S. 724, 741 (1985) ("Unless Congress intended to include laws regulating insurance contracts within the scope of the insurance saving clause, it would have been unnecessary for the deemer clause explicitly to exempt such laws from the saving clause when they are applied directly to benefit plans.").

[4] For an extended treatment of this framework see, generally Craig J. Konnoth, Drugs' Other Side Effects, 104 Ia. L. Rev. 171 (2019).

[5] 21 U.S.C. § 321(h).

support or sustain human life and do not unreasonably risk injury; Class II devices are somewhere in the middle, as they support or sustain human life and present a higher risk; Class III devices present a high risk of injury.[6] FDA controls are commensurate with device risk. Class I devices are subject to "general controls" – for example, prohibitions on misbranding. Class II devices are subject to some additional, discretionary controls. Class III devices require premarket approval from the Secretary, though there are methods for obtaining exemptions.[7]

Turning next to EHRs, these consist of software that offers various kinds of functionality, including data entry, storage, retrieval, transmission, and CDS, among others.[8] In the late 1980s and early 1990s, EHRs began to take on their modern form, offering functions such as computerized order entry, CDS, and medical device interfaces – even though the early computer systems were slow, had low storage capacity, and paper was omnipresent.[9]

On my account, the FDA regulates EHRs in whole or in part when it takes on regulation of these functions, including when these functions appear in an EHR context. Thus, if the FDA declares authority over CDS regulation, it engages in regulation of EHRs to some degree because of the ubiquity of CDS in EHR contexts. Starting in the late 1980s, as EHRs took on their modern form, the FDA offered various reasons both for and against regulating EHRs and EHR-type products.

On one hand, the reasons for regulating EHRs seem obvious – it falls within the medical device definition. It seems that EHRs constitute an "apparatus" or "contrivance" that is "intended for use" in the process of disease diagnosis, as well as in "the cure, mitigation, treatment, or prevention of disease." Thus, when data from bloodwork is fed into an EHR, and a medical professional looks at the EHR to make a diagnosis, and also looks at the EHR to determine what other medication a patient is taking, so that they can determine what should be prescribed, the EHR plays a role in both the process of diagnosis and treatment. Prominent data regulation scholars, Sharona Hoffman and Andy Podgurski, similarly conclude: "Given that they feature decision support, order entry, and other care delivery and management functions, one might reasonably conclude that EHR systems are as essential to patient care as are many regulated devices. Furthermore, their software can be more complicated than that found in many computer-controlled medical devices that are subject to FDA jurisdiction."[10]

6 21 U.S.C.A. § 360c(a)(1).

7 Id.; Sharona Hoffman & Andy Podgurski, Finding a Cure: The Case for Regulation and Oversight of Electronic Health Record Systems, 22 Harv. J. L. & Tech. 103, 137 (2009).

8 R.S. Evans, Electronic Health Records: Then, Now, and In the Future, Yearbook Med. Inform. S48–61 (2016), www.ncbi.nlm.nih.gov/pmc/articles/PMC5171496/; see also HealthIT.gov, Clinical Decision Support, www.healthit.gov/topic/safety/clinical-decision-support ("The majority of CDS applications operate as components of comprehensive EHR systems").

9 See Evans, supra note 8.

10 Hoffman & Podgurski, supra note 7at 130. They raise concerns about FDA authority and would give the oversight to the Centers for Medicare and Medicaid Services, another subagency in HHS.

This understanding appears to have undergirded the thinking of at least one senior FDA official, who, a decade ago, suggested that EHRs should be regulated as medical devices. As he explained, Health Information Technology – in this case, it would appear from context, specifically EHRs, are vulnerable to various errors that affect patient safety. These include "(1) errors of commission, such as accessing the wrong patient's record ... (2) errors of omission or transmission, such as the loss or corruption of vital patient data (3) errors in data analysis, including medication dosing errors of several orders of magnitude and (4) incompatibility between multi-vendor software applications and systems, which can lead to any of the above."[11] Two years later, a dissenting view in an Institute of Medicine Report advanced similar reasons for regulating EHRs as medical devices.[12] EHR "components participate directly in diagnosis, cure, mitigation, treatment, and prevention of specified individual human beings" squarely falling within the definition of medical devices.[13] Indeed, for reasons I will not engage here, the dissent argued that EHRs should be regulated as Class III devices.

On the other hand, over the years, regulators have offered various reasons against regulating EHRs as devices, though none seem to overcome the squarely textual reasoning above. First, the FDA has noted EHR outputs are subject to independent clinical judgment. Physicians can use their independent experience and knowledge to evaluate the EHR output and make their own decisions concerning patients.[14] Second, "health IT is constantly being upgraded and modified to reflect new evidence and clinical interventions, changing work flows, and new requirements ... Constantly evolving systems ... don't lend themselves to discontinuous oversight mechanisms such as those used for medical devices."[15] Third, the FDA lacks "capacity" to regulate;[16] and fourth, that "regulation of health IT

However, the Cures Act allows the Secretary to entrust authority to the FDA. See also Nicolas Terry, Pit Crews with Computers: Can Health Information Technology Fix Fragmented Care?, 14 Hous. J. Health L. & Pol'y 129, 183 (2014) ("In straining to avoid untimely over-regulation, the FDA may have under-regulated. If the agency had asserted its jurisdiction over EMRs rather than backing down to ONC and CMS during MU, maybe better, safer products would have been brought to market (admittedly later).").

11 Jeffrey Shuren, Dir. of FDA's Ctr. for Devices and Radiological Health, Testimony at the Health Info. Tech. Policy Comm. Adoption/Certification Workgroup (Feb. 25, 2010) (acknowledging the receipt of 260 reports of malfunctioning EHR systems since 2008), www.cchfreedom.org/pdfs/Health%20IT%20Deaths%20-%20FDA%20jeffrey%20Shuren.pdf.

12 Inst. of Med., Health IT and Patient Safety: Building Safer Systems for Better Care 194 (2012), www.ncbi.nlm.nih.gov/books/NBK189661/pdf/Bookshelf_NBK189661.pdf [hereinafter IOM Report].

13 Id.

14 This remarkably stable rationale has spanned the last thirty years. Compare 52 Fed. Reg. 36,104 (1987) with Bipartisan Policy Center Health Innovation Initiative, An Oversight Framework for Assuring Patient Safety in Health Information Technology 15 (2013), https://bipartisanpolicy.org/wp-content/uploads/2019/03/Patient-Safety-Health-IT.pdf; See also infra note 42 (describing recently released guidance pertaining to the Cures Act).

15 Bipartisan Policy Center, supra note 14, at 16.

16 IOM Report, supra note 12, at 154.

[including EHRs] by FDA as a Class III device could have" an impact "on innovation."[17]

But there are problems with these rationales. The independent review rationale also founders because professionals are just as reliant on EHRs as they are on many other devices (and relatedly, unable to carry out fully independent reviews). Indeed, depending on the error, a professional may be more likely to see if an x-ray machine malfunctioned – because the image is fuzzy, perhaps – than if an EHR contains wrong data. Similarly, as Hoffman and Podgurski note, "in the midst of surgery or in the intensive care unit" it would be hard for a provider to reflect on the data that the EHR has provided.[18] Further, the concept of "intervention" is hard to suss out. Does "intervention" require the practitioner to follow the EHR's output or recommendation only if it accords with their assessment, but ignore it otherwise? If so, the value-add of the EHR is unclear – if the practitioner is going to stick to their judgment no matter what.

Similarly, the other rationales also fail. On the second objection, medical devices generally are subject to various kinds of upgrades and "constant[] evol[ution]"; the FDA has offered a preliminary discussion regarding upgrading different kinds of software, with different tracks for "locked" versus continuously evolving algorithms.[19] As for the third, FDA funding and support can be increased. And the fourth concern goes to the kind of regulation that would be appropriate for EHRs as medical devices – it does not speak to whether EHRs are devices, and whether the FDA should have control.

Thus, while it is clear that many stakeholders have concerns with giving the FDA full control over EHR regulation, they have not provided strong rationales.

3.2 ADDITIONAL RATIONALE: NETWORKED VERSUS NONNETWORKED ASPECTS OF EHR USE

In this section, I argue that fundamental aspects of EHRs – namely, their systemwide interconnectedness – render at least some important EHR functionalities foreign to FDA expertise. Thus, I argue that the FDA should refrain from regulation on aspects of EHRs that directly implicate data networks. That regulation should remain in the hands of the ONC, which has relationships with data networks and EHR developers.[20] However, FDA regulation may be appropriate where the subject of regulation is the point at which the EHR interacts directly with patient care.

17 Id.

18 Hoffman & Podgurski, supra note 7.

19 US Food & Drug Admin., Proposed Regulatory Framework for Modifications to Artificial Intelligence/Machine Learning (AI/ML) Based Software as a Medical Device (SaMD): Discussion Paper and Request for Feedback 3 (2019), www.fda.gov/media/122535/download [hereinafter SaMD Discussion Paper].

20 See generally Craig Konnoth & Gabriel Scheffler, Can Electronic Health Records Be Saved?, 46 Am. J.L. & Med. 7, 7–19 (2020).

In other work, I have explained that EHR use occurs at two levels: at the individual level, and a population-based level.[21] At the individual level, a medical professional uses EHR for the care of a specific patient. They look up a patient's medical history, past medical conditions, treatments and the like. They can use the data to treat the patient, ensuring that there are no adverse drug interactions.

At a systemwide level, many EHRs are connected in ways that allow the data they contact to be pulled together and analyzed to draw conclusions on the safety and effectiveness of treatments and procedures, among other purposes, across vast populations. For this purpose, troves of data are cleaned, collated, and analyzed. The goal of a so-called learning health system would be to pull together data – much, if not most of it, in the form of EHRs – in real-time to figure out what interventions work best based on current knowledge, to reenter data back into the system, which in turn, is then used to refine the outcome for future interventions on other patients in an iterative feedback loop.[22] While not all EHRs can carry out these functions, many of them do so, and the goal is to have full interconnectivity.

Further, it is not just the uses of EHRs that invite population and systemwide considerations. Pulling together EHRs involves other population- and system-level considerations. For example, the data formats and elements that one EHR uses have ramifications for how other, unrelated EHR systems work – if they do not use the same formats and elements, the overall system cannot function properly.[23] Thus, as one regulatory entity put it: "[i]ndividual health IT components may meet their stated performance requirements, yet the system as a whole may yield unsafe outcomes."[24]

These questions of population-level data and interconnected networks should determine the bounds of FDA jurisdiction. The operation of EHRs in a certain instance, then, is fundamentally interconnected to a broader system. When a doctor deploys an EHR in a particular context, their action draws on data, data formats, users (who may have input the data years ago), and networks. More than that, their engagement with the EHR can have implications for patient care – not just that of their patient, but, if the EHR is agglomerated and used elsewhere, on that of other patients.

This is the key difference between most devices and EHRs. As long as other devices are integrated into the relevant medical system of which they are a part, they fulfil their primary function. Safety considerations therefore focus on the particular context in which the device is used – while there may be downstream effects, they are less important. The purpose of EHRs however, is to record, transmit, aggregate,

21 Craig Konnoth, Data Collection, EHRs, and Poverty Determinations, 46 J.L., Med. & Ethics 622, 625–6 (2018).

22 Craig Konnoth, Health Information Equity, 165 U. Penn. L. Rev. 1317, 1319 (2017).

23 Craig Konnoth, Regulatory De-arbitrage in Twenty-First Century Cures Act's Health Information Regulation, 29 Ann. of Health L. & Life Sci. 136, 137 (2020).

24 US Food & Drug Admin., FDASIA Health IT Report: Proposed Strategy and Recommendations for a Risk-Based Framework 10 (Apr. 2014), www.fda.gov/media/87886/download [hereinafter, FDASIA Report].

and use information downstream. At a fundamental level EHRs must engage with other systems and subsequent patients – or the same patient in subsequent visits.

Because of this interconnected nature, unlike with other devices, where the safety of a particular MRI is not (within reason) dependent upon which supplier the provider obtained it from, it is harder to tease EHR and their data away from how it was delivered and sourced, and how it may play with other systems. In regulating EHRs, the FDA would not have to just consider the particular EHR system at hand. It would have to consider how the EHR system works with other EHR systems and formats, and other users. It would have to consider downstream uses of the data thus input, as it may be used for future analyses.

Limiting the FDA's ability to engage with the third party and indirect effects of EHRs fits in with the broader approach it currently takes. In previous work, I have argued that the FDA generally lacks expertise and has limited authority to regulate inter alia indirect drug effects and drug effects on third parties. As I explain, an indirect cause is one which is "separated from an effect by an intervening cause. This intervening cause must 1) be independent of the original act, 2) be a voluntary human act or an abnormal natural event, and 3) occur in time between the original act and the effect."[25] Thus, the use of birth control may lead (some claim) to higher incidents of STDs, since individuals may have condomless sex. But such condomless sex is a voluntary, intervening act. Similarly, "[t]hird-party harm occurs when the drug is prescribed for use, and actually used by person A, but person B is harmed by the use either directly or indirectly."[26] Such harm includes, for example, secondhand smoke directly inhaled by third parties who do not use cigarettes. Some harms are both indirect and third party, such as downstream partners who may contract an STD caused by condomless sex that some claim occurs due to the availability of birth control.[27] I explain that while the FDA should sometimes regulate indirect and third-party harm, its expertise and authority are at its nadir when it does so, and its intervention should be limited. That is the situation in which EHRs reside.

Without considering its implications for regulatory control, two regulatory entities have recognized that EHRs raise questions of indirect and third-party harms. They are part of "a complex sociotechnical system."[28] Yet, they do not distinguish the networked and nonnetworked aspects of EHRs. Rather, they focus on the interaction of users with EHRs, and the error that results. As they emphasize, the interactive nature of EHRs, organizational workflow, and user understanding, determine safety.[29] Scholars, such as Sara Gerke and coauthors, writing in the context of artificial intelligence (AI), have

25 Craig J. Konnoth, Drugs' Other Side Effects, 105 Ia. L. Rev. 171, 197 (2019).

26 Id. at 200.

27 Richard J. Fehring et al., Influence of Contraception Use on the Reproductive Health of Adolescents and Young Adults, 85 Linacre Q. 167, 167–77 (2018).

28 FDASIA report, supra note 24, at 10.

29 IOM Report, supra note 12, at 61–2.

similarly argued that AI in health implicates a "system" view, by which they mean the intersection of humans, and organizational workflow, with technology.[30]

But in the EHR context,[31] the distinguishing factor is not user-technology interaction. After all, other devices raise concerns regarding user-technology interactions, and the errors that result, and the FDA has, to some degree at least, sought to regulate such concerns by reviewing labeling, and the like.[32] There are limits – for example, the FDA cannot "regulate the practice of medicine."[33] But the user-error concerns here arise with respect to all medical devices. They are not unique to EHRs (or, for that matter, to medical software more generally). Rather, the relevant boundary is between networked and nonnetworked EHR functions.

Separating EHR use into two aspects allows us to determine the bounds of FDA jurisdiction. On one hand, it may make sense for the FDA to regulate certain aspects of the EHR as they pertain to a specific patient – subject to the limits on regulating the practice of medicine. But when networked aspects of the EHR are involved, the FDA should step back. In that situation, the ONC, which has developed relationships with EHR developers, national data networks, and indeed, has created a process to create a voluntary national health data network, should step in and regulate. How might this play out? Let us consider a taxonomy developed by various HHS agencies and see how the approach works.

3.3 APPLYING THE FRAMEWORK

The Food and Drug Administration Safety and Innovation Act (FDASIA) required the FDA, ONC, and the Federal Communications Commission (FCC) to develop "a report that contains a proposed strategy and recommendations on an appropriate, risk-based regulatory framework pertaining to health information technology, including mobile medical applications, that promotes innovation, protects patient safety, and avoids regulatory duplication."[34]

The report separated Health IT into three sets of functions:

> 1) administrative health IT functions [namely 'billing and claims processing, practice and inventory management, and scheduling'], 2) health management health IT functions [namely 'health information and data exchange, data capture and encounter documentation, electronic access to clinical results, most clinical decision support, medication management, electronic communication and coordination, provider order entry, knowledge management, and patient identification and

30 Sara Gerke et al., The Need for a System View to Regulate Artificial Intelligence/Machine Learning-Based Software as Medical Device, 3 npj Digital Med. (2020), www.nature.com/articles/s41746-020-0262-2?lead_type=mba.

31 And I emphasize that the scholars above were not considering the EHR context.

32 US Food & Drug Admin., Device Labeling, www.fda.gov/medical-devices/overview-device-regulation/device-labeling.

33 Gerke et al., supra note 30.

34 FDASIA Report, supra note 24.

matching'], and 3) medical device health IT functions [namely 'computer aided detection software, remote display or notification of real-time alarms from bedside monitors, and robotic surgical planning and control'].[35]

The report suggested that only category 3) functions were subject to FDA regulation. That seems correct, but not for the reasons in the Report.

First, administrative functions – "billing and claims processing, practice and inventory management, and scheduling" – are not patient facing, and can be separated on that ground.

Next, health management health IT functions include "health information and data exchange, data capture and encounter documentation, electronic access to clinical results, most clinical decision support, medication management, electronic communication and coordination, provider order entry, knowledge management, and patient identification and matching."[36] The Report concluded that it did not have to regulate these functions because they presented a lower risk.[37] In so concluding, it cited little evidence. The better reason is that these functions all have to do with EHR integration with other systems and its interaction with multiple users. They all have to do with EHR as a networked product – networked with both technology and system users. The FDA, which rarely regulates at a systemwide level, focused primarily on the interaction between device and patient, is ill-suited for such regulation. Rather, the ONC, which has developed relationships with multiple players in the health data world, should take the lead role.[38]

Finally, medical device health IT functions include "computer aided detection software, remote display or notification of real-time alarms from bedside monitors, and robotic surgical planning and control."[39] The Report suggested that these functions are higher risk, and therefore fall within the FDA's purview. On my account, these functions are more focused on HIT functionality as it pertains to specific patients, rather than networking aspects. It therefore falls more within FDA expertise.

Similar issues arise in the context of CDS regulation. Cures Act Section 520(o)(1)(C) excludes software that is meant to display medical information about a patient and the like, as long as the "health care professional [can] independently review the basis for such recommendations that such software presents so that it is not the intent that such health care professional rely primarily on any of such recommendations to make a clinical diagnosis or treatment decision regarding an individual patient."[40] In guidance, the FDA explained that whether a professional exercised such judgment depended on "[t]he purpose or intended use of the software function; The

35 Id. at 11–12.
36 Id. at 13.
37 Id. at 12.
38 See IOM Report, supra note 12, at 20–1 (describing the ONC's relationship with stakeholders).
39 FDASIA Report, supra note 24, at 13.
40 21 U.S.C. § 360j(o)(E)(iii).

intended user (e.g., ultrasound technicians, vascular surgeons); The inputs used to generate the recommendation (e.g., patient age and gender); and [t]he rationale or support for the recommendation. In order for the software function to be excluded from the definition of device, the intended user should be able to reach the same recommendation on his or her own without relying primarily on the software function."[41]

Commenters responded with confusion.[42] As Professor Efthimios Parasidis noted, "The FDA's statement does not represent a reasonable interpretation of the statute, because it focuses on the physician's ability to come up with a treatment decision independent of the CDS program, rather than focusing on the ability of the physician to independently review 'the basis of such recommendation that such software presents.' It is one thing to be able to diagnose a patient independent of a CDS program, and another to understand and independently review the output of a CDS program. The statute covers the latter, while the FDA's draft guidance appears to cover the former."[43]

In 2019, the FDA doubled down on this approach, however.[44]

On my account, CDS should fall within the FDA's purview to the extent it involves the quality of an algorithm and the outputs it produces. The ONC has little expertise on issues of algorithmic quality, while the FDA encounters such issues in its regulation of other devices apart from EHR.[45] However, CDS relies on the data collected from a range of different EHRs. To the extent that a CDS problem arises with data quality, transmission, or input from EHRs – that is, issues relating to

41 US Food & Drug Admin., Clinical and Patient Decision Support Software: Draft Guidance for Industry and Food and Drug Administration Staff 8 (2017), www.regulations.gov/document?D=FDA-2017-D-6569-0002.

42 See Barbara Evans & Pilar Ossorio, The Challenge of Regulating Clinical Decision Support Software After 21st Century Cures, 44 Am. J. L. and Med. 237, 239–40 (2018) ("The Cures Act singles out CDS software that recommends diagnoses or actions to treat or prevent disease. It defines a standard for deciding when such software can be excluded from FDA regulation. Congress excludes CDS software from FDA regulation if the software is intended to enable the 'health care professional to independently review the basis for such recommendations that such software presents so that it is not the intent that such health care professional rely primarily on any of such recommendations to make a clinical diagnosis or treatment decision regarding an individual patient.' To escape FDA regulation, the software vendor/manufacturer must intend for the software to make it possible for health care professionals to override its recommendations by explaining its rationale in terms that a clinician could understand, interrogate, and possibly reject. Whether CDS software is subject to FDA regulation potentially turns on the software's ability to answer the quintessential epistemological question: How do we know?").

43 Efthimios Parasidis, Comment on Clinical and Patient Decision Support Software: Draft Guidance for Industry and Food and Drug Administration Staff, 82 Fed. Reg. 53,987 (Dec. 8, 2017), www.regulations.gov/document?D=FDA-2017-D-6569-0010; Am. Med. Informatics Ass'n, Comment on Clinical and Patient Support Software: Draft Guidance for Industry and Food and Drug Administration Staff, 82 Fed. Reg. 53,987 (Dec. 8, 2017), www.regulations.gov/document?D=FDA-2017-D-6569-0016.

44 US Food & Drug Admin., Clinical Decision Support Software: Draft Guidance for Industry and Food and Drug Administration Staff 12 (2019), www.fda.gov/media/109618/download.

45 See generally SaMD Discussion paper, supra note 19.

the quality of networking across the national health information network – it falls under the ONC's authority. The HHS Secretary should use their authority to recalibrate the relevant authority between the two agencies in this way.

3.4 CONCLUSION

I have argued that the delineation of authority between the FDA and the ONC should not be based on the extent of provider intervention or control over HIT, which involves conceptually hard distinctions. It should not be based on how risky a piece of HIT is as such outcomes are highly context-dependent and still empirically hard to ascertain. Rather, they should be based on whether the aspect of the HIT subject to regulation involves its ability to network with other systems and users. To the degree that it does, the HIT should fall within ONC regulation. However, as long as the focus of the HIT function does not implicate networking – such as the quality of algorithmic analysis – FDA jurisdiction is appropriate. The line between the categories can be blurry – after all, the analysis of algorithmic quality might implicate questions of data collection and standardization. But if history is any guide, such blurriness will inevitably be the case, no matter what standard is adopted, as we move to more and more automated health systems.

PART II

European Regulation of Medical Devices

Introduction

Timo Minssen

Similar to the United States' Food and Drug Administration (FDA), regulators in other jurisdictions also seek to address the increasing significance of data-driven digital health products and their interface with medical AI and machine learning. This also holds true for the European Union (EU) and its member states, as well as the United Kingdom. To be lawfully marketed within the European Union, all medical devices and in vitro diagnostic medical devices must meet the CE marking requirements under the relevant EU regulatory frameworks.[1] On May 25, 2017, two major regulatory changes simultaneously entered into force, which are highly relevant for medical device manufacturers: EU Regulation 2017/745 on medical devices (MDR) and EU Regulation 2017/746 on in vitro diagnostic medical devices (IVDR).[2] In reaction to the COVID-19 pandemic's impact on medical device stakeholders, and with patient health and safety as a guiding principle, the application date for the EU Medical Device Regulation (2017/745) (MDR) had been postponed from May 2020 to May 2021.[3] This decision was met with a sigh of relief since it gave stakeholders more time to prepare for – and comply with – the new regulatory framework. However, in light of new technical developments and capabilities many uncertainties and challenges remain to be addressed.

As the contributions in this part demonstrate, this also concerns the broader legislative framework within which the European medicine agencies and the so-called notified bodies will have to operate. In addition to product-specific regulations, these authorities will have to consider a great number of recent laws, guidance documents, policy papers, strategy announcements, and initiatives, such as the

[1] Timo Minssen et al., Regulatory Responses to Medical Machine Learning, 7 Journal of Law the Biosciences (2020), https://doi.org/10.1093/jlb/lsaa002.

[2] See Regulation 2017/745 of the European Parliament and of the Council of 5 April 2017 on medical devices, amending Directive 2001/83/EC, Regulation (EC) No 178/2002 and Regulation (EC) No 1223/2009 and repealing Council Directives 90/385/EEC and 93/42/EEC [2017], art. 20, O.J. (L 117/1) (EU) [hereinafter MDR]; see also Regulation 2017/746 of the European Parliament and of the Council of 5 April 2017 on in vitro diagnostic medical devices and repealing Directive 98/79/EC and Commission Decision 2010/227/EU [2017], art. 18, O.J. (L 117/176) (EU) [hereinafter IVDR].

[3] See Commission postpones application of the Medical Devices Regulation to prioritize the fight against coronavirus, https://ec.europa.eu/commission/presscorner/detail/en/ip_20_589.

European Health Data Space (EHDS). They will have to deal with a broad variety of relevant topics ranging from health data protection, social justice, and cybersecurity to liability, competition law, and intellectual property rights. These interacting initiatives are expected not only to have a major impact on the specific regulation, but also on the wider governance of medical devices and health data uses. To achieve the most beneficial outcome for patients and to alleviate potential risks, it is important to consider these developments from a holistic perspective. After all, most systems are only as strong as their weakest link in both regional and international contexts.

That this holds particularly true in the cybersecurity context is highlighted by Elisabetta Biasin and Erik Kamenjasevic's chapter, "Cybersecurity of Medical Devices: Regulatory challenges in the European Union." In light of recent cyberattacks on digital hospital systems and medical devices, which has also become a major issue during the COVID-19 pandemic, their chapter delivers an important contribution to the laws of medical devices and cybersecurity. In particular, the authors analyze and discuss the interface of the EU medical devices' legal framework with the EU cybersecurity policy objectives. Highlighting a great number of recent threats and challenges, the authors conclude that "the adequate level of cybersecurity and resilience of medical devices is one of the crucial elements for maintaining the daily provision of health care services." In order to provide a step forward in mitigating these challenges, the authors provide several recommendations that EU regulators should consider, ranging from better guidelines on specific security standards to improving the cooperation between competent national authorities.

This certainly also applies to the health data protection context, as it is explained by Hannah van Kolfschooten in the next chapter, "The mHealth Power Paradox: Improving Data Protection in Health Apps through Self-Regulation in the European Union." The author asks, "whether and to what extent self-regulation by app stores may contribute to the level of health data protection in the European Union?" To answer this question, she explores health data protection issues regarding mHealth apps, and analyzes the EU legal framework governing mHealth apps. Concentrating on the most relevant stipulations of the EU's General Data Protection Regulation (GDPR),[4] the author discusses the "benefits and risks of industry self-regulation as an alternative means to protect data protection rights in light of current mHealth regulation practices by Apple's App Store and Google's Google Play." This allows her to propose several improvements to self-regulation in this field.

The GDPR is also at the center of the next chapter by Janos Meszaros, Marcelo Corrales Compagnucci and the author of this introduction. In their chapter, "The

[4] Regulation 2016/679 of the European Parliament and of the Council of 27 April 2016 on the protection of natural persons with regard to the processing of personal data and on the free movement of such data, and repealing Directive 95/46/EC (General Data Protection Regulation), 2016 O.J. (L 119) 4.5, 1–88 (EU).

Interaction of the Medical Device Regulation and the GDPR: Do European Rules on Privacy and Scientific Research Impair the Safety and Performance of AI Medical Devices?," the authors analyze a variety of GDPR stipulations on deidentification and scientific research that help "research organizations to use personal data with fewer restrictions compared to data collection for other purposes." Under these exemptions, organizations may process specific types of data for a secondary purpose without consent. However, the authors admonish the definition and legal requirements of scientific research that differ among EU Member States. Since the new EU Medical Device Regulations 2017/745 and 2017/746 require compliance with the GDPR, they argue that this legal uncertainty "might result in obstacles for the use and review of input data for medical devices," and call for "more harmonized rules, to balance individuals' rights and the safety of medical devices."

Next, Barry Solaiman and Mark Bloom consider a topic that has become increasingly important in recent years: "AI, Explainability, and Safeguarding Patient Safety in Europe: Towards a Science-Focused Regulatory Model." Their chapter examines "the efforts made by regulators in Europe to develop standards concerning the explainability of artificial intelligence (AI) systems used in wearables." Recent attempts by governments to monitor and contain the spread of the COVID-19 pandemic has certainly accelerated the increasingly invasive use of such wearables and hence the need for such standards. The authors also point out that "one key challenge for scientists and regulators is to ensure that predictions are understood and explainable to legislators, policymakers, doctors, and patients to ensure informed decision making." Examining the operation of AI networks, the authors welcome a series of recent UK and EU guidelines for such networks and applications. But they also point out that those guidelines will ultimately be restricted by the available technology. The authors therefore argue that European legislators and regulators should spend more efforts on developing minimum standards on explainability of such technologies, which should be "leveled-up progressively as the technology improves." Acknowledging the need for appropriate human oversight and liability, they contend that those standards should be "informed by the computer science underlying the technology to identify the limitations of explainability," and that "the technology should advance to help them decipher networks intelligibly."

Finally, Helen Yu's chapter "Regulation of Digital Health Technologies in the European Union: Intended versus Actual Use," focuses on "how the classification rules and postmarket surveillance system provisions of the EU Medical Devices Regulation (MDR) need to anticipate and address the actual use of DHTs." She warns that courts and regulators have so far not been "consistent on the circumstances under which manufacturers are held responsible for known or encouraged 'misuse' of their products." She therefore stresses the importance of adequately addressing "the potential harm caused to consumers who use digital health technologies (DHTs) beyond the manufacturer's intended purpose" and highlights the "need for a framework to re-classify and regulate DHTs based on evidence of actual use."

Overall, the authors' contribution in this section demonstrates clearly how the EU and US regulators, legislators, developers, and users of medical devices are facing very similar challenges. This applies to both the micro level – with regard to the evaluation of particular medical devices – as well as on the macro level concerning the wider legal frameworks and ramifications that are so very important for the safe and efficient functioning of such devices. However, it was also shown that some aspects of the various attempts to address these and to reach acceptable trade-offs with regard to safety, efficacy, privacy, and other values differ across the pond. Against this background and considering the great variety of opportunities and risks in the increasingly complex value chains of modern medical devices, it seems more important than ever to improve international collaboration in the area and to align regulatory and legislative approaches across the globe.

4

Cybersecurity of Medical Devices

Regulatory Challenges in the European Union

Elisabetta Biasin and Erik Kamenjasevic

4.1 INTRODUCTION

4.1.1 *Context*

Ensuring cybersecurity in the health care sector is a growing concern. The increasing digitalization of health care service providers has enabled cyberattack techniques toward them to become more liquid, flexible, and able to exploit all the possible paths of entry rapidly.[1] For example, one such attack may target critical assets of hospitals which include both the IT infrastructure and connected-to-network medical devices. A successful cyberattack toward IT infrastructure may cause significant disruptive effects for the provision of essential health care services.[2] When a cyberattack concerns a medical device, it may put at severe risk the health and safety of patients.[3] This disquiet appears to be even greater at the time of a worldwide COVID-19 outbreak. Reports on cyberattacks toward medical devices issued during this pandemic revealed how hackers use various techniques to get access to individuals' sensitive health-related information for different gains.[4]

The authors wish to thank: Prof. W. Nicholson Price II, Charlotte Ducuing, and Jessica Schroers for their helpful comments and feedback. The research leading to these results has received funding from the European Union's Horizon2020 Research and Innovation Programme, under Grant Agreement no 787002.

1 Enrico Frumento, Cybersecurity and the Evolutions of Healthcare: Challenges and Threats Behind its Evolution, in m_Health Current and Future Applications 115 (Giuseppe Andreoni et al. eds., 2019).

2 This happened, for instance, during the Wannacry malware attacks for several trustees of the UK National Healthcare System (NHS). See Finnian Bamber et al., Nat'l Audit Office, Investigation: Wannacry Cyber-Attack and the NHS (2018).

3 As was demonstrated in 2018 by a team of researchers, an attacker could cause pacemakers to deliver a deadly shock or stop an insulin pump from providing the needed insulin to a patient. See Sally Shin & Josh Lipton, Security Researchers Say They Can Hack Medtronic Pacemakers, CNBC (Aug. 17, 2018), www.cnbc.com/2018/08/17/security-researchers-say-they-can-hack-medtronic-pacemakers.html.

4 See Laurens Cerulus, Hackers Use Fake WHO Emails to Exploit Coronavirus Fears, POLITICO (Mar. 13, 2020), www.politico.eu/article/hackers-use-fake-who-emails-to-exploit-coronavirus-fears-for-gain/?fbclid=IwAR379JroScZEggppneFxEQqMpYfKP9MoRg90k1lB-xziGkIH_3Byy1NtKjE; Mathew M. Schwartz, COVID-19 Complication: Ransomware Keeps Hitting Healthcare, Bank Info Security

Regulators around the globe have started increasingly to pursue medical device cybersecurity as a policy objective over the past years. For example, the US Food and Drug Administration (FDA) issued its first general principles for Networked Medical Devices Containing Off-the-Shelf Software in 2005, followed by the 2014 and 2016 Guidance for Premarket Submission and Postmarket Management of Cybersecurity in Medical Devices. In March 2020, the International Medical Devices Regulators Forum (IMRDF) issued its medical devices principles and practices on medical devices' cybersecurity, while in the European Union (EU), the first piece of guidance was issued only in July 2020 (with the first version from December 2019) by the European Commission's (EC) Medical Devices Coordination Group (MDCG).

4.1.2 *Ambition*

Discussions evolving around the regulation of medical devices and their cybersecurity are a recent trend in academic literature.[5] Many contributions analyze the US system, while fewer concern the EU one.[6] This chapter aims to contribute to the literature dealing with the law of medical devices and cybersecurity by assessing the level of maturity of the EU medical devices legal framework and EU cybersecurity policy objectives.[7] The analysis starts with an outline of cybersecurity-related aspects of EU Medical Devices Regulation (MDR).[8] This is followed by a critical analysis of regulatory challenges stemming from the MDR, through the lens of the MDCG Guidance. The following section concerns the regulatory challenges stemming from other legal frameworks, including the Cybersecurity Act,[9] the Network and Information Systems (NIS) Directive,[10] the General Data Protection Regulation

(Mar. 16, 2020), www.bankinfosecurity.com/covid-19-complication-ransomware-keeps-hitting-hospitals-a-13941.

5 See Deborah Eskenasy, Le dispositif médical à la recherche d'un nouveau cadre juridique 38 (Nov. 30, 2016) (unpublished PhD dissertation) (remarks on legal literature on medical devices law).

6 See, for example, Charlotte A. Tschider, Enhancing Cybersecurity for the Digital Health Marketplace, 26 Ann. Health L. 1 (2017); Louiza Doudin, Networked Medical Devices: Finding a Legislative Solution to Guide Healthcare into the Future, 40 Seattle U. L. Rev. 1085 (2017).

7 Joint Communication to the European parliament, the Council, the European Economic and Social Committee and the Committee of the Regions Cybersecurity strategy of the European union: an open, safe and secure cyberspace, JOIN (2013) 1 final (Feb. 7, 2013) [hereinafter EC 2013 Cybersecurity Strategy].

8 Regulation (EU) 2017/745 of the European Parliament and of the Council of 5 April 2017, on medical devices, amending Directive 2001/83/EC, Regulation (EC) No 178/2002 and Regulation (EC) No 1223/2009 and repealing Council Directives 90/385/EEC and 93/42/EEC, 2017 O.J. (L 117/1) [hereinafter MDR].

9 Regulation (EU) 2019/881 of the European Parliament and of the Council of 17 April 2019 on ENISA (the European Union Agency for Cybersecurity) and on information and communications technology cybersecurity certification and repealing Regulation (EU) No 526/2013 (Cybersecurity Act), 2019 O.J. (L 151) [hereinafter CSA].

10 Directive (EU) 2016/1148 of the European Parliament and of the Council of 6 July 2016, concerning measures for a high common level of security of network and information systems across the Union, 2016 O.J. (L 194) [hereinafter NISD].

(GDPR),[11] and the Radio Equipment Directive (RED)[12] since they all become applicable when it comes to ensuring the cybersecurity of medical devices. Here the analysis demonstrates that regulatory challenges persist due to regulatory specialization,[13] which has led to regulatory overlapping, fragmentation risks, regulatory uncertainty, and duplication.[14] In the final section, the chapter provides conclusive remarks as well as recommendations for regulators dealing with the cybersecurity of medical devices in the European Union.

4.2 HOW DOES THE EU MEDICAL DEVICES REGULATION DEAL WITH THE CYBERSECURITY OF MEDICAL DEVICES?

The provisions of the EU Medical Devices Regulation (MDR)[15] primarily address manufacturers of medical devices who are defined as "the natural or legal person who manufactures or fully refurbishes a device or has a device designed, manufactured, or fully refurbished and markets that device under its name or trademark."[16] No explicit reference to cybersecurity is provided in the main part of the MDR. However, it provides some essential cybersecurity-related requirements that manufacturers have to implement in a medical device.[17]

When putting a medical device on the market or into service, Article 5(1) of the MDR obliges its manufacturer to ensure that the device is compliant with the MDR obligations when used in accordance with its intended purpose. According to Article 5(2) of the MDR, "a medical device shall meet the general safety and performance requirements" (also including the cybersecurity-related requirements)[18] "set out in Annex I [of the MDR] ... taking into account the

[11] Regulation (EU) 2016/679 of the European Parliament and of the Council of 27 April 2016 on the protection of natural persons with regard to the processing of personal data and on the free movement of such data, and repealing Directive 95/46/EC (General Data Protection Regulation), 2016 O.J. (L 119) [hereinafter GDPR].

[12] Directive 2014/53/EU of the European Parliament and of the Council of 16 April 2014 on the harmonization of the laws of the Member States relating to the making available on the market of radio equipment and repealing Directive 1999/5/EC, 2014 O.J. (L 153) [hereinafter RED].

[13] See Emmanuelle Mathieu et al., 2011, Regulatory Agencies and Multi-Actor Regulatory Governance: A Method to Study Regulatory Fragmentation, Specialization, Coordination and Centralization (unpublished manuscript) (2011), www.academia.edu/20494619/Regulatory_agencies_and_multi-actor_regulatory_governance_A_method_to_study_regulatory_fragmentation_specialization_coordination_and_centralization (on the notion of specialization and fragmentation).

[14] In this chapter, we will refer to "cybersecurity" in two different ways. In a general way, we mean "cybersecurity" as a policy objective pursued by the European Union – having regard to the EC 2013 Cybersecurity Strategy (see supra note 7). When used in a specific way, we refer to the definition provided by the CSA, art. 4: "a set of activities to protect network and information systems the users of such systems, and other persons affected by cyber threats."

[15] MDR, supra note 8.

[16] Id. art. 2(30).

[17] See Medical Devices Coordination Group, Guidance on Cybersecurity of medical devices (Dec. 2019) [MDCG, Guidance] (complete list of the cybersecurity requirements).

[18] Id.

intended purpose."[19] The intended purpose is defined in Article 2(12) as "the use for which a device is intended according to the data supplied by the manufacturer on the label, in the instructions for use or in promotional or sales materials or statements and as specified by the manufacturer in the clinical evaluation." As part of the general requirements set in Annex I of the MDR, "devices shall achieve the performance intended by the manufacturer"[20] and be designed in a way suitable for the intended use. They shall be safe and effective, and associated risks shall be acceptable when weighed against the benefits of the patients and level of protection of health and safety while taking into account the state of the art.[21]

Moreover, "[m]anufacturers shall establish, implement, document, and maintain a risk management system."[22] Part of this system also includes risk-control measures to be adopted by manufacturers for the design and manufacture of a device, and they shall conform to safety principles and state of the art.[23] A medical device designed to be used with other devices/equipment as a whole (including the connection system between them) has to be safe and should not impair the specified performance of the device.[24]

Furthermore, a medical device shall be designed and manufactured in a way to remove, as far as possible, risks associated with possible negative interaction between software and the IT environment within which they operate.[25] If a medical device is intended to be used with another device, it shall be designed so the interoperability and compatibility are reliable and safe.[26] A medical device incorporating electronic programmable systems, including software or standalone software as a medical device, "shall be designed to ensure repeatability, reliability, and performance according to the intended use,"[27] and "appropriate means have to be adopted to reduce risks or impairment of the performance."[28] A medical device should be developed and manufactured according to the state of the art and by respecting the principles of the development lifecycle, risk management (including information security), verification, and validation.[29] Lastly, manufacturers shall "set out minimum requirements concerning hardware, IT network characteristics, and IT security measures, including protection against unauthorized access."[30] Concerning information to be supplied together with the device,

19 MDR, supra note 8, art. 5(2).
20 Id. Annex I, req. 1.
21 Id.
22 Id. req. 3.
23 Id. req. 4.
24 Id. req. 14.1.
25 Id. req. 14.2.(d).
26 Id. req. 14.5.
27 Id. req. 17.1.
28 Id.
29 Id. req. 17.2.
30 Id. req. 17.4.

manufacturers must inform about residual risks,[31] provide warnings requiring immediate attention on the label[32] and, for electronic programmable system devices, give information about minimum requirements concerning hardware, IT networks' characteristics, and IT security measures (including protection against unauthorized access), necessary to run the software as intended.[33]

4.3 REGULATORY CHALLENGES STEMMING FROM THE MDR ANALYZED THROUGH THE LENS OF THE MDCG GUIDANCE ON CYBERSECURITY FOR MEDICAL DEVICES

The Medical Device Coordination Group (MDCG) of the European Commission endorsed Guidance on Cybersecurity for Medical Devices (Guidance) in December 2019[34] where it dealt with the cybersecurity-related provisions embedded in the MDR. Already, it is necessary here to mention that this MDCG Guidance is not a legally binding document. Hence, in case of disagreement, manufacturers could decide not to follow it – which might have an impact on the overall harmonizing purpose of the MDR and lead to a divergence of application of the EU principles and laws on a Member State level. Nevertheless, being the first guiding document on this topic issued by the EC for the medical devices sector, it is an essential step in further elaborating on specific MDR cybersecurity-related provisions.

As already mentioned in the previous section, the MDR does not expressly refer to cybersecurity.[35] Nor does the MDCG Guidance define the terms "cybersecurity," "security-by-design," and "security-by-default." Instead, the latter document only provides an outline of its provisions relating to cybersecurity of medical devices and points out conceptual links between safety and security.[36] Leaving these terms theoretical and undefined does not facilitate their implementation in practical terms by the stakeholders concerned.

Moreover, no reference in the MDCG Guidance is given to definitions provided by the Cybersecurity Act (CSA).[37] Establishing a connection in the soft-law instrument (i.e., the Guidance) with the latter would imply a reference to a hard law definition. This link could serve to reduce the ambiguity of the term, and it might help in achieving more coherence within the EU cybersecurity regulatory framework as a whole.[38] The

31 Id. req. 23.1.(g).

32 Id. req. 23.2.(m).

33 Id. req. 23.4.(ab).

34 MDCG, Guidance, supra note17.

35 See Elisabetta Biasin, Medical Devices Cybersecurity: A Growing Concern?, CITIP Blog (Sept. 26, 2019), www.law.kuleuven.be/citip/blog/medical-devices-cybersecurity-a-growing-concern/, (a concise overview of cybersecurity, EU guidance and the MDR).

36 MDCG, Guidance, supra note 17, at 7.

37 Id. at 9.

38 See Gloria González Fuster & Lina Jasmontaite, Cybersecurity Regulation in the European Union: The Digital, the Critical and Fundamental Rights, in The Ethics of Cybersecurity 119 (Markus

proposed approach would be ultimately beneficial for manufacturers as it would bring more clarity in the interpretation of MDR requirements.

The MDCG Guidance stresses the importance to "recognize the roles and expectations of all stakeholders"[39] on joint responsibility and states its "substantial alignment" with International Medical Device Regulators Forum (IMRDF) Principles and Practices for Medical Devices Cybersecurity.[40] To this end, achieving a satisfactory level of the cybersecurity of a medical device concerns manufacturers, suppliers, health care providers, patients, integrators, operators, and regulators. Manufacturers are bound by the majority of the provisions in the MDR. Integrators of a medical device are, among others, responsible for assessing a reasonable level of security while operators need to ensure the required level of security for the operational environment, and that personnel are properly trained on cybersecurity issues. At the same time, health care professionals are responsible for a device being used according to the description of the intended use, while patients and consumers need to "employ cyber-smart behaviour."[41] All of these stakeholders are an equally important part of the cybersecurity chain,[42] and each is responsible for ensuring a secured environment in which a device could smoothly operate for the ultimate benefit of patients' safety.

Nevertheless, the MDCG Guidance failed to elaborate on how exactly the joint responsibility of different stakeholders is influenced or conflicted by other applicable laws, in particular, when it comes to the Network and Information Systems (NIS) Directive,[43] the General Data Protection Regulation (GDPR),[44] and the Cybersecurity Act (CSA).[45] Since the expert group did not tackle them in detail in theory, it is also hard to imagine how the interested stakeholders operating within the medical devices domain are supposed to implement in practice different pieces of legislation divergent in scope and applicability.[46] Hence, the MDCG should consider adopting a more holistic approach in the future when determining the meaning of "joint responsibility" as this would help in analyzing relevant aspects of other

Christen et al. eds., 2020) (for an overview of the coherence problem in the EU cybersecurity legal framework).

39 MDCG, Guidance, supra note 17, at 12.

40 Id.

41 Id. at 13.

42 See Erik Kamenjasevic, Protect the Weakest Link in a Cyber-Security Chain – Protect the Human, CITIP Blog (Mar. 20, 2018), www.law.kuleuven.be/citip/blog/protect-the-weakest-link-in-a-cyber-security-chain-protect-the-human/.

43 NISD, supra note 10.

44 GDPR, supra note 11.

45 CSA, supra note 9.

46 Further elaboration on these laws could have been done, by the same expert group, based on art. 3(5) and 12 of the Medical Devices Coordination Group Rules of Procedure. art. 3(5) states that the Chair of the MDCG or the working group may invite, on a case-by-case basis, experts and other third parties with specific competence in a subject on the agenda to participate in the meetings or provide written contributions. art. 12 provides that the Commission services shall provide technical, scientific, and logistical support for the MDCG and any of its working groups.

horizontal legislation and, eventually, in achieving a more coherent cybersecurity regulatory framework.

Finally, what seems to be heavily overlooked for unclear reasons is the applicability of the Radio Equipment Directive (RED),[47] which has not even been mentioned in the MDCG Guidance. The RED cybersecurity-related provisions and their interaction with MDR as well as the other laws applicable to the cybersecurity of medical devices are explained below.

4.4 REGULATORY CHALLENGES STEMMING FROM OTHER LEGAL FRAMEWORKS APPLICABLE TO MEDICAL DEVICES

Regulation of cybersecurity is a complex task. Cybersecurity is an area in which different policy fields need to be combined (horizontal consistency), and where measures need to be taken at both levels – the European Union and Member States (vertical consistency).[48] Regulation of medical devices is complex, too, as it is a multi-level[49] legal framework characterized by specialization and fragmentation.[50] Regulating the cybersecurity of medical devices implies bearing the complexities of both legal frameworks. In this regard, we identified four regulatory challenges: regulatory overlapping; fragmentation risks; regulatory uncertainty; and duplication. We clarify the first two challenges as relating to horizontal consistency requirements, the third to vertical requirements, and the fourth to a combination thereof. Finally, we envisage specialization and fragmentation as a common denominator of all four challenges.

4.4.1 *Regulatory Overlapping: CSA Certification Schemes and the MDR*

On the one hand, the MDR provides the possibility to obtain a certificate for demonstrating compliance with its security requirements. On the other hand, the CSA set up a new and broader framework for cybersecurity certifications for ICT products, processes, and services. The CSA appears to be inevitably relevant for medical devices' cybersecurity since medical devices may fall under the definition of an ICT product.[51]

Some stakeholders have questioned the applicability of CSA rules and the operability of European Cybersecurity Certification Schemes (ECCS) for health care.[52] They expressed concerns as regards to overlaps between MDR and cybersecurity

[47] RED, supra note 12.

[48] Ramses Wessel, Towards EU Cybersecurity Law: Regulating a New Policy Field in Research Handbook on Int'l Law & Cyberspace 405 (Nicholas Tsagourias et al. eds., 2015).

[49] See Nupur Choudhoury & Ramses Wessel, Conceptualising Multilevel Regulation in the EU: A Legal Translation of Multilevel Governance?, 18(3) Eur. L.J. 335 (2012).

[50] See supra Section 4.1.2.

[51] CSA, art. 2(12).

[52] See, e.g., COCIR, Advancing Cybersecurity of Health and Digital Technologies (Mar. 27, 2019), www.cocir.org/uploads/media/19036_COC_Cybersecurity_web.pdf.

certification schemes and requirements.[53] For instance, COCIR (the European trade association representing the medical imaging, radiotherapy, health ICT and electromedical industries) claimed that "[a] specific certification scheme for medical devices is ... not necessary as the MDR introduces security requirements that will become part of the certification for receiving the CE mark."[54] Such a scenario may bring duplication in requirements for manufacturers on the one hand, as well as for authorities having the oversight on manufacturers' compliance. Ultimately, this could also imply conflicts in authorities' respective competence.

The MDCG Guidance did not provide clarifications on the applicability of the CSA in this context. It provides only one reference to the CSA in the whole body of the document.[55] The reference is purely descriptive[56] and does not resolve the applicability question. Against this background, the CSA clarifies that the health care sector should be one of its priorities.[57] The MDCG or the EU regulator should provide further guidance tackling aspects relevant to the cybersecurity certification schemes for medical devices. This could be done, for instance, by explaining how MDR cybersecurity-related requirements apply when the ICT product is considered to be a medical device and what type of certification schemes would be relevant. Furthermore, regulators could specify that, for ICT products not qualifying as a medical device, the CSA should remain the general rule.

4.4.2 *Fragmentation Risks: Voluntariety of Certification Mechanisms*

As seen in Section 4.4.1, the CSA has established certification mechanisms for ensuring the cybersecurity of ICT products. Manufacturers of medical devices may join them voluntarily.[58] However, EU Member States may establish a mandatory certification mechanism in their territories since the CSA provides that "[t]he cybersecurity certification shall be voluntary *unless otherwise specified by Union law or Member State law*" (emphasis added).[59] In practice, this provision implies that some Member States may impose the obligation of obtaining a cybersecurity certification, while others would leave it as a voluntary fulfilment. Manufacturers would be obliged to obtain a cybersecurity certificate for a device to market it within one Member State while at the same time, the same would not be required in another Member State.

53 See id.
54 Id. at 6.
55 See MDCG, Guidance, supra note 17.
56 Id.
57 CSA, art. 56(3).
58 CSA, art. 56(2).
59 Id.

This hypothesis could provoke diverging mechanisms in the internal market and could lead to regulatory shopping.[60] Manufacturers could also face additional compliance costs for aligning with different national requirements. Moreover, this could lead to fragmentation risks for the EU market. National requirements could diverge, and supervisory authorities could interpret different rules following different interpretative approaches.[61] Therefore, the overarching regulatory strategies to bring more consistency amongst the Member States should aim at ensuring coordination and cooperation amongst competent authorities.

4.4.3 *Regulatory Uncertainty: Security Requirements between the MDR and the Radio Equipment Directive (RED)*

The RED establishes a regulatory framework for making available on the EU market and putting into service of radio equipment. Certain types of medical devices (such as pacemakers or implantable cardioverter defibrillators) are likely to fall under the scope of the Directive and thus be subject to its security requirements.[62] The RED's simultaneous application with the MDR may imply issues in practice. Notably, such parallel application may lead to the question of whether RED security rules are complementary or redundant to the MDR.[63]

The European Commission developed guidance (the RED Guide)[64] to assist in the interpretation of the RED. However, the RED Guide only states that an overlap issue covering the same hazard might be resolved by giving preference to the more specific EU legislation.

Similarly, more general EC guidelines on EU product rules (the Blue Guide)[65] explains first, that two or more EU legislative acts can cover the same product, hazard, or impact. Second, it provides that the issue of overlap might be resolved by

60 DIGITALEUROPE, Cybersecurity Act: DIGITALEUROPE Urges Colegislators to Ensure Certification Schemes Do Not Lead to More Market Fragmentation in Europe (June 11, 2018), www.digitaleurope.org/wp/wp-content/uploads/2019/01/DIGITALEUROPE%20Cybersecurity%20Act%2011%20June.pdf (stakeholders' concerns over the CSA's fragmentation risks).

61 See Jan Rommel et al., Specialisation and Fragmentation in Regulatory Regimes, in Government of Public Management 69–71 (Patrick Lægreid et al. eds., 2010).

62 Amongst the many other aspects, the RED foresees technical features for the protection of privacy, personal data, misuse, interoperability, network functioning, and compliance regarding the combination of radio equipment and software. See RED, art. (3)(3), lett. (d) and (e). Since they relate to network and information systems, the two articles are considered for the purposes of the present chapter as cybersecurity-related requirements.

63 Due to overlapping elements, manufacturers must refer to different notified bodies to meet obligations stemming from different legislations. In practice this adds another level of complexity. See BSI, Medical Devices complying with the Radio Equipment Directive, www.bsigroup.com/meddev/LocalFiles/ja-jp/Technologies/BSI-md-Radio-devices-ja-JP.pdf.

64 European Commission, Guide to the Radio Equipment Directive 2014/53/EU, Version of 19 December 2018 (2018) [hereinafter EC, RED Guide].

65 European Commission, The 'Blue Guide' on the EU Interpretation of EU Product Rules (2014) [hereinafter EC, Blue Guide].

giving preference to the more specific law. This, explains the EC, "usually requires a risk analysis of the product, or sometimes an analysis of the intended purpose of the product, which then determines the applicable legislation."[66] In other words, except for the cases where the applicability of one law has obvious priority over the other, a medical device's manufacturer is left with a choice of the applicable legislation. On the one hand, this approach could imply a significant burden for virtuous manufacturers in justifying the applicable law. On the other hand, such kind of regulatory uncertainty could lead less-virtuous manufacturers to exploit somehow "functional overlaps" of the two regulations and bring them to "choose only" compliance with RED. This could be particularly significant for low-risk medical devices, for which a decision on the intended medical purpose – and thus, law's scrutiny – is left to the responsibility of the manufacturer.[67]

The MDCG Guidance does not provide any help in this regard. For no apparent reasons, it overlooked the applicability of the RED while it should be present in the Guidance. For example, the MDCG could provide an example of cases to which the RED applies, together with its opinion of the relevance of RED cybersecurity-related requirements. This solution would help to resolve regulatory uncertainty and help manufacturers in their decision concerning the applicability of requirements stemming from different pieces of legislation.

4.4.4 *Duplication: The Notification of Medical Devices Security Incidents*

Incident notification is an evident example of how specialization and decentralization have provoked the proliferation of administrative authorities with supervisory tasks. This is particularly true for the framework of medical devices where three different legal frameworks for incident notification apply: the MDR (on serious incident notification),[68] the GDPR (on data breach notification),[69] and the NISD (on security incident notification obligations).[70] Every piece of legislation requires notification to different authorities: the MDR to competent authorities, the GDPR to supervisory authorities, the NISD to national authorities or Computer Security Incident Response Teams (CSIRTs) (depending on the incident reporting model chosen by the Member State).[71] Criteria for which an incident must be notified to an authority differ in scope and objectives pursued by different pieces of legislation.

66 EC, Blue Guide, 22.

67 See Eugenio Mantovani & Pedro Cristobal Bocos, Are mHealth Apps Safe? The Intended Purpose Rule, Its Shortcomings and the Regulatory Options under the EU Medical Devices Framework, in Mobile E-Health 251–76 (Hannah R. Marston et al. eds., 2017) (on pitfalls of the "intended purpose" notion in medical devices law).

68 MDR, art. 87.

69 GDPR, art. 33–4.

70 NISD, art. 14.

71 There are four different incident reporting models: centralized, distributed, decentralized, hybrid. See ENISA, EU MS Response Development Status Report (2019) 8–9.

None the less, it could happen that in practice, a security incident concerning a medical device should be notified at the same time to MDR, NISD and GDPR competent and/or supervisory authorities.[72]

In this case, notification of a security incident implies administrative oversight by three (or more) different authorities. Such a circumstance could cause duplication of tasks and costly compliance procedures for manufacturers and health care stakeholders in general.[73] Some stakeholders already pointed out that "increasing numbers of organizations . . . need to be informed about a single security incident," and "[i]n some examples, multiple competent authorities in a single country."[74]

A possible approach that could simplify the whole process would be to "adopt a more centralized approach to avoid duplication and confusion."[75] A step further could be done by enhancing cooperation mechanisms between these authorities, harmonizing security incidents notification procedures at a vertical level across the Member States as well as at a horizontal level by considering different policy fields and their regulatory objectives.

4.5 CONCLUSIONS AND RECOMMENDATIONS

The adequate level of cybersecurity and resilience of medical devices is one of the crucial elements for maintaining the daily provision of health care services. Above all, it is pivotal to mitigate risks relating to patients' health and safety. On the one hand, the ongoing debate on the topic in the United States and, more recently in the European Union, shows an increasing level of awareness amongst regulators, manufacturers, health care professionals, and other involved stakeholders. On the other hand, the research presented in this chapter shows that the existing EU legal framework dealing with medical devices' cybersecurity brings significant regulatory challenges. In order to provide a step forward in mitigating these challenges, the EU regulator might consider the following recommendations:

1. Establish a more robust connection of the MDCG Guidance with EU cybersecurity (hard) laws, especially the CSA and its definitions of cybersecurity, security-by-design, and security-by-default. Ensuring consistent use of terminology across different pieces of legislation (binding and non-binding) would

72 According to NISD, art. 4(1)(7), a security incident is an event having an actual adverse effect on the security of network and information systems. Such an event, if it involves the processing of personal data, could also qualify as a "personal data breach" (cfr GDPR, art. 4(1)(12). Finally, a security incident could also be a "serious incident" under the MDR meaning art. 4(1)(54), for instance, when the incident directly or indirectly leads to a serious public health threat, or the death of a patient. See MDCG Guidance, Annex II (examples of cybersecurity incidents/serious incidents).

73 Including health care providers, when considered as "operators of essential services," according to NISD (art. 4(1)(4)).

74 See COCIR, supra note 52, at 8.

75 Id.

also help manufacturers in meeting the requirements as it would bring more clarity in the interpretation of the MDR cybersecurity-related provisions.

2. Clarify the meaning and implications of "joint responsibility" in the intertwining with other applicable laws (in particular when it comes to the NISD, GDPR, and CSA). Further explanations on how exactly the responsibility stemming from one piece of legislation applicable to a specific stakeholder is influenced or conflicted with the responsibility of another stakeholder (stemming from the same or different piece of legislation) would represent a meaningful tool to guide manufacturers in complying with all the relevant laws.
3. Clarify the scope of application of the CSA for certification mechanisms and MDR security requirements. In particular, the EU regulator should explain how the MDR cybersecurity-related requirements apply to an ICT product which also falls under a definition of a medical device, and what type of certification schemes would be relevant.
4. Provide guidance on the application of the RED, its interaction with the MDR and other laws applicable to the cybersecurity of medical devices.
5. Ensure cooperation between competent national authorities (i.e., for incident notifications) in order to achieve timely respect of the requirements, and to avoid compliance duplication.

5

The mHealth Power Paradox

Improving Data Protection in Health Apps through Self-Regulation in the European Union

Hannah van Kolfschooten

5.1 INTRODUCTION: MHEALTH APPS: PROMISE OR THREAT?

An increasing number of European Union (EU) citizens use mobile apps to monitor their own fitness, lifestyle, or general health to take control over their health outside of a clinical setting.[1] This growing trend is reflected in the content of mobile app stores: self-monitoring mobile health (mHealth) apps such as running trackers and medication reminders are omnipresent. While mHealth apps are said to hold great potential for empowering individuals, the apps also constitute threats to users' fundamental rights in the European Union.[2] The main risk is posed by the extensive processing and sharing of health data with third parties by mHealth apps. Users have limited awareness of, and control over, who has access to their health data.[3] This leads to a paradox: users turn to mHealth to increase self-empowerment, but at the same time surrender power due to this lack of data control.[4]

These risks are further compounded by the lack of effective EU regulation. The EU legal framework on health and protection of patients' rights does not apply to self-monitoring mHealth app users.[5] Furthermore, while the EU's General Data Protection Regulation (GDPR) provides a solid legal framework for the protection of health data, in practice, many mHealth apps do not comply with its provisions.[6]

[1] Incisive Health International, Taking the Pulse of eHealth in the EU: An Analysis of Public Attitudes to eHealth Issues in Austria, Bulgaria, Estonia, France, Germany, Italy, and the UK (2017).

[2] European Commission, Green Paper on mobile Health ("mHealth") (2014).

[3] Keith Spiller et al., Data Privacy: Users' Thoughts on Quantified Self Personal Data, in Self-Tracking: Empirical and Philosophical Investigations 111–24 (Btihaj Ajana ed., 2018).

[4] Federica Lucivero & Karin R. Jongsma, A Mobile Revolution for Healthcare? Setting the Agenda for Bioethics, 44 J. Med. Ethics 685, 685–9 (2018).

[5] Commission Staff Working Document on the existing EU legal framework applicable to lifestyle and wellbeing apps Accompanying the document Green Paper on mobile Health ("mHealth") (2014); See also Recital 19 of the MDR.

[6] Quinn Grundy et al., Data Sharing Practices of Medicines Related Apps and the Mobile Ecosystem: Traffic, Content, and Network Analysis, 364 BMJ l920 (2019); Achilleas Papageorgiou et al., Security and Privacy Analysis of Mobile Health Applications: The Alarming State of Practice, PP IEEE Access 1–1 (2018).

When traditional legislative regulation does not lead to the intended effect, complementary alternative forms of regulation may be the solution.[7] In the context of health data protection in mHealth apps, mobile app distribution platforms (app stores) may be well positioned to improve health data protection by means of self-regulation. App stores in the European Union already occupy an important place in this regard by offering a top-down regulation of third-party mHealth apps distributed on their platforms by means of app review procedures. App stores require app developers to comply with certain rules as part of a preapproval process and remove noncompliant apps. This "gatekeeping function" empowers app stores to influence app developers' conduct: a form of industry self-regulation.[8] Starting from this premise, the purpose of this chapter is to evaluate whether and to what extent self-regulation by app stores may contribute to the level of health data protection in the European Union.

The chapter is structured as follows. First, it outlines health data protection issues concerning mHealth apps (Section 5.2). Next, it describes the EU legal framework governing mHealth apps, focusing on the GDPR (Section 5.3). Subsequently, it discusses the benefits and risks of industry self-regulation as an alternative means to protect data protection rights in light of current mHealth regulation practices by Apple's App Store and Google's Google Play (Section 5.4). Finally, this chapter proposes several improvements to self-regulation in this field (Section 5.5), which will provide the basis for conclusions (Section 5.6).

5.2 HEALTH PRIVACY ISSUES IN SELF-MONITORING MHEALTH APPS

Popular examples of mHealth apps include calorie counters, apps to monitor menstruation cycles, and running trackers. These types of apps continuously monitor users' behavior over an extended period of time. While the focus of mHealth apps ranges from health to fitness and lifestyle, all of them collect large amounts of health-related data, such as biometric data, data concerning vital body functions, and health indicators. Most of these data qualifies as "data concerning health" within the meaning of the GDPR.[9] Health data should be understood in a broad manner.[10] The GDPR's definition of health data implies that information about users' weight, blood pressure, tobacco, and alcohol consumption is considered health data because this information is scientifically linked to health or disease risks.[11] Furthermore, certain types of information may not be health data as such, but may transform into health data when monitoring takes place over a longer period of time (i.e., average steps per

7 Anil K. Gupta & Lawrence J. Lad, Industry Self-Regulation: An Economic, Organizational, and Political Analysis, 8 AMR 416, 416–25 (1983).
8 Adrian Fong, The Role of App Intermediaries in Protecting Data Privacy, 25 Int'l J.L. & Info. Tech. 85, 85–114 (2017).
9 GDPR, 2016 O.J. (L 119) Recital 35.
10 Art. 29 Data Protection Working Party, Annex – health data in apps and devices (2015) 2.
11 Id.

month), or the data is combined with other data sources (i.e., daily calorie intake and social media profile).[12]

The risk for a violation of the users' fundamental rights is high, since misuse of health data may be irreversible and have long-term effects on data subjects' lives and social environments.[13] Several studies show that the extensive processing of health data by mHealth apps poses numerous threats to privacy.[14] This is mainly caused by the fact that health data is a valuable commodity: big data companies are increasingly interested in health data as it is scarce because of the expensive collection process.[15] Therefore, mHealth apps may encourage users to provide more health data in order to make more profit. Passively collected data, such as calculated overviews of average steps, are regularly collected beyond users' control.[16] Moreover, mHealth apps often use a standard Terms of Service, setting the rules on a "take it or leave it" basis.[17] Consequently, users are often unaware of the exact type and volume of collected data.[18]

Additional concerns are raised with regard to the user's control over access to the collected health data. Most apps provide for the possibility to disclose information to an "undefined (future) audience."[19] For example, many apps share health data among unspecified users to provide comparisons, and app operators may sell health data to third parties, such as advertisers and insurance companies.[20] Apps often do not provide the option to consent granularly: users have to consent to all receivers and all types of data at once.[21] In conclusion, the extensive processing and third-party sharing of health data by mHealth apps compromises users' control and therefore poses threats to users' privacy rights.

5.3 THE EFFECTIVENESS OF EU LEGAL PROTECTION OF HEALTH DATA IN MHEALTH APPS

5.3.1 *Inapplicability of the EU Health Framework*

In the European Union, health privacy in technology is regulated via multiple legal instruments. At the national level, health privacy is protected through patients' rights

12 Id. at 3–5.
13 Z v. Finland (1997) 25 Eur. Ct. H.R. 371, 94–6.
14 See generally Dominik Leibenger et al., Privacy Challenges in the Quantified Self Movement – An EU Perspective, 2016 Proc. on Privacy Enhancing Techs. 315, 315–34 (2016).
15 Grazia Cecere et al., Economics of Free Mobile Applications: Personal Data as a Monetization Strategy 45 (2018).
16 Papageorgiou et al., supra note 6.
17 Id.
18 Kirsten Ostherr et al., Trust and Privacy in the Context of User-Generated Health Data, 4 Big Data & Soc'y (2017).
19 Marjolein Lanzing, The Transparent Self, 18 Ethics & Info. Tech. 9, 9–16 (2016).
20 Leibenger et al., supra note 14.
21 Commission Staff Working Document, supra note 5.

frameworks. One basic right can be identified in all Member States: medical confidentiality. Medical confidentiality entails both the patient's right to confidentiality of personal data and the duty for health professionals to keep this data confidential.[22] However, mHealth app users are generally not considered patients by app developers nor in their own experience, as the apps do not serve a medical purpose and health professionals are not involved.[23] Therefore, users are not protected under the patients' rights framework.

At the EU level, health technology is mainly regulated through regulation of medical devices under the Medical Devices Regulation (MDR).[24] Software, including apps, may also fall under the MDR.[25] However, in order to qualify as a medical device, the intended purpose of the app needs to fall within one of the medical purpose categories stipulated by the MDR.[26] As most self-monitoring mHealth apps (monitoring fitness, general health, or wellbeing) are not intended for medical purposes but instead focus on general health, they usually do not qualify as medical devices.[27] The MDR specifically excludes software intended for general purposes and lifestyle and wellbeing purposes.[28] However, when apps do have an intended medical purpose, for example, self-monitoring apps prescribed by a physician, the MDR may apply. In any case, the MDR protects health privacy primarily with reference to the GDPR.[29]

5.3.2 *The GDPR Protects Health Data in Theory*

The main instrument for health privacy protection in the European Union is the GDPR. The GDPR provides individuals with several rights concerning personal data processing.[30] The GDPR applies to mHealth apps available in the European Union.[31] The basic premise of the GDPR is that every processing of personal data must be underpinned by a legal basis.[32] Moreover, it imposes duties on data processors and controllers and confers rights on data subjects in order to increase control.[33]

22 Tamara K. Hervey & Jean V. McHale, European Union Health Law (2015).
23 Commission Staff Working Document, supra note 5.
24 NB: Regulation (EU) 2017/745 (MDR) will replace the current Directive 93/42/EEC in May 2020.
25 CJEU, Case C-329/16 (SNITEM).
26 See Helen Yu, Regulation of Digital Health Technologies in the EU: Intended versus Actual Use, in The Future of Medical Device Regulation: Innovation and Protection (I. Glenn Cohen et al. eds., 2021).
27 European Commission, Guidance Document Medical Devices – Scope, Field of Application, Definition – Qualification and Classification of Stand Alone Software (2016).
28 MDR, Recital 19.
29 MDR, art. 109–10.
30 GDPR, 2016 O.J. (L 119) Recitals 7, 63 GDPR.
31 GDPR, art. 2–3, 2016 O.J. (L 119); European Data Protection Supervisor, Opinion 1/2015 Mobile Health: Reconciling technological innovation with data protection (2015).
32 GDPR, art. 6, 2016 O.J. (L 119).
33 GDPR. 2016 O.J. (L 119) Chapter III.

Data subjects' rights include the right to information,[34] the right to access,[35] and the right to withdraw consent.[36] Furthermore, the GDPR provides for a special data protection regime for health data, which stipulates a general prohibition on the processing of health data but provides for limited derogations.[37] However, these derogations are arguably inapplicable to mHealth apps, because app developers do not process health data in the public interest[38] and are not bound by professional secrecy.[39] Therefore, typically, health data can only be processed in mHealth apps when users provide their explicit consent.[40] This implies that the data subject must give an "express statement of consent."[41] The GDPR's extensive protection of data rights in combination with the strict health data regime gives it the potential to sufficiently protect mHealth users' health data.

5.3.3 *But the GDPR Does Not Effectively Protect Health Data in Practice*

However, several empirical studies show that many mHealth apps do not comply with relevant GDPR provisions related to health data.[42] For example, from a study on twenty mHealth apps available in the European Union, it was found that the majority of mHealth apps do not comply with provisions on user consent: 55 percent of the analyzed apps provide information about the app provider's privacy policy before registration, only 5 percent ask for consent every time the user shares additional personal information, none of the apps comply with the requirement of expressing "explicit" consent by specific questions or an online form and only 35 percent offer the possibility to withdraw consent and thereby delete their health data.[43] Another analysis of privacy policies of thirty-one EU mHealth apps shows that none complied with the right to information: only 42 percent mentioned the right to object and 58 percent the right to rectification and access.[44] A different study on twenty-four mHealth apps shows that 79 percent send users' health data to third parties in a nontransparent manner.[45]

Thus, in practice, many mHealth apps do not seem to comply with the GDPR. This can be explained by the fact that apps are often developed by individuals located all over the world, with little understanding of applicable data protection

34 GDPR, art. 12–13, 2016 O.J. (L 119).
35 GDPR, art. 15, 2016 O.J. (L 119).
36 GDPR, art. 7(3), 2016 O.J. (L 119).
37 GDPR, art. 9, 2016 O.J. (L 119).
38 GDPR, art. 9(2)(b–j), 2016 O.J. (L 119).
39 GDPR, art. 9(3), 2016 O.J. (L 119).
40 GDPR, art. 9(2)(a), 2016 O.J. (L 119).
41 Data Protection Working Party, art. 29, 2016 O.J. (L 119), Guidelines on consent under Regulation 2016/679 (2018) 18–19; GDPR, art. 32.
42 See generally Grundy et al., supra note 6.
43 Papageorgiou et al., supra note 6.
44 Trix Mulder, Health Apps, Their Privacy Policies and the GDPR, 10 Eur. J. L. and Tech. (2019).
45 Grundy et al., supra note 6.

legislation.[46] Furthermore, due to the great number of available apps, regulatory oversight is difficult because of insufficient resources.[47] The majority of Member States do not have an entity that is responsible for the regulatory oversight of mHealth apps.[48] Knowledge of lack of oversight may also result in lower compliance. In sum, the GDPR offers a relevant and sufficient legal framework for protection of health data, but lack of compliance and enforcement make the GDPR a practically ineffective instrument to protect mHealth users. Therefore, as long as compliance is not strengthened, traditional legislative regulation does not suffice.

5.4 SELF-REGULATION BY APP STORES AS A SOLUTION TO IMPROVE HEALTH DATA PROTECTION

When traditional (legislative) regulation does not lead to the intended effect, complementary alternative forms of regulation, such as self-regulation, may be the solution.[49] While the important role of app stores in securing GDPR compliance has been recognized by the European Union on several occasions,[50] and the role of digital platforms in protecting fundamental rights online is a popular topic in legal scholarship, the discussion seems to focus mainly on social media platforms and does not elaborate on app stores.[51] However, app stores may be well positioned to improve health data protection by means of self-regulation.

5.4.1 *Self-Regulation in Data Protection*

Industry self-regulation can be defined as "a regulatory process whereby an industry-level, as opposed to a governmental- or firm-level, organisation ... sets and enforces rules and standards relating to the conduct of firms in the industry."[52] Often-mentioned benefits of self-regulation are flexibility in adapting rules to technological changes, greater quality of rules, and more commitment to the rules.[53] However, self-regulation also has its limitations, specifically with regard to fundamental rights protection. Self-regulation instruments often lack effective enforcement and monitoring mechanisms. Furthermore, in some cases, self-regulation instruments are not consistent with other existing regulation, which makes the

46 Fong, supra note 8, at 98.

47 David Wright, Enforcing Privacy: Regulatory, Legal and Technological Approaches 29–31 (David Wright & Paul De Hert eds., 2016).

48 Carrie Beth Peterson et al., From Innovation to Implementation: eHealth in the WHO European Region (2016).

49 OECD, Alternatives to Traditional Regulation (2013) at 4–7; Gupta & Lad, supra note 7, at 417.

50 European Union Agency for Cybersecurity, Privacy and Data Protection in Mobile Applications 16 (2018); Data Protection Working Party, art. 29, supra note 41, at 11–12.

51 See, e.g., Christina Angelopoulos et al., Study of Fundamental Rights Limitations for Online Enforcement through Self-Regulation 96 (2015).

52 Gupta & Lad, supra note 7, at 417.

53 Rebecca Ong, Mobile Communication and the Protection of Children 247–9 (2010).

overall regulatory system increasingly complex. Other challenges include risks for favoritism and lack of accountability.[54]

In the context of data protection, self-regulation by the industry is becoming more common. Companies often choose to complement existing legislation with self-regulatory instruments for reasons of protecting consumer interests, increasing public trust and reputation, and combatting negative public opinions.[55] Also, self-regulation has been given prominence in the context of data protection at the EU level: the GDPR supports and encourages self-regulation by businesses in the form of codes of conduct and Binding Corporate Rules.[56] Moreover, the European Commission has (so far unsuccessfully) taken steps to set up a voluntary Privacy Code of Conduct on mHealth apps for app developers.[57]

5.4.2 *App Stores as Privacy Regulators*

With regard to industry self-regulation of mHealth apps in the European Union, we see that app stores already play an important role by top-down regulating third-party mHealth apps distributed on their platforms by means of app review procedures.[58] The app-ecosystem works as follows: in order for app developers to distribute their apps to the general public, they need to publish their app in app stores for consumers to download onto their mobile devices. App stores require app developers to comply with certain rules as part of a preapproval process and remove noncompliant apps. This "gatekeeping function" empowers app stores to influence app developers' conduct.[59] Therefore, app stores are the central orchestrators in the app-ecosystem and have a large amount of control over consumers.[60]

App stores are not regulated under the GDPR. They do not qualify as data processors or controllers under the GDPR themselves, as they do not exercise any control over personal data of users, but simply provide a platform for app providers to offer their apps.[61] However, app stores can impact the manner in which third-party apps – who do qualify as data processors – handle data protection.[62] Moreover, they are encouraged by

54 OECD, supra note 49, at 6–7, 42.

55 Artyom Dogtiev, App Stores List (2019), Business of Apps 131–2 (2017), www.businessofapps.com/guide/app-stores-list/.

56 GDPR, art. 40, 47, 2016 O.J. (L 119).

57 European Commission, supra note 27.

58 Apple App Store, App Store Review Guidelines (2019), https://developer.apple.com/app-store/review/guidelines/; Google Play, Google Play Developer Distribution Agreement (2019), https://play.google.com/intl/ALL_uk/about/developer-distribution-agreement.html/.

59 Fong, supra note 8, at 96–8; Luis Hestres, App Neutrality: Apple's App Store and Freedom of Expression Online, 7 Int'l J. Comm. (2013) at 1265–80.

60 The Netherlands Authority for Consumers & Markets, Market Study into Mobile App Stores 40 (2019).

61 European Union Agency for Cybersecurity, supra note 50.

62 Id.

the GDPR to fulfil this role.[63] In this regard, app stores conduct a form of industry self-regulation.[64] While app stores voluntarily impose these rules on third-party apps, although encouraged by the GDPR, self-regulation is not voluntary from the point of view of the app developers. In order to examine these app stores' behavior toward privacy of mHealth apps and to assess the effectiveness of these existing practices for health data protection in mHealth apps, this chapter performs a case-study analysis on Apple App Store and Google Play, today's leading app stores.[65]

5.4.3 *Case Studies*

5.4.3.1 Apple App Store

In order for app developers to submit apps to the Apple App Store, they must register to the Apple Developer Program, governed by the Apple Developer Program

TABLE 5.1 *Health data protection in app store policies*

	Apple App Store	Google Play
Operating system	iOS (e.g. iPhone)	Android (e.g. Samsung Galaxy)
Amount of apps	+– 2.2 million apps	+– 2.6 million apps
Pre-approval procedure	✓	✓
Deletion of non-compliant apps	✓	✓
Requirement to comply with privacy legislation	✓	✓
Requirement to integrate privacy policy	✓	✓
Explicit inclusion of the GDPR data protection principles	✓	✗
Explicit inclusion of data subjects' rights	✓	✗
Explicit rules on user consent	✓	✓
Rules on mHealth apps	✓	✗
Rules on health data	✓	✗
Requirement of explicit consent for health data processing	✗	✗

Source: author's analysis (2020)

63 GDPR, 2016 O.J. (L 119) Recital 78.
64 Fong, supra note 8.
65 Dogtiev, supra note 55.

License Agreement.[66] Furthermore, Apple App Store reviews all submitted apps and app updates according to the App Store Review Guidelines.[67] As shown in Table 5.1 above, these Guidelines contain specific rules on mHealth apps and state that these apps may be reviewed with greater scrutiny.[68] The guidelines also contain general provisions on processing of personal data and privacy. First, apps must include a privacy policy, explaining how users can exercise their rights to data retention, deletion, and withdraw consent.[69] Second, data collection must be based on user consent and users must be provided with an easily accessible and understandable option to withdraw consent.[70] Third, apps should minimize data collection.[71] With regard to sharing of data with third parties, user consent is required.[72] Furthermore, apps should not attempt to build a user profile on the basis of collected data.[73] The Apple Developer Program License Agreement also states that app developers must take into account user privacy and comply with privacy legislation.[74]

Furthermore, as can be seen in Table 5.1, the guidelines contain explicit rules on health data processed by mHealth apps.[75] First, apps may not use or disclose collected health data to third parties for the purpose of advertising, marketing, or other data-mining purposes.[76] In addition, apps may not use health data for targeted or behavioral advertising.[77] However, they may use or disclose health data for the purposes of improving health management and health research, but only with user permission.[78] Second, app developers may not write inaccurate data into mHealth apps.[79] Third, mHealth apps may not store health information in the iCloud.[80]

5.4.3.2 Google Play

Google Play's review criteria are outlined in the Developer Distribution Agreement and Developer Program Policies.[81] The Agreement functions as a legally binding

66 Apple App Store, Apple Developer Program License Agreement (2020), www.imperial.ac.uk/media/imperial-college/staff/web-guide/public/Apple-Developer-Agreement.pdf.
67 Apple.com, supra note 58.
68 Id. at § 1.4.1.
69 Apple App Store, App Store Review Guidelines (Sept. 12, 2019), https://developer.apple.com/app-store/review/guidelines/, § 5.1.1 (i).
70 Id. at § 5.1.1 (ii).
71 Id. at § 5.1.1 (iii).
72 Id. at § 5.1.2 (i)–(ii).
73 Id. at § 5.1.2 (iii).
74 Apple Developer Program License Agreement 2020, supra note 66, at § 3.3.7–3.3.11.
75 App Store Review Guidelines Sept. 12, 2019, supra note 69, at § 5.1.3.
76 Id. at § 5.1.3 (i).
77 Id. at § 3.1.7.
78 Id. at § 5.1.3 (i).
79 Id. at § 5.1.3 (ii).
80 Id.
81 Google Play, Google Play Developer Distribution Agreement (Nov. 5, 2019), https://play.google.com/intl/ALL_uk/about/developer-distribution-agreement.html/.

contract between the app developer and Google.[82] With regard to processing of personal data, the Agreement states that apps should comply with applicable data protection laws.[83] More specifically, apps must inform users of what personal data is processed, provide a privacy notice, and offer adequate data protection. Furthermore, apps may only use personal data for the purposes the user has consented to.[84] As shown in Table 5.1 above, the Agreement does not specifically mention mHealth apps or health data.

The Developer Program Policies provide more guidance on processing of personal (health) data. With regard to processing of personal data, the Policies state that apps that are intended to abuse or misuse personal data are strictly prohibited.[85] Furthermore, apps must be transparent about the collection, use, and sharing of personal data.[86] As to sensitive personal data, which probably also include health data, the Policies state that collection and use should be limited to purposes directly related to functionality of the app. Furthermore, an accessible privacy policy must be posted within the app itself. It must also disclose the type of parties the sensitive data is shared with.[87] Moreover, the in-app disclosure must contain a request for users' consent prior to data processing, requiring affirmative user action. These permission requests must clearly state the purposes for data processing or transfers. Furthermore, personal data may only be used for purposes that the user has consented to.[88] The Policies do not contain explicit provisions on mHealth apps, except for a prohibition on false or misleading health claims.[89]

5.4.3.3 Case Study Analysis

The above examination of app stores' guidelines shows that app stores are indeed concerned with privacy issues. However, it is questionable whether this leads to a higher level of protection of mHealth app users' health privacy. Both app stores' guidelines state that apps must comply with privacy legislation and integrate a privacy policy. However, the level of detail of the respective app stores' privacy provisions differs significantly. While Apple App Store specifically recalls most of the GDPR's data protection principles and data subjects' rights, Google Play's privacy guidelines are formulated in somewhat vague terms and do not mention data subjects' rights. Therefore, Google Play's guidelines do not offer app developers the needed guidance on how to protect personal data, specifically with regard to data subjects' rights. This

82 Id. at § 2.1.
83 Id. at § 4.6.
84 Id. at § 4.8.
85 Google Play, Google Play Developer Program Policies (2019), https://play.google.com/about/developer-content-policy/ under "Privacy, security and deception."
86 Id.
87 Id.
88 Id.
89 Id. under "Unapproved Substances."

entails a strong risk that users' rights will simply end up in the app's privacy policy fine print and will not lead to better privacy protection in practice.

Furthermore, while Apple App Store has specific guidelines on health data processing, Google Play's Policies only mention "sensitive personal data." This lack of specific regulation of health data does not reflect the risky nature of this type of data and therefore does not increase awareness of the need for protection. Most notably, both guidelines miss a provision on "explicit consent" for health data processing, which is required for app developers under the GDPR. While both guidelines contain provisions on user consent, no distinction is made between "regular" and "explicit" consent and thus no clarification on how to obtain explicit consent is offered. This puts privacy at risk, as control over health data is not sufficiently protected.

Both guidelines state that noncompliant apps will be removed, but do not elaborate on the structure of the monitoring process. Therefore, actual enforcement of the guidelines faces risks of uncertainty and inconsistency, which does not ensure compliance with the GDPR. After all, app stores are likely facing the same capacity problems as data protection authorities, and it could take months before noncompliant apps are taken down. Compliance issues also come into play in the differences between the respective guidelines, as this leads to the risk of unequal standards of protection of iOS and Android users.

Taken together, it can be concluded that the current self-regulation practices, Google Play's especially, do not live up to their potential and do not adequately ensure mHealth app users' control over their health data. However, due to the central position of app stores, self-regulation by app stores may still contribute to a higher level of health data protection if certain amendments are made to the content and form of their policies. Recommendations on how to improve the policies are touched upon in the next section.[90]

5.5 RECOMMENDATIONS TO IMPROVE CURRENT APP STORE SELF-REGULATION PRACTICES

App stores have a powerful position in the mHealth app sector. By setting requirements for mHealth apps to be listed on and removed from their platforms they hold the most promising means to improve the level of health data protection of users. Their current self-regulation practices could be improved on multiple fronts. First, app stores could provide app developers with clearer guidelines on data processing obligations and data subjects' rights. This should include stating all applicable obligations and rights under the GDPR and providing practical guidance on how to adequately implement this in apps. For example, app stores could issue technical guidelines on how to include consent withdrawal mechanisms in the apps. Translating privacy rights to technical measures will enhance adequate understanding

90 This section does not consider intermediary liability under the e-Commerce Directive.

and implementation by app developers.[91] Furthermore, app stores could make data subject rights and principles part of their contractual agreements with app developers to further strengthen compliance.[92]

Second, specific provisions on health data protection should be included, in order to point out its importance and increased privacy risks. These provisions should at least include the requirement to obtain explicit consent on health data processing and provide technical guidance on how to implement this.[93] There should also be specific provisions on limiting sharing of health data with third parties and possible commercial use. Additionally, app stores can further strengthen users' control by requiring apps to include user report tools on data protection infringement or provide for these tools in the app store itself.[94] Furthermore, app stores should commit to raising awareness of the risks of health data processing. For instance, a standard text on the risks could be provided for in the guidelines, which app developers would be required to include in their privacy policies. App stores could educate users of the risks by adding "health data processing warnings" to the downloading environment.

Moreover, app stores could strengthen user protection if they would mainstream their policies and engage in a shared EU Code of Conduct under the GDPR.[95] The GDPR codes are voluntary tools that set out specific data protection rules. They provide a detailed rulebook for controllers and processors in a specific sector. Bodies representing a sector – such as app stores – can create codes to aid GDPR compliance.[96] Codes have to be approved by the European Data Protection Board (EDPB) and compliance will be monitored by an accredited, independent supervisor.[97] Consequently, present self-regulation would turn into coregulation, and current guidelines would be replaced or supplemented by this GDPR code. App stores could make adherence to the code by app developers a requirement to offer apps on their platforms. This would have more effect than current self-regulation initiatives as preapproval of the code by the EDPB will give the code greater authority and the monitoring mechanism will lead to better compliance. Moreover, the unequal level of protection and risks of legal uncertainty and inconsistency would be minimized.[98] For mHealth app users' health privacy, a GDPR code will provide for more transparency regarding apps' approaches to data

91 Data Protection Working Party, art. 29, supra note 41.

92 Fong, supra note 8, at 108–11.

93 Masooda Bashir et al., Online Privacy and Informed Consent: The Dilemma of Information Asymmetry, 25 Proc. of the Assc'n for Info. Science and Tech., 1, 1–10 (2015).

94 Daithi Mac Sithigh, App Law Within: Rights and Regulation in the Smartphone Age, 21 Int'l J. L. & Info. Tech. 154, 154–86 (2013).

95 GDPR, art. 40, 2016 O.J. (L 119).

96 European Data Protection Board, Guidelines 1/2019 on Codes of Conduct and Monitoring Bodies under Regulation 2016/679 (2019) 6.

97 Id. at 8; GDPR, art. 40(5), 40(9), 41(1), 2016 O.J. (L 119).

98 Maximilian von Grafenstein, Co-Regulation and the Competitive Advantage in the GDPR: Data Protection Certification Mechanisms, Codes of Conduct and the "State of the Art" of Data

processing.[99] For example, the code would have to include specification of all applicable rights related to control over health data, explicit consent included.[100]

The preceding sections allow for the conclusion that app stores could positively impact GDPR compliance and thus strengthen mHealth users' health privacy by engaging in a GDPR code with specific health data safeguards. While there is no guarantee that app stores will make these changes, there are compelling reasons for them to do so. Foremost, the increased legal certainty offers app stores a competitive advantage. It reduces the complexity of app developers' entrepreneurial process, which may positively impact app stores' businesses.[101] For app developers, a code would be beneficial because it could be used to demonstrate compliance with the GDPR.[102] Furthermore, app stores will benefit from good privacy practices by third-party apps because this will likely also enhance their own trustworthiness. In this regard, privacy can be seen as a positive marketing statement.[103] Moreover, both Apple and Google were stakeholders in the European Commission's attempt at a voluntary mHealth Privacy Code of Conduct, which shows their interest in such an initiative.

5.6 CONCLUSION: IMPROVED APP STORE SELF-REGULATION STRENGTHENS HEALTH PRIVACY

Paradoxically, the wish to achieve self-empowerment by using mHealth apps leads to users surrendering power due to a lack of control over their health data. While the GDPR offers a solid solution for the protection of mHealth app users' health data in theory, it lacks practical effectiveness. Self-regulation of third-party apps by app stores by means of review procedures could fill the regulatory gap and thereby contribute to the level of health data protection in the European Union. However, the performed case-studies show that current self-regulation does not fulfil this promise. None the less, given the platforms' central and powerful position in the sector, complementary regulation of mHealth apps by app stores may still be the most promising means to improve the level of health data protection of mHealth app users. This conclusion sheds light on the heavily debated role of the European Union in regulating technological phenomena and related fundamental rights risks: in some cases, the sector itself is in a better position to regulate these risks and enforce legal compliance than independent supervisory authorities. This finding is in line with the European Union's growing tendency to promote and support self-regulation structures to supplement EU legislation.

Protection-by-Design, in Research Handbook on Privacy and Data Protection Law: Values, Norms and Global Politics (Forthcoming).

99 European Data Protection Board, supra note 96, at 7–9.

100 GDPR, art. 40(2), 2016 O.J. (L 119).

101 von Grafenstein, supra note 98.

102 See GDPR, art. 24(3), § 3.2.3; 2016 O.J. (L 119); European Data Protection Board, supra note 96, at 9.

103 Mulder, supra note 44.

Despite the important role of app stores in achieving this, in the end, the ultimate responsibility for safeguarding users' health privacy lies with the mHealth app developers and providers that process health data. mHealth apps should provide users with the adequate means to exercise privacy rights by ensuring concrete and effective opportunities to have control over decisions regarding health data processing. In this regard, effective possibilities for actual enforcement of self-regulation standards are of key importance. While app store self-regulation may steer mHealth app developers in the right direction by translating the GDPR's privacy provisions into technical pre-approval requirements, compliance with the relevant privacy provisions is also aided by increased awareness among both mHealth users, developers, and health data brokers as to the risks mHealth apps entail for individual fundamental rights. The European Union could play a central role in accomplishing this, in order to assist mHealth users to achieve the highly desired self-empowerment by bringing the GDPR to life in mHealth apps.

6

The Interaction of the Medical Device Regulation and the GDPR

Do European Rules on Privacy and Scientific Research Impair the Safety and Performance of AI Medical Devices?

Janos Meszaros, Marcelo Corrales Compagnucci, and Timo Minssen

Stipulations on deidentification and scientific research in the European General Data Protection Regulation (GDPR) help research organizations to use personal data with fewer restrictions compared to data collection for other purposes. Under these exemptions, organizations may process specific data for a secondary purpose without consent. However, the definition and legal requirements of scientific research differ among EU Member States. Since the new EU Medical Device Regulations 2017/745 and 2017/746 require compliance with the GDPR, the failure to come to grips with these concepts creates misunderstandings and legal issues. We argue that this might result in obstacles for the use and review of input data for medical devices. This could not only lead to forum shopping but also safety risks. The authors discuss to what extent scientific research should benefit from the research exemption and deidentification rules under the GDPR. Furthermore, this chapter analyzes recently released guidelines and discussion papers to examine how input data is reviewed by EU regulators. Ultimately, we call for more harmonized rules to balance individuals' rights and the safety of medical devices.

6.1 INTRODUCTION

Artificial intelligence (AI) and big data have a significant impact on society,[1] as many aspects of our lives have become subject to data processing.[2] This "datafication" has

Acknowledgement: This research is supported by a Novo Nordisk Foundation grant for a scientifically independent Collaborative Research Program in Biomedical Innovation Law (grant agreement number NNF17SA0027784).

1 Marcelo Corrales Compagnucci, Big Data, Databases and 'Ownership' Rights in the Cloud 4, 38, 40 (2020); Marcelo Corrales & Paulius Jurčys, Nudging Cloud Providers through Intermediary Services in New Technology, Big Data and the Future of Law, 154–5 (Marcelo Corrales et al. eds., 2017).

2 Viktor Mayer-Schönberger & Kenneth Cukier, Big Data: A Revolution that Will Transform How We Live, Work, and Think (Mariner Books ed., 2013).

also led to a rapid transformation in the delivery of health care services.[3] The new generation of medical devices represents one example of technological advance that could substantially protect and improve public health.[4] Many of these rely heavily on data and AI algorithms to prevent, diagnose, treat, and monitor sources of epidemic diseases.[5]

Though opening a world of new opportunities, rapid advances in AI medical devices have resulted in a number of highly complex dilemmas, tradeoffs, and uncertainties regarding the applicability and appropriateness of the current legal framework. Many of these legal and ethical issues relate to privacy and data protection. The European General Data Protection Regulation (GDPR)[6] is of particular importance in that respect. Focusing on the GDPR, the following chapter discusses the risk that AI medical device systems may run afoul of sufficiently informed consents of data subjects since they collect, process, and transfer sensitive personal data in unexpected ways without giving adequate prior notice, choices of participation, and other options.[7] At the same time, such data can be important to ensure the safety and effectiveness of such devices. Considering the consequential need for reasonably sound tradeoffs, we argue that current legal frameworks and definitions need to be harmonized and refined. We refer to the typical lifecycle in the collection and processing of health data via medical devices (Section 6.2) to highlight the challenges and legal risks at each phase. Section 6.3 examines the new EU regulations for Medical Devices (MDR)[8] and In Vitro Diagnostic Medical Devices (IVDR)[9] with a special focus on the MDR. In this section, we seek in particular to identify and iron out the missing links between the GDPR and the MDR.

3 Alessandro Blasimme & Effy Vayena, Towards Adaptive Governance in Big Data Health Research: Implementing Regulatory Principles (Oct. 2019), https://papers.ssrn.com/sol3/papers.cfm?abstract_id=3501545; Marcelo Corrales Compagnucci, Big Data, Databases and 'Ownership' in the Cloud 4, 39, 40, 299 (2019).

4 Ugo Pagallo et al., The Rise of Robotics & AI: Technological Advances and Normative Dilemmas 1–13 (2018).

5 Marcelo Corrales Compagnucci et al., Homomorphic Encryption: The Holy Grail for Big Data Analytics and Legal Compliance in the Pharmaceutical and Healthcare Sector, 3 EPLR 144, 145–55 (2019).

6 Regulation 2016/679 of the European Parliament and of the Council of 27 April 2016 on the protection of natural persons with regard to the processing of personal data and on the free movement of such data, and repealing Directive 95/46/EC (General Data Protection Regulation) (Text with EEA relevance), 2016 O.J. (L 119) 4.5, at 1–88 (EU) [hereinafter GDPR].

7 Timo Minssen et al., The EU-US Privacy Shield Regime for Cross-Border Transfers of Personal Data Under the GDPR: What Are the Legal Challenges and How Might These Affect Cloud-Based Technologies, Big Data, and AI in the Medical Sector?, 4 EPLR 34, 34–50; Marcelo Corrales Compagnucci et al., Lost on the High Seas without a Safe Harbor or a Shield? Navigating Cross-Border Data Transfers in the Pharmaceutical Sector after Schrems II Invalidation of the EU-US Privacy Shield, 4 EPLR 153, 153–160.

8 Regulation 2017/745 of the European Parliament and of the Council of 5 April 2017 on medical devices, amending Directive 2001/83/EC, Regulation (EC) No 178/2002 and Regulation (EC) No 1223/2009 and repealing Council Directives 90/385/EEC and 93/42/EEC, 2017 O.J. (L 117) 5.5, at 1–175 (EU) [hereinafter MDR].

9 Regulation 2017/746 of the European Parliament and of the Council of 5 April 2017 on in vitro diagnostic medical devices and repealing Directive 98/79/EC and Commission Decision 2010/227/EU,2017 O.J. (L 117) 5.5, at 176–332 (EU) [hereinafter IVDR].

Section 6.4 discusses our main findings and summarizes recommendations. This provides the basis for our conclusions in Section 6.5.

6.2 COLLECTION AND PROCESSING OF HEALTH DATA UNDER THE GDPR

Modern health care systems and medical devices collect and process vast amounts of data, which may enhance an individual's health care experience directly and indirectly through scientific research and policy planning. Nevertheless, obtaining informed consent[10] or authorization from a large number of data subjects can be challenging and result in disproportionate cost and effort.[11] For instance, the Italian government provided the health data[12] of 61 million Italian citizens to IBM Watson Health, without obtaining patient consent.[13] The agreement between the Italian government and IBM underlined that IBM alone would retain rights to the results of the research, which it could then license to third parties.[14] Instead of acquiring consent for the secondary processing, the most realistic option for privacy protection is providing the option to opt-out for the citizens, such as the national data opt-out system[15] in England.[16]

In general, the processing of sensitive data (e.g., health data) is prohibited under the GDPR. This can be a crucial issue in the case of AI-augmented medical devices since the sensitivity and specificity of an algorithm are only as good as the data that they are trained on. For instance, if an algorithm is only trained on the genetic material derived from European Caucasians, it may not provide accurate information that can be generalized to individuals of other groups. However, the GDPR enables the processing of sensitive data for public interest, public health, and scientific research purposes, if there are appropriate safeguards for the rights and freedom of individuals. While the GDPR does not fully specify what those

[10] Consent is defined by GDPR, art. 4(11), as "any freely given, specific, informed and unambiguous indication of the data subject's wishes by which he or she, by a statement or by a clear affirmative action, signifies agreement to the processing of personal data relating to him or her."

[11] Paul R. Burton et al., Policies and Strategies to Facilitate Secondary Use of Research Data in the Health Sciences, 46 International Journal of Epidemiology 1732, 1732–3 (2017).

[12] The health data included demographic data; all medical conditions, diagnoses, and their treatment; emergency and other hospital visits, including dates and times; prescriptions and their costs; genomic data and information about any cancers; and much else besides.

[13] Elad Leshem, IBM Watson Health AI gets access to full health data of 61m Italians, Medium (Jan. 18, 2018), https://medium.com/@qData/ibm-watson-health-ai-gets-access-to-full-health-data-of-61m-italians-73f85d90f9c0.

[14] Glyn Moody, Detailed Medical Records of 61 Million Italian Citizens to Be Given to IBM for Its "Cognitive Computing" System Watson, Privacy News Online (May 22, 2017), www.privateinternetaccess.com/blog/detailed-medical-records-61-million-italian-citizens-given-ibm-cognitive-computing-system-watson/.

[15] NHS Digital, National Data Opt-out, https://digital.nhs.uk/services/national-data-opt-out.

[16] Janos Meszaros & Chih-Hsing Ho, Building Trust and Transparency? Challenges of the Opt-Out System and the Secondary Use of Health Data in England, 19 Med. L. Int'l 159, 159–81 (2019).

safeguards are, it indicates that their purpose is to "ensure that technical and organizational measures are in place in order to ensure respect for the principle of data minimization."[17] Such measures may include de-identification methods (for example, anonymization and pseudonymization) provided that the intended use of the data can still be fulfilled. However, differing requirements of national laws toward the application of these exemptions and de-identification methods often hinder the application of AI medical devices at the EU level. In Sections 6.2.1–6.2.3, we consider the most salient problems.

6.2.1 *Public Interest and Public Health*

Public interest and public health can be a legal basis for the secondary use of health data. The GDPR posits several levels of public interest, such as general and important.[18] However, the level of public interest in AI medical devices is still not clear and may fall under different categories. This could create problems to identify whether personal data might be processed with or without consent to develop and update these devices. Deciding on the level of public interest is as challenging as it is relevant. Medical devices need to be safe and reliable. Malfunctions could potentially cost lives. Therefore, the public interest and public health could be linked to the intended use and classification of these devices.

6.2.2 *Scientific Research*

There are situations when data was not collected for research or health care purposes initially. For instance, when a smartwatch measures a wearer's heart rate. This data can be useful later for research purposes, to find unseen correlations. The collected data provides valuable information for future research but reaching users for getting their approval for the secondary purpose would pose a significant burden, if it is possible at all. This can lead to controversial scenarios, such as the Google DeepMind[19] case in the United Kingdom, where the Royal Free Hospital under the National Health Service (NHS)[20] provided the personal data of 1.6 million patients to Google DeepMind without their consent. Google's AI medical device was an app, which could monitor an acute kidney injury disease. The app called "Streams" was used as part of a trial to test, diagnose, and detect the disease. Public

[17] GDPR, art. 89(1).

[18] Janos Meszaros & Chih-Hsing Ho, Big Data and Scientific Research: The Secondary Use of Personal Data Under the Research Exemption in the GDPR, *Acta Juridica Hungarica* 403, 403–19 (2018).

[19] DeepMind Technologies is a British artificial intelligence company founded in 2010, currently owned by Google through Alphabet Inc.

[20] Royal Free is one of the largest health care providers in Britain's publicly funded National Health Service.

concerns and corroborative research suggested that Google DeepMind failed to comply with the provisions enshrined by data protection law.[21]

The GDPR aims to ease the restrictions on the processing of sensitive data by explicitly allowing the processing for research purposes. To use this legal basis, the data controllers need to apply appropriate safeguards (e.g., pseudonymization and anonymization) under EU and Member State laws.[22] The GDPR defines scientific research in a broad manner, which includes "technological development and demonstration, fundamental research, applied research and privately funded research" conducted by both public and private entities.[23] However, the definition of research can be found in the Recitals[24] of the GDPR, which are not legally binding by themselves. Several EU Member States, such as Germany and Finland, do not define "scientific research" in their laws. Instead, these States define the limits and requirements of research through the regulation of their authorities responsible for this field.[25] Other Member States such as Austria regulate scientific research by referring to the OECD's Frascati Manual.[26,27] The OECD Frascati Manual includes definitions of basic concepts, data collection guidelines, and classifications for compiling research and development statistics. However, the Frascati Manual never defines "scientific research" as such, even though it makes use of the term in a number of instances throughout the text. Furthermore, the application of the research exemption can lead to different interpretations. For instance, in Ireland, the application of the research exemption by the Health Research Consent Declaration Committee is significantly stricter than in the United Kingdom, by the Medical Research Council.[28] Hence, the Member States need to restrict the scope of scientific research, since overly broad interpretations might undermine the goals of the GDPR. These diverse rules on data collection pose hurdles for improving the safety of medical devices, since processing new data for updating is crucial, and the different requirements and barriers in Member States undermine the

21 Janos Meszaros et al., Nudging Consent and the New Opt-Out System to the Processing of Health Data in England, in Legal Tech and the New Sharing Economy, 61, 68 (Marcelo Corrales Compagnucci et al. eds., 2019).

22 GDPR, art. 9(2)(j).

23 GDPR, Recital 159.

24 In EU law, Recitals are usually placed at the beginning of the legal text. They introduce the legislation and explain the reasons for the provisions and clarify legislative goals. Recitals are normally not binding as such. Recitals may, however, influence interpretations of the law by Courts or further legislation and may in that way achieve binding effect.

25 See, e.g., German Research Foundation requirements for funding scientific research, www.dfg.de/en/research_funding/principles_dfg_funding/index.html.

26 Organisation for Economic Co-operation and Development (OECD), Frascati Manual: Guidelines for Collecting and Reporting Data on Research and Experimental Development (2015).

27 515th Regulation on Research, Austria, www.ffg.at/sites/default/files/downloads/service/forschungspraemienverordnung_bgbla_2012_ii_515.pdf.

28 Mary Donnelly & Maeve McDonagh, Health Research, Consent and the GDPR Exemption (Apr. 2, 2019). This is a pre-edited version of M. Donnelly & M. McDonagh Health Research, Consent and the GDPR Exemption, 26 Eur. J. Health L. 97, 97–119 (2019).

collection of reliable and diverse datasets. Germany's new Digital Healthcare Act[29] is a good example of promoting the use of low-risk medical devices and ensuring better usability of health data for research purposes. The Act entitles persons covered by statutory health insurance to benefit from digital health applications and contains provisions to make demographic data from health insurers more usable for research purposes.[30]

6.2.3 *Deidentification*

Deidentification methods represent a broad spectrum of tools and techniques to protect the data subject's privacy. In general, the strength of the deidentification scales with a loss in data utility and value.[31] The two ends of this spectrum are clear: personal data without any deidentification, which can directly identify the data subject and anonymous data, which cannot identify individuals.[32] Between these two ends, there is a wide range of methods and techniques, which need further clarification. The GDPR clarifies that pseudonymized data is a type of personal data.[33] However, the definition of pseudonymization is too broad to know the requirements to reach an adequate level of deidentification. Recognizing the broad spectrum of deidentification techniques and acknowledging them as an "appropriate safeguard" enables the development of regulatory guidance that encourages the maximum use of deidentification, and it may open the door for the safe secondary use of data in scientific research.

Public interest, public health, and scientific research represent a broad exemption from the prohibition of the processing of sensitive data in the GDPR. These legal bases also require safeguards, such as deidentification techniques. However, the application of them in the Member States is not unified. This may trigger

[29] Gesetz für eine bessere Versorgung durch Digitalisierung und Innovation (Digitale-Versorgung-Gesetz – DVG) [Digital Healthcare Act] of 9 December 2019, BGBl I at 2562 (Germany, 2019). Compare also Germany's new Hospital Future Act, Gesetz für ein Zukunftsprogramm Krankenhäuser (Krankenhauszukunftsgesetz – KHZG), G. v. 23.10.2020 BGBl. I S. 2208 (Nr. 48).

[30] Sara Gerke et al., Germany's Digital Health Reforms in the COVID-19 Era: Lessons and Opportunities for Other Countries, 3 npj Digit. Med. 94 (2020).

[31] Paul Ohm, Broken Promises of Privacy: Responding to the Surprising Failure of Anonymization, 57 UCLA L. Rev. 1706 (Aug. 13, 2009); U. of Colorado Law Legal Studies Research Paper No. 9–12, https://ssrn.com/abstract=1450006.

[32] The GDPR has strict expectations towards anonymization. Unlike the Health Insurance Portability and Accountability Act (HIPAA) in the United States, which sets forth a rule exempting data from regulation if eighteen specific identifiers are removed, the GDPR applies the standard that data is anonymous only when it cannot be identified by any means by any person (GDPR, Recital 26).

[33] However, many scholars are challenging the idea that pseudonymized data constitutes personal data in all cases. For instance: Miranda Mourby, Elaine Mackey, Mark Elliot, et al., Are "Pseudonymised" Data Always Personal Data? Implications of the GDPR for Administrative Data Research in the UK, 34 (2) *Computer Law and Security Review* 222–33 (2018); Anne Bahr & Irene Schlünder, Code of Practice on Secondary Use of Medical Data in European Scientific Research Projects, 5 *International Data Privacy Law* 279, 279–91 (2015).

unnecessary legal risks in the development and deployment of AI medical devices and takes us directly to what has been called the "update problem":[34] how can regulators, as well as reliable developers and producers, determine when the updated AI behaves differently enough that a new assessment is needed? It is challenging to ensure that AI medical devices conform to all the rules and technical issues without posing new risks than those assessed during the premarket review.[35] Considering that the essence of updating medical devices potentially introduces new risks without constant approval, it is crucial to validate the data they are learning from. Therefore, regulators and product manufacturers need to implement a risk reassessment and incident-report framework, which includes ongoing evaluation and mitigation strategies throughout the whole lifecycle of AI medical devices, in particular, during service deployment and operation phases. For this, harmonized rules on the collection and processing of health data as well as review systems and processes of medical devices would be necessary in the EU Member States.

6.3 THE EU MEDICAL DEVICE REGULATION

To keep up with advances in science and technology, two new EU regulations on medical devices and in vitro diagnostic medical devices entered into force on May 25, 2017.[36] They will progressively replace the existing directives[37] after a staggered transitional period.[38]

The MDR clarifies that data protection rules need to be applied when medical devices process personal data.[39] Therefore, if a medical device regulated by the MDR collects personal data, it also falls under the GDPR. The MDR differentiates among three classes of medical devices, depending on their level of risk:

1. Class I devices, posing low/medium risk (e.g., wheelchairs);
2. Class IIa and IIb devices, representing medium/high-level risk (e.g., x-ray devices);

34 B. Babic et al., Algorithms on Regulatory Lockdown in Medicine. Prioritize Risk Monitoring to Address the "Update Problem," 366 Science 1202, 1202–4 (2019).

35 Glenn Cohen et al., The European AI Strategy: Implications and Challenges for Digital Health (forthcoming LANCET-Digital Health).

36 Supra notes 9 & 10.

37 Council Directive 90/385/EEC on Active Implantable Medical Devices (AIMDD) (1990); Council Directive 93/42/EEC on Medical Devices (MDD) (1993); Council Directive 98/79/EC on in vitro Diagnostic Medical Devices (IVDMD) (1998).

38 The Council and the Parliament adopted on 23 April 2020 Regulation 2020/561 amending Regulation 2017/745 on medical devices regarding application dates of certain of its provisions. This Regulation postpones the date of application for most Medical Devices Regulation provisions by one year – until 26 May 2021. This postponement alleviates the pressure off national authorities, notified bodies, manufacturers, and other actors so they can focus fully on urgent priorities related to the COVID-19 crisis. The IVDR Regulation 2017/746 corresponding date of application remains the same (May 2022).

39 Regulation 2017/745 Recital 47, arts. 62(4)(h), 72(3), 92(4), 110(1)–(2) (EU).

3. Class III, high-risk devices (e.g., pacemakers).

In the case of low-risk level (Class I) medical devices, such as a smartwatch, privacy might often prevail over the secondary use of personal data to develop and improve these devices. In the case of high-risk level (Class III), the safety of medical devices might outweigh patient privacy. AI medical devices with a medium risk level (Class II), such as medical image processing software, may be considered to have at least a general level of public interest. However, developing high-risk devices does not mean that manufacturers could automatically process health data without consent. Careful consideration is necessary on a case-by-case basis with strong safeguards, under the oversight of authorities.

Medical devices in the European Union need to undergo a conformity assessment to demonstrate that they meet legal requirements. The conformity assessment usually involves an audit of the manufacturer's quality system and, depending on the type of device, a review of technical documentation from the manufacturer on the safety and performance of the device.[40] Manufacturers can place a CE (Conformité Européenne) mark on their medical device after passing the assessment. The EU Member States can designate accredited notified bodies to conduct conformity assessments. A notified body within the European Union is an entity designated by an EU competent authority to assess the conformity of medical devices before being placed on the market. Companies are free to choose the notified body they engage with.[41] There are more than fifty EU notified bodies in total that can certify according to Medical Device Directives. However, not all of these notified bodies can certify according to all categories of medical device products. When the authorities start to scrutinize the AI/ML medical device during the approval process, it is challenging to know clearly how the AI application and algorithms developed and evolved due to their opaque nature.[42] It is not clear how notified bodies can review the input data of AI medical devices. First, reviewing large and complex datasets requires special knowledge and technical expertise, which might be lacking or not at the same level within all the notified bodies of the European Union. Second, there are medical devices developed outside of the European Union. Reviewing the datasets used for developing them might trigger data protection and data transfer jurisdictional issues. The datasets might contain sensitive data of individuals from countries outside Europe, thus data sharing is challenging, posing a hurdle for part of the review process. For instance, the Health Insurance Portability and Accountability Act (HIPAA) and state regulations in the

[40] EMA, Medical devices, www.ema.europa.eu/en/human-regulatory/overview/medical-devices.

[41] European Medicines Agency, Questions & Answers on Implementation of the Medical Devices and In Vitro Diagnostic Medical Devices Regulations, ((EU) 2017/745 and (EU) 2017/746) (Oct. 21, 2019) Rev.1 EMA/37991/2019.

[42] US Food & Drug Admin., Executive Summary for the Patient Engagement Advisory Committee Meeting, Artificial Intelligence (AI) and Machine Learning (ML) in Medical Devices (Oct. 22, 2020). William Nicholson Price II, Regulating Black-Box Medicine, 116 Mich. L. Rev. 421 (Mar. 21, 2017).

United States, and Japanese regulations on personal data[43] might not allow the sharing of sensitive data with the notified bodies in the EU Member States. Moreover, sharing anonymized data might not be sufficient to review input data thoroughly. Third, there is a great variety of data-processing software and methods among companies operating in different countries, which makes it extremely challenging to review these devices uniformly on the same level.

The European Medicines Agency and several notified bodies are already preparing for the change of AI medical devices. The European Medicines Agency and the Heads of Medicines Agencies (HMA) Big Data Task Force (BDTF)[44] released two reports[45] recently for the European regulators and stakeholders to realize the potential of big data in terms of public health and innovation. Since the biggest issues in the European Union currently are the decentralization of health data and regulatory tasks, the reports focus on providing guidance and resources for data quality and discoverability to build up computing and analytical capacity. Thus, the most ambitious recommendation of the BDTF is the establishment of an EU platform: Data Analysis and Real World Interrogation Network (DARWIN) to access and analyze health care data from across the European Union. This platform would create a European network of databases with verified quality and strong data security. It is intended to be used to inform regulatory decision making with robust evidence from health care practice. The reports highlight the following actions for the European Union:

1. Ensuring sufficient expertise and capacities within the European network (in all the notified bodies in the Member States), in order to ensure that AI medical devices can be assessed appropriately.
2. Enable regulatory evaluation of clinical data submitted by drug manufacturers for approval where the data has been processed by AI algorithms or if part of the analysis, such as patient selection, involved AI methods.
3. Enable regulatory use of AI in internal processes at authorities and notified bodies. For instance, applying Natural Language Processing of received texts, or reviewing image data submitted to support a clinical claim from a drug manufacturer.
4. Approval of AI-based Health Apps in devices intended for clinical decision making.

The reports also clarify that the European Union cannot accept opaque algorithms performing without checks and balances. Algorithm code should be

43 Act on the Protection of Personal Information (Act No. 57 of May 30, 2003, as amended, APPI).

44 The HMA/EMA Task Force on Big Data was established in 2017 to report on the challenges and opportunities posed by big data in medicine regulation.

45 See, e.g., HMA-EMA Joint Big Data Taskforce Phase I and Phase II reports on "Evolving Data-Driven Regulation" (2019), www.ema.europa.eu/en/documents/other/hma-ema-joint-big-data-taskforce-phase-ii-report-evolving-data-driven-regulation_en.pdf.

more transparent (feature selection, code, original data set) and available for targeted review by regulators and notified bodies. The report states that the outcomes and changes to algorithm use (safety and efficacy) need to be subject to post-marketing surveillance mechanisms, in a similar way as monitoring drug safety after marketing authorization. By way of comparison, the European Union's approach for the assessment of medical devices is slightly different from the FDA's in the United States. While the reports suggest that the European Union is still focusing on the transparency of AI applications, the FDA also pays special attention to the excellence and trustworthiness of the companies developing AI medical devices during the precertification process.[46] Figure 6.1 below shows the flow of health data for developing AI medical devices in the European Union.

6.4 DISCUSSION

The effective collection and processing of relevant health data is the first step to making AI medical devices that work properly. This is particularly relevant during the COVID-19[47] outbreak as the foreseeable reuse of health data for scientific purposes leads to a rise in the number of organizations manufacturing AI medical devices.[48] The US Sentinel system is a great example of monitoring the safety of medical devices and securely sharing and reusing the collected information.[49] Our analysis suggests, however, that the processing and review of input data for medical devices, as well as the definition of specific data uses, are not fully harmonized in the European Union. This issue stems from the fact that the health care systems and scientific research are mainly regulated by the EU Member States, resulting in diverse legal environments and barriers for processing health data. Thus, the GDPR and Medical Device Regulation have not reached a sufficient level of harmonization in this field. This may result in unnecessary legal risks in the development and deployment of AI medical devices, which is crucial in the case of the "update problem."[50] Therefore, harmonized rules on the collection and processing of health data, as well as review systems and processes of medical devices, would be necessary in the EU Member States.

46 US Food & Drug Admin., Proposed Regulatory Framework for Modifications to Artificial Intelligence/Machine Learning (AI/ML)-Based Software as a Medical Device (SaMD) – Discussion Paper and Request for Feedback (2019).

47 Guidelines 04/2020 on the use of location data and contact tracing tools in the context of COVID-19 outbreak adopted on 21 April 2020.

48 European Data Protection Supervisor, A Preliminary Opinion on Data Protection and Scientific Research (Jan. 6, 2020), https://edps.europa.eu/sites/edp/files/publication/20-01-06_opinion_research_en.pdf.

49 US Food & Drug Admin., FDA's Sentinel Initiative, https://www.fda.gov/safety/fdas-sentinel-initiative (Nov. 26, 2020).

50 B. Babic et al., Algorithms on Regulatory Lockdown in Medicine. Prioritize Risk Monitoring to Address the "Update Problem," 366 Science 1202, 1202–4 (2019).

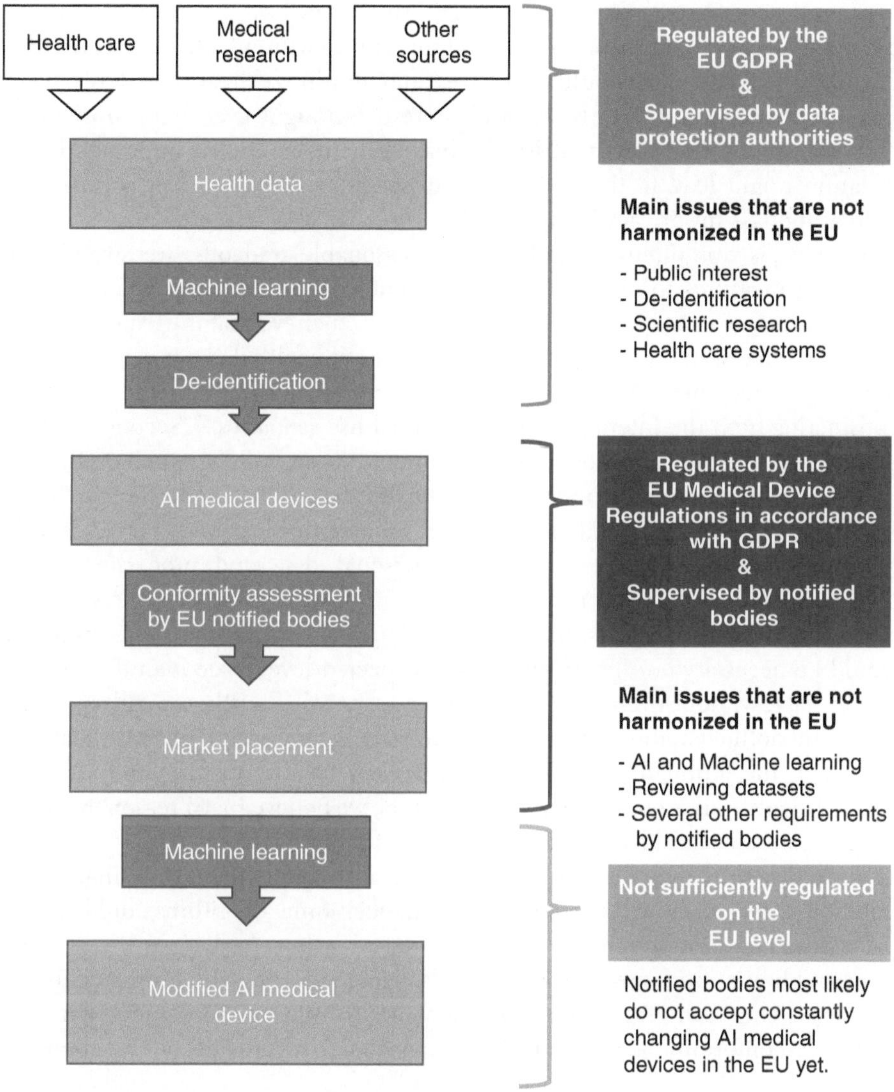

FIGURE 6.1. The processing of health data for developing AI medical devices

The "update problem" is still not sufficiently addressed and little work has thoroughly examined how AI medical devices are developed and built from the perspectives of public interest and data protection law. To build these devices, data-intensive research is necessary. However, at what cost? Strong privacy protection may hinder the development, effectiveness, and precision of AI products and services. Globally, there is a drive to create competitive pharmaceutical and health care industries. As a result, the developers of AI medical devices and services have enjoyed a privileged position since they have been able to further use health data with less restrictions, and sometimes without adequate consent.[51] On the one hand, this could save lives and minimize treatment costs.[52] An increased precision due to better and more data, might even help to identify, monitor, and correct potential risks for bias in the data. On the other hand, this situation might lead to the further use of sensitive data with less control and increasing risks for privacy breaches.

To address this dilemma and achieve reasonable tradeoffs, we suggest the following measures to advance the assessment of the safety and efficacy of AI medical devices in the European Union. First, we believe that the expected level of public interest in the case of the secondary use of health data for developing AI medical devices must be clarified for different categories of medical devices, considering both the intended and unintended use scenarios.[53] Second, we propose to regulate the definition and requirements of scientific research on the EU level to harmonize the secondary use of health data. This would be crucial for providing a sufficient amount of quality data for machine learning in the case of AI medical devices. Moreover, collecting personal data and processing it for a purpose with public interest should not result in a product or service that negatively affects the data subject's rights. Third, we think that more guidance would be necessary on the safeguards and expected level of de-identification on health data, without overconfidently relying on them. Fourth, we call upon the EMA and notified bodies to be properly prepared for the review of (large) datasets since it is the foundation of AI medical devices. While opening and assessing opaque algorithms is challenging for regulators, we believe that a reasonable level of transparency should be required to allow for sufficient regulatory review of medical device systems.[54] This does not necessarily imply that every single computational step must be traceable.[55] For instance, some algorithms could still be utilized to construct a transparent and trusted AI system "as long as the assumptions and limitations, operational protocols, data properties, and output decisions can be systematically examined and validated."[56] Fifth, we recommend harmonizing the conformity assessment of notified bodies to provide safety, allow for

[51] Julia Powles & Hal Hodson, Google DeepMind and Healthcare in an Age of Algorithms, 7 Health Tech. 351, 351–67 (Dec. 2017).

[52] Jonathan H. Chen & Steven M. Asch. , Machine Learning and Prediction in Medicine – Beyond the Peak of Inflated Expectations, 376 N. Engl. J. Med. 2507 (Jun. 2017).

[53] Helen Yu, Regulation of Digital Health Technologies in the EU: Intended vs Actual Use, in Future of Medical Device Regulation: Innovation and Protection (Cambridge University Press ed., Oct. 2020); see also Timo Minssen et al., When Does Stand-Alone Software Qualify as a Medical Device in the European Union? – The Cjeu's Decision in Snitem and What It Implies for the Next Generation of Medical Devices, 28 Med. L. Rev. 615, 615–24 (2020).

[54] Timo Minssen, Regulating Digital Health, Gary Humphreys Report (2020), www.who.int/bulletin/volumes/98/4/20-020420.pdf.

[55] Id.

[56] Id.

European-wide reports on unwanted incidents, and avoid forum shopping. Sixth, and finally, we propose to develop special regulation and oversight for AI research to allow for a better coordination and compliance assessment in view of the great variety of separate regulations concerning data protection, health care, and medical research.

6.5 CONCLUSION

Harnessing the full benefits of AI-driven medical devices offers many opportunities, in particular in health crisis situations, such as the ongoing COVID-19 pandemic. However, many legal risks and lingering questions remain unsolved. The European Union does not yet have the means to fully exploit the benefits of this data due to heterogeneous health care systems with different content, terminologies, and structures.[57] In addition, the European Union currently has no pan-European data network and is lagging behind other regions in delivering answers for health care-related regulatory questions.[58] Although the GDPR and Medical Device Regulations aim to address some of these challenges by harmonizing the processing of data and risk assessment of AI medical devices in the European Union, these areas still remain diversified. To enhance the performance and safety of medical devices, it will be important to improve the dialogue between data protection authorities, ethical review boards, notified bodies, and medicine agencies. The proposed recommendations discussed in this chapter attempt to enhance this dialogue for a better understanding and alignment between the medical device sector, regulators, public research programs, and data protection standards.[59] This could form the basis for a legal debate on the circumstances under which access by researchers to health data by private companies can be justified based on public interest and research exemptions.[60] Considering the increasing importance of public-private partnerships and AI-driven medical devices proactive initiatives to that effect appear more important than ever.[61] The ongoing implementation of the EU strategies concerning AI, Data and medical innovation plays an important role in that regard. This has not only resulted in the

57 European Medicines Agency, A Common Data Model for Europe? Why? Which? How? Workshop report from a meeting held at the European Medicines Agency 10, 10–11 (Dec. 2017), www.ema.europa.eu/en/documents/report/common-data-model-europe-why-which-how-workshop-report_en.pdf.

58 Id. at 31.

59 Cf. European Data Protection Supervisor, A Preliminary Opinion on Data Protection and Scientific Research, EDPS (Jan. 6, 2020), https://edps.europa.eu/sites/edp/files/publication/20-01-06_opinion_research_en.pdf.

60 Id.

61 Press release. Commission and Germany's Presidency of the Council of the EU underline importance of the European Health Data Space, https://ec.europa.eu/commission/presscorner/detail/en/IP_20_2049 (Nov. 11, 2020).

evolving formation of the European Health Data Space,[62] but also in the adoption of a new EU Data Governance Act[63] and the proposal of an AI Regulation,[64] which provides for regulatory sandboxes for low-risk devices. It is the hope of the authors that these developments will improve the current situation.

62 Press release. Commission and Germany's Presidency of the Council of the EU underline importance of the European Health Data Space, https://ec.europa.eu/commission/presscorner/detail/en/IP_20_2049 (Nov. 11, 2020).

63 Proposal for a REGULATION OF THE EUROPEAN PARLIAMENT AND OF THE COUNCIL on European data governance (Data Governance Act) COM/2020/767 final. Cf. www.euractiv.com/section/digital/news/data-governance-new-eu-law-for-data-sharing-adopted/.

64 Proposal for a REGULATION OF THE EUROPEAN PARLIAMENT AND OF THE COUNCIL LAYING DOWN HARMONISED RULES ON ARTIFICIAL INTELLIGENCE (ARTIFICIAL INTELLIGENCE ACT) AND AMENDING CERTAIN UNION LEGISLATIVE ACTS, COM/2021/206 final.

7

AI, Explainability, and Safeguarding Patient Safety in Europe

Toward a Science-Focused Regulatory Model

Barry Solaiman and Mark G. Bloom

7.1 INTRODUCTION

This chapter explores the efforts made by regulators in Europe to develop standards concerning the explainability of artificial intelligence (AI) systems used in wearables. Diagnostic health devices such as fitness trackers, smart health watches, ECG and blood pressure monitors, and other biosensors are becoming more user-friendly, computationally powerful, and integrated into society. They are used to track the spread of infectious diseases, monitor health remotely, and predict the onset of illness before symptoms arise. At their foundation are complex neural networks making predictions from a plethora of data. While their use has been growing, the COVID-19 pandemic will likely accelerate that rise as governments grapple with monitoring and containing the spread of infectious diseases. One key challenge for scientists and regulators is to ensure that predictions are understood and explainable to legislators, policymakers, doctors, and patients to ensure informed decision making.

Two arguments are made in this chapter. First, regulators in Europe should develop minimum standards on explainability. Second, those standards should be informed by the computer science underlying the technology to identify the limitations of explainability. Recently, several reports have been published by the European Commission and the National Health Service (NHS) in the United Kingdom (UK). This chapter examines the operation of AI networks alongside those guidelines finding that, while they make good progress, they will ultimately be limited by the available technology. Further, despite much being said about the opaqueness of neural networks, human beings have significant oversight over them. The finger of liability will remain pointed toward humans, but the technology should advance to help them decipher networks intelligibly. As computer scientists enhance the technology, lawmakers should set minimum standards that are leveled-up progressively as the technology improves.

7.2 WEARABLES IN HEALTH CARE

Wearables are devices designed to stay on the body and collect health data such as heart rate, temperature, and oxygenation levels.[1] Smartwatches, chest belts, clothing, ingestible electronics, and many others are converging with the internet-of-things (IoT) and cloud computing to become powerful diagnostics for more than seventy conditions.[2] The technology has advanced rapidly, with GPUs, CPUs, and increasing RAM being adopted, opening possibilities for deep learning.[3] Despite these advances, adoption remains low in the health care setting overall, being in the early stages of the Gartner Hype Cycle.[4] Nevertheless, the trend is moving toward greater adoption. The COVID-19 pandemic in 2020 may accelerate the development of telemedicine, monitoring patients remotely, predicting disease, and mapping the spread of illnesses.[5] An example of the technology's use can be seen in England under an NHS pilot program where patients were fitted with a Wi-Fi-enabled armband. This monitored vital signs remotely, such as respiratory rates, oxygen levels, pulse, blood pressure, and body temperature. AI was able to monitor patients in real-time, leading to a reduction in readmission rates, home visits, and emergency admissions. Algorithms were able to identify warning signs in the data, alerting the patient and caregiver.[6] This example aligns with a broader trend of adoption.[7] The largest NHS hospital trusts have signed multiyear deals to increase the number of wearables used for remote digital health assessments and monitoring.[8] This allows doctors to monitor their patients away from the hospital setting, both before and after medical procedures.

[1] Aras D. Dargazany et al., Wearable DL: Wearable Internet-of-Things and Deep Learning for Big Data Analytics-Concept Literature and Future, 1 Mobile Info. Systems 4 (2018).

[2] NHSX, Artificial Intelligence: How to Get it Right – Putting Policy into Practice for Safe Data-Driven Innovation in Health and Care, 18 (Oct. 2019), www.nhsx.nhs.uk/media/documents/NHSX_AI_report.pdf; Sara Gerke et al., Ethical and Legal Issues of Ingestible Electronic Sensors, 2 Nature Electronics 329 (2019).

[3] Sourav Bhattacharya et al., From Smart to Deep: Robust Activity Recognition on Smartwatches Using Deep Learning, IEEE (2016), https://userpages.umbc.edu/~nroy/courses/shhasp18/papers/From%20Smart%20to%20Deep%20Robust%20Activity%20Recognition%20on%20Smartwatches%20Using%20Deep%20Learning.pdf.

[4] NHSX, supra note 2, at 20; Department of Health and Social Care (UK), The AHSN Network: Accelerating Artificial Intelligence in Health and Care (2018), https://wessexahsn.org.uk/img/news/AHSN%20Network%20AI%20Report-1536078823.pdf.

[5] Fight Covid-19 through the Power of the People, Stan. Med. (2020), https://innovations.stanford.edu.

[6] Moni Miyashita & Michael Brady, The Health Care Benefits of Combining Wearables and AI, Harv. Bus. Rev. (2019), https://hbr.org/2019/05/the-health-care-benefits-of-combining-wearables-and-ai.

[7] Such adoption may lead to unintended consequences, such as unregulated yet sophisticated apps marketed as low-level medical devices which may lead to doctors becoming overburdened with requests. See Helen Yu, Regulation of Digital Health Technologies in the EU: Intended versus Actual Use, in Innovation and Protection: The Future of Medical Device Regulation (I. Glenn Cohen et al. eds., 2021).

[8] Laura Donnelly, NHS Experiment in AI Will See Whole City Offered Virtual Hospital Appointments and Diagnosis by Chatbot, Telegraph (Jan. 23, 2020), www.telegraph.co.uk/news/2020/01/23/nhs-experiment-ai-will-see-whole-city-offered-virtual-hospital/.

7.3 HUMAN NEURAL NETWORKS?

Underpinning such technologies is complex computer science. A device can predict illness, but it cannot explain why it made a prediction, which raises several legal issues. A targeted legal strategy cannot be realistically devised without understanding the technology driving it. Lawyers are unlikely to become master coders or algorithm developers, but they can have a reasonable understanding of where most efforts are needed. By examining what drives AI, more technically aware discussions can be generated in the legal sphere.

AI is an umbrella term used for different forms of "machine learning." This includes "supervised" and "unsupervised" learning, which entails making predictions by analyzing data.[9] The former involves predefined labels used to assign the data to relevant groups, whereas the latter searches for common features in the data to classify it. A subset of "machine learning" is "deep learning," which consists of artificial neural networks (ANNs) used for autonomous learning. There are various architectures, but the primary example here is of a deep supervised learning network with labeled data.[10] Such networks are the most numerous in operation and can illustrate how deep learning works and where the legal issues may arise.

Figure 7.1 depicts a neural network. An ANN begins with an "input layer" on the left.[11] The example is an image of a cerebellum, which the ANN converts into many "neurons" (represented by the grid of squares). Each neuron is assigned a value (for black and white images) called the "activation" number. The number could, for example, be higher for brighter neurons (where the cerebellum is) and lower for darker neurons (outside the cerebellum). Every neuron is represented in the input layer. The example shows four neurons, but the ANN will have as many neurons as there are pixels in the image.

The example also shows two hidden layers in the middle, but there will be numerous in practice. In reality, the layers are not hidden to the programmer, but their numerousness makes the ANN virtually undecipherable – much like a human brain. The activations in the input layer (the black circles) will influence what is activated in the first hidden layer (the light grey circles) which will influence further activations. At the end is the output layer with several choices (Cerebellum, frontal lobe, or pituitary gland). The ANN gives the highest value to its choice (here, Cerebellum, the dark grey circle). Between the neurons are connections called "weights" (represented as lines) whose values are determined by a mathematical function. The sum of the weights in one layer determines which neurons are

9 Also "reinforcement" learning. Stuart Russell & Peter Norvig, Artificial Intelligence: A Modern Approach 830 (3rd ed. 2010).

10 See, e.g., deep Boltzmann machine, spike neural networks. Aras, 7.

11 But What Is Neural Network?, YouTube (Oct. 5, 2017), www.youtube.com/watch?v=aircAruvnKk; Russell & Norvig, supra note 9; Ron Sun, Connectionism and Neural Networks, in The Cambridge Handbook of Artificial Intelligence (Keith Frankish & William M. Ramsey eds., 2014).

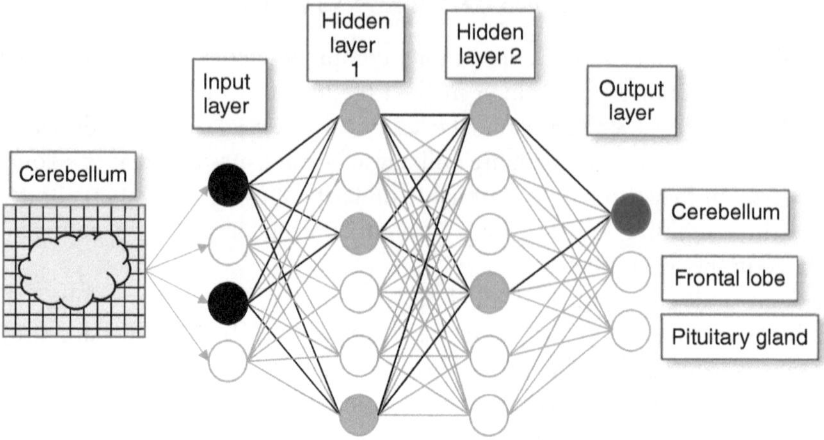

FIGURE 7.1: Example of an ANN

activated in the next layer. For example, the sum of the weights in the input layer has activated the first, third, and sixth neurons in the first hidden layer. Humans can also influence those activations by adding a "bias" to alter the value required for an activation.

In practice, the numerousness and complexity of the connections create an undecipherable matrix of distinct weights and biases. The choice of output cannot be explained, which is where the term "black box" algorithms arises. Despite this, humans play a central role. They give the network training data consisting of many prelabeled images of cerebellums, pituitary glands, and frontal lobes. The network is trained on that data. The process of data moving from left to right is called "forward propagation," and the weights between the neurons are initially random, which produces random outputs. To correct the ANN, a validation data set is used with labels indicating the correct answer. In response, the ANN works backward (back-propagation) from the output layer, through the hidden layers to the input layer, adjusting the weights and biases as it moves along. The network becomes more accurate through repetition.

Deep supervised learning networks are well suited to diagnostics. Inputs, such as scans, are in a standardized format, which is a useful source of structured input data, training, and validation. The process becomes highly accurate because of the numerous hidden layers and connections. However, the black-box nature of an ANN should not be overstated. Humans have significant involvement, labeling data, giving it to the network, providing feedback, computing biases, interpreting data, and putting it into practice.

Most studies of wearable data have focused on supervised learning architectures.[12] However, data derived from wearables is often unlabeled and unstructured, which

[12] See, e.g., Oscar D. Lara et al., A Survey on Human Activity Recognition Using Wearable Sensors, 15 IEEE Commc'n Surveys & Tutorial 1199 (2012).

benefits unsupervised learning that identifies patterns to make predictions.[13] These techniques raise more complex legal issues because humans are less involved. They are a work in progress at present, but they will become more prominent.[14] Indeed, there are increasing studies that analyze wearable data using unsupervised ANNs. One study proposes an unsupervised ANN to classify and recognize human activities.[15] It was able to recognize human activities through a combination of data obtained from magnetometers and accelerometers in wearables.[16] Another study analyzed data from 3D accelerometers on the wrist and hip, a skin temperature sensor, an ECG electrode, a respiratory effort sensor, and an oximeter amongst others.[17] The unsupervised network yielded 89 percent accuracy in detecting human activities (walking, cycling, playing football, or lying down).[18] Another approach has analyzed gestures to detect daily patterns that might indicate when older persons require assistance.[19]

These are a small sample of studies increasingly utilizing unsupervised learning architectures in wearables. The underlying point is that such technologies are being used more frequently, which raises legal issues surrounding explainability. At the same time, humans must still train the networks. The processes within the hidden layers are complex to decipher, but humans pretrain and oversee the process.[20] Consequently, while the legal implications must be deciphered, the autonomous nature of these systems should not be overstated.

7.4 EXPLAINABILITY AND THE LAW

Explainability refers to ex-ante explanations of an ANN's functionality, and ex-ante or ex-post explanations of the decisions taken, such as the rationale, the weighting, and the rules.[21] It requires that humans can understand and trace decisions.[22] However, the regulation of an ANN is as complex as its operation, which is problematic in health care. While shortcomings in explainability of AI systems will not necessarily lead to liability, it is one important factor. The key point of

13 Aras, 5–6; Stuart Russell & Peter Norvig, supra note 9, at 695.
14 Aras, 15; Stanford.
15 Lukun Wang, Recognition of Human Activities Using Continuous Autoencoders with Wearable Sensors, 16 Sensors 189, 2–3 (2016).
16 Id. at 15.
17 Miikka Ermes et al., Detection of Daily Activities and Sports with Wearable Sensors in Controlled and Uncontrolled Conditions, 12 IEEE Transactions on Information Technology in Biomedicine 20, 21 (2008).
18 Id. at 24–5.
19 Alessandra Moschetti et al., Towards an Unsupervised Approach for Daily Gesture Recognition in Assisted Living Applications, 17 IEEE Sensors Journal 8395, 8402 (2017).
20 Sourav, 2.
21 Sandra Wachter et al., Why a Right to Explanation of Automated Decision-Making Does Not Exist in the General Data Protection Regulation, 7 Int'l Data Privacy L. 76, 78 (2017).
22 European Commission, Ethics Guidelines for Trustworthy AI: High-Level Expert Group on Artificial Intelligence 18 (Apr. 8, 2019).

interaction between explainability and liability is at the fact finding or evidence stage. It may be difficult to factually prove the harm caused by a neural network because one cannot explain how a certain input resulted in a specific output, and that a deficiency resulted due to that process.[23] The circumstances in which explainability becomes important in liability analyses are broad.

Problems may arise where harm is caused to a patient because the doctor did not follow the appropriate standard of care.[24] Price notes how, in the current climate, the risk of liability for doctors relying on AI recommendations is significant because the practice is "too innovative to have many adherents."[25] Algorithm developers might be liable as well. However, in Europe, the laws are incoherent. The Product Liability Directive (1985/374/EEC) holds manufacturers liable for defective products. Proving that an ANN was defective requires technical expertise, but even experts cannot explain the hidden layers of a network.[26] There is also the problem of ANNs being autonomous and changing. While the European Union has taken a strict approach on manufacturers being liable for the safety of products throughout their lifecycle, it acknowledges that the Directive should be revisited to account for products that may change or be altered thereby leaving manufacturers in legal limbo.[27]

There are also medical device regulations, but half of developers in the United Kingdom do not intend to seek CE Mark classification because it is uncertain whether algorithms can be classified as medical devices.[28] There are medical device conformity assessments, but there are no standards for validating algorithms nor regulating adaptive algorithms.[29] Also, while manufacturers must carry out risk

23 Expert Group on Liability and New Technologies, Liability for Artificial Intelligence and Other Emerging Digital Technologies, European Commission 1, 54 (2019), https://op.europa.eu/en/publication-detail/-/publication/1c5e30be-1197-11ea-8c1f-01aa75ed71a1/language-en/format-PDF; European Commission, White Paper on Artificial Intelligence – A European Approach to Excellence and Trust, 13 (2020), https://templatearchive.com/ai-white-paper/.

24 W. Nicholson Price II et al., Potential Liability for Physicians Using Artificial Intelligence, 322 JAMA 1765, 1765 (2019).

25 W. Nicholson Price II, Medical Malpractice and Black-Box Medicine, in Big Data, Health Law, and Bioethics 301 (I. Glenn Cohen et al. eds., 2018).

26 European Commission, supra note 22, at 13.

27 European Commission, Report on the Safety and Liability Implications of Artificial Intelligence, the Internet of Things and Robotics (2020), https://ec.europa.eu/info/sites/info/files/report-safety-liability-artificial-intelligence-feb2020_en_1.pdf; this is known as the "update problem." See I. Glenn Cohen et al., The European Artificial Intelligence Strategy: Implications and Challenges for Digital Health, 2 Lancet Digital Health e376, e377 (2020), www.thelancet.com/action/showPdf?pii=S2589-7500%2820%2930112-6; on "system view" approach to regulation, see Sara Gerke et al., The Need for a System View to Regulate Artificial Intelligence/Machine Learning-Based Software as Medical Device, 3 Digital Me. 1 (2020); Timo Minssen et al., Regulatory Responses to Medical Machine Learning, J. L. & Biosciences 1, 6 (2020).

28 Regulation on Medical Devices (Regulation 2017/745) (EU); In Vitro Diagnostic Medical Device Regulation (IVDR) (Regulation 2017/746) (EU); NHSX, How to Get It Right, supra note 2, at 22.

29 Id.

assessments before products are placed on the market, they quickly become outdated because ANNs continuously evolve.[30] For doctors, they may be negligent when advising patients based on AI recommendations that later cause harm. There are also questions about whether a person can consent to flawed medical advice from an ANN. These challenges are recognized in Europe where several reports were published in 2019 and 2020.

7.5 GUIDELINES

In the European Union, there are Guidelines, a White Paper, and an Assessment List regarding AI geared toward developing a future regulatory framework. On the guidelines, the EU Commission set up an "independent group" which released the Ethics Guidelines for Trustworthy AI in 2019 seen as a "starting point" for discussions about AI premised on respect for human autonomy, prevention of harm, fairness, and explicability.[31] The White Paper (which builds upon the Guidelines) was published in 2020 and outlines an approach to AI based on "excellence and trust."[32] It notes that while AI can improve prevention and diagnosis in health care, black box algorithms create difficulties of legal enforcement.[33] The Assessment List for Trustworthy Artificial Intelligence (ALTAI) is a self-assessment list published in July 2020.[34]

7.5.1 *Guidelines, Explainability, and the GDPR*

In the Guidelines, the principle of "explicability" is of primary relevance. It requires that AI processes and decisions are transparent and explainable to those involved.[35] The Guidelines emphasize that this may not always be possible with black box algorithms and, "in those circumstances, other explicability measures (e.g., traceability, auditability, and transparent communication on system capabilities) may be required."[36] Auditability and transparent communication are likely within easiest reach from a technical standpoint. The accuracy of the training data used can be verified, and the specific tasks undertaken by humans developing the network can be checked. Traceability is the greatest challenge owing to the hidden layers.

The Guidelines highlight several principles that may help in realizing explainability. First, "human agency," which refers to humans understanding AI systems

30 European Commission, supra note 27, at 6.
31 European Commission, supra note 22, at 3.
32 European Commission, supra note 23.
33 European Commission, supra note 23, at 1, 10.
34 European Commission, The Assessment List for Trustworthy Artificial Intelligence (ALTAI) for Self Assessment (2020), https://ec.europa.eu/digital-single-market/en/news/assessment-list-trustworthy-artificial-intelligence-altai-self-assessment.
35 Id. at 13.
36 Id.

and challenging them.[37] AI can shape human behavior and should support informed decision making.[38] The issue is whether a doctor is liable for advice given that was informed by AI recommendations. Of relevance is Article 22 of the General Data Protection Regulation (GDPR) concerning automated decision making and profiling which protects individuals from decisions "based solely on automated processing, including profiling, which produces legal effects."[39] The Information Commissioner's Office (ICO) in the United Kingdom requires that individuals must have the right to obtain human intervention, express their point of view, an explanation of the decision and the ability to challenge it.[40]

Taken at its most extreme, there would be an automatic infringement of a medical decision based solely on the automated processing of an ANN, and a right to an explanation. However, it has been argued that a "right to explanation" does not exist under the GDPR, but rather a limited right to be "informed" of system functionality.[41] In other words, a right only to ex ante explanations of system functionality at the data collection stage, rather than ex post explanations of the decisions that have been made once the data has been propagated and an output generated.[42] Furthermore, a right to explanation has existed for many years in different jurisdictions but has not led to greater transparency because copyright protections have precluded algorithms from being revealed.[43] The general distinction is that persons might be entitled to know of specific data used in a neural network, but are not entitled to know the weights, biases and, statistical values.[44] The extent of the right is very narrow and would, in any case, be limited to those bringing a claim rather than general laws on explainability setting minimum standards.

Further, it would be a rare scenario indeed for a decision to be made "solely" by AI as required under Article 22. In practice, AI is used to supplement informed decisions rather than make them. It is also unlikely that AI outputs can result solely from "automated" processing because humans are always involved in some capacity.[45] Most fundamentally, the wording of Article 22 requires that automated processing has "legal effects" on the individual. However, an ANN will not interfere with the right not to consent, nor to withdrawing consent once it has been given. Although,

37 Id. at 16.

38 Id.

39 GDPR 2016/679 and the UK Data Protection Act 2018 (DPA).

40 Information Commissioner's Office, Right Not to Be Subject to Automated Decision-Making (2020), https://ico.org.uk/for-organisations/guide-to-data-protection/guide-to-law-enforcement-processing/individual-rights/right-not-to-be-subject-to-automated-decision-making/ [hereinafter ICO].

41 Wachter et al., supra note 21, at 79, 90; Further, an individual's right to know about how personal data is evaluated, is significantly curtailed by ECJ jurisprudence. See Sandra Wachter & Brent Mittelstadt, A Right to Reasonable Inferences: Re-thinking Data Protection Law in the Age of Big Data and AI, 1 Colum. Bus. L. Rev. 1, 6–7 (2019).

42 Id. at 82.

43 Id. at 86.

44 Id. at 87.

45 Id. at 92.

the law might protect those relying on wearable tech giving flawed advice that would interfere with their right to informed consent.

Matters are further complicated by an interrelated provision in the GDPR concerning "profiling," which is any "automated processing of personal data" used to predict aspects concerning a person's health.[46] Wearables may combine individual health data with broader user data to provide individualized advice. Users relying on them would be unable to assess why the advice was given nor challenge it, which undermines the aims of "human agency" in the Guidelines. Additionally, nothing in the law appears to preclude automated processing where the individual consents.[47] The law could protect individuals by requiring a minimum level of explainability in such cases.

A related matter is "human oversight and autonomy." This is most practically achieved through "human-on-the-loop" or "human-in-command" approaches.[48] The former requires that humans can both intervene in designing a system and monitor it. The latter refers to holistic oversight over a network. The Guidelines recommend that the less oversight a human has, the more extensive testing and stricter governance is required.[49] However, for neural networks to work, humans must intervene and monitor a system, both granularly and holistically. Without such oversight, the neural network would produce "garbage" outputs. Networks can be tricked easily, and even slight changes to the data can cause them to fail.[50] The Guidelines, therefore, overstate the significance of these principles.

Other principles are "technical robustness and safety" and "human oversight and autonomy." Networks could be required to change procedures or ask for human intervention before continuing an operation when encountering a problem. A network should indicate the likelihood of errors occurring, be reliable, and have reproducible outputs.[51] This requires adequate transparency, which entails principles of "traceability" and "communication."[52] Traceability means documenting outputs of the ANN, the labeled data, the datasets, and data processes.[53] Communication means revealing the AI's capabilities and limitations.[54] Returning to the GDPR, Article 22(3) requires "the right to obtain human intervention on the part of the controller, to express his or her point of view and to contest the decision."

Two matters arise here. First, what human involvement means. Second, when should humans get involved? The former could mean humans replacing automated decisions without algorithmic help; a human decision taking into account the

46 GDPR, art. 4(4); see also ICO, supra note 40.
47 GDPR, art. 22(2)(C), art. 9(2).
48 European Commission, supra note 22, at 16.
49 Id.
50 Jory Heckman, DARPA: Next Generation Artificial Intelligence in the Works, Federal News Network (Mar. 1, 2018), https://federalnewsnetwork.com/technology-main/2018/03/darpa-next-generation-artificial-intelligence-in-development/.
51 European Commission, supra note 22, at 17.
52 Id. at 18.
53 Id.
54 Id.

algorithmic assessment, or humans monitoring the input data based on a person's objections and a new decision made solely by the network.[55] It could also mean that a data controller must provide ex-ante justifications for any inferences drawn about the subject's data to determine whether the inference was unreasonable.[56] A risk-based approach could determine the latter. Thus, the riskier the recommendation by an ANN, the more checks required.[57] However, this would be limited to procedural rather than substantive validation, such as appropriately training doctors for using AI.[58] Further, a risk-based approach would still be unable to assess the reasons for AI recommendations.

Much remains undetermined regarding what these factors mean in practice for explainability. The White Paper recognizes that these principles are not covered under current legislation and promises feedback later.[59] For now, it proposes distinct forms of human oversight such as blocking AI systems not reviewed and validated by humans; allowing systems to operate temporarily as long as human intervention occurs afterward; ensuring close monitoring of networks by humans once they are in operation and that networks can be deactivated when problems arise; or imposing operational constraints on networks during the design phase.[60] Such oversight could assist in finding inaccurate input data, problematic inferences, or other flaws in the algorithm's reasoning.[61] It could form part of procedural evaluations of black-box algorithms noted by Price.[62] However, a key question is how such factors may apply in practice, which is why the Commission also released an Assessment List (ALTAI). The ALTAI list contains two questions on explainability, but they are minimalist. The first asks whether the decision of a neural network was explained to users. The second asks whether users were continuously surveyed about whether they understood the decisions of a network.[63] There are other potentially useful questions regarding human oversight and the other principles noted above, but it is the NHSX approach that is of most practical significance.

7.5.2 *Practical Implementation*

The NHS Code of Conduct for Data-Driven Health and Care Technology may provide a practical solution. Principle 7 focuses on explainability. It states: "Show what type of algorithm is being developed or deployed, the ethical examination of

55 Sandra Wachter et al., Counterfactual Explanations without Opening the Black Box: Automated Decisions and the GDPR, 31 Harv. J. L. & Tech. 842, 873 (2018).
56 Wachter & Mittelstadt, supra note 41, at 7.
57 By developers and independent external auditors. Price, supra note 25, at 295, 301.
58 Id. at 304.
59 European Commission, supra note 22, at 9.
60 Id. at 21.
61 Wachter, supra note 55, at 37.
62 Price, supra note 25, at 305.
63 European Commission, supra note 34, at 14–15.

how the data is used, how its performance will be validated and how it will be integrated into health and care provision."[64] The outputs should be explained to those relying on them, the learning methodology of the ANN should be transparent, the learning model and functionality specified, its strengths and limitations and compliance with data protection.[65]

To assist developers, there is a "how-to" guide detailing what is expected when developing AI.[66] Four processes are relevant here. First, reporting the type of algorithm developed, how it was trained and demonstrating that adequate care was given to ethical considerations in the input data.[67] For this, a "model card" or checklist approach is proposed for explaining those aspects of the ANN.[68] Second, provide evidence of the algorithm's effectiveness through external validation, communicating early with NHSX on the proposed method of continuous audit of inputs and outputs, and how they were determined.[69] Third, explain the algorithm to those relying on their outputs, detail the level of human involvement, and develop languages that are understandable to the layperson.[70] Fourth, explain how a decision was "made on the acceptable use of the algorithm in the context of it being used."[71] This may involve speaking to patient groups to assess their thinking on the acceptable uses of AI and monitor their reactions to gauge acceptance of the technology.[72]

The Code is significant because it indicates how minimum standards for explainability might operate in the context of an ANN. However, it is undetermined how the factors might be realized or whether a uniform approach would work for all neural networks. A pilot Trustworthy AI Assessment List has been proposed in the Commission's Guidelines with questions on traceability and explainability.[73] The questions on traceability concern detailing the method of programming and testing – those on explainability concern the ability to interpret outputs and ensuring that they can be explained. The questions are useful but remain idealistic for deriving sense from the hidden layers. The technological limitations mean that other ideas in the Guidelines are more practicable at present. This includes a "white list" of rules

64 NHSX Code of Conduct, https://www.gov.uk/government/publications/code-of-conduct-for-data-driven-health-and-care-technology/initial-code-of-conduct-for-data-driven-health-and-care-technology.

65 Id.

66 Id. at 29.

67 Id. at 31.

68 Id. at 31; Margaret Mitchell et al., Model Cards for Model Reporting, FAT* '19: Conference on Fairness, Accountability, and Transparency 1, 3 (Jan. 2019).

69 NHSX, How to Get It Right, supra note 2, at 32; this approach aligns with Leong Tze Yun's recommendation that AI systems should be systemically examined and validated; see Gary Humphreys, Regulating Digital Health, 98 Bulletin of the World Health Organization 235, 235 (2020), www.who.int/bulletin/volumes/98/4/20-020420.pdf.

70 Id.

71 Id.

72 Id.

73 European Commission, supra note 22, at 24–31.

that must always be followed and "black list" restrictions that must never be transgressed.[74]

While such requirements could provide minimum standards for explainability, there are some aspects of neural networks that remain unexplainable. If networks do not provide insight into their continuously evolving reasoning, it will be impossible to achieve detailed insight arising from any checklist. For this reason, researchers are developing new technologies surrounding "algorithmic transparency." This includes auditing techniques and interactive visualization systems.[75] It is beyond the scope of this chapter to explore these in detail, but one example involves the creation of a "deep visualization" toolbox that examines the activation of individual neurons.[76] Working backward, researchers can map out different neurons and determine which one influences the other. The activated neurons can be viewed in real-time to see which parts of an image the neuron is highlighting.[77] As this technology develops further, lawyers and policymakers should remain alert to incorporating standards developed in this field into the explainability requirements of guidelines and regulations. One day, they could form part of the minimum standards for explainability.

7.6 CONCLUSION

The foundations for setting minimum standards concerning explainability have now been established. However, there are shortcomings in AI-enhanced technology, such as wearables, which undermine informed decision-making for doctors, patients, and others. This is problematic because wearables will become ever more heavily relied upon for a wide variety of medical purposes. Further, doctors and patients ought to know why neural networks produce specific outputs. In time, scientists will develop more sophisticated models of explainability. Regulators, doctors, patients, and scientists should work together to ensure that those advances filter into the relevant guidelines as they develop – a gradual and flexible "leveling up" that keeps apace with the science. In this manner, lawyers and policymakers should take responsibility for better understanding the technology underlying those systems. As such, they should become more familiar with and knowledgeable about neural networks, the use of input data, training data, how data propagates, and how "learning" occurs. This will be key for creating standards that are relevant, sound, and justified. While laws and guidelines in the future will indicate the path to be pursued, some matters will take concerted interdisciplinary efforts to resolve.

74 Id. at 21.

75 Information Commissioner's Office (UK), Big Data, Artificial Intelligence, Machine Learning and Data Protection 86 (2017), https://ico.org.uk/media/for-organisations/documents/2013559/big-data-ai-ml-and-data-protection.pdf.

76 Jason Yosinski et al., Understanding Neural Networks through Deep Visualization, Deep Learning Workshop, 31st International Conference on Machine Learning (2015).

77 Id.

8

Regulation of Digital Health Technologies in the European Union

Intended versus Actual Use[*]

Helen Yu

The functionality of digital health technologies (DHTs), such as wearable devices and virtual assistants, is increasingly being used to make personal health and medical decisions. If manufacturers of DHTs are able to avoid regulation of their products as medical devices by marketing them as "lifestyle and well-being" devices, the potential harm caused to consumers who use DHTs beyond the manufacturer's intended purpose will not be adequately addressed. This chapter argues the need for a framework to reclassify and regulate DHTs based on evidence of actual use.

This chapter focuses on how the classification rules and postmarket surveillance system provisions of the EU Medical Devices Regulation (MDR) need to anticipate and address the actual use of DHTs. To date, courts and regulators have not been consistent on the circumstances under which manufacturers are held responsible for known or encouraged "misuse" of their products. By defining a postmarket surveillance requirement for manufacturers of DHTs to acquire knowledge of the actual use of their products, informed regulatory decisions based on impact can be made. Actual use information can also help establish that the risk caused by a reasonably foreseeable misuse of DHTs was known to the manufacturer in a liability claim should consumers suffer harm from relying on statements or representations, made or implied, when using DHTs to self-manage their health. Moreover, if data generated by DHTs will be used to make regulatory decisions under the 2020 revision of the Good Clinical Practice, the MDR must proactively regulate technologies that have an actual impact on public health.

* This chapter has been adapted from an article originally published in BMJ Innovations (Digital Health Technologies Under the New EU Medical Devices Regulation: Monitoring and Governing Intended versus Actual Use, 7 BMJ Innovation 637–41 2021).

8.1 INTRODUCTION

The functionality of digital health technologies (DHTs), such as wearable devices and virtual assistants, is being promoted as essential tools to empower people to take control and responsibility of their own health and wellness. Examples of wearable devices referred to in this chapter include devices that track health and fitness-related data such as heart rate, activity level, sleep cycles, caloric intake, and the like. An example of a virtual assistant includes Amazon Echo with its technology to analyze the user's voice to detect and determine "physical or emotional abnormality" and provide targeted content related to a particular medicine sold by a particular retailer to address the detected problem.[1]

There is significant literature on the potential benefits of DHTs in reducing costs and the burden on the health care system, for example, by providing patients with options to self-manage health from home.[2] DHTs are also attributed with the ability to help detect early warning signs of potentially serious health conditions, alerting users to irregularities, leading to investigations to detect illnesses that may otherwise have gone unnoticed with potentially tragic consequences.[3] While health care providers generally recognize DHTs as useful tools, there is also evidence that these very same technologies are increasingly being used by the public in a manner that potentially increases health care costs in the long run.[4] One study reported an increase in physician-"digitalchondriac" interaction where patients demand immediate attention from medical professionals based on troubling key health indicators detected by wearable devices, which may or may not be accurate.[5] On the other end of the spectrum, some patients elect to by-pass traditional health service structures and formalities and take medical and health decisions into their own hands at great risk to themselves instead of consulting a medical professional. Some doctors recount stories of patients taking prescription medication in response to an irregular reading from their wearable device without

1 Issued US patent US10096319B1 entitled voice-based determination of physical and emotional characteristics of users, https://patents.google.com/patent/US10096319B1/en.

2 See, e.g., Melinda Beeuwkes Buntin et al., The Benefits of Health Information Technology: A Review of the Recent Literature Shows Predominantly Positive Results, 30 Health Aff. 464–71 (2011).

3 See, e.g., Apple Watch Saves Man's Life after Warning Him of Heart Problems, The Telegraph (Jul. 16, 2019), www.telegraph.co.uk/news/2019/07/16/apple-watch-saves-mans-life-warning-heart-problems/; see also D.C. Ioannidis et al., Wearable Devices: Monitoring the Future?, Oxford Med. Case Reps. 492–4 (2019).

4 See, e.g., Alex Matthews-King, Apple Watch and Fitbits Wrongly Sending Healthy People to Doctors Could Overwhelm NHS, Report Warns, Independent, www.independent.co.uk/news/health/nhs-apple-watch-fitbits-ai-waiting-times-gp-misdiagnosis-a8749876.html; Artificial Intelligence in Healthcare, Acad. Med. Royal Colls., www.aomrc.org.uk/wp-content/uploads/2019/01/Artificial_intelligence_in_healthcare_0119.pdf.

5 See, e.g., D. Lupton, The Digitally Engaged Patient: Self-monitoring and Self-Care in the Digital Health Era, 11 Soc. Theory & Health 256–70 (2013).

understanding or inquiring about the risk of taking a higher than recommended dosage of medication.[6]

DHTs have been setting off alarms for users to take note and control of their health, but there are also data and reports that suggest many of those alarms turn out to be false. As consumers increasingly engage in self-monitoring and self-care with the help of DHTs, health practitioners need to respond to patient confusion and anxiety created by data generated by DHTs.[7] Because the accuracy of DHTs can vary greatly with a margin of error as high as 25 percent across different devices,[8] health practitioners have the added burden of treating patients without medical training who nevertheless seek medical intervention for self-diagnosed illnesses derived from the internet by attributing symptoms detected by unreliable DHTs. The next section will examine the applicable regulatory framework in the European Union to better understand what oversight mechanisms are available to ensure the safety and efficacy of DHTs in view of evidence of how consumers actually use these devices to make personal health and medical decisions.

8.2 THE EU MEDICAL DEVICES REGULATION

Medical devices are recognized as essential to the health and wellbeing of European citizens and legislation is essential to ensure the safety and efficacy of medical devices for the protection of public health.[9] The new EU Medical Devices Regulation (MDR)[10] will come into force in May 2021, replacing the existing Medical Devices Directive (MDD).[11] The MDR attempts to modernize the MDD by introducing new concepts, definitions, and rules that may be applicable to DHTs. For example, the definition of a medical device in the MDR includes new qualifying language "prediction and prognosis of disease."[12] In principle, this definition should capture the collection, monitoring, processing, and evaluation of physiological data associated with DHTs since they claim to be capable of potentially predicting or providing a prognosis of potential future disease identification from the data collected.

6 See, e.g., K.J. Compton-Thweatt, Physicians or Facebook? The Effects of Do-It-Yourself Healthcare on Modern Society, Integrated Studies 171 (2018); A. Robeznieks, 4 Mistakes Your Patients Should Avoid With Wearables, AMA, www.ama-assn.org/practice-management/digital/4-mistakes-your-patients-should-avoid-wearables.

7 Lukasz Piwek et al., The Rise of Consumer Health Wearables: Promises and Barriers, 13 PLoS Med. (2016).

8 M.A. Case et al., Accuracy of Smartphone Applications and Wearable Devices for Tracking Physical Activity Data, 313 JAMA 10–11 (2015).

9 European Commission, New EU rules to ensure safety of medical devices, MEMO/17/848 (2017).

10 Regulation 2017/745 of the European Parliament and of the Council of 5 April 2017 on medical devices, amending Directive 2001/83/EC, Regulation (EC) No 178/2002 and Regulation (EC) No 1223/2009 and repealing Council Directives 90/385/EEC and 93/42/EEC, 2017 O.J. (L 117) 5.5 (EU).

11 Council Directive 93/42/EEC of 14 June 1993 concerning medical devices, 1993 O.J. (L 169) 12.7.

12 Regulation 2017/745, supra note 10, at art. 2.

However, the MDR clearly states "software for general purposes, even when used in a health care setting, or software intended for lifestyle and well-being purposes is not considered a medical device."[13] It is the intended purpose, as opposed to the technological features and capabilities of a device that determines whether a DHT will be regulated under the MDR. Intended purpose is defined as "the use for which a device is intended according to the data supplied by the manufacturer on the label, in the instructions for use or in promotional or sales materials or statements and as specified by the manufacturer in the clinical evaluation."[14] Because the regulatory framework can be challenging for many startups with limited resources, the ability to market the intended use of DHTs as health and wellness devices as opposed to a medical device that requires a higher degree of regulatory compliance is a pragmatic business decision, but at what potential cost to public health? Even for larger companies, Apple CEO Tim Cook stated that the regulatory process and degree of adherence required for the Apple Watch would prevent Apple from continuing to innovate and remain competitive in the medical product marketplace.[15]

In brief, the classification rules and procedures under the MDR are based on the potential risk a particular device poses to the user, having regard to the technical design and manufacture of the device.[16] Currently, a significant number of wearables are classified as Class I noninvasive devices.[17] However, under the MDR, the introduction of a more nuanced classification system and a more involved assessment procedure may increase the regulatory scrutiny of DHTs. For example, software intended to monitor physiological processes will be considered Class IIa, and software intended to monitor vital physiological parameters would be classified as Class IIb.[18] As the classification level increases, the applicable safety rules and conformity assessments also become stricter. However, the increased classification level applies only to "active devices intended for diagnosis and monitoring," which again does not include DHTs that manufacturers self-declare as intended for "lifestyle and well-being purposes."[19]

13 Id. at p. 19.

14 Id. at art. 2(12); see also Case C-329/16 Syndicat national de l'industrie des technologies médicales (SNITEM), Philips France v. Premier ministre, Ministre des Affaires sociales et de la Santé Confédération paysanne and Others v. Premier ministre and Ministre de l'Agriculture, de l'Agroalimentaire et de la Forêt [2017] ECLI:EU:C:2017:947; see also T. Minsssen et al., When Does Stand-Alone Software Qualify as a Medical Device in the European Union? – The CJEU's Decision in SNITEM and What It Implies for the Next Generation of Medical Devices, 28 Med. L. Rev. 615–24 (2020).

15 A. Heath, Apple's Tim Cook Declares the End of the PC and Hints at New Medical Product, Telegraph, www.telegraph.co.uk/technology/2016/01/21/apples-tim-cook-declares-the-end-of-the-pc-and-hints-at-new-medi/.

16 Regulation 2017/745, supra note 10, at p. 58, art. 51, Annex VIII.

17 European Commission, DG for Communications Network, Content and Technology Smart Wearables: Reflection and Orientation Paper (2016).

18 European Commission, supra note 9, at Annex VIII.

19 Id.

While efforts continue to focus on what types of innovations fall into the definition of a medical device and within which classification level, this chapter focuses on how the public actually uses and interfaces with these products, regardless of the regulatory classification. There is increasing evidence to suggest that consumers use DHTs to help with medical care decision making despite the manufacturer's stated intent.[20] Although the MDR attempts to establish a contemporary legislative framework to ensure better protection of public health and safety, the point where DHTs "not intended for medical purposes" and the use of pharmaceuticals intersect, raises a myriad of legal, ethical, and policy implications. Pharmaceuticals, which are highly regulated, are reportedly being used by the public to make self-determined medication decisions based solely on information derived from DHTs,[21] which are not as well regulated under the MDR. Understandably, the regulatory framework should focus on technologies that pose the greatest risk to patients and their data security. However, as discussed in greater detail below, "misuse" of lower-risk devices beyond the manufacturer's intended use could raise significant public health risks not previously contemplated. Some DHTs proclaim medical benefits but disclaim that the device is intended for health and wellbeing purposes only.[22] If manufacturers of DHTs are able to avoid the higher regulatory burden associated with having their products classified as medical devices, the question is what legal framework exists to hold manufacturers responsible for known "misuse" of their products and whether consumer protection laws will provide adequate redress to the potential harm caused to consumers who nevertheless use DHTs beyond the manufacturer's stated purpose to make personal health and medical decisions.

Although the vast majority of DHTs pose a very low risk of harm to consumers, there is increasing evidence that many of these devices are not as accurate as described or fail to work at all.[23] Without an oversight mechanism to detect and respond to the health risk arising from the actual use of low-risk devices beyond the manufacturer's stated intended use means many consumers could be adversely affected throughout the lifecycle of the product without recourse. To bring medical devices onto the EU market, the CE approval process is required to verify that a device meets all the regulatory requirements under the MDR. However, for Class I devices, the manufacturer is responsible for self-certification for the CE marking process.[24] Policy proposals related to permitting lower-risk devices to be brought to

[20] S.S. Bhuyan et al., Use of Mobile Health Applications for Health-Seeking Behavior Among US Adults, 40 J. Med. Sys. 153 (2016); see also Sean Day & Megan Zweig, Beyond Wellness for the Healthy: Digital Health Consumer Adoption 2018, Rock Health, https://rockhealth.com/insights/beyond-wellness-for-the-healthy-digital-health-consumer-adoption-2018/.

[21] Compton-Thweatt, supra note 6.

[22] See, e.g., Casey Erdmier et al., Wearable Device Implications in the Healthcare Industry, 40 J. Med. Eng'g & Tech. 141–8 (2016).

[23] See, e.g., B. Bent, Investigating Sources of Inaccuracy in Wearable Optical Heart Rate Sensors, 3 NPJ Digit. Med. 1–9 (2020).

[24] Regulation 2017/745, supra note 10, at Annex VIII.

market more efficiently on the condition that postmarketing data on safety and effectiveness is collected as part of mandatory renewal or reevaluation process has previously been considered.[25] While postmarket safety and efficacy data may be used to assess whether a DHT continues to qualify for a low-risk classification level, it falls short of providing an evidence-based reason to reclassify a DHT based on the potential risk arising from how consumers actually use these devices, regardless of their safety and efficacy profile.

8.3 INTENDED VERSUS ACTUAL USE

While DHTs are intended to modify behavior to improve health and wellness, an unintended consequence of the functionalities of these devices is that consumers are increasingly using them to make personal health and medical decisions.[26] DHTs offer to collect and monitor physiological data that medical devices do and can be used in combination with apps to interpret such data to provide medical advice. The line between DHTs and medical devices therefore increasingly becomes blurred, particularly to the consumer, as new devices and new improvements of well-established wearables allow the monitoring and assessing of a range of medical risk factors.[27] According to a recent survey, 71 percent of physicians say they use digital health data to inform their own personal health decisions,[28] and another survey found that consumers are increasingly using wearables to make critical health care decisions instead of monitoring physical activity and lifestyle.[29]

However, the majority of manufacturers provide no empirical evidence to support the effectiveness of their products, in part, because the applicable regulation does not require them to do so.[30] Recent reports indicate an increase in incidents of wearables sending otherwise healthy people to doctors due to incorrect and inaccurate readings.[31] Meanwhile, popular consumer devices continue to insist that their product, unless otherwise specified, is not a medical device and should not be held

25 M.B. Hamel et al., FDA Regulation of Mobile Health Technologies, N. Eng. J. Med., 371, 372 (2014).

26 Compton-Thweatt, supra note 6; see also J. Dunn et al., Wearables and the Medical Revolution. 15 Personalized Med 429–48 (2018).

27 Piwek et al., supra note 7.

28 Stanford Medicine 2020 Health Trends Report, http://med.stanford.edu/content/dam/sm/school/documents/Health-Trends-Report/Stanford%20Medicine%20Health%20Trends%20Report%202020.pdf.

29 Day & Zweig, supra note 20.

30 Case et al., supra note 8; see also Sara Chodosh, "FDA approved" Medical Devices Don't Actually Have to Do What They Promise, Popular Science, www.popsci.com/fda-approved-medical-devices/.

31 Matthews-King, supra note 4; see also Dora Allday & Stephen Matthews, Fitbits Are Putting a Strain On Doctors "Because the Exercise Trackers Are Incorrectly Telling Wearers They Are ILL," Daily Mail, www.dailymail.co.uk/health/article-6639305/Hypochondriacs-rely-data-Fitbits-piling-extra-pressure-NHS.html; Emily Clarkson, Is Your Fitness Tracker Helping or Hurting Your Health?, The Manifest, https://themanifest.com/app-development/fitness-tracker-helping-hurting-health.

to such a standard[32] despite marketing their devices as being able to "help improve wellness, disease management and prevention."[33] Experts agree that wearable devices cannot be expected to give medical grade accuracy, nor should consumers demand such high scientific quality from DHTs. However, as users become increasingly more reliant on DHTs that may provide a false sense of security on one spectrum to misguided self-diagnosis on the other, the need for legal solutions and regulatory oversight has been called for to address issues of consumer harm and accountability.[34]

To avoid liability, manufacturers typically rely on disclaimers even though it is known that users tend to ignore such information.[35] Legal measures are available to address direct-to-consumer marketing practices relating to fraudulent or misleading advertising. For example, in the 2018 dispute against Fitbit's Purepulse heart rate tracker for being grossly inaccurate, alleging false advertising, common law fraud, and breach of implied warranty among other claims, the court allowed the class action to proceed, stating that "[g]iven the magnitude of the aberrant heart rate readings and multiple allegations that the devices under-report heart rate, [plaintiff] has plausibly alleged an 'unreasonable safety hazard' that may arise when users rely on Fitbit heart rate readings during exercise."[36] Similarly, the FDA also monitors medical product communications to make sure they are consistent with the product's regulatory authorization.[37] However, the FDA has stated that it will only oversee "medical devices whose functionality could pose a risk to patient safety if the [device] were to not function as intended."[38] More specifically, the FDA stated that it does not intend to regulate general wellness products.[39] In other words, if the manufacturer's stated intention is for DHTs to be used for "life-style and well-being"

32 See, e.g., Important Safety and Product Information, Fitbit, www.fitbit.com/dk/legal/safety-instructions.

33 See, e.g., Fitbit Launches Fitbit Care, A Powerful New Enterprise Health Platform for Wellness and Prevention and Disease Management, Fitbit, https://investor.fitbit.com/press-releases/press-release-details/2018/Fitbit-Launches-Fitbit-Care-A-Powerful-New-Enterprise-Health-Platform-for-Wellness-and-Prevention-and-Disease-Management/default.aspx.

34 See, e.g., M. Schukat et al., Unintended Consequences of Wearable Sensor Use in Healthcare, 25 Y. B. Med. Informatics 73–86 (2016); see also A.B. Cohen & K. Safavi, The Oversell and Undersell of Digital Health, Health Aff. Blog 442, 443 (2019) and Jenny McGrath, Lack of Regulation Means Wearables Aren't Held Accountable for Health Claims, Digit. Trends, www.digitaltrends.com/wearables/wearable-devices-leading-to-over-diagnosis/.

35 Akshay et al., Wearable Healthcare Technology – the Regulatory Perspective, 4 Int'l J. Drug Reg. Aff. 1–5 (2016).

36 McLellan v. Fitbit, Inc., Case No. 16-cv-36, (N.D. Cal. 2018).

37 US Food & Drug Admin., Medical Product Communications That Are Consistent with the FDA-Required Labeling – Questions and Answers Guidance for Industry (2018).

38 See US Food and Drug Admin., Policy for Device Software Functions and Mobile Medical Applications: Guidance for Industry and Food and Drug Administration Staff, www.fda.gov/downloads/MedicalDevices/DeviceRegulationandGuidance/GuidanceDocuments/UCM263366.pdf.

39 US Food and Drug Admin., General Wellness: Policy for Low Risk Devices, www.fda.gov/media/90652/download.

purposes, then any use by the public outside the intended use falls outside the scope of the FDA regulatory framework.

Courts and policy makers seem to support the consumer demand for reliability of DHTs.[40] However, courts have not always been consistent on the circumstances under which manufacturers are held responsible for known or encouraged "misuse" of their products.[41] Nor have they provided clear or predictable guidance on what constitutes reasonably foreseeable misuse that manufacturers should have known that their product is being used for a purpose for which it is not intended.[42] Because of the legal duty to anticipate and take precautions against unintended but reasonably foreseeable use of products, manufacturers have always been expected to be apprised of the potential "misuses" of their products. Generally, under the reasonable foreseeability standard, manufacturers can be held liable for injuries caused by a product even if the consumer fails to use the product as intended, but the consumer must show the actual use rendered the product defective, which was known or should have been known to the manufacturer.[43] In practice, it can be difficult to determine what unintended uses and what harms arising from such unintended uses are reasonably foreseeable, with some responsibility of prudence being placed on the consumer.[44] It would likely be difficult to establish legal liability under the consumer protection framework for harms arising from the known use of DHTs by consumers who rely on these devices to make medical and health decisions instead of using them for health and wellness purposes only.

There is an opportunity for the MDR to implement a reclassification framework based on evidence of actual use to provide better regulatory oversight, especially as the functionality of DHTs continues to expand their focus toward health care by detecting and measuring an increasing number of physiological parameters associated with health conditions. Manufacturers should not be able to circumvent and avoid higher regulatory burdens by being willfully blind to the increasing evidence of consumers who feel empowered by promotional statements or representations made or implied that they can use DHTs as a means to take control of and responsibility for their own health and wellness.[45] However, according to the Court of Justice of the European Union "[where] a product is not conceived by its manufacturer to be used for medical purposes, its certification as a medical device

40 See European Commission, Assessing the Impact of Digital Transformation of Health Services (2018); see also World Health Org., Draft global strategy on digital health 2020–4 (2019).

41 See, e.g., E. Timmerman & B. Reid, The Doctrine of Invited Misuse: A Societal Response to Marketing Promotion, 4 J. Macromarketing 40–8 (1984).

42 W.L. Trombetta & T.L. Wilson, Foreseeability of Misuse and Abnormal Use of Products by the Consumer, 39 J. Marketing 48–55 (1975).

43 Id.

44 Infra note 45.

45 Clarkson, supra note 31; see also Brian Fung, Is Your Fitbit Wrong? One Woman Argued Hers Was – and Almost Ended Up in a Legal No-Man's Land, Washington Post, www.washingtonpost.com/technology/2018/08/02/is-your-fitbit-wrong-one-woman-argued-it-was-almost-ended-up-legal-no-mans-land/.

cannot be required."[46] In other words, how a device is actually used should have no bearing on how the device is regulated if the stated intention of the manufacturer is that the product is not a medical device. Nevertheless, the postmarket surveillance (PMS) requirement under the MDR may be used to require manufacturers to proactively understand how their products are being used by the public to better align regulatory purposes with public health objectives.

8.4 POSTMARKET SURVEILLANCE (PMS) UNDER THE MDR

Under the MDR, the PMS system is a proactive procedure where manufacturers act in cooperation with other economic actors to collect, review, and report on experiences of devices on the market with the aim of identifying any need for corrective or preventative measures.[47] One of the new features of the MDR is the concept of a PMS plan that requires manufacturers to define the process of collecting, assessing, and investigating incidents and market-related experiences reported by health care professionals, patients, and users on events related to a medical device.[48] According to the MDR, the PMS plan "shall be suited to actively and systematically gathering, recording and analysing relevant data on the quality, performance and safety of a device throughout its entire lifetime, and to drawing the necessary conclusions and to determining, implementing and monitoring any preventive and corrective actions."[49] Because of a growing demand to adopt a more proactive as opposed to the current passive reactive approach to PMS,[50] the implementation of the PMS plan under the MDR may be an avenue to address the concerns associated with the actual use of DHTs beyond the manufacturer's stated intended use. The ability to identify risks and take corrective measures in a timely manner is vital for any regulatory framework. Clear guidance on the implementation of the PMS plan is essential to improve the delivery of health care to consumers through the help of DHTs.

Arguably, the PMS plan can be interpreted to include an obligation to collect postmarketing data on consumer use of DHTs as part of a mandatory reevaluation process to assess the appropriate classification level and regulatory compliance the DHT must adhere to in order to continue to remain on the market. By defining a PMS requirement for manufacturers of DHTs to acquire knowledge of actual use of their products in order to maintain their lower classification status, informed regulatory decisions based on data and evidence can be made. Actual use information can also help establish that the risk caused by a reasonably foreseeable misuse of

[46] Case C-219/11 Brain Products GmbH v. Biosemi VOF and Others.
[47] Regulation 2017/745, supra note 10, at art. 2(60).
[48] Id. at arts. 83–6, Annex III.
[49] Id. at § 1.1 of Annex III.
[50] See, e.g., Josep Pane et al., Evaluating the Safety Profile of Non-active Implantable Medical Devices Compared with Medicines, 40 Drug Safety 37, 37–47 (2017).

DHTs was known to the manufacturer in a liability claim should consumers suffer harm from relying on statements or representations, made or implied, when using DHTs to self-manage their health.

However, the MDR is not particularly clear on the extent of the PMS obligation, stating that the PMS plan should be "proportionate to the risk class and appropriate for the type of device."[51] For Class I devices, a PMS report based on the PMS plan shall be "updated when necessary and made available to the competent authority upon request,"[52] and there is no clarification of how often information should be collected. The elements and type of information that shall be collected for the PMS plan include adverse events, data on nonserious incidents and undesirable side effects, safety updates, trend reporting, relevant specialist or technical literature, and feedback and complaints from users.[53] Although information about actual use is not specifically mentioned, it may be captured under trend reporting, which is intended to include incidents "that could have a significant impact on the benefit analysis ... which may lead to risks to the health or safety of patients, users or other persons that are unacceptable when weighed against the intended benefits."[54] The reclassification of devices is contemplated for reasons of public health based on new scientific evidence or based on information that becomes available in the course of vigilance and market surveillance.[55] Evidence of actual use collected as part of the PMS plan can therefore be used as grounds for reclassification to anticipate and address the actual use of DHTs. However, even with the ability to reclassify, the classification rules and definition of noninvasive versus active devices based on intended use renders this process a vicious cycle. Furthermore, the reclassification of devices based on PMS requires a request to the commission by a Member State and consultation with the Medical Device Coordination Group,[56] making the process bureaucratically cumbersome and unlikely to be used in practice. Without clearer implementation guidelines and a better alignment of the PMS objectives with the classification rules, the PMS plan could become a toothless oversight mechanism.

PMS allows for continuous vigilance, not only to ensure quality, safety, and efficacy of the devices but to ensure the appropriate level of regulatory adherence based on how a device is actually being used. With the rapid proliferation and advancement of DHTs, it will require a collaborative effort between manufacturers, regulators, health care providers, and consumers to strike the right balance between the appropriate regulatory burden and the benefit that DHTs promise to bring to the public health system. DHTs could prove to be a good secondary diagnostic tool with

51 Regulation 2017/745, supra note 10, at art. 83(1).
52 Id. at art. 85.
53 Id. at Annex III.
54 Id. at art. 88.
55 Id. at art. 51(3).
56 Id. at art. 51.

its ability to constantly monitor and collect data and provide detailed longitudinal data to monitor progress and understand patterns.[57] A deeper understanding of patients through their health data is one of the keys to improving health, especially in managing chronic conditions that are primarily driven by leading an unhealthy lifestyle.[58] As the International Council for Harmonization of Technical Requirements for Pharmaceuticals for Human Use continues to consider revisions to the Good Clinical Practice (GCP) to enable the use of real-world evidence, such as patient data derived from or influenced by consumer use of DHTs, reliable oversight and regulation of DHTs become even more pressing to ensure the data are reliable and appropriately collected and interpreted to serve as evidence for informing future regulatory decisions. The underlying presumption that data derived from DHTs can be transformed into meaningful real-world evidence to be used for the intent contemplated by the GCP is that the data is reliable and that there is a relationship between the use of the DHT and the clinical relevance of the data.[59] A PMS system that is aligned with the classification rules to adapt regulatory oversight of DHTs based on actual use and actual impact on consumer health will better support the use of real-world evidence or data derived from DHTs for the purposes of the GCP. The interpretation of the PMS plan to include a proactive requirement on manufacturers to self-report and be informed of not only the safety and efficacy of their products but also how their products are being used will help users and regulators make more informed decisions. This requirement also aligns with the EU responsible research and innovation policy objectives to ensure the innovation process is interactive, transparent, and responsive to public interests and concerns.[60] The PMS plan may be resource intensive; however, innovation will still be encouraged by allowing manufacturers to continue to benefit from easier access to the market without imposing a higher regulatory burden at the outset. Furthermore, the collection of actual use information may constitute know-how that can be used to facilitate follow-on innovation and ultimately increase competition. A risk-based regulatory framework that promotes innovation, protects patient safety, and avoids overregulation of DHTs can be achieved if the clear objectives and a robust structure are defined for the PMS system.

8.5 CONCLUSION

With the introduction of the PMS plan in the MDR, industry, regulators, health care professionals, and consumers have the opportunity to work together to define

57 Piwek et al., supra note 7.

58 Dinesh Puppala, Regulatory Standpoint: Wearables and Healthcare, Hopkins Biotech Network, https://hopkinsbio.org/biotechnology/regulatory-standpoint-wearables-healthcare/.

59 Determining Real-World Data's Fitness for Use and the Role of Reliability, Duke-Margolis Center for Health Policy.

60 H. Yu, Redefining Responsible Research and Innovation for the Advancement of Biobanking and Biomedical Research, 3 J. L. & Biosciences 611–35 (2016).

oversight parameters and mechanisms to realize the potential of DHTs as a health care tool. If consumer DHTs are being advertised as providing medical grade results[61] and therefore being used by consumers as a medical device, the MDR needs to provide adaptive mechanisms to respond to how DHTs are actually used. Leveraging the PMS plan to require manufacturers to proactively monitor, collect, and report on the actual use of DHTs by consumers in order to continue to qualify for classification and regulation as a lower-risk device will convey accountability and provide an evidence-based oversight mechanism within the MDR to garner public trust. Interpreting the PMS plan to require manufacturers to report on how their products are actually used as part of a mandatory reevaluation process to continually assess the classification of the device, regardless of the device's safety and efficacy profile, will ensure greater consumer protection. To achieve this, the MDR must provide clearer implementation guidelines that better align PMS obligations with the classification rules applicable to DHTs. As advocated by some medical professionals, if medical decisions will be made from information generated by DHTs, then such DHTs will require proportionate regulatory oversight.[62]

61 See, e.g., KardiaMobile, which advertises to be "the most clinically-validated personal EKG in the world. Now a medical-grade EKG can become part of your daily routine. Enjoy peace of mind," www.alivecor.com/kardiamobile. Kardia is FDA cleared. See https://alivecor.zendesk.com/hc/en-us/articles/115015799808-Is-Kardia-FDA-cleared-and-CE-marked.

62 Kenneth R. Foster & John Torous, The Opportunity and Obstacles for Smartwatches and Wearable Sensors, 10 IEEE Pulse 22, 22–5 (2019).

PART III

Designing Medical Device Regulations

Introduction

I. Glenn Cohen

In English, as in many (all?) languages there exists a grammatical category known as the "irrealis moods" – a set of grammatical categories that refer to a situation or action that is not known to have happened at the moment the speaker is talking. Andre Aciman has poetically described them as "verbal moods that indicate that certain events have not happened, may never happen, or should or must or are indeed desired to happen, but for which there is no indication that they will happen . . . the might be and the might have been."[1] Some of these are familiar in English like the subjunctive (for unlikely events) or conditional (for events that depend on another condition) mood. Others are more common in non-English languages like the optative (for events that are hoped for or expected),[2] the dubitative (events whose occurrence is doubted or dubious),[3] and jussive (events that are pleaded or asked for)[4] moods.

The irrealis mood is always an exercise in imagined alternatives, and the same is true in each of the chapters in this part – indeed all, in one way or another, imagine a counterfactual world where the FDA rethinks its regulatory approach. Each also has at its core a view that an FDA device regulatory approach that was good (or at least workable) in one context, is a failure as applied to a new set of technologies.

For Mateo Aboy and Jake S. Sherkow's chapter "IP and FDA Regulation of De Novo Medical Devices" the problem arises in the intersection of the FDA's recent policy clarifications on permitting a De Novo device as a "predicate" for a follow-on device application under the 510(k) pathway. While from a safety and efficacy perspective it makes sense to require the second applicant to show that the device is "substantially equivalent" to its predicate device including an assessment that it uses the "*same* technological characteristics" as the predicate, that requirement creates trouble when the relevant aspect of the predicate device is patented, creating

1 Andre Aciman, Homo Irrealis: *Essays* 1 (2020).

2 See Optative, Merriam-Webster Dictionary Online, https://www.merriam-webster.com/dictionary/optative.

3 See Dubitative, Merriam-Webster Dictionary Online, https://www.merriam-webster.com/dictionary/dubitative.

4 See Jussive, Merriam-Webster Dictionary Online, https://www.merriam-webster.com/dictionary/Jussive.

a tactic that is as clever as it is problematically anticompetitive: "device manufacturers use patents to protect the very controls required for regulatory approval."

For Sara Gerke's chapter, "Digital Home Health During the COVID-19 Pandemic: Challenges to Safety, Liability, and Informed Consent and the Way to Move Forward," the problem is the intersection with the Emergency Use Authorization (EUA) regime created by the PREP act and activated in COVID-19 and the only partial coverage of digital home health products within the FDA's regulatory review. Because many digital home health products do not require FDA review, they thus do not require authorization under an EUA (a benefit to the maker) but also do not qualify for the immunity protections of the PREP act (a drawback to the maker). From the perspective of the end user, though, the details of what the FDA reviews or not is at best mysterious and more likely totally unknown, such that their understanding of the liability ramifications are paltry at best. While Gerke discusses whether such gaps can be filled with more robust informed consent processes, in particular during the COVID-19 pandemic one wonders if this is an unlikely might have been!

In some of the chapters in this part, determining which irrealis mood the authors intend is trickier. Matthew Herder and Nathan Cortez offer a chapter on "A 'DESI' for Devices? Can a Pharmaceutical Program from the 1960s Improve FDA Oversight of Medical Devices?," but should we take those question marks and their framing as optative or dubitative? Their chapter takes inspiration from the history of the Drug Efficacy Study Implementation program (DESI) triggered by a major existential shift at the FDA to examine drug effectiveness more which required relying on third parties to examine the effectiveness of more than 3,000 drugs between 1963–84. They argue for a Desi 2.0, reasoning that "[i]f the FDA's inability to encourage high-quality evidence production are ultimately reflective of a kind of incumbency – *both* in terms of who is involved in producing and how it is appraised – then regulation may take as its inspiration DESI's disruptive move to bring outside actors into the regulatory fold." Perhaps in an attempt to move the reader from dubitative to optative they suggest precursors in the treatment of digital health technologies by the FDA at the moment, in particular the precert program and the involvement of the National Evaluation System for health Technology (NEST).

As a group these chapters also raise the interesting question about the role of the scholar and the irrealis moods. Legal and policy scholarship tends to focus on existing initiatives and regulatory processes, primarily concerned with the "here and now." Then again, if past is prologue, perhaps we should not be so dubitative about large changes to the FDA's approach to device regulation – these chapters chart both major sea changes in the past and strong tail winds in the present toward novel regulatory approaches.

9

IP and FDA Regulation of De Novo Medical Devices

Mateo Aboy and Jacob S. Sherkow

If recent changes to the US Food & Drug Administration's (FDA's) authority are an indication, the future of medical device regulation could largely be shaped by intellectual property (IP). In an effort to "accelerate innovation of and patient access to novel technologies,"[1] the FDA now has authority to clear medical devices under its "De Novo Pathway," a shortened path to market for new, innovative devices.[2] This authority also includes the ability for follow-on applicants (referred to as "510(k) applicants" after the pertinent statutory section) to use approved De Novo devices as predicates upon which to base their devices' safety and efficacy.[3] But the Agency's guidance in the area – in combination with devices' increasingly technological sophistication – put De Novo devices' IP protections at the forefront of the approval process. This raises a host of questions about the intersection of IP and medical devices, including standard essential patents covering medical devices, IP protections for medical device software, and products liability's relationship with medical device IP.[4]

Section 9.1 of this chapter provides a brief overview of medical device regulation in the United States and, in particular, the De Novo and 510(k) premarketing

1 Aaron S. Kesselheim & Thomas J. Hwang, Breakthrough Medical Devices and the 21st Century Cures Act, 164 Annals Internal Med. 500, 501 (2016).

2 See US Food & Drug Admin., Acceptance Review for De Novo Classification Requests: Guidance for Industry and Food and Drug Administration Staff [hereinafter "De Novo Acceptance Guidance"] (Sept. 9, 2019), https://www.fda.gov/media/116945/download [https://perma.cc/7YBQ-FWUM]; US Food & Drug Admin., De Novo Classification Process (Evaluation of Automatic Class III Designation): Guidance for Industry and Food and Drug Administration Staff [hereinafter "De Novo Classification Guidance"] (Oct. 30, 2017), https://www.fda.gov/media/72674/download [https://perma.cc/8US4-QEG7].

By convention, FDA capitalizes "De Novo" in its guidance documents, a convention we follow here.

3 See 21st Century Cures Act, Pub. L. No. 144–255, 130 Stat. 1033 (2016); De Novo Classification Guidance, supra note 2, at 5 ("The granting of the De Novo request allows the device to be marketed immediately, creates a classification regulation for devices of this type, and permits the device to serve as a predicate device."); US Food & Drug Admin., Premarket Notification 510(k) (Sept. 27, 2018), https://www.fda.gov/medical-devices/premarket-submissions/premarket-notification-510k [https://perma.cc/EDK4-SB9N] ("A legally marketed [predicate] device is a device . . . that was granted marketing authorization via the De Novo classification process").

4 JS Sherkow, M Aboy, "The FDA De Novo medical device pathway, patents and anticompetition" Nature Biotechnology 38 (9), 1028–1029.

pathways. It includes a discussion of recent FDA guidance in the area that lend themselves to a variety of intellectual property strategies to potentially hinder follow-on 510(k) applications, as discussed in Section 9.2. Section 9.3 examines the implications for such strategies and explores three areas for future attention: standards essential patents covering core technological features of De Novo devices; intellectual property protection for software critical for medical devices; and products liability regimes that incorporate this approval–infringement gambit.

9.1 MEDICAL DEVICE PREMARKETING PATHWAYS

Recent attempts to modernize and speed up the FDA's premarketing clearance and classification process for medical devices have included both new device classifications and new ways of filing abbreviated applications. The FDA's "De Novo" classification and "Breakthrough Devices" programs, in particular, allow applicants to create entirely new medical device "types," complete with their own fleet of standardized safety and effectiveness checklists, including sets of specifications on software, hardware, and energy sources.[5] These safety and effectiveness checklists are enumerated for each device type in the FDA's rolls under "general" or "special controls." General controls are a list of safety checks required of all medical devices – proper labeling, for example.[6] Special controls, by contrast, are safety and effectiveness checks specific to a device type, e.g., a requirement that external cardiac pacemakers deliver a current at a pulse amplitude no greater than 200 mA.[7] The De Novo pathway, in particular, allows the clearance of devices that can demonstrate a "reasonable assurance" of fidelity to its device type's general and special controls.[8]

The De Novo and Breakthrough pathways are still a novelty, however, and the vast majority of medical devices – over 85 percent by some metrics – are cleared through what is known as the "510(k) pathway," named so after the pertinent section in the Food, Drug & Cosmetics Act (FDCA).[9] Up to now, the 510(k) pathway has been the most widely employed medical device premarket submission program since the enactment of the Medical Device Amendments of 1976 to the FDCA.[10] Significant for

5 De Novo Classification Guidance, supra note 2; 21st Century Cures Act, supra note 3(codifying breakthrough device review); US Food & Drug Admin., Breakthrough Devices Program: Guidance for Industry and Food and Drug Administration Staff [hereinafter "Breakthrough Device Guidance"] (Dec. 18, 2018), https://www.fda.gov/media/108135/download [https://perma.cc/P24U-HHHU].

6 21 C.F.R. § 860.3(c)(1) (West 2020).

7 Id. § 860.3(c)(2) (West 2020) (special controls, generally); id. § 870.5550(b)(2) (external cardiac pacemakers).

8 21 U.S.C.A. § 360c(f)(2)(A)(v) (West 2020).

9 See US Food & Drug Admin., FY 2018: Performance Report to Congress for the Medical Device User Fee Amendments at 18 https://www.fda.gov/media/130598/download [https://perma.cc/MWU2-JPUT] (noting that the Agency received 3,591 510(k) notifications during the 2018 fiscal year, compared to 619 applications for other approvals – 85 percent of the total).

10 See Vinay K. Rathi & Joseph S. Ross, Modernizing the FDA's 510(k) Pathway, 381 N. Engl. J. Med. 1891 (2019); see also Medical Device Amendments of 1976, Pub. L. 94–295, 90 Stat. 539 (1976).

the 510(k) pathway is the process by which a new device is categorized into one of three classes based on its risk: Class I, the least risky devices; Class II; or Class III, the most risky devices.[11] This initial classification determines the requirements a device must meet prior to market introduction. In particular, non-exempt Class I and Class II devices for which a "predicate" device exists can rely on the 510(k) pathway toward clearance if the new device can show it is "substantially equivalent" to the predicate device.[12] By contrast, Class III devices, for the most part, must instead use the significantly more onerous Premarket Approval ("PMA") pathway, which may require costly clinical tests.[13] Accordingly, over the last forty years, the 510(k) program became the preferred and dominant premarketing pathway for medical device manufacturers, and especially those concerning Class II devices.[14]

In an effort to encourage innovation and competition, the 21st Century Cures Act allows De Novo devices to serve as "predicates" for subsequent 510(k) submissions, so long as such devices use the same general and special controls as their De Novo predicates, and possess, in most cases, "the same" technological characteristics as the predicate De Novo device.[15] This allows the 510(k) applicant to demonstrate "substantial equivalence" between it and the De Novo device.[16] The substance of the substantial equivalence determination is based primarily on satisfying two inquiries: first, "Do the devices have the same intended use?"; and second, "Do the devices have the same technological characteristics?"[17] The result of failing to satisfy both of these inquiries is a "not substantially equivalent" determination, which traditionally automatically classified the new device as a Class III, that is, high-risk, device, depriving the applicant of the convenience, cost, and speed of the 510(k) pathway.[18]

Until recently, this approval structure encouraged applicants to characterize their new medical devices as having the "same intended use" and "same technological characteristics" as a predicate device, independently of their devices' degree of novelty.[19] Applicants of low- and moderate-risk devices needed to be cautious of introducing significant innovations, however, as these could result in an NSE

11 21 U.S.C.A. § 360c(a)(1) (West 2020).

12 Id. § 360c(i).

13 Id. § 360e(b)(1).

14 Rathi & Ross, supra note 11.

15 See 21 U.S.C.A. § 360c(i) (West 2020) (mandating these requirements for all 510(k) applications).

16 Id. § 360c(f)(2)(B)(i) (West 2020) (authorizing "any device classified under [the De Novo pathway] shall be a predicate device for determining substantial equivalence under paragraph (1)"); De Novo Classification Guidance, supra note 2, at 12 ("Once a De Novo request is granted, then the subject device may be used as a predicate for any future 510(k) submissions.").

17 US Food & Drug Admin., The 510(k) Program: Evaluating Substantial Equivalence in Premarket Notifications [510(k)] Guidance for Industry and Food and Drug Administration Staff Document, at 27 [hereinafter "510(k) Flowchart"] www.fda.gov/media/82395/download [https://perma.cc/3DF6-FN29].

18 See id. at 3 ("A determination that a new device is not substantially equivalent (NSE) to a predicate device results in the new device being classified into Class III.").

19 Inst. of Med. of the Nat'l Academies, Medical Devices and the Public's Health: The FDA 510(k) Clearance Process at 35 Years, [hereinafter IOM 510(k) report] 193–4 (2011) ("The committee found

determination and shunting to the PMA route of approval.[19] Some have argued that – at least for some devices – this encouraged slow and incremental changes to preexisting devices at the expense of radical innovation.[21]

On December 7, 2018, however, the FDA published new draft guidance for the De Novo classification process under the 21st Century Cures Act.[22] The agency followed the guidance with a September 9, 2019 "Acceptance Guidance" to further support the De Novo process as a pathway to classify novel medical devices for which there is no legal marketed predicate device.[23] This alternative pathway for low- and moderate-risk devices (i.e., Class I and Class II devices) is now available for either applicants who received an NSE determination in a prior 510(k) application; or applicants claiming that there is no legally marketed predicate device upon which to base a 510(k) application.[24] This second option, in effect, creates a new regulatory pathway for approval of novel medical devices: the direct submission of a device under a De Novo classification request.[25] 510(k) applicants, in turn, may use these "direct" De Novo devices as predicates for their applications.[26]

At best, this procedure is hoped to accelerate the development of truly novel medical devices. Criticism of the prior regime centered on a flight not to innovation but to mimicry – the fear of innovating too much at the risk of an NSE determination.[27] Allowing the rapid entry of truly novel devices through the De Novo and Breakthrough programs, followed by slight variation and market competition through the 510(k) pathway seeks to encourage both innovation and competition.[28] Whether this will meet its mark remains to be seen. A 2011 Institute of Medicine report raised hopes that the De Novo pathway "offers a potential basis of a better regulatory model for premarket review of Class II devices."[29] But as of this writing there were fewer than 300 marketed De Novo devices in the United States.[30]

that the 510(k) clearance process was not designed to reward, recognize, or encourage innovation. At most, promotion of innovation was a byproduct of a process that, by minimizing unnecessary regulatory burdens, facilitated the entry into the market of new devices that do not raise novel questions of safety or effectiveness.").

20 Id.

21 See Christopher Buccafusco, Disability and Design, 95 NYU L. Rev. 952, 974–6 (2020) (recounting this with respect to wheelchairs).

22 De Novo Classification Guidance, supra note 2.

23 De Novo Acceptance Guidance, supra note 2.

24 De Novo Classification Guidance, supra note 2, at 4.

25 Id.

26 Id. at 12; see also 21 U.S.C. § 360c(f)(2)(B)(i) (West 2020).

27 IOM 510(k) Report, supra note 20, at 193–4.

28 Id. at 195–6.

29 Id. at 11.

30 US Food & Drug Admin., Device Classification under Section 513(f)(2)(de novo), www.accessdata.fda.gov/scripts/cdrh/cfdocs/cfPMN/denovo.cfm?start_search=1&Center=&

9.2 INTELLECTUAL PROPERTY CONSIDERATIONS

9.2.1 *IP and Competition*

These premarketing pathways, while rooted in classic considerations of safety and effectiveness, lend themselves to a potential intellectual property strategy with the effect of – or designed for – preventing 510(k) applicants from using De Novo devices as predicates. The strategy begins with the general and special controls certification required for the submission of a De Novo application. The application must include "a description of why . . . general and special controls provide reasonable assurance of safety and effectiveness."[31] This certification of "reasonable assurance" based on these controls is, of course, the impetus behind the De Novo pathway: if general and special controls really can ensure a device's safety and effectiveness, then requiring an applicant to demonstrate safety and effectiveness through robust clinical trials even though there is no appropriate predicate is wasteful.[32] Additionally, this certification requirement raises an epistemic problem: how can one be reasonably assured that a device's special controls will make it safe and effective if there are no other device types like it? To use a new type of pacemaker, for example, how can one know, without robust testing, whether a 200-mA limit, or 250 mA, or 350 mA, provides "reasonable assurance" that the new type of pacemaker is both safe and effective? In an attempt to resolve this question, the FDA, in 2017, began to ask De Novo applicants to propose their own special controls for their own devices.[33] Some of these controls, according to the Agency's De Novo Acceptance Guidance, can be quite specific and technologically oriented, such as the device's performance standards, materials used to ensure biocompatibility, its design to ensure safe use, the energy source of the device, data requirements (clinical studies), or its use of software.[34] If these controls are accepted by the FDA, and if the device is approved, as noted above, this establishes a new device type, for which any follow-on applications must either use the same controls or otherwise demonstrate substantial equivalency.[35]

These same technological features, that is, key technological characteristics and the special controls necessarily tied to these technological characteristics through performance standards, can be patented by the De Novo applicant. This establishes an IP barrier of entry for 510(k) applicants wishing to use De Novo devices as predicates for

Panel=&ProductCode=&KNumber=&DenKNumber=&Applicant=&DeviceName=&Type=&ThirdPartyReviewed=&ClinicalTrials=&ExpeditedReview=&Decision=&DecisionDateFrom=&DecisionDateTo=04%2F21%2F2020&DeNovo=on&IVDProducts=&CombinationProducts=&ZNumber=&PAGENUM=500, [https://perma.cc/HH5A-J59A].

31 De Novo Acceptance Guidance, supra note 2, at 18.

32 IOM 510(k) Report, supra note 20, at 17–18.

33 De Novo Classification Guidance, supra note 2, at 16 ("For class II devices, provide proposed special controls along with cross-references to other information within the request demonstrating that the device meets these special controls.").

34 Id. at 18.

35 Id. at 5–6.

their applications: in determining whether a 510(k) application is "substantially equivalent" to its predicate device, the FDA assesses whether the 510(k) device uses the "same technological characteristics" as the predicate, that is, the same "materials, design, [and] energy source, and other device features" of the predicate device.[36] This requires most 510(k) applications to provide "engineering drawings or other figures," "a complete identification of the detailed chemical formulation used in the materials of construction," an identification of "energy delivery that is part of the functional aspect of the device," and a recitation of the device's "software/hardware features . . . as appropriate for the specific device technology."[37] To the degree these aspects of the predicate device are patented, this is not just a potential admission of patent infringement but possibly a detailed roadmap of how the De Novo applicant can prove its infringement case.[38]

All is not lost for proposed 510(k) devices that do not use the same technological characteristics as their De Novo predicates; their applicants can still demonstrate substantial equivalency if their devices' technological characteristics use the same "performance characteristics" and do not "raise different questions of safety and effectiveness."[39] But these performance characteristics – the De Novo predicates' "device design, material[s] used, and physical properties" – can substantially overlap with predicates' special controls, which, if patented, puts 510(k) applicants back in the same trap as before: in order to demonstrate substantial equivalency to the FDA, 510(k) applicants must either admit to patent infringement or confess to the FDA that their proposed devices are not substantially equivalent to their predicates.

In summary, marketers of De Novo devices can tell the FDA which special controls to use to assess their devices, controls that De Novo applicants can then also patent.[40] If these special controls overlap with a De Novo device's performance characteristics, this makes filing a 510(k) application on the entire De Novo device type impossibly unattractive; the 510(k) applicant must either essentially admit to infringing the De Novo device predicate's special controls or choose to acknowledge its device is not substantially equivalent, thus sinking their 510(k) application.

9.2.2 *An Example: Alternate Controller Insulin Pumps*

Admittedly, this seems like a rather tortuous pathway to quelling competition. But a real-life example proves how easy – and powerful – the strategy can be. As of this

36 Id. at 18–19.

37 Id. at 19–20.

38 Cf. Shashank Upadhye, Understanding Patent Infringement Under 35 U.S.C. § 271(e): The Collisions Between Patent, Medical Device, and Drug Laws, 17 Santa Clara Computer & High Tech. L. J. 1, 28 (2000) ("[S]ince the 510(k) process requires a comparison of the products, then perhaps this is also an admission of at least equivalency infringement.").

39 510(k) Flowchart, supra note 18.

40 See De Novo Classification Guidance, supra note 2, at 16 ("For class II devices, provide proposed special controls along with cross-references to other information within the request demonstrating that the device meets these special controls.").

writing, Tandem Diabetes Care, Inc. markets, as a De Novo device, the t:slim X2 Insulin Pump, an automatic pediatric insulin pump given the generic device type of "alternate controller enabled infusion pump."[41] To allow patients control over when they receive insulin, the pump can be operated by a connected smartphone – the "alternate controller" – that raises several concerns over safety and effectiveness for which Tandem identified several special controls.[42] Those controls include, among other things, the "[s]haring of necessary state information between the pump and any digitally connected alternate controllers" and "[a] detailed process and procedure for sharing the pump interface specification with digitally connected devices."[43] These special controls overlap with the device's performance controls, which include "validated software protocols intended to ensure secure, accurate, and reliable communication with digital interfacing devices."[44] As an illustrative example, these aspects of the device's communication protocols that have been patented by Tandem, which owns over fifty patents covering various aspects of its insulin pump technology.[45] Take, for example, US Patent No. 10,478,551, which claims a broad method "of delivering a medicament bolus with a medical infusion pump" via "a remote consumer electronic device."[46] Presumably, almost any overlap between the "remote consumer electronic device" enumerated in the claims and a "digitally connected device" that uses a "validated software protocol" to connect to the pump, would at least colorably infringe. US Patent No. 9,833,177, also owned by Tandem, similarly claims a detailed system that includes a "controller communicatively coupled to the pump."[47] Again, there is likely little daylight between the "secure, accurate, and reliable communication" protocol identified in the device's performance characteristics and the detailed system for controller communications in the patent. And US Patent No. 9,492,608 claims a variety of methods of "infusing insulin" using a programmed controller, making design-arounds for follow-on applicants difficult.[48]

[41] Letter from Kellie B. Kelm, Acting Director, Division of Chemistry and Toxicology Devices, FDA, to Michael Sarrasin, Senior Director of Regulatory and Clinical Affairs, Tandem Diabetes Care, Inc. (Dec. 3, 2019) [hereinafter "t:slim X2 De Novo Order"] at 1, www.accessdata.fda.gov/cdrh_docs/pdf18/DEN180058.pdf [https://perma.cc/AD2F-8LS6].

[42] Id. at 3–6.

[43] Id. at 4.

[44] US Food & Drug Admin., Evaluation of Automatic Class III Designation For t:slim X2 Insulin Pump with Interoperable Technology – Decision Summary [hereinafter "t:slim X2 Decision Summary"], at 13, www.accessdata.fda.gov/cdrh_docs/reviews/DEN180058.pdf [https://perma.cc/S4G4-HXFJ].

[45] Conducted doing a search, using the U.S.P.T.O.'s Public PAFT database, on all patents originally assigned to Tandem Diabetes. http://patft.uspto.gov/netacgi/nph-Parser?Sect1=PTO2&Sect2=HITOFF&u=%2Fnetahtml%2FPTO%2Fsearch-adv.htm&r=0&p=1&f=S&l=50&Query=an%2F%22tandem+diabetes%22&d=PTXT [https://perma.cc/9DDY-E6HW].

[46] US Patent No. 10,478,551, at col. 14, ll. 10–11.

[47] US Patent No. 9,833,177, at col. 14, l. 53.

[48] US Patent No. 9,492,608, at col. 14, l. 44.

Ultimately, any 510(k) applicant seeking to market a follow-on alternate controller enabled infusion pump would need either to admit it uses the same "process and procedure for sharing the pump interface specification" with the controller – a likely admission of infringement of Tandem Diabetes' patents – or that it uses different special controls but nonetheless hews to the device's performance characteristics – which are also patented. Denial on both counts, under the FDA's own guidelines, means the two devices are not substantially equivalent. To be clear, there is currently one approved 510(k) application for an "alternate controller enabled infusion pump" – currently marketed by Insulet Corporation, the Omnipod DASH[49] – but it seems clear that Tandem Diabetes considers Insulet to be a direct competitor.[50] Insulet's 510(k) application, meanwhile, states that while it has different technological characteristics from Tandem's device, it nonetheless meets the predicate's performance controls.[51] Whether this will result in a patent infringement suit, or not, remains to be seen, but for now, the pathway presented for any follow-on developer, as with Insulet, seems fraught.

9.3 MORE COMPLEX STRATEGIES

In some sense, the anticompetitive trap described above is simple: device manufacturers use patents to protect the very controls required for regulatory approval. But several areas of intellectual property practice intersect with this strategy in complex ways. Standard essential patents trouble the relationship between IP and device requirements. IP protection covering medical device software may be both better and worse for follow-on applicants. And patents may exacerbate the role that products liability plays in designing follow-on devices. These more complex forms of protection further demonstrate the thick ties between IP and medical device approval.

9.3.1 *Standards Essential Patents*

Where patents cover a De Novo device's special controls or performance characteristics, the patents may be narrow enough to allow 510(k) applicants to design around them. But this becomes greatly complicated – if not downright impossible – where the patents are standards essential patents ("SEPs") for standards explicitly required to meet safety and efficacy standards.[52] Certifying

49 Letter from Kellie B. Kelm, Acting Director, Division of Chemistry and Toxicology Devices, FDA, to Julie Perkins, Senior Director, Quality Assurance and Regulatory Affairs, Insulet Corp. (Sept. 20, 2019) [hereinafter "Insulet 510(k)"], available at www.accessdata.fda.gov/cdrh_docs/pdf19/K191679.pdf [https://perma.cc/68Z2-YY4L].

50 Tandem Diabetes Care, Inc., 2019 Annual Report (Form 10-K) (Feb. 24, 2020), at 11, http://investor.tandemdiabetes.com/static-files/ca84169a-f9d8-4cdd-a759-373252385ea9 [https://perma.cc/CKU9-3S3G] (listing "Insulet Corporation" as "Competition").

51 Insulet 510(k), supra note 50at *6–*11.

52 See generally Jorge L. Contreras, Essentiality and Standards-Essential Patents, in The Cambridge Handbook of Technical Standardization Law: Competition, Antitrust, and Patents 209–30 (Jorge L. Contreras ed., 2017) (reviewing the "essentiality" of patents covering certain standards).

that a 510(k) device meets such a standard is, in essence, a certification of infringement of the SEPs.[53] Here is an example: the FDA's evaluation for alternate controller enabled infusion pumps specifically references the use of a Bluetooth Low Energy radio as the means for reliably and securely connecting the controller to the pump.[54] But the Bluetooth Low Energy technology is, itself, a standard established by the Bluetooth Special Interest Group ("BSIG"), and covered by specific SEPs.[55] As with the patent strategy describe, above, a 510(k) applicant would need to use the same technology and, therefore, obtain a patent license from BSIG. Where the De Novo marketer has participated in developing the standard or contributing its patents to the SEPs, this makes noninfringing 510(k) applications all but a dream.

At the same time, SEPs may present less of a concern than non-SEP patents held by the De Novo device marketer because SEPs are typically licensed on fair, reasonable, and non-discriminatory terms to all comers; injunctions are rare.[56] But a recent policy statement from a variety of government agencies recently questioned the wisdom of dispensing with injunctions for SEPs.[57] If injunctions do begin to become commonplace for SEPs, and if De Novo device marketers robustly participate in setting device standards, 510(k) applicants may find it all but impossible to demonstrate substantial equivalency without facing the threat of an injunction from standards organizations. The future of this area will turn on the effect of this injunction policy and device marketers' participation in standards setting.

9.3.2 *Software IP*

A substantial proportion of the De Novo applications are for SaMDs ("Software as Medical Devices"),[58] "software intended to be used for one or more medical purposes that perform these purposes without being part of a hardware medical device" (e.g., a medical device software application that runs on a consumer grade

53 See Jorge L. Contreras, Much Ado About Hold-Up, U. Ill. L. Rev. 875, 881–2 (2019) ("With standards-compliant products, however, the manufacturer's options are more limited; designing around the patent may prevent the product from complying with the standard, thus reducing its functionality or making it unmarketable . . . Thus, in order to sell a standards-compliant product, the prudent manufacturer must obtain permission from the patent holder (known as a license).").

54 t:slim X2 Decision Summary, supra note 45, at *1.

55 Bluetooth, Learn About Bluetooth – Radio Versions, www.bluetooth.com/learn-about-bluetooth/bluetooth-technology/radio-versions/ [https://perma.cc/9L44-YQHR].

56 Jorge L. Contreras, Global Rate Setting: A Solution for Standards-Essential Patents, 94 Wash. L. Rev. 701, 747–8 (2019).

57 USPTO, DOJ & NIST, Policy Statement on Remedies for Standards-Essential Patents Subject to Voluntary F/RAND Commitments (Dec. 19, 2019), www.justice.gov/atr/page/file/1228016/download [https://perma.cc/VT68-QPXB].

58 US Food & Drug Admin., Device Classification under Section 513(f)(2)(de novo), supra note 31; see also Timo Minssen et al., Regulatory Responses to Medical Machine Learning, J.L. Biosci., https://academic.oup.com/jlb/advance-article/doi/10.1093/jlb/lsaa002/5817484.

hardware such as a smartphone).[59] Such De Novo SaMDs raise important questions at the intersection of IP and the medical device premarket pathways in situations where the key computer-implemented inventions are patented and become the key technological characteristics (i.e., the SaMD itself). Even in the cases of "Software *in* a Medical Device" (i.e., software that drives or is required by a hardware medical device to achieve its intended function), the interactions between IP, De Novo, and 501(k) can be problematic. De Novo medical devices typically include software, some of which constitute devices' core technological characteristics or special controls tight to key performance characteristics. Using the t:slim X2, again, as an example, the insulin pump uses a suite of software to ensure that the device's various functions – basal delivery, bolus delivery, and occlusion detection, for example – functioned properly.[60] These software controls are, indeed, performance characteristics of the device, follow-on applications of which would need to replicate.[61]

Using IP to protect De Novo devices' controls and performance characteristics adds nuance to how effectively it could potentially hinder 510(k) applications. With respect to patents, many "software" patents – admittedly, a nettlesome term without clear definition – have been rendered invalid after the Supreme Court of the U.S.' opinion in *Alice Corp. v. CLS Bank International.*[62] This is true in both post-issuance proceedings at the US Patent and Trademark Office and in litigation in federal court.[63] 510(k) applicants may, therefore, give less credence to software patents covering De Novo devices' special controls or performance characteristics.[64] In other instances, due to peripheral claiming practice and software patents' often overly general claim elements, 510(k) may be able to easily design software patents protecting the features of their predicate devices.[65]

But certain forms of software can be copyrighted as well, a substantially more difficult problem for 510(k) applicants.[66] Unlike patents, copyrights' infringement ambit is central rather than peripheral, rooting itself in whether the accused software

59 US Food & Drug Admin., Software as a Medical Device, https://www.fda.gov/medical-devices/digital-health/software-medical-device-samd [https://perma.cc/4L2Y-SNJ8].

60 t:slim X2 Decision Summary, supra note 45, at 5.

61 Id.

62 134 S. Ct. 2347 (2014); see also Ryan T. Holte, The Trespass Fallacy in the "Software Patent" Debate, 65 Fla. L. Rev. F. 46, 49 (2014) ("[T]he debate about 'software patents' lacks any clear standard perhaps because the term 'software patent' itself lacks any settled definition. Indeed, there is no legal definition for the term 'software patent' used by courts and scholars.").

63 Stuart Graham & Saurabh Vishnubhakat, Of Smart Phone Wars and Software Patents, 27 J. Econ. Perspectives 67, 70–3 (2013).

64 Cf. Colleen V. Chien, Holding Up and Holding Out, 21 Mich. Telecomm. & Tech. L. Rev. 1 (2014) (defining "hold out" as the practice of ignoring patent assertion demands because the risk of liability is small).

65 See Mark A. Lemley, Software Patents and the Return of Functional Claiming, Wis. L. Rev. 905, 947 (2013) (requiring the disclosure of specific algorithms in software patents "will leave room for later entrants to design around the patent and develop different algorithms to achieve the same result").

66 See, e.g., Oracle Am., Inc. v. Google Inc., 750 F.3d 1339, 1363–8 (2014) (allowing copyright protection to Oracle's Java API packages).

possesses "substantial similarity" to the copyrighted one.[67] This also means that "designing around" software copyright is much more difficult.[68] Assuming that software copyrights cover a De Novo device's special controls or performance characteristic, it would be extremely difficult for a 510(k) applicant to argue that its device is "substantially equivalent" to the De Novo predicate but does not possess "substantial similarity" to its special controls.

With this said, the vitality of copyright covering software – specifically, application program interfaces ("APIs") – is in dispute. The Supreme Court of the US is, as of this writing, slated to decide the issue in an upcoming case, *Google LLC v. Oracle America, Inc.*, concerning software covering Java APIs.[69] Given APIs' functional nature, many commentators think the Court will ultimately do away with such protections.[70] Regardless, the case will be important for De Novo and 510(k) applicants alike. Perhaps it is strange to think that the future of medical device competition may substantially turn on the copyrightability of Java APIs, but that may best encapsulate the issues confronting medical device regulation for the twenty-first century.

9.3.3 *Patents and Products Liability*

Even assuming that 510(k) applicants could design around De Novo predicates' protected controls and performance characteristics, it is not clear how far they would go. Marketers of 510(k) devices, just like marketers for their predicate devices, are liable for design defects in their devices.[71] This is more than a mere worry – medical device products liability cases are some of the most damage-heavy in the American legal system.[72]

Fear of products liability suits has dispirited the adventurousness of many follow-on device manufacturers.[73] Christopher Buccafusco has recently recounted the ploddingly slow incremental improvements behind wheelchairs, even long after their principal patents had expired.[74] Wheelchair manufacturers "continued to make wheelchairs following [the patented] established design . . . [ensuring users]

67 Amini Innovation Corp. v. Anthony California, Inc., 439 F.3d 1365, 1368 (Fed. Cir. 2006).

68 See Joseph P. Fishman, Creating Around Copyright, 128 Harv. L. Rev. 1333, 1386–7 (2015) (noting this problem with copyright's peripheral claiming structure).

69 Certiorari Order, Google LLC v. Oracle Am., Inc., No. 18–956 (Nov. 15, 2019), available at www.supremecourt.gov/orders/courtorders/111519zr_8n59.pdf [https://perma.cc/5Q2Q-MQRE].

70 E.g., Pamela Samuelson & Clark D. Asay, Saving Software's Fair Use Future, 31 Harv. J.L. & Tech. 535 (2018).

71 Restatement (Third) of Torts: Prod. Liab. § 6(c) (1998).

72 See, e.g., Tina Bellon, Johnson & Johnson Hit with $247 Million Verdict in Hip Implant Trial, Reuters (Nov. 16, 2017), www.reuters.com/article/us-johnson-johnson-verdict/johnson-johnson-hit-with-247-million-verdict-in-hip-implant-trial-idUSKBN1DG2MB [https://perma.cc/L7VP-D8HH].

73 Buccafusco, supra note 22, at 981–2.

74 Id.

would have a difficult time arguing that the product was fundamentally unsafe."[75] By contrast, follow-on manufacturers expressed the belief that "introducing new products, without established safety records, could subject them to massive liability should people get hurt."[76] Even with the absence of patent protection and fifty years' worth of real-world safety data, Buccafusco's lesson from the wheelchair case is that follow-on manufacturers may not use all of the runway IP otherwise affords them. As applied to De Novo devices, this instruction is likely to have even more force. De Novo devices are, by definition, those without a predicate, devices that are likely to be more novel and potentially more dangerous than wheelchairs. Orthopedic injuries from wheelchair misuse should not be discounted. But faulty insulin pumps are likely to be fatal.

Patents are likely to exacerbate this in the context of 510(k) applications to De Novo devices. If the only path toward noninfringing approval is a radical transition to the predicate device's design, 510(k) applicants may forgo the opportunity altogether for fear of liability. At the same time, incremental innovation – like that historically characterized by the wheelchair industry – may be enough to gain regulatory approval and avoid products liability suits, but not enough to avoid infringement. This puts an added constraint on 510(k) applicants seeking to design around De Novo predicates – the invisible force of products liability suits for redesigns of approved devices.

9.4 CONCLUSION

Allowing De Novo or breakthrough device applicants to patent their devices' special controls and performance characteristics creates an anticompetitive gauntlet for 510(k) device applicants. Those 510(k) applicants seeking to use De Novo or breakthrough devices as predicates are hemmed into either admitting their devices are "substantially equivalent" to their predicates – effectively an admission of patent infringement – or that they use different technological or performance characteristics, a regulatory concession sinking their own applications. These difficulties may be exacerbated in more complex cases involving standards essential patents, IP covering medical software, or design-arounds that raise products liability concerns. This cannot be what Congress intended when it opened the 510(k) pathway to De Novo devices. The FDA should consequently be warier about De Novo applicants that propose special controls or performance covered by the applicants' own patents. If left unchecked, the future of medical regulation may turn not on innovation of devices' safety and effectiveness, but strategic avoidance of others' intellectual property.

75 Id. at 981.
76 Id.

10

A "DESI" for Devices?

Can a Pharmaceutical Program from the 1960s Improve FDA Oversight of Medical Devices?

Matthew Herder and Nathan Cortez

The US Food and Drug Administration (FDA) has embraced "real-world evidence" (RWE) to evaluate the safety and efficacy of medical devices and drugs. However, the turn towards RWE remains controversial. Securing high-quality evidence after market entry can be a significant challenge. And concerns about the safety of several medical devices – discovered only after real-world use – have renewed calls for more rigorous pre and postmarket evaluation. Here, we discuss the shift toward RWE and the attendant challenges and concerns. Then, through a historical examination of the "Drug Efficacy Study Implementation" program (DESI), we argue that changing how RWE studies are conducted and who evaluates them might mitigate some concerns. Distributing the responsibility for designing, conducting, and assessing RWE beyond industry sponsors and the FDA is critical to producing – and acting upon – more clinically useful information about these products. We explore how the DESI program, which used third parties to examine the effectiveness of more than 3,000 drugs between 1963–1984, coupled with existing flexibilities in the law governing medical devices, provide both the inspiration and necessary conditions to support a DESI 2.0.

10.1 INTRODUCTION

A defining dilemma in regulating health products is balancing upfront scrutiny of safety and effectiveness prior to marketing with ongoing oversight during everyday use. Reliable evidence from both the premarket and postmarket phases is essential for both informed regulation and optimal clinical use. Yet the standards for evaluating this evidence are underspecified by law, challenged by innovation, and contested by a range of actors. In this chapter, we bring into conversation two types of products that have traditionally been subject to divergent regulation – drugs and devices – to illustrate both the challenges of, and potential opportunities associated with, increasing reliance upon what can be learned from the real world, so-called "real-world evidence" (RWE).

Since the mid-20th century, the US Food and Drug Administration (FDA) has relied on premarket data collection to demonstrate that products are safe and effective. In recent years, however, the agency has gradually relied more on evidence gathered on the postmarket side of the equation, typically under the auspices of expedited reviews designed to speed up market access to promising (if yet unproven) drugs.[1] Moreover, since the 1976 Medical Device Amendments, the vast majority of devices have gained entry into the US market by demonstrating substantial equivalence to a previously marketed device,[2] thus inviting the FDA to infer safety and efficacy on the basis of previous clinical use of older devices. Nevertheless, after a number of high-profile cases in which devices entered the market as substantially equivalent to older devices but later proved to carry significant risks,[3] the agency is under some pressure to revisit how it sets the evidentiary bar.

The FDA's evidentiary standards, particularly the important balance between pre and postmarket evidence, are in flux. Section 10.2 details this shift and develops an argument that medical devices are especially ripe for regulatory experimentation. In Section 10.3 we pull from historical experience with drugs to describe key features of a new regulatory approach for devices. We theorize that the "Drug Efficacy Study Implementation" (DESI) program, which the FDA initiated in the 1960s, could be refashioned to improve both the quality of the evidence and the regulatory decisions made about medical devices. We see particular promise in expanding both evidence gathering and evidence evaluation to third parties outside both the FDA and industry. In concluding, Section 10.4 outlines potential stumbling blocks for a "DESI 2.0" for devices, which we hope will guide further development of this idea.

10.2 EVOLVING STANDARDS FOR DRUGS AND DEVICES

10.2.1 *Lifecycle Regulation and Real-World Evidence at the FDA*

The idea that a product's safety or efficacy profile might change significantly once used widely in the "real world" is far from new. Although controlled experiments help evaluate the safety and efficacy of a product in a target population, they may also mask important risks or exaggerate benefits that become apparent when the product is used over longer periods, in larger populations, and beyond the confines of strict trial protocols. Thus, the FDA has always been somewhat alert to how pre

1 Matthew Herder, Pharmaceutical Drugs of Uncertain Value, Lifecycle Regulation at the US Food and Drug Administration, and Institutional Incumbency, 97 Milbank Q. 820–57 (2019).

2 Inst. of Med., Medical Devices and the Public's Health: The FDA 510(k) Clearance Process at 35 Years (2011), www.nap.edu/catalog/13150/medical-devices-and-the-publics-health-the-fda-510k-clearance.

3 Int'l Consortium of Investigative Journalists, The Implant Files: A Global Investigation into Medical Devices, ICIJ (2018), www.icij.org/investigations/implant-files/.

and postmarket experience with a product might differ. Even so, the FDA's recent shift from pre- to postmarket data gathering and evaluation is both marked and remarkable. New sources of postmarket data are influencing the FDA's upstream decisions about whether, and on what terms, to approve health products.[4]

Of course, postmarket studies that are required by the FDA, or voluntarily undertaken by the sponsor, may still take the form of a randomized clinical trial (RCT). That is not what the FDA and others mean when they refer to real-world evidence (RWE) and real-world data (RWD). The former is essentially any evidence generated outside typical clinical research settings. The latter comes in multiple forms, including "electronic health records (EHRs), claims and billing activities, product and disease registries, patient-generated data including in home-use settings, and data gathered from other sources that can inform on health status, such as mobile devices."[5] Some researchers are trying to replicate RCT findings using RWD,[6] and within at least some corners of the FDA, including recent FDA Commissioners,[7] the appetite for RWE is growing.[8]

One linear account of this change is that Congress and others outside the agency have pushed the FDA toward a "lifecycle" approach to regulation that incorporates RWE. While the process has been mostly gradual, dating back to the HIV/AIDS crisis of the 1980s, the 21st Century Cures Act of 2016 marked a tipping point. The landmark legislation directed the FDA to consider nontraditional study designs and data analysis to streamline drug reviews;[9] apply the "least burdensome means" of approving devices, for instance, by factoring in the likelihood of RWD clarifying safety and effectiveness;[10] remove certain medical software from medical devices subject to FDA oversight;[11] establish an expedited regulatory pathway for "breakthrough" devices;[12] and develop guidance to incorporate RWE and patient experience data into its decision making for drugs and devices alike.[13]

4 Joshua D. Wallach et al., Postmarket Studies Required by the US Food and Drug Administration for New Drugs and Biologics Approved Between 2009 and 2012: Cross Sectional Analysis, BMJ 361, 361 (2018); Herder, supra note 1.

5 Rachel E. Sherman et al., Real-World Evidence – What Is It and What Can It Tell Us?, 375 N. Engl. J. Med. 2293–7 (2016).

6 Elisabetta Patorno et al., Using Real-World Data to Predict Findings of an Ongoing Phase IV Cardiovascular Outcome Trial – Cardiovascular Safety of Linagliptin vs. Glimepiride, Diabetes Care (forthcoming), early access available at https://care.diabetesjournals.org/content/early/2019/06/19/dc19-0069. Cf. Victoria L. Bartlett et al., Feasibility of Using Real-World Data to Replicate Clinical Trial Evidence, 2 JAMA Network Open e1912869 (2019).

7 Robert M. Califf, Expedited and Facilitated Drug Evaluations and Evidence of Benefit and Risk: The Cup is Half-Full, 15 Clin. Trials 235–9 (2018).

8 Herder, supra note 1; Gregory Pappas et al., Determining Value of Coordinated Registry Networks (CRNs): a Case of Transcatheter Valve Therapies, 1 BMJ Surg. Interv. Health Tech. 1, 1 (2019).

9 Jerry Avorn & Aaron S. Kesselheim, The 21st Century Cures Act – Will It Take Us Back in Time?, 372 N. Engl. J. Med. 2473–5 (2015).

10 21st Century Cures Act, Pub. L. No. 114–255, 130 Stat. 1033 (2016) § 3058 [hereinafter "Cures Act"].

11 Id. § 3060.

12 Id. § 3051.

13 Center for Devices and Radiological Health, Use of Real-World Evidence to Support Regulatory Decision-Making for Medical Devices, US Food & Drug Admin. (2019), www.fda.gov/

Another reading of this shift toward lifecycle regulation and RWE suggests that the FDA itself has shaped this regulatory arc. For example, the FDA established the accelerated approval process for drugs and the breakthrough program for devices years before Congressional direction – perhaps to safeguard the agency's central role in pharmaceutical governance.[14]

Whatever the motivations, the shift toward lifecycle regulation and RWE remains a work in progress. Postmarket studies regularly take years to complete[15] and seldom improve the evidence already gathered.[16] The FDA rarely threatens to impose fines or withdraw authorization when postmarket studies are delayed or the evidence does not confirm efficacy.[17] Moreover, the FDA's legal authorities and resources to enforce postmarketing requirements are inadequate and the continuing dominance of the FDA's reviewing divisions over its postmarket monitoring divisions compromises the agency's ability to revisit initial decisions.[18] Meanwhile, numerous studies show – notwithstanding agency claims to the contrary – that the FDA has been applying a lower regulatory bar for approval of drugs, and the vast majority of medical devices escape formal scrutiny of safety and efficacy.[19]

In sum, the FDA's capacity to spur sponsors to generate reliable information about their products[20] and to adjust regulatory decisions as the evidence evolves are each in serious question. It is time to consider new mechanisms to counter these shortfalls. The remainder of Section 10.2 details why medical devices, especially digital health products, offer an opportunity for the FDA to pursue this very sort of regulatory experimentation.

10.2.2 *Signs of Regulatory Experimentation in Digital Health and Beyond*

The FDA's framework for regulating devices has not changed much since the 1976 Medical Device Amendments, despite radical technological advances.[21] Although

regulatory-information/search-fda-guidance-documents/use-real-world-evidence-support-regulatory-decision-making-medical-devices.

14 Herder, supra note 1.

15 Wallach et al., supra note 4; Steven Woloshin et al., The Fate of FDA Postapproval Studies, 377 N. Engl. J. Med. 1114–17 (2017); Huseyin Naci et al., Characteristics of Preapproval and Postapproval Studies for Drugs Granted Accelerated Approval by the US Food and Drug Administration, 318 JAMA 626–36 (2017).

16 Bishal Gyawali et al., Assessment of the Clinical Benefit of Cancer Drugs Receiving Accelerated Approval, 179 JAMA Intern. Med. 906–13 (2019).

17 Herder, supra note 1.

18 Id.

19 Benjamin N. Rome, FDA Premarket Approval Supplements and Medical Device Safety and Effectiveness (2016) (PhD dissertation, Harvard University), https://dash.harvard.edu/handle/1/40620251; Nathan Cortez, Digital Health and Regulatory Experimentation at the FDA 23 Yale J. Health Pol'y, L. & Ethics 6(2019); Medicine, supra note 3.

20 Amy Kapczynski, Dangerous Times: The FDA's Role in Information Production, Past and Future, 102 Minn. L. Rev. 2357 (2018).

21 Nathan Cortez, Digital Health and Regulatory Experimentation at the FDA, 18 Yale J. Health Pol'y, L. & Ethics 6, 21 (2019).

a consensus now favors reform,[22] Congress has done little apart from calling for task force recommendations for how to regulate health IT products,[23] and trying to clarify which products fall within FDA jurisdiction.[24]

In the absence of reform, the FDA itself has begun to experiment with new approaches. The agency's 2017 Digital Health Innovation Action Plan[25] articulates three key departures from the FDA's longstanding framework for devices: 1) shifting evidence gathering and evaluation from the premarket to the postmarket phase; 2) scrutinizing firms rather than products, using a new "Software Pre-Certification Program" to evaluate companies offering products; and 3) outsourcing market certification to independent, third-party reviewers, moving away from centralized agency review. While the first departure mirrors the agency's lifecycle approach to drug regulation, the other two departures are unique, as centralized, product-specific reviews have been the lodestar of FDA regulation for roughly a century.[26,27]

Although the details of these new approaches are still in flux, they revolve around a few core ideas. First, shifting evidence gathering to the postmarket setting effectively grants sponsors a kind of conditional or phased authorization, with the expectation that postmarket evidence might confirm the device's safety and efficacy.[28] The FDA has assigned the task of gathering such evidence to NEST, the National Evaluation System for health Technology,[29] a public-private initiative led by the FDA's Center for Devices and Radiological Health (CDRH).[30] NEST is charged with collecting RWE from multiple sources, including electronic health records, insurance claims, pharmacy records, device registries, and patient-generated data (PGD).[31] As of 2019, the NEST network includes over 195 hospitals, 3,942 outpatient clinics, and fifteen coordinated registry networks that

22 Id. at 11–13; Nathan Cortez, The Mobile Health Revolution?, 47 U.C. Davis L. Rev. 1173 (2014).

23 Pub. L. No. 112–144 § 618, 112th Cong. 2012, 126 Stat. 993, 1063.

24 Cures Act, supra note 10, § 3060.

25 US Food & Drug Admin., Digital Health Innovation Action Plan (June 2017), www.fda.gov/media/106331/download; Scott Gottlieb, Comm'r of Food and Drugs, Fostering Medical Innovation: A Plan for Digital Health Devices (June 15, 2017), www.fda.gov/NewsEvents/Newsroom/FDAVoices/ucm612019.htm; Scott Gottlieb, Comm'r of Food and Drugs, FDA Announces New Steps to Empower Consumers and Advance Digital Healthcare (July 27, 2017), www.fda.gov/NewsEvents/Newsroom/FDAVoices/ucm612014.htm.

26 Daniel Carpenter, Reputation and Power: Organizational Image and Pharmaceutical Regulation at the FDA 544–84 (2010).

27 Jeffrey Shuren et al., FDA Regulation of Mobile Medical Apps, JAMA E1 (July 2, 2018); US Food & Drug Admin., Developing a Software Precertification Program: A Working Model v0.1 (Apr. 2018), www.fda.gov/downloads/MedicalDevices/DigitalHealth/DigitalHealthPreCertProgram/ucm605685.pdf.

28 US Food & Drug Admin., Challenge Questions, www.fda.gov/downloads/MedicalDevices/DigitalHealth/DigitalHealthPreCertProgram/ucm605686.pdf.

29 US Food & Drug Admin., Developing a Software Precertification Program: A Working Model v1.0 (Apr. 2018), www.fda.gov/downloads/MedicalDevices/DigitalHealth/DigitalHealthPreCertProgram/ucm605685.pdf.

30 See Medical Device Innovation Consortium, About Us, https://mdic.org/about/mission-purpose/.

31 Id.

curate and analyze data.[32] NEST will organize data "into several standardized common data models (including domains such as demographics, diagnoses, procedures, and laboratory tests)."[33] Importantly, while NEST was originally proposed as a way to conduct postmarket surveillance to identify safety issues early,[34] it has broadened its focus to collecting data throughout the entire product lifecycle, using it not only for postmarket surveillance, but also for premarket review.[35] For example, the FDA said such evidence could be used to support a sponsor's petition for device reclassification.[36] The data could also be used, ideally, to inform insurance coverage and reimbursement decisions, clinical practice, and patient adoption.[37]

In 2018 and 2019, NEST solicited proposals for test cases to evaluate how well such data can be used to answer specific questions.[38] The latest round includes, for example, a study using insurance claims data to evaluate whether to expand the label for cardiac devices in children with congenital heart disease, and a trial using electronic health records and patient data to evaluate how well the Apple Watch ECG can detect irregular heart rhythms, to inform premarket submissions and postmarket surveillance.[39] The twenty approved test cases span a range of therapeutic devices (oncology, cardiology, vascular, orthopedic, etc.), a range of risk profiles (from low-risk 510(k) devices to higher-risk PMA devices), a range of data (retrospective and prospective), and a range of proposed uses (premarket, postmarket, and coverage decisions).[40] The test cases will also allow NEST to address concerns over the validity of studies using RWE, with expert committees focusing on the quality of the source data and designing appropriate methodologies for data analysis.[41]

32 Rachael L. Fleurence & Jeffrey Shuren, Advances in the Use of Real-World Evidence for Medical Devices: An Update from the National Evaluation System for Health Technology, 106 Clin. Pharmacology & Therapeutics 30–33 (2019).

33 Id.

34 Jeffrey Shuren & Robert M. Califf, Need for a National Evaluation System for Health Technology, 316 JAMA 1153 (2016).

35 Center for Devices and Radiological Health (CDRH), US Food and Drug Administration (FDA), National Evaluation System for Health Technology (NEST), www.fda.gov/about-fda/cdrh-reports/national-evaluation-system-health-technology-nest.

36 US Food & Drug Admin., Guidance for Industry and Food and Drug Administration Staff: Use of Real-World Evidence to Support Regulatory Decision-Making for Medical Devices (Aug. 31, 2017), www.fda.gov/regulatory-information/search-fda-guidance-documents/use-real-world-evidence-support-regulatory-decision-making-medical-devices.

37 Fleurence & Shuren, supra note 32.

38 Id.

39 NEST Coordinating Center, Press Release: NESTcc Announces 12 New Real-World Evidence Test-Cases (June 4, 2019), www.businesswire.com/news/home/20190604006034/en/National-Evaluation-System-health-Technology-Coordinating-Center.

40 Id.; Fleurence & Shuren, supra note 32.

41 Fleurence & Shuren, supra note 32; Recommendations for a National Medical Device Evaluation System: A Report from the Medical Device Registry Task Force & the Medical Devices Epidemiology Network (2015), at https://goo.gl/hSQPhn.

While the FDA's shift toward lifecycle regulation has been the subject of growing critique,[42] NEST can add significant scientific rigor to the process of collecting and analyzing RWE to the benefit of "regulatory, clinical, and coverage decision making" not to mention "the health and the quality of life of patients."[43] However, there are also reasons to be skeptical that this will occur, underscoring the need for even more radical experimentation, which we describe in Section 10.3.

10.3 A DESI FOR DEVICES?

Though the FDA has experimented with medical device regulation in recent years, mounting evidence that the move toward lifecycle regulation and RWE carries serious tradeoffs suggests more radical changes may be required. We draw inspiration from a historical program, designed and implemented by the FDA in the wake of 1962 legislative reforms, to envision even more modern advances to medical device regulation. We first describe the DESI program, then argue that existing legal authorities can and should be repurposed to support a DESI 2.0 for devices.

10.3.1 *The "Drug Efficacy Study Implementation" Experiment*

Although the 1962 Kefauver-Harris Amendments are widely considered to be foundational, the requirement that drug manufacturers show "substantial evidence" of effectiveness were preconfigured by agency practice. Safety, the sole criterion for market entry from 1938 to 1962, was understood by the FDA to encompass clinical utility or effectiveness beginning in the early 1950s.[44] Administrative innovation prestaged congressional legislation.

The 1962 amendments likely emboldened the FDA, not only in terms of justifying heightened expectations for evidence of efficacy, but also in terms of using its administrative discretion to fashion solutions to problems perceived in the marketplace. Central among them was the question of what to do about the thousands of "old drugs" that had entered the market between 1938 and 1962, which were not formally evaluated for effectiveness prior to Kefauver-Harris. Congress did not explicitly require the FDA to review these old drugs,[45] but the agency read multiple sections of the legislation as all the mandate they needed.[46] Within a few years "DESI" was born.

42 Herder, supra note 1.

43 Fleurence & Shuren, supra note 32.

44 Carpenter, supra note 26.

45 Former FDA chief counsel Peter Barton Hutt and his co-authors acknowledge, "There actually was no direct requirement that FDA review all pre-1962 NDAs for effectiveness." Peter Barton Hutt et al., Food and Drug Law: Cases and Materials 776 (4th ed. 2014). However, they write that because Section 107 deemed such NDAs approved in perpetuity, "FDA had no choice but to begin a process of reviewing each pre-1962 NDA to determine whether it was shown to be an effective as well as a safe drug." Id. at 776.

46 29 Fed. Reg. 2790 (Feb. 28, 1964).

DESI would come to evaluate some 3,400 old drugs for over 16,000 therapeutic indications over twenty-plus years.[47] To accomplish that feat, the agency understood that it needed a remarkable new structure. In 1966, under the leadership of Commissioner James Goddard, the FDA contracted the work to the National Academy of Sciences (NAS) and National Research Council (NRC).[48] The FDA not only lacked sufficient personnel for the task, but its personnel lacked the clout that NAS/NRC experts could command if and when difficult decisions had to be made to pull products from the market. The FDA created a centralized Policy Advisory Committee to define DESI's procedures, which in turn spawned thirty review panels assigned to the therapeutic categories of the day. Each panel was comprised of a chair and approximately six NAS/NRC experts. They worked in confidence, delivering recommendations to the FDA about whether a given drug was "effective," "probably effective," "possibly effective," or "ineffective." Even though the panels did not conduct new research, each panel reviewed the medical literature for roughly 150 drugs, requiring 10,000 hours of expert scientific labor.[49]

DESI drew lawsuits from industry as the FDA followed through on panel recommendations, announcing hundreds of drug withdrawals via the Federal Register.[50] The litigation was less about the involvement of outside NAS/NRC experts, and more to do with the summary-type procedures that the FDA had adopted in the name of efficiency. Notwithstanding firms' legal challenges, the litigation ultimately failed. The Supreme Court largely validated the agency's approach in the 1973 "*Hynson* quartet" of cases involving challenges to NDA withdrawals for preamendment drugs.[51] Even without explicit statutory authorization, in *Hynson* the Supreme Court refers to DESI as a "statutory mandate,"[52] and a Senate Report from 1972 refers to DESI as being "required by the Drug Amendments of 1962."[53] Further, the Supreme Court upheld the FDA's power to use summary procedures, ruling that firms' expectations of a full administrative hearing to decide the fate of a drug was conditional upon having first produced "substantial evidence" of effectiveness. Where such evidence is lacking, the Court held, a full hearing need not follow.

The implications of DESI are manifold. But the move to engage outside actors in the decision-making process is underexamined. If the FDA's inability to encourage high-quality evidence production are ultimately reflective of a kind of

47 Carpenter, supra note 26.

48 Daniel Carpenter et al., The Drug Efficacy Study and Its Manifold Legacies, in FDA in the Twenty-First Century: The Challenges of Regulating Drugs and New Technologies 310 (Holly Fernandez Lynch & I. Glenn Cohen eds., 2015).

49 Id. at 312.

50 Carpenter, supra note 26.

51 Weinberger v. Hynson, Westcott & Dunning, 412 U.S. 609 (1973); Weinberger v. Bentex Pharmaceuticals, Inc., 412 U.S. 645 (1973); Ciba Corp. v. Weinberger, 412 U.S. 640 (1973); USV Pharmaceutical Corp. v. Weinberger, 412 U.S. 455 (1973).

52 Hynson, 412 U.S. at 615.

53 S. Rep. No. 92–924 at p. 2; Bentex, 412 U.S. at 650.

incumbency – both in terms of who is involved in producing and how it is appraised[54] – then regulation may take as its inspiration DESI's disruptive move to bring outside actors into the regulatory fold. In the realm of medical devices, recent FDA initiatives such as NEST show some willingness to do this.

But the success of a DESI 2.0 for devices may depend on coupling 1) third-party evidence generation with 2) third-party reviews of that evidence – two functions which neither the original DESI nor more recent initiatives like NEST have sought to combine. Third-party evidence generation and reviews might significantly strengthen the use of "real-world" signals beyond what the FDA and/or industry is either capable or willing to do, making more meaningful recent odes to total lifecycle regulation and postmarket surveillance.

10.3.2 *Repurposing Existing Legal Authorities to Support a "DESI 2.0"*

Allowing third parties to both generate evidence and conduct rigorous product reviews is a less radical idea than we might think. Data are now available through many different sources, including massive device registries.[55] And the sheer volume of devices introduced into the market, particularly in digital health, augers in favor of outsourcing some portion of review of safety and efficacy. It is the joining of these two functions and empowering third parties to fulfill them that is crucial.

A threshold question is whether a DESI 2.0 would be legally permissible. Just as the Kefauver-Harris Amendments were interpreted by the FDA as authorizing the original DESI, the current statute is flexible enough to support both device reviews and evidence generation by third parties. First, the statute very broadly requires the FDA to "consider, in consultation with the applicant, the least burdensome appropriate means of evaluating device effectiveness that would have a reasonable likelihood of resulting in approval," unless "contrary to public health."[56] Moreover, as with DESI, the statute entrusted initial review and classification of pre-1976 devices to expert panels, and envisioned that the FDA could turn to expert panels to review classification petitions.[57] In both cases, panel decisions are recommendations published and reviewed by the FDA.[58] Likewise, the statute authorizes the FDA to withdraw or suspend PMA approvals, particularly when "new information" is presented.[59] FDA rules make clear that the agency "may seek advice on scientific matters from any appropriate FDA advisory committee" and "may use information other than that submitted by the applicant" in deciding whether to withdraw approval of a PMA.[60]

54 Herder, supra note 1.
55 Pappas et al., supra note 8.
56 21 U.S.C. § 360c(a)(3)(D), 360e.
57 Id. § 360c(b), (c), (f).
58 Id.
59 Id. § 360e(e).
60 21 C.F.R. § 814.46(b)(1)–(2).

Section 523 of the FDCA provides more specific authority for the kind of dual-function third-party mechanism we imagine. In 1997 Congress amended the statute to codify a five-year pilot program to allow the FDA to accredit third parties to review 510(k)s and make nonbinding recommendations to the agency.[61] The FDA initiated the pilot in 1996, before it received statutory authorization.[62] The idea was to provide manufacturers of certain devices "an alternative 510(k) review process that could yield more rapid marketing clearance decisions" and preserve FDA review for higher-risk devices.[63] The FDA published accreditation criteria in 1998,[64] and the pilot has been renewed by Congress every five years since 2002.[65] Currently, only eight entities are accredited for the renamed "3P Review Program."[66] Although 510(k) user fees are waived and FDA clearance is 29 percent faster when recommended by an accredited third party, the program remains underutilized.[67]

Despite possessing sufficient legal authority to create a DESI 2.0, the FDA might seek more clear statutory authorization from Congress in order to act upon third-party evidence and recommendations. Although the FDA's authority to adopt summary-type procedures for devices would be supported by the *Hynson* quartet of Supreme Court decisions, more aggressive reliance on third-party reviews might need clearer statutory support. To wit, after the FDA announced its Digital Health Action Plan and software precertification program, several Senators sent a letter to the FDA questioning the agency's statutory authority to do so.[68] Indeed, the FDA's announcement of the Action Plan itself acknowledged that it may lack statutory authority for third-party precertification.[69] However, there is a long history of the FDA relying on panels and advisory committees to make nonbinding

61 Food and Drug Administration Modernization Act (FDAMA), Pub. L. No. 105–115 § 210, 111 Stat. 2342 (Nov. 21, 1997) (creating new FDCA § 523; 21 U.S.C. § 360m).

62 US Food & Drug Admin., Implementation of Third Party Programs Under the FDA Modernization Act of 1997, Final Guidance for Staff, Industry, and Third Parties (Feb. 2001), www.fda.gov/regulatory-information/search-fda-guidance-documents/implementation-third-party-programs-under-fda-modernization-act-1997-final-guidance-staff-industry.

63 Id.

64 63 Fed. Reg. 28,388 (May 22, 1998).

65 Medical Device User Fee and Modernization Act of 2002 (MDUFMA) § 202, Pub. L. No. 107–250, 116 Stat. 1609; FDAAA (2007); FDASIA § 611 (2012); FDA Reauthorization Act of 2017, Pub. L. No. 115–52 § 206.

66 US Food & Drug Admin., Current List of Accredited Persons for 510(k) Review under the FDA Modernization Act of 1997, www.accessdata.fda.gov/scripts/cdrh/cfdocs/cfThirdParty/Accredit.cfm (database updated as of Feb. 24, 2020); US Food & Drug Admin., Draft Guidance: 510(k) Third Party Review Program (Sept. 14, 2018), www.fda.gov/media/85284/download.

67 Hutt, Merrill, & Grossman, supra note 45.

68 Letter from Sen. Elizabeth Warren, Sen. Patty Murray, & Sen. Tina Smith to Scott Gottlieb, FDA Commissioner, and Jeffrey Shuren, Director of the FDA Center for Devices and Radiological Health of Oct. 10, 2018 at 3–4.

69 Scott Gottlieb, Commissioner of Food and Drugs, Fostering Medical Innovation: A Plan for Digital Health Devices (June 15, 2017), www.fda.gov/NewsEvents/Newsroom/FDAVoices/ucm612019.htm; Scott Gottlieb, Commissioner of Food and Drugs, FDA Announces New Steps to Empower Consumers and Advance Digital Healthcare (July 27, 2017), www.fda.gov/NewsEvents/Newsroom/FDAVoices/ucm612014.htm.

recommendations regarding product approvals, classifications, and withdrawals. A similar system, whereby NEST (or some other third party) would be empowered not only to analyze newly collected data but also make recommendations to the agency about appropriate regulatory actions in light of that evidence – ranging from label changes to product withdrawal – would seem to be within FDA authority. Advisories and recommendations are, by their very nature, nonbinding, though their publication would force the FDA to offer compelling justifications for making decisions contrary to the recommendations.

Thus, the stars seem well aligned for a DESI 2.0 for devices. Agency practice presages it. Intense cooperation with third parties to develop new sources of RWE and deploy them for regulatory decisions presages it. The statutory authority remains broad and arcs in that direction. And, perhaps most importantly, the need is clear. The FDA itself remains unable to give adequate attention to the sheer volume and variety of new devices. If vogue ideas like RWE, RWD, and total product lifecycles are to gain real traction, formalizing and inviting third-party participation seems crucial.

10.4 POTENTIAL OBSTACLES AND FUTURE RESEARCH

While the law may not be an immediate obstacle to creating a DESI 2.0, industry, institutional, and scientific obstacles remain. For starters, medical device manufacturers are likely to challenge any such initiative in Court. In *Hynson*, industry contested the agency's authority to adopt summary procedures, which the Supreme Court upheld. In recent years, lower courts have, at times, endorsed exceedingly low standards for what constitutes "substantial evidence."[70] If a mere scintilla of evidence was sufficient to trigger a formal evidentiary hearing before any decision to withdraw a device from the market, any efficiencies to be gained from third-party reviews would be seriously undermined.

A second set of obstacles is more institutional in nature. On one hand, the external academic researchers affiliated with NEST have incredible credentials, but it is not obvious that they command the level of deference from the FDA that the NAS/NRC once did. Elite universities have established relationships with the FDA;[71] how critically these academic units would approach the task of generating robust new evidence and, when warranted, reversing prior agency decisions, is not known. In this regard, potential conflicts of interest (especially financial conflicts) are a potential concern. The work of FDA advisory committees has been plagued by conflicts, so ensuring that a DESI 2.0 retains a strong independence[72] with respect to each device

70 Amarin Pharma, Inc. v. US Food & Drug Admin., 119 F. Supp. 3d 196 (S.D.N.Y. 2015).

71 Maya Dutta-Linn, Keeping Watch, Harv. Med. School News & Research (2019), https://hms.harvard.edu/news/keeping-watch.

72 For a discussion of the importance of "independence" or "disinterestedness" among decision-makers, see Matthew Herder, Toward a Jurisprudence of Drug Regulation, 42 J. Am. Soc. Law. Med. & Ethics 244, 256 (2014).

evaluated may prove critical to the initiative's success. More generally, nongovernment certification has a spotty track record, from longstanding critiques of Joint Commission accreditation of hospitals for Medicare,[73] to familiar critiques of third-party certification of "meaningful use" for electronic health records (EHRs),[74] to more recent critiques of the Federal Aviation Administration (FAA) allowing Boeing to self-certify its 737 Max aircraft (later recalled after multiple crashes).[75] These examples demonstrate the need for traditional regulatory compliance monitoring and enforcement as a backstop to any third-party recommendations.[76]

Thirdly, there are also scientific obstacles to implementing a DESI 2.0. As noted above, standards for generating RWE from a variety of real-world data are a work in progress. There is serious scientific debate about the strength of different kinds of RWE for different types of health interventions, not to mention when such evidence should motivate regulatory action. Anticipating these debates, the major trade associations like AdvaMed and BIO have commented on the FDA's use of RWE.[77] Committing DESI 2.0 to transparency – in terms of the data it generates, its analyses, and recommendations – can serve not only to enhance trust, but also to refine scientific standards.[78]

DESI was a watershed moment in the history of medical product regulation, using outside review panels to evaluate evidence of clinical efficacy for thousands of products. Although DESI was encouraged by watershed legislation, the Kefauver-Harris Amendments did not clearly authorize it. Today, the FDA is being pushed toward lifecycle regulation and reliance on so-called "real world evidence" to evaluate products. Whether this shift is successful or not depends, we think, on whether the FDA can learn important lessons from the DESI experiment with pharmaceuticals in the 1960s–80s. In particular, third parties may be useful not only in generating RWE on specific products but also evaluating such evidence to support the FDA's regulatory decision making.

73 See, e.g., Timothy S. Jost, Medicare and the Joint Commission on Accreditation of Healthcare Organizations: A Healthy Relationship?, 57 L. & Contemp. Probs. 15, 39–40 (1994).

74 See, e.g., Erin McCann, Many ONC-Certified EHRs Actually Fail to Meet Certification Standards, Healthcare IT News (Sept. 9, 2015).

75 See, e.g., Brian Naylor, Boeing's Not Alone in Companies that Government Agencies Have Let Self-Regulate, NPR, All Things Considered (Apr. 2, 2019).

76 Cortez, supra note 22 at 23; Nathan Cortez, Analog Agency in a Digital World, in FDA in the 21st Century: the Challenges of Regulating Drugs and New Technologies 438 (2015).

77 Biotechnology Innovation Organization (BIO), Incorporating Real-World Evidence Within the Label of an FDA-Approved Drug: Perspectives from BIO Membership, www.advamed.org/wp-content/uploads/2017/03/advamed-principles-regarding-use-real-world-evidence.pdf; Advanced Medical Technology Association (AdvaMed), AdvaMed Principles Regarding the Use of Real-World Evidence ("RWE") in the National Evaluation System for Health Technology ("NEST") and Similar Systems, www.advamed.org/sites/default/files/resource/advamed-principles-regarding-use-real-world-evidence.pdf.

78 Matthew Herder, Denaturalizing Transparency in Drug Regulation, 8 McGill J. L. Health S57–S143 (2015).

11

Digital Home Health During the COVID-19 Pandemic

Challenges to Safety, Liability, and Informed Consent, and the Way to Move Forward

Sara Gerke

11.1 INTRODUCTION

Artificial intelligence (AI) and other digital health products, such as smart pills, are rapidly entering clinical practice.[1] We live in the age of big data, where massive amounts of data are collected and used to develop or update digital health products and are shared with third parties for research or commercial purposes. Moreover, we can already see a shift in health care from hospitals to people's homes, for example through the use of medical apps, Fitbits, and other wearables. This line between clinic and home will likely become more and more blurry in the near future. According to one estimate, the smart home health care market size is projected to grow from $6.1 billion in 2018 to over $30 billion in 2025.[2]

In particular, the COVID-19 pandemic has propelled the adoption of health AI and digital health across multiple applications.[3] For example, the development and use of digital home health products have been expedited to reduce exposure to the coronavirus SARS-CoV-2, such as through remote patient monitoring, and to better control its spread, such as through exposure-notification apps.[4] At the same time, the regulation of medical devices is more flexible during the public health emergency. However, the acceleration of launching new digital home health devices on the US

[1] For more information on the ethics and law of health AI, see, e.g., Sara Gerke et al., Ethical and Legal Challenges of Artificial Intelligence-driven Healthcare 295 (Adam Bohr & Kaveh Memarzadeh eds., 1st ed. 2020); for more information on the ethical and legal issues of smart pills, see, e.g., Sara Gerke et al., Ethical and Legal Issues of Ingestible Electronic Sensors, 2 Nature Electron. 329 (2019).

[2] Global Market Insights, Smart Home Healthcare Market, www.gminsights.com/industry-analysis/smart-home-healthcare-market.

[3] MarketsandMarkets, Artificial Intelligence in Healthcare Market, www.marketsandmarkets.com/Market-Reports/artificial-intelligence-healthcare-market-54679303.html.

[4] Sara Gerke et al., Regulatory, Safety, and Privacy Concerns of Home Monitoring Technologies During COVID-19, 26 Nature Med. 1176 (2020). For more information on exposure-notification apps, see, e.g., I. Glenn Cohen et al., Digital Smartphone Tracking for COVID-19: Public Health and Civil Liberties in Tension, 323 JAMA 2371 (2020); Alessandro Blasimme & Effy Vayena, What's Next for COVID-19 Apps? Governance and Oversight, 370 Science 760 (2020).

market combined with less regulatory oversight also raises some challenges, including post-pandemic questions.

In this chapter, I will first give an overview of the promise of digital home health. I will then discuss the regulation of digital home health before and during COVID-19 in the context of the US Federal Food, Drug, and Cosmetic Act (FDCA). This will be followed by a discussion of three digital home health challenges during the pandemic: 1) safety, 2) liability, and 3) informed consent. In this context, I will also make suggestions on how to move forward.

11.2 THE PROMISE OF DIGITAL HOME HEALTH

The term "digital health" is broadly defined by the US Food and Drug Administration (FDA) and encompasses categories such as telehealth, health information technology, mobile health, AI/machine learning, wearable devices, and precision medicine.[5] Digital health technologies harness software, connectivity, sensor, and computing platforms for health care and associated uses.[6] They are used for several applications, ranging from general wellness to medical devices.[7] The hope is that digital health will revolutionize health care by enabling precision medicine, increasing quality, improving access, and reducing costs and inefficiencies.[8]

I define "digital home health" as digital health that is related to the patient's or consumer's home. The term "home" has a broad scope here. It encompasses patients' or consumers' homes in the narrow sense of the term, such as their apartment, house, and so forth. In addition, it also refers to any other location in which there is no personal contact with and direct supervision by a health care provider. For example, digital home health includes telehealth visits as the conversation between the physician and the patient is virtual. It also refers to general wellness apps, such as an app for weight management,[9] and mobile medical apps, such as an app that detects heart function irregularities,[10] used by consumers or patients. Another example is COVID-19 exposure-notification apps that consumers use – without physicians' supervision – to receive notifications in cases where they may have been exposed to SARS-CoV-2. The term also covers remote patient monitoring – regardless of whether the monitoring takes place in the patient's

[5] US Food & Drug Admin., What is Digital Health?, www.fda.gov/medical-devices/digital-health-center-excellence/what-digital-health.

[6] Id.

[7] Id.

[8] Id.

[9] US Food & Drug Admin., General Wellness: Policy for Low Risk Devices – Guidance for Industry and Food and Drug Administration Staff (2019), at 3, www.fda.gov/media/90652/download.

[10] US Food & Drug Admin., Policy for Device Software Functions and Mobile Medical Applications – Guidance for Industry and Food and Drug Administration Staff (2019), at 5, www.fda.gov/media/80958/download.

apartment or house or even in a hospital – since the data are collected remotely and transferred digitally, and thus there is no personal contact with and direct supervision by a health care provider.[11]

Digital home health holds great promise in enabling patients to self-manage their health issues, keeping them out of the hospital as long as possible, and easing the already overburdened health care system. More than sixty million Americans (who are over sixty-five or younger people with disabilities or certain conditions) are already receiving insurance coverage by Medicare, and it is expected that this number will further increase to more than eighty million beneficiaries in 2030.[12] As the American population is aging, digital home health can serve as a useful tool to help patients to stay independent as long as possible.[13] For example, Best Buy Health offers assisted living technology, including remote patient monitoring devices placed in people's home.[14] A recent study predicts that the global remote patient monitoring market will increase from $23.2 billion in 2020 to $117.1 billion by 2025.[15] Remote monitoring devices can collect a variety of health data, including body temperature, pulse rate, blood pressure, respiration rate, and weight. Digital home health can be used for various applications, such as fall prevention and detection, memory aids, and nutrition, diet, or health status monitoring.[16] For example, researchers at the Massachusetts Institute of Technology developed a radio-frequency-based system, BodyCompass, that provides sleep posture monitoring overnight in a person's home.[17] This system may be applied to track Parkinson's disease progression, reduce apnea events, or avoid bedsores after surgery. In the era of big data, people are also increasingly using apps, fitness trackers, and other wearables to manage their health.

In particular, the COVID-19 pandemic has only highlighted the potential of digital home health. Over the last one and a half years, the development and launching of digital home health products on the US market have been accelerated to ease overcrowding in the hospitals and reduce personal contacts between patients

[11] The umbrella term for remote patient monitoring is "home monitoring"; see Gerke et al., supra note 4, at 1176. The term "digital home health" is broader than home monitoring; it is an umbrella term that also encompasses "home monitoring."

[12] Centers for Medicare & Medicaid Services, CMS Fast Facts, www.cms.gov/Research-Statistics-Data-and-Systems/Statistics-Trends-and-Reports/CMS-Fast-Facts/index; Steven Landers et al., The Future of Home Health Care: A Strategic Framework for Optimizing Value, 28 Home Health Care Manag. & Pract. 262 (2016).

[13] Gerke et al., supra note 4, at 1176.

[14] Best Buy Health, Assisted Living Technology, https://healthcare.bestbuy.com/site/bbhealth/products-technology/pcmcat1600181550900.c?id=pcmcat1600181550900.

[15] MarketsandMarkets, Remote Patient Monitoring (RPM) Market, www.marketsandmarkets.com/Market-Reports/remote-patient-monitoring-market-77155492.html.

[16] Global Market Insights, supra note 2.

[17] Shichao Yue et al., BodyCompass: Monitoring Sleep Posture with Wireless Signals, https://people.csail.mit.edu/scyue/projects/bodycompass.

and physicians and the risk for infection with SARS-CoV-2.[18] For example, physicians can use Alivecor's KardiaMobile 6L, an electrocardiogram device, to measure QTc in patients both at home and in the hospital for the duration of COVID-19.[19] Moreover, telehealth rates have skyrocketed. For example, from March through June 2020, more than 34.5 million telehealth services were delivered to Medicaid and Children's Health Insurance Program's beneficiaries, suggesting a 2,632 percent growth compared to the same time in 2019.[20]

11.3 REGULATION OF DIGITAL HOME HEALTH

11.3.1 *Pre-COVID-19*

The FDA regulates digital home health products if they are classified as medical devices under FDCA Section 201(h). This is usually the case when such a product is

> intended for use in the diagnosis of disease or other conditions, or in the cure, mitigation, treatment, or prevention of disease, in man . . . and which does not achieve its primary intended purposes through chemical action within or on the body of man . . . and which is not dependent upon being metabolized for the achievement of its primary intended purposes.[21]

Software plays an essential role in digital home health. There are three different software types associated with medical devices:

1. Software as a Medical Device (SaMD) – that is, standalone software that is a medical device on its own;
2. Software in a Medical Device (SiMD) – that is, software, which is integral to a medical device; and
3. software used in the maintenance or manufacture of a medical device.[22]

In particular, a variety of digital home health medical devices are SaMD. For example, AliveCor's Kardia Band System is SaMD that is intended to store, record, and transmit single-channel electrocardiogram rhythms and detect the presence of normal sinus rhythm and atrial fibrillation.[23] The Kardia Band System consists of

18 See Gerke et al., supra note 4, at 1176.
19 Alivecor, AliveCor to Provide QTc Measurement for Clinicians Treating COVID-19 Patients, www.alivecor.com/press/press_release/alivecor-to-provide-qtc-measurement-for-clinicians-treating-covid-19-patients.
20 Centers for Medicare & Medicaid Services, Services Delivered via Telehealth Among Medicaid & CHIP Beneficiaries During COVID-19, www.medicaid.gov/resources-for-states/downloads/medicaid-chip-beneficiaries-COVID-19-snapshot-data-through-20200630.pdf.
21 Food, Drug, and Cosmetic Act § 201(h), sentence 1 [hereinafter FDCA].
22 US Food & Drug Admin., Software as a Medical Device (SaMD), www.fda.gov/medical-devices/digital-health-center-excellence/software-medical-device-samd.
23 Letter from the FDA to AliveCor (Nov. 16, 2017), www.accessdata.fda.gov/cdrh_docs/pdf17/K171816.pdf.

a watchband with a sensor, the Kardia phone app software installed on the Apple iPhone, and the Kardia watch app software installed on the Apple Watch.[24] Other examples are Apple's Electrocardiogram App[25] and Apple's Irregular Rhythm Notification Feature,[26] both of which are SaMD and intended for use with the Apple Watch.

There are three different classes of medical devices – that is, Class I, Class II, and Class III. While Class I medical devices have the lowest risk, Class III medical devices have the highest risk. Depending on the class, medical devices are subject to general controls (all classes), special controls (Class II), and premarket approval (PMA, Class III) to ensure reasonable assurance of their safety and effectiveness.[27] In particular, there are three main premarket pathways for medical devices:

1. 510(k)/clearance – for Class I or II devices, unless exempt;
2. De Novo Classification Request – for novel medical devices of low/moderate risk; and
3. PMA – for Class III medical devices.[28]

Digital home health medical devices can be found in all premarket pathways. For example, AliveCor's Kardia Band System is a Class II medical device that received FDA clearance via the 510(k) pathway in November 2017 as the first device add-on for the Apple Watch.[29] Apple's Electrocardiogram App and Irregular Rhythm Notification Feature are also Class II medical devices, and both received FDA marketing authorization via the De Novo pathway in September 2018.[30]

Some digital home health products are not classified as medical devices under the FDCA and hence are not subject to FDA regulation. The 21st Century Cures Act, signed into law in December 2016, introduced FDCA Section 520(o), which excludes certain medical and clinical decision support software from the medical device definition.[31] In the context of digital home health products, Section 520(o)(1)(B) is relevant:

> The term device, as defined in section 201(h), shall not include a software function that is intended ... for maintaining or encouraging a healthy lifestyle and is

24 Id.

25 Letter from the FDA to Apple (Sept. 11, 2018), www.accessdata.fda.gov/cdrh_docs/pdf18/DEN180044.pdf.

26 Letter from the FDA to Apple (Sept. 11, 2018), www.accessdata.fda.gov/cdrh_docs/pdf18/DEN180042.pdf.

27 FDCA § 513(a)(1).

28 For more information, see, e.g., US Food & Drug Admin., How to Study and Market Your Device, www.fda.gov/medical-devices/device-advice-comprehensive-regulatory-assistance/how-study-and-market-your-device.

29 Letter from the FDA to AliveCor, supra note 23.

30 Letters from the FDA to Apple, supra notes 25 & 26. This new competition likely also led to AliveCor's decision in the summer of 2019 to stop selling the Kardia Band System. However, AliveCor intends to continue supporting the system for people who have already bought it. See Dave Muoio, AliveCor Ends Sales of KardiaBand, Its ECG Accessory for Apple Watches, Mobile Health News (Aug. 19, 2019), www.mobihealthnews.com/about.

31 Pub. L. 114–255, § 3060(a) (2016).

unrelated to the diagnosis, cure, mitigation, prevention, or treatment of a disease or condition.

This exception covers digital home health products with a general wellness intended use that maintains or encourages a "general state of health or a healthy activity."[32] For example, apps used by consumers for weight management, relaxation or stress management, physical fitness, self-esteem, sexual function, mental acuity, or sleep management are not considered medical devices, as long as they are not related to "the diagnosis, cure, mitigation, prevention, or treatment of a disease or condition."[33] The FDA also does not regard most software apps and systems for public health surveillance and communication as medical devices, such as COVID-19 exposure-notification apps.[34] Moreover, software for videoconferencing intended for use in telehealth is also not a medical device under the FDCA and thus is not subject to FDA regulation.[35]

For low-risk software functions that are medical devices or may meet the medical device definition, the FDA also intends to practice enforcement discretion and thus does not intend to enforce compliance with the requirements under the FDCA.[36] An example is software functions that guide users through questionnaires of symptoms and signs to recommend the most appropriate health care facility for their needs.[37]

11.3.2 *During COVID-19*

During the COVID-19 pandemic, there are two other pathways for digital home health medical devices available: 1) Emergency Use Authorizations (EUAs) and 2) COVID-19 guidance documents.

11.3.2.1 EUAs

The FDA can issue EUAs for medical devices during COVID-19. In February 2020, the then Secretary of Health and Human Services Alex Azar determined a public health emergency[38] and, based on this determination, has issued the following three EUA Declarations related to medical devices:

[32] US Food & Drug Admin., supra note 9; US Food & Drug Admin., Changes to Existing Medical Software Policies Resulting from Section 3060 of The 21st Century Cures Act – Guidance for Industry and Food and Drug Administration Staff (2019), at 4–5, www.fda.gov/media/109622/download.

[33] US Food & Drug Admin., 21st Century Cures Act – Guidance, supra note 32, at 5.

[34] US Food & Drug Admin., Digital Health Policies and Public Health Solutions for COVID-19, www.fda.gov/medical-devices/coronavirus-covid-19-and-medical-devices/digital-health-policies-and-public-health-solutions-covid-19; Gerke et al., supra note 4, at 1177.

[35] US Food & Drug Admin., supra note 34; See also US Food & Drug Admin., supra note 10, at 19.

[36] US Food & Drug Admin., supra note 10, at 2, 9, 12.

[37] Id. at 23.

[38] Determination of Public Health Emergency, 85 Fed. Reg. 7316, www.federalregister.gov/documents/2020/02/07/2020-02496/determination-of-public-health-emergency.

1. "in vitro diagnostics for detection and/or diagnosis of the novel coronavirus";[39]
2. "personal respiratory protective devices";[40] and
3. "medical devices, including alternative products used as medical devices."[41]

Due to the broad scope of the latter EUA Declaration, the FDA can issue EUAs under FDCA Section 564 for unapproved or uncleared digital home health medical devices for commercial distribution or for unapproved or uncleared uses of approved or cleared digital home health medical devices.[42] This is the case if the following four criteria are fulfilled:

1. serious or life-threatening condition or disease;
2. evidence of effectiveness;
3. benefit/risk analysis; and
4. no alternatives.[43]

The first criterion is met during the COVID-19 pandemic – SARS-CoV-2 can cause COVID-19, a serious or life-threatening disease. The second criterion requires a "may be effective" standard as evidence, and thus a lower level than an "effectiveness" standard.[44] More precisely, it must be "reasonable to believe" that the digital home health medical device "may be effective" to treat, diagnose, or prevent COVID-19.[45] The third criterion is given if it is "reasonable to believe" that the potential and known benefits of the digital home health medical device outweigh its known and potential risks, taking into account the material threat posed by SARS-CoV-2.[46] For both the second and third criteria, the assessment must be "based on the totality of scientific evidence available," including – if available – data from well-controlled and adequate clinical trials.[47] Lastly, the fourth criterion is fulfilled when there is "no adequate, approved, and available alternative" to the digital home health medical device for treating, diagnosing, or preventing COVID-19.[48] An

39 Id.

40 Emergency Use Declaration, 85 Fed. Reg. 13907, www.federalregister.gov/documents/2020/03/10/2020-04823/emergency-use-declaration.

41 Emergency Use Authorization Declaration, 85 Fed. Reg. 17335, www.federalregister.gov/documents/2020/03/27/2020-06541/emergency-use-authorization-declaration; see also FDCA § 564(b); Gerke et al., supra note 4, at 1177.

42 See FDCA § 564(a)(2).

43 FDCA § 564(c); see also US Food & Drug Admin., Emergency Use Authorization of Medical Products and Related Authorities, Guidance for Industry and Other Stakeholders (2020), at 7–8, www.fda.gov/media/97321/download.

44 US Food & Drug Admin., supra note 43, at 8.

45 FDCA § 564(c)(2)(A).

46 FDCA § 564(c)(2)(B).

47 FDCA § 564(c)(2).

48 FDCA § 564(c)(3).

approved alternative may be considered "unavailable" if there are insufficient supplies to fully encounter the emergency need and may be considered "inadequate" if SARS-CoV-2 is or may be resistant to it.[49]

With the issuance of an EUA, the FDA may also, for example, waive the requirements concerning current good manufacturing practice.[50] An EUA can be revised or revoked under specific conditions, such as when the issuance criteria are no longer met.[51] In general, an EUA also becomes ineffective with the termination of the Secretary of Health and Human Services' corresponding EUA Declaration.[52]

The FDA has already issued EUAs for digital home health medical devices, namely for certain wearable or remote patient monitoring devices to help reduce personal contacts between patients and health care providers and thus exposure to COVID-19.[53] For example, in April 2020, the FDA issued an EUA for VitalConnect's VitalPatch Biosensor.[54] This wireless remote monitoring system is intended to be used by health care professionals to detect QT interval changes of an electrocardiogram in adult COVID-19 patients who are not in the ICU but are undergoing treatment with drugs that may cause arrhythmias.[55] The device is used in the hospital setting to remotely monitor such patients to decrease health care professionals' exposure to SARS-CoV-2.[56] VitalPatch Biosensor is a 510(k)-cleared device for continuous collection of physiological data in health care settings and in the patients' homes.[57] However, its clearance does not include the use for automated arrhythmia detection of an electrocardiogram's QT interval.[58] Thus, the FDA authorized here an emergency use of a cleared device for an uncleared use.

11.3.2.2 COVID-19 Guidance Documents

The FDA has released numerous enforcement discretion guidance documents related to digital home health medical devices that apply during the COVID-19 pandemic.[59] These guidance documents represent the agency's current thinking

49 US Food & Drug Admin., supra note 43, at 8.
50 FDCA § 564(e)(3).
51 FDCA § 564(f)–(g).
52 FDCA § 564(f), (b)(2).
53 US Food & Drug Admin., Remote or Wearable Patient Monitoring Devices EUAs, www.fda.gov/medical-devices/coronavirus-disease-2019-covid-19-emergency-use-authorizations-medical-devices/remote-or-wearable-patient-monitoring-devices-euas.
54 Letter from the FDA to VitalConnect (Apr. 26, 2020), at 1, www.fda.gov/media/137397/download.
55 Id.
56 Id.
57 Id.
58 Id.
59 For all guidance documents related to medical devices, including digital home health medical devices, see US Food & Drug Admin., Coronavirus (COVID-19) and Medical Devices, www.fda.gov/medical-devices/emergency-situations-medical-devices/coronavirus-covid-19-and-medical-devices#guidance.

and should be seen as nonbinding recommendations, unless particular statutory or regulatory requirements are cited.[60]

For example, the FDA issued a guidance document for certain legally marketed noninvasive remote monitoring devices to help expand the capability and availability of such devices to facilitate patient monitoring, while decreasing health care provider and patient contact and exposure to SARS-CoV-2.[61] This guidance document contains a list of applicable device types, such as breathing frequency monitors, noninvasive blood pressure measurement systems, cardiac monitors, and oximeters.[62] All of these devices can be connected to a wireless network through, for example, Wi-Fi or Bluetooth to transfer a patient's collected health data directly to the health care provider or another monitoring party.[63] Some of these devices also apply algorithms.[64] The guidance document states that, during the public health emergency, the FDA does not intend to disapprove of limited modifications to claims, functionality, indications, software, or hardware of the listed devices, without prior 510(k) submission, where this premarket notification submission would usually be necessary.[65] Suppose a noninvasive remote monitoring device was previously marketed exclusively for use in hospitals. During the COVID-19 pandemic, the manufacturer can modify the device for use in the home setting without submitting a 510(k).[66] In addition, the FDA also clarifies that the agency does not anticipate to enforce compliance with the special controls for two device types listed in the guidance document, namely non-electroencephalogram physiological signal-based seizure monitoring systems and computerized cognitive assessment aids.[67] The guidance document also contains recommendations, such as on labeling, and emphasizes that the modification of a legally marketed noninvasive monitoring device must not create an undue risk.[68]

Another example of a COVID-19 guidance document related to digital home health medical devices is for certain noninvasive maternal and fetal monitoring devices.[69] This enforcement policy aims to foster monitoring of pregnant women at home during COVID-19, while decreasing potential exposure for health care

60 See, e.g., US Food & Drug Admin., Enforcement Policy for Non-Invasive Remote Monitoring Devices Used to Support Patient Monitoring During the Coronavirus Disease 2019 (COVID-19) Public Health Emergency (Revised), at 5, https://www.fda.gov/regulatory-information/search-fda-guidance-documents/enforcement-policy-non-invasive-remote-monitoring-devices-used-support-patient-monitoring-during.

61 Id.

62 Id. at 6–7.

63 Id. at 7.

64 Id. at 8.

65 Id.

66 Id.

67 Id.

68 Id. at 9–11.

69 US Food & Drug Admin., Enforcement Policy for Non-Invasive Fetal and Maternal Monitoring Devices Used to Support Patient Monitoring During the Coronavirus Disease 2019 (COVID-19) Public Health Emergency, www.fda.gov/media/137286/download.

providers and their patients to SARS-CoV-2.[70] Some of these devices can be connected to Wifi or Bluetooth to directly transmit the measurements, such as the fetal or maternal heart rate, to the patient's health care provider or another monitoring party.[71] The FDA clarifies that 510(k)-cleared noninvasive maternal and fetal monitoring devices listed in the guidance document can be modified to a limited extent in their functionality, indications, software, and/or hardware without submitting a new 510(k).[72] This only applies, however, when the modification of the device does not create an undue risk.[73] This guidance document also contains recommendations, such as on labeling.[74] Other examples of COVID-19 enforcement discretion guidance documents related to digital home health medical devices include guidance for digital health devices for treating psychiatric disorders[75] and guidance for remote ophthalmic assessment and monitoring devices.[76]

11.4 DISCUSSION

While the acceleration of launching new digital home health products on the US market or modifying legally marketed devices is needed to address the COVID-19 pandemic, it also raises several challenges. In the following, I will discuss three of them, namely safety, liability, and informed consent,[77] and make suggestions on how to move forward.

11.4.1 *Safety*

The two additional regulatory pathways available during the COVID-19 public health emergency, namely EUAs and COVID-19 enforcement discretion guidance documents, are vital to act swiftly and combat COVID-19, but at the same time also pose safety risks. In particular, digital home health medical devices that are FDA authorized for emergency use concerning COVID-19 under an EUA have not undergone a "full" review that intends to provide reasonable assurance of their

70 Id. at 4–5.
71 Id. at 5, 7.
72 Id. 7.
73 Id.
74 Id. 11–12.
75 US Food & Drug Admin., Enforcement Policy for Digital Health Devices for Treating Psychiatric Disorders During the Coronavirus Disease 2019 (COVID-19) Public Health Emergency, www.fda.gov/media/136939/download.
76 US Food & Drug Admin., Enforcement Policy for Remote Ophthalmic Assessment and Monitoring Devices During the Coronavirus Disease 2019 (COVID-19) Public Health Emergency, www.fda.gov/media/136733/download.
77 Other issues beyond this article's scope include privacy, surveillance, security, and access. For more information, see, e.g., Gerke et al., supra note 4, at 1180–1; Marcello Ienca & Effy Vayena, On the Responsible Use of Digital Data to Tackle the COVID-19 Pandemic, 26 Nature Med. 463; Carmel Shachar et al., AI Surveillance during Pandemics: Ethical Implementation Imperatives, 50 Hastings Cent. Rep. 18 (2020).

safety and effectiveness, as is the case of FDA-cleared or approved medical devices. Instead, as seen above,[78] the FDA can already issue an EUA when the digital home health medical device "may be effective" to treat, diagnose, or prevent COVID-19. Thus, an EUA does not suggest that the device is safe and effective.[79]

It is imperative that – even in times of a pandemic – the FDA does not make too many tradeoffs when carrying out the benefit/risk analysis and determining whether the digital home health medical device's potential and known benefits outweigh its known and potential risks.[80] For example, the agency has recently been criticized for its decision in March 2020 to issue an EUA for chloroquine phosphate and hydroxychloroquine sulfate for the treatment of COVID-19, when used under certain conditions, due to a lack of adequate scientific evidence at the time of issuance.[81] The FDA revoked the EUA in June 2020 after case reports in April 2020 have shown death and serious heart-related adverse events in COVID-19 patients receiving these medicines.[82] This case example also holds valuable lessons for EUAs for digital home health medical devices as it highlights the importance of a robust benefit/risk analysis based on the totality of scientific evidence even in times of crisis. In particular, more transparency in the decision-making process of EUAs is needed. For example, the FDA has issued EUAs for wearable or remote patient monitoring devices "based on bench testing and reported clinical experience," but without giving any further information on such reports in the letters of authorization.[83] Thus, it would be helpful if the FDA disclosed the scientific evidence used to reach an EUA decision in more detail in its letter of authorization.[84] Transparency is crucial to promote public trust in the agency, which has been tremendously shaken during the COVID-19 pandemic, such as most recently in vaccines.[85]

78 See supra Section 11.3.2.1.

79 See letter from the FDA to VitalConnect, supra note 54, at 7; Gerke et al., supra note 4, at 1178.

80 For more information on the criteria of issuance an EUA, see supra Section 11.3.2.1.

81 See, e.g., Liam Bendicksen et al., Increase Transparency at the FDA: We Need Sunlight to Fight the Pandemic, STAT (Sept. 29, 2020), www.statnews.com/2020/09/29/increase-transparency-at-the-fda-we-need-sunlight-to-fight-the-pandemic; see also letter from the FDA to the Biomedical Advanced Research and Development Authority (Mar. 28, 2020), www.fda.gov/media/136534/download.

82 Letter from the FDA to the Biomedical Advanced Research and Development Authority (June 15, 2020), www.fda.gov/media/138945/download; US Food & Drug Admin., Coronavirus (COVID-19) Update: FDA Revokes Emergency Use Authorization for Chloroquine and Hydroxychloroquine, www.fda.gov/news-events/press-announcements/coronavirus-covid-19-update-fda-revokes-emergency-use-authorization-chloroquine-and; US Food & Drug Admin., Hydroxychloroquine or Chloroquine for COVID-19: Drug Safety Communication – FDA Cautions Against Use Outside of the Hospital Setting or a Clinical Trial Due to Risk of Heart Rhythm Problems, www.fda.gov/safety/medical-product-safety-information/hydroxychloroquine-or-chloroquine-covid-19-drug-safety-communication-fda-cautions-against-use.

83 See letter from the FDA to VitalConnect, supra note 54, at 2; letter from the FDA to PhysiolGuard Corporation (May 5, 2020), at 2, www.fda.gov/media/137693/download.

84 See also Bendicksen et al., supra note 81.

85 See, e.g., Michael Barbaro, The Vaccine Trust Problem, www.nytimes.com/2020/07/21/podcasts/the-daily/coronavirus-vaccine.html?showTranscript=1.

There are likely additional safety risks when the development of digital home health products – devices and non-devices – is rushed to quickly put them on the market in response to the COVID-19 pandemic. In particular, digital home health products are prone to false-positive results that may be caused, for example, by inaccurate measurements.[86] Suppose an authorized remote monitoring device for emergency use under an EUA is used in the hospital to monitor a COVID-19 patient remotely, thereby reducing clinicians' exposure to SARS-CoV-2, and has too many false positives due to its rapid development. Suppose the device alerts the patient's physician each time it detects an irregular heart rhythm. Thus, due to the high false-positive ratio, the device sends several false alerts, which can easily lead to alert fatigue of the physician.[87] Moreover, digital home health products also bear the risk of false-negative results. If the device in the hypothetical example fails to detect an irregular heart rhythm, the patient's treatment may be delayed, and this can have adverse effects on the patient's health.[88]

The COVID-19 guidance documents related to digital home health medical devices mainly apply to certain limited modifications of particular legally marketed devices.[89] Thus, in general, the risks associated with such modifications may likely be lower than the risks associated with EUAs, which may also authorize emergency use of uncleared or unapproved medical devices.[90] In addition, the COVID-19 guidance documents contain an additional safeguard as the limited modifications must not create an undue risk.[91] Nevertheless, one also needs to acknowledge that accelerated modifications of devices in compliance with the COVID-19 guidance documents bring additional risks, especially when such devices are now used in people's homes. For example, even if patients receive instructions for home use with appropriate lay terminology,[92] patients may over-rely on the device's output, mishandle the device, and also not know when to seek medical help.[93]

Many digital home health products are not considered medical devices, and thus the FDA did not review them – even before the COVID-19 pandemic.[94] Thus, it is essential that – irrespective of whether a product undergoes no review, a "light"

86 Gerke et al., supra note 4, at 1178.

87 For more information on alert fatigue, see, e.g., Sara Gerke et al., The Need for a System View to Regulate Artificial Intelligence/Machine Learning-Based Software as Medical Device, 3 npj Digit. Med. (2020).

88 See also Gerke et al., supra note 4, at 1178.

89 For more information on COVID-19 guidance documents, see supra Section 11.3.2.2. An exception of a COVID-19 guidance document that applies to specific uncleared devices is US Food & Drug Admin., Enforcement Policy for Clinical Electronic Thermometers During the Coronavirus Disease 2019 (COVID-19) Public Health Emergency, www.fda.gov/media/136698/download. For more information on this guidance, see also Gerke et al., supra note 4, at 1179.

90 Gerke et al., supra note 4, at 1179. For more information on EUAs, see supra Section 11.3.2.1.

91 Gerke et al., supra note 4, at 1179; see also US Food & Drug Admin., supra note 60, at 9; FDA, supra note 69, at 7–9.

92 See, e.g., FDA, supra note 60, at 10; US Food & Drug Admin., supra note 69, at 11.

93 Gerke et al., supra note 4, at 1178.

94 For more information, see supra Section 11.3.1.

review, or a "full" review – digital home health companies should mitigate safety risks to patients and consumers as much as reasonable. They should – during the pandemic and post-pandemic – practice "ethics by design."[95] This approach requires, among other things, that the companies develop products that mitigate biases, adequately protect individuals' privacy, and have proper security safeguards in place. Moreover, digital home health companies should also practice "ethics maintenance" of their products during and after the COVID-19 pandemic. This is particularly important for so-called adaptive algorithms that can learn and adapt to new conditions and therefore hold great promise to realize the full potential of AI in the future.[96] However, since these algorithms constantly learn and change, it will be crucial to make sure that the products will remain safe and effective. An "ethics maintenance" approach ensures, for instance, that companies monitor their digital home health products continuously and that the monitoring is carried out by a department other than the one that developed it.[97]

On January 8, 2021, the then Secretary of Health and Human Services Alex Azar signed a proposal making some regulatory flexibilities provided during the COVID-19 pandemic permanent.[98] This proposal was published in the Federal Register on January 15, 2021, only five days before President Joe Biden's inauguration. It intended, among other things, to exempt eighty-three Class II medical devices from the 510(k) premarket notification requirement, including several devices related to digital home health such as fetal cardiac monitors and computerized behavioral therapy devices for psychiatric disorders.[99] The proposal suggested that the 510(k) premarket notification requirement was no longer necessary for such devices to assure their safety and effectiveness because they were apparently associated with few adverse event reports.[100] But few adverse event reports should not be a primary reason to justify 510(k) exemptions. Digital home health medical devices interact with their user, and it can be challenging to detect issues with them straightaway.[101] As we have seen above, digital home health medical devices are,

95 Gerke et al., Ethical and Legal Issues of Ingestible Electronic Sensors, supra note 1; see also Gerke et al., supra note 4, at 1180.

96 Boris Babic et al., Algorithms on Regulatory Lockdown in Medicine: Prioritize Risk Monitoring to Address the "Update Problem," 366 Science 1202 (2019).

97 Id. at 1204 (where Babic et al. suggest an appropriate division of labor for AI/machine learning systems).

98 Department of Health & Human Services, Making Permanent Regulatory Flexibilities Provided During the COVID-19 Public Health Emergency by Exempting Certain Medical Devices From Premarket Notification Requirements; Request for Information, Research, Analysis, and Public Comment on Opportunities for Further Science and Evidence-Based Reform of Section 510(k) Program, 86 Fed. Reg., 4088, www.govinfo.gov/content/pkg/FR-2021-01-15/pdf/2021-00787.pdf.

99 Id. at 4088, 4096–8.

100 Id. at 4096.

101 For medical AI tools, see also Casey Ross, "Slippery Slope Territory": Health Officials Propose Waiving Regulatory Review of Medical AI Tools, STAT (Jan. 16, 2021), www.statnews.com/2021/01/16/slippery-slope-territory-health-officials-propose-waiving-regulatory-review-of-medical-ai-tools.

for example, prone to false-positive and false-negative results. Patients and consumers may also over-rely on their outputs and may unknowingly not seek medical care although necessary. In a Notice from April 16, 2021, the Department of Health and Human Services and the FDA luckily withdrew, among other things, the proposed exemptions for the eighty-three Class II medical devices.[102] The main reason for the withdrawal was "that the proposed exemptions and bases for them are flawed."[103]

11.4.2 *Liability*

The use of digital home health products during the COVID-19 pandemic also raises questions of liability. Suppose a remote monitoring device that is authorized for emergency use concerning COVID-19 under an EUA fails to detect an irregular heart rhythm in a COVID-19 patient, and the patient dies as a result. Can the manufacturer be held liable under current law? The then Secretary of Health and Human Services Alex Azar issued a Declaration under the Public Readiness and Emergency Preparedness Act (PREP Act), effective as of February 4, 2020, "to provide liability immunity for activities related to medical countermeasures against COVID-19."[104]

[102] Department of Health & Human Services & FDA, Making Permanent Regulatory Flexibilities Provided During the COVID-19 Public Health Emergency by Exempting Certain Medical Devices From Premarket Notification Requirements; Withdrawal of Proposed Exemptions, 86 Fed. Reg. 20174, www.govinfo.gov/content/pkg/FR-2021-04-16/pdf/2021-07760.pdf.

[103] Id. at 20174.

[104] Declaration Under the Public Readiness and Emergency Preparedness Act for Medical Countermeasures Against COVID-19, 85 Fed. Reg. 15198, www.govinfo.gov/content/pkg/FR-2020-03-17/pdf/2020-05484.pdf; see also Amendment to Declaration Under the Public Readiness and Emergency Preparedness Act for Medical Countermeasures Against COVID-19, 85 Fed. Reg. 21012, www.govinfo.gov/content/pkg/FR-2020-04-15/pdf/2020-08040.pdf; Second Amendment to Declaration Under the Public Readiness and Emergency Preparedness Act for Medical Countermeasures Against COVID-19, 85 Fed. Reg. 35100, www.govinfo.gov/content/pkg/FR-2020-06-08/pdf/2020-12465.pdf; Department of Health and Human Services, Third Amendment to Declaration Under the Public Readiness and Emergency Preparedness Act for Medical Countermeasures Against COVID-19, 85 Fed. Reg. 52136, www.govinfo.gov/content/pkg/FR-2020-08-24/pdf/2020-18542.pdf; Fourth Amendment to the Declaration Under the Public Readiness and Emergency Preparedness Act for Medical Countermeasures Against COVID-19 and Republication of the Declaration, 85 Fed. Reg. 79190, www.govinfo.gov/content/pkg/FR-2020-12-09/pdf/2020-26977.pdf; Fifth Amendment to Declaration Under the Public Readiness and Emergency Preparedness Act for Medical Countermeasures Against COVID-19, 86 Fed. Reg. 7872, www.govinfo.gov/content/pkg/FR-2021-02-02/pdf/2021-02174.pdf; Sixth Amendment to Declaration Under the Public Readiness and Emergency Preparedness Act for Medical Countermeasures Against COVID-19, 86 Fed. Reg. 9516, www.govinfo.gov/content/pkg/FR-2021-02-16/pdf/2021-03106.pdf; Sixth Amendment to Declaration Under the Public Readiness and Emergency Preparedness Act for Medical Countermeasures Against COVID-19, 86 Fed. Reg. 10588, www.govinfo.gov/content/pkg/FR-2021-02-22/pdf/2021-03526.pdf; Seventh Amendment to Declaration Under the Public Readiness and Emergency Preparedness Act for Medical Countermeasures Against COVID-19, 86 Fed. Reg. 14462, www.govinfo.gov/content/pkg/FR-2021-03-16/pdf/2021-05401.pdf; Eighth Amendment to

Under the PREP Act,

> a *covered person* shall be immune from suit and liability under Federal and State law with respect to all *claims for loss* caused by, arising out of, relating to, or resulting from the administration to or the use by an individual of a *covered countermeasure* if a declaration ... has been issued with respect to such countermeasure (emphasis added).[105]

However, there is no immunity in cases of willful misconduct that proximately caused serious injury or death.[106] A covered person is, for example, a manufacturer of a covered countermeasure or a "qualified person" (for example, a licensed health professional or other person who is authorized to administer, prescribe, or dispense covered countermeasures under the State law in which the countermeasure was administered, prescribed, or dispensed).[107] The term "loss" includes, for instance, death and personal injury.[108] Covered countermeasures are, for example, FDA cleared or approved medical devices used to prevent, mitigate, treat, cure, diagnose, or limit the harm of COVID-19, medical devices authorized for emergency use concerning COVID-19 under an EUA, and investigational medical devices that are permitted to be used under an investigational device exemption to treat COVID-19.[109] Consequently, PREP Act immunity may apply in cases of digital home health medical devices authorized for emergency use concerning COVID-19 under an EUA. However, devices that are modified under the COVID-19 enforcement discretion guidance documents are not covered countermeasures, and thus there is a priori no PREP Act immunity.[110] Further, digital home health

Declaration Under the Public Readiness and Emergency Preparedness Act for Medical Countermeasures Against COVID-19, 86 Fed. Reg. 41977, www.govinfo.gov/content/pkg/FR-2021-08-04/pdf/2021-16681.pdf; Ninth Amendment to Declaration Under the Public Readiness and Emergency Preparedness Act for Medical Countermeasures Against COVID-19, 86 Fed. Reg. 51160, www.govinfo.gov/content/pkg/FR-2021-09-14/pdf/2021-19790.pdf; Declaration Under the Public Readiness and Emergency Preparedness Act for Medical Countermeasures Against COVID-19; Correction, 86 Fed. Reg. 54696, www.govinfo.gov/content/pkg/FR-2021-10-04/pdf/2021-21652.pdf.

105 42 U.S.C. § 247d–6d(a)(1).

106 42 U.S.C. § 247d-6d(c)(3); see also Department of Health and Human Services, Declaration Under the Public Readiness and Emergency Preparedness Act for Medical Countermeasures Against COVID-19, supra note 104; Department of Health and Human Services, Advisory Opinion on the Public Readiness and Emergency Preparedness Act and the Mar. 10, 2020 Declaration under the Act (Apr. 17, 2020, as Modified on May 19, 2020), at 7, www.hhs.gov/sites/default/files/prep-act-advisory-opinion-hhs-ogc.pdf.

107 42 U.S.C. § 247d–6d(i)(8); see also Department of Health and Human Services, Declaration Under the Public Readiness and Emergency Preparedness Act for Medical Countermeasures Against COVID-19, supra note 104; Department of Health and Human Services, supra note 106, at 5–6.

108 42 U.S.C. § 247d–6d(a)(2)(A).

109 42 U.S.C. 247d–6d(i)(1) and (7); see also Department of Health and Human Services, Declaration Under the Public Readiness and Emergency Preparedness Act for Medical Countermeasures Against COVID-19, supra note 104; Department of Health and Human Services, supra note 106, at 3–5.

110 See also Peter S. Spivack & Emily M. Lyons, Liability Immunity Under the Prep Act for COVID-19 Countermeasures: What Manufacturers Need to Know, at 6, www.hoganlovells.com/~/media/hogan-lovells/pdf/2020-pdfs/2020_03_23_liability_immunity_under_the_prep_act-for_covid_19_countermea

products that are not classified as medical devices are likewise not covered countermeasures, and PREP Act immunity does not apply from the outset.[111] Such products will likely be governed under product liability law if they are defective.[112]

The Department of Health and Human Services Office of the General Counsel (Counsel) has emphasized in its first Advisory Opinion from May 2020 the broad scope of the PREP Act immunity.[113] Even in cases where not all of the requirements are fulfilled, a "reasonably-could-have-believed" standard may confer immunity.[114] For instance, suppose the medical product is not a covered countermeasure (for example, is counterfeit), but an individual or entity "reasonably could have believed" that it was a covered countermeasure (for example, the individual or entity has taken reasonable steps to substantiate the product's authenticity).[115] Such an individual or entity will not lose PREP Act immunity so long as the individual or entity complies with all other conditions of the Secretary of Health and Human Services' Declaration and the PREP Act.[116]

If all conditions of the Secretary of Health and Human Services' Declaration and the PREP Act are fulfilled, immunity will cover claims for loss sounding in contract and tort and claims for loss relating to compliance with federal, state, or local laws, regulations, or other legal conditions.[117] The Counsel clarifies in its first Advisory Opinion that

> immunity applies when a covered person engages in activities *related to an agreement or arrangement with the federal government, or when a covered person acts*

sures.pdf; Gerke et al., supra note 4, at 1178. For more information on COVID-19 enforcement discretion guidance documents, see supra Section 11.3.2.2.

111 See also Gerke et al., supra note 4, at 1180.

112 Id.

113 Department of Health and Human Services, supra note 106, at 4. For other advisory opinions, see Department of Health and Human Services, Advisory Opinion 20-02 on the Public Readiness and Emergency Preparedness Act and the Secretary's Declaration under the Act (May 19, 2020), www.hhs.gov/guidance/sites/default/files/hhs-guidance-documents/advisory-opinion-20-02-hhs-ogc-prep-act.pdf; Department of Health and Human Services; Advisory Opinion 20-03 on the Public Readiness and Emergency Preparedness Act and the Secretary's Declaration under the Act (Oct. 22, 2020, as modified on Oct. 23, 2020), www.hhs.gov/guidance/sites/default/files/hhs-guidance-documents/AO3.1.2_Updated_FINAL_SIGNED_10.23.20.pdf; Department of Health and Human Services, Advisory Opinion 20-04 on the Public Readiness and Emergency Preparedness Act and the Secretary's Declaration under the Act (Oct. 22, 2020, as modified on Oct. 23, 2020), www.hhs.gov/guidance/sites/default/files/hhs-guidance-documents/AO%204.2_Updated_FINAL_SIGNED_10.23.20.pdf; Department of Health and Human Services, Advisory Opinion 21-01 on the Public Readiness and Emergency Preparedness Act Scope of Preemption Provision (Jan. 8, 2021), www.hhs.gov/guidance/sites/default/files/hhs-guidance-documents/2101081078-jo-advisory-opinion-prep-act-complete-preemption-01-08-2021-final-hhs-web.pdf; Department of Health and Human Services, Advisory Opinion 21-02 on the Public Readiness and Emergency Preparedness Act and the Secretary's Declaration under the Act (Jan. 12, 2021), www.hhs.gov/guidance/sites/default/files/hhs-guidance-documents/AO-21-02-PREP-Act_1-12-2021_FINAL_SIGNED.pdf.

114 Department of Health and Human Services, supra note 106, at 4–5; see also 42 U.S.C. § 247d–6d(a)(4)(B).

115 Department of Health and Human Services, supra note 106, at 2, 4, 5, 7.

116 Id.

117 Id at 2.

> *according to an Authority Having Jurisdiction to respond to a declared emergency* (emphasis added).[118]

The Counsel interprets such two conditions broadly.[119] The first condition includes "any arrangement with the federal government."[120] The second condition means "any activity that is part of an authorized emergency response at the federal, regional, state, or local level."[121] These activities can be authorized, for example, through agreements, requests for assistance, guidance, or other arrangements.[122]

The Fourth Amendment to the Declaration under the PREP Act, published in the Federal Register on December 9, 2020, added a third distribution channel that extends liability coverage to additional private-distribution channels.[123] To qualify for this channel, the "Covered Person must manufacture, test, develop, distribute, administer, or use the Covered Countermeasure pursuant to the FDA licensure, approval, clearance, or authorization (or pursuant to an Investigational New Drug Application or Investigational Device Exemption), or the NIOSH approval."[124]

If liability immunity is provided to covered persons, individuals who die or suffer a serious physical injury as a direct outcome of the use or administration of a covered countermeasure may receive compensation under the Countermeasures Injury Compensation Program.[125] In order to assess whether PREP Act immunity applies, each case will need to be evaluated individually, taking into account the particular circumstances and facts. The Fourth Amendment to the Declaration under the PREP Act also clarified that the Declaration must be construed pursuant to the Counsel's advisory opinions.[126] However, the advisory opinions only set forth the Counsel's current views.[127] It is thus highly recommended that digital home

118 Id.; see also Department of Health and Human Services, Declaration Under the Public Readiness and Emergency Preparedness Act for Medical Countermeasures Against COVID-19, supra note 104.

119 Department of Health and Human Services, supra note 106, at 2.

120 Id.

121 Id.

122 Id.

123 Department of Health and Human Services, Fourth Amendment to the Declaration Under the Public Readiness and Emergency Preparedness Act for Medical Countermeasures Against COVID-19 and Republication of the Declaration, supra note 104, at 79191.

124 Id. at 79194. For more information on the Fourth Amendment to the Declaration, see, e.g., Cortney M. Godin & Kaitlyn M. Hansen, Fourth Amendment to the PREP Act Expands Protection and Adopts Guidance, www.peabodyarnold.com/fourth-amendment-to-the-prep-act-expands-protection-and-adopts-guidance.

125 Department of Health and Human Services, Declaration Under the Public Readiness and Emergency Preparedness Act for Medical Countermeasures Against COVID-19, supra note 104; Department of Health and Human Services, supra note 106, at 8.

126 Department of Health and Human Services, Fourth Amendment to the Declaration Under the Public Readiness and Emergency Preparedness Act for Medical Countermeasures Against COVID-19 and Republication of the Declaration, supra note 104, at 79191.

127 See, e.g., Department of Health and Human Services, Advisory Opinion 21-02 on the Public Readiness and Emergency Preparedness Act and the Secretary's Declaration under the Act, supra note 113, at 3.

health companies, for example, continue to apply best record-keeping practices and recording justifications for decision-making concerning devices that could be used as countermeasures to fight COVID-19.[128]

Digital home health products will also continue to raise liability questions post-pandemic. In particular, health AI presents new challenges for the liability ecosystem,[129] and it will be decisive to figure out how to ensure a balanced liability system in the future.

11.4.3 *Informed Consent*

Informed consent is important to respect the patient's autonomy and includes that health care providers disclose relevant information to competent patients who can voluntarily decide whether they want to accept or refuse a treatment, research study, and so forth.[130] For example, during the COVID-19 pandemic, a meaningful discussion between the physician and the patient is crucial in cases in which a wearable or remote patient monitoring device that is authorized for emergency use under an EUA shall be used in the treatment of a COVID-19 patient (for example, in a hospital setting) to help reduce personal contacts.[131] Most prominently, the physician should inform the patient that the device has not undergone a "full" FDA review and that the EUA does not suggest that it is safe and effective.[132] The physician should also explain to the patient, among other things, the significant known and potential risks and benefits of the use of the device, the patient's option to refuse or accept its use, and available alternatives, including their benefits and risk.[133]

The FDA requires sponsors to develop two fact sheets – one for health care providers and one for patients – that contain relevant information, such as on COVID-19, the device and its use, the device's potential and known risks and benefits, alternatives, length of the monitoring, the device's limitations, and an

[128] See Duane Morris, Department of Health & Human Services Clarifies Broad Scope of Immunity Protection Under the PREP Act, www.duanemorris.com/alerts/department_health_human_services_clarifies_broad_scope_immunity_protection_prep_act_0420.html; Department of Health and Human Services, supra note 106, at 8.

[129] See., e.g., W. Nicholson Price II, Medical Malpractice and Black-Box Medicine 295 (I. Glenn Cohen et al. eds., 1st ed. 2018); A. Michael Froomkin et al., When AIs Outperform Doctors: Confronting the Challenges of a Tort-Induced Over-Reliance on Machine Learning, 61 Ariz. L. Rev. 33 (2019); W. Nicholson Price II et al., Potential Liability for Physicians Using Artificial Intelligence, 322 JAMA 1765 (2019); A. Selbst, Negligence and AI's Human Users, 100 B.U. L. REV. 1315 (2020); W. Nicholson Price II et al., How Much Can Potential Jurors Tell Us about Liability for Medical AI?, 62 J. Nucl. Med. 15 (2021); Kevin Tobia et al., When Does Physician Use of AI Increase Liability?, 62 J. Nucl. Med. 17 (2021).

[130] Paul S. Appelbaum, Assessment of Patients' Competence to Consent to Treatment, 357 N. Eng. J. Med. 1834 (2007).

[131] For more information on EUAs, see supra Section 11.3.2.1.

[132] See also Gerke et al., supra note 4, at 1179.

[133] Id.; see also FDCA § 564(e).

EUA.[134] An informed consent conversation between the physician and patient may also be carried out via telehealth, such as by phone or video call, to discuss, inter alia, the patient's questions concerning the fact sheet or any other questions.[135] In particular, the current fact sheets are only available in English, and their translation in other languages would be helpful for patients who may not be fluent in English.[136] The physician also needs to communicate with the patient through a qualified interpreter to ensure that a patient with limited English proficiency can give voluntary and informed consent.[137]

Transparency about the EUA and its criteria for issuance is essential to promote trust in the physician-patient relationship. The same applies to post-pandemic scenarios. Regardless of the legal requirements, the clinical translation of new technologies like AI and wearable or remote patient monitoring devices can only succeed if health care providers are frank with their patients from the outset about the technology's use, its benefits, and shortcomings.[138] The era of big data also requires that physicians are adequately educated about AI and digital health, including scientific, ethical, and legal considerations. Education in this field is crucial so that physicians can, for instance, explain to their patients what AI is, with what type of data the algorithm was trained, what data is collected and shared with third parties, and why it is shared. Moreover, this knowledge will not only help physicians to identify the best available treatment option for their patients but also to recognize potential biases in an AI/machine learning system.

Another challenge of most digital home health products is user agreements. For example, in response to COVID-19, Apple developed together with the White House, the Centers for Disease Control and Prevention, and the Federal Emergency Management Agency, a COVID-19 screening tool app. This app aims to help users understand what steps to take next about COVID-19, such as self-isolating. However, with the app's installation or use, users also agree to be bound by

134 See, e.g., Letter from the FDA to VitalConnect (Apr. 26, 2020), supra note 54, at 4. For examples of such fact sheets, see, e.g., VitalConnect, Fact Sheet for Healthcare Providers, www.fda.gov/media/137399/download; VitalConnect, Fact Sheet for Patients, www.fda.gov/media/137400/download. For a best-practice list with information that fact sheets of EUA home monitoring devices should contain, see Gerke et al., supra note 4, at 1179.

135 For more information on telehealth coverage policies during COVID-19 and post-pandemic considerations, see Sara Gerke et al., Germany's Digital Health Reforms in the COVID-19 Era: Lessons and Opportunities for Other Countries, 3 npj Digit. Med. (2020); Carmel Shachar et al., Implications for Telehealth in a Postpandemic Future: Regulatory and Privacy Issues, 323 JAMA 2375 (2020).

136 See also Gerke et al., supra note 4, at 1179.

137 For more information on the right to language services, see Gaurab Basu et al., Clinicians' Obligations to Use Qualified Medical Interpreters When Caring for Patients with Limited English Proficiency, 19 Am. J. Ethics 245 (2017).

138 See, e.g., I. Glenn Cohen, Informed Consent and Medical Artificial Intelligence: What to Tell the Patient? 108 Geo. L. J. 1425 (2020) (who concludes that "the existing legal doctrine of informed consent does not robustly support an obligation to disclose the use of medical AI/ML," at 1467). For the importance of transparency concerning ambient intelligence in hospitals, see Sara Gerke et al., Ethical and Legal Aspects of Ambient Intelligence in Hospitals, 323 JAMA 601 (2020).

the terms of Apple's software license agreement. The issue with user agreements is that they are lengthy and difficult to understand, especially for nonlawyers. In contrast to an informed consent conversation between a physician and patient, a user agreement is nonnegotiable, and the user either accepts it or has to refrain from using the app.[139] In addition, user agreements often change. Moreover, in most cases of digital home health apps, such as in the case of Apple's screening tool app, sensitive data are collected. Such data may then be shared with third parties for different purposes, including commercial ones.[140]

Thus, during the COVID-19 pandemic and after the pandemic, more transparency is needed concerning software license agreements and the respective privacy policies when users install and use digital home health apps, such as COVID-19 exposure-notification apps, wellness apps, and mobile medical apps. App developers can do a better job in making the terms more accessible to the average user. For example, icons and a few sentences with lay terminology could be additionally used to present relevant information – such as the app's goal, information to data collection, use and sharing, and cybersecurity safeguards – to users once they have installed and opened the app. If this key information changes (for example, the app is now sharing data with third parties for commercial purposes), users should be notified in a similar manner so that they can make an informed decision about whether to continue using the app. User-friendly design options not only increase transparency, but also promote user trust in companies, which is necessary to ensure the success of digital home health in the future.

11.5 CONCLUSION

Digital home health holds great promise in enabling individuals to manage their own health. However, the adoption of digital home health products has been hastened during the COVID-19 pandemic to reduce exposure to SARS-CoV-2. This acceleration has also raised several challenges, including safety, liability, and informed consent. It is important that the identified issues are dealt with as best as possible during the COVID-19 public health emergency and will be overcome post-pandemic to release digital home health's full potential in the future.

139 For more information on user agreements and their relationship to informed consent, see, e.g., Craig M. Klugman, The Ethics of Smart Pills and Self-Acting Devices: Autonomy, Truth-Telling, and Trust at the Dawn of Digital Medicine, 18 AJOB 38, 40–1 (2018).

140 The Health Insurance Portability and Accountability Act of 1996 (HIPAA), for example, has gaps and may not adequately protect the health data privacy of individuals. Most users currently need to rely on the privacy laws of the states in which they live as to whether their privacy is adequately protected when using apps. For more information on such data privacy issues, see, e.g., I. Glenn Cohen & Michelle M. Mello, Big Data, Big Tech, and Protecting Patient Privacy, 322 JAMA 1141 (2019); Gerke et al., Ethical and Legal Challenges of Artificial Intelligence-Driven Healthcare, supra note 1, at 317–19; Gerke et al., supra note 4, at 1180–1; W. Nicholson Price II & I. Glenn Cohen, Privacy in the Age of Medical Big Data, 25 Nature Med. 37 (2019); Shachar et al., supra note 77, at 18–19.

PART IV

The Impact of Medical Device Regulation on Patients and Markets

Introduction

Christopher Robertson

What do we know about the products we put in our bodies? It is hard enough to determine the safety and efficacy of drugs, which go through a premarket approval process. In contrast, many medical devices are not subject to premarket approval, and even those that are approved tend to undergo iterative changes during their lifecycle, such that the versions now being used may be quite different designs than the versions originally proposed to, and reviewed by, the FDA. Or the same designs may be used for an altogether new purpose or a new patient population.

Unfortunately, the evidence is not very good. To peek into just one part of the medical device ecosystem, consider panel-track supplements. Of the six different pathways for reviewing modification to approved devices, the "panel track" is the only one that always requires submission of clinical data, because the manufacturer is proposing a "significant change in design or performance of the device, or a new indication for use of the device." In 2017, JAMA published a report by Sarah Zheng, Sanket Dhruva, and Rita Redberg reviewing the clinical studies used by the US Food and Drug Administration to approve such modifications to high-risk medical devices over nearly a decade.[1] Of the eighty-three clinical studies for all seventy-eight panel-track supplements approved between 2006 and 2015, less than half (45 percent) were randomized clinical trials, less than a third were at least somewhat blinded, and all but a fifth (19 percent) used surrogates rather than mortality and morbidity as primary endpoints. And most disconcertingly, all but 38 percent lacked control groups, which is typically a necessity for causal inference. If we cannot isolate the effects caused by the device, what is the point?

On the basis of this relatively weak data, it is hard to know if these devices are actually safe and effective for their intended purposes. Without that information, it is hard for patients and their doctors to know whether the devices are right for them, and it is hard for payors to determine whether the products are worth their prices.[2]

[1] Sarah Y. Zheng et al., Characteristics of Clinical Studies Used for US Food and Drug Administration Approval of High-Risk Medical Device Supplements, 318 JAMA 619 (2017).

[2] Sarah Fontenay et al., Quality of Economic Evaluations of Ventricular Assist Devices: A Systematic Review, 36 Int'l J. Tech. Assessment in Health Care 380 (2020).

Frankly, that is exactly the situation that rational purveyors of these devices desire, trading on hope and conjecture, while they selectively release whatever information is favorable to their product. The chapters in this section pick up this theme around proof and value.

In their chapter, Jody Lyneé Madeira and colleagues are worried about the relationship of the drug and device industry with specialized drug courts, in the era of opioid abuse. Here the primary medical device is called "the Bridge" and it provides neurostimulation as a preliminary step to reduce cravings in the treatment of substance use disorder. A 2020 review of the literature on such devices yielded only five studies meeting inclusion criteria, with a combined total subjects of N=150 across all five studies.[3] The review authors conclude that, "the studies that have been performed have suffered from small sample sizes and poor characterization of the study population and their substance use patterns, as well as inadequate attempts at participant masking and controlling sources of bias. As such, there is a paucity of high-quality, rigorously-conducted research."[4] Only one of these studies focused on the Bridge device itself, and it was coauthored by the patent holder for the device, who also serves as consultant for the company marketing it. The Bridge is a great example of how the FDA is a weak gatekeeper for medical devices, and how weak regulation begets weak evidence.

Kate Kraschel is also concerned with unproven medical products, specifically those used for fertility services. Preimplantation genetic screening is one such service, which can be used to select embryos that are more likely to yield healthy babies, but it has a false-negative problem, often screening out healthy embryos. In this domain, the FDA has been largely silent, due to complicated political questions and the fact that the devices themselves are secondary to clinicians' decisions about whether and how to use them. Accordingly, since no regulator requires proof of safety and efficacy, no such reliable evidence is produced. In this regulatory gap, money flows in to exploit the hopes of patients who are eager to become parents of healthy babies.

Preeti Mehrotra and colleagues take on the problem of dirty devices. Specifically, how should duodenoscopes be disinfected, and what role should the FDA have in setting those standards? This chapter exposes the problems with a binary approach to regulatory approval, where the device itself may be safe and effective, but only if downstream users properly sterilize it. This chapter also reflects a fragmentation of entities providing guidance in this space, including hospital policymakers, professional associations, and governmental regulators.

Wendy Netter Epstein focuses on the safety/innovation tradeoff for the FDA's policy setting. Not unlike driving a car, the faster one goes, the greater the risk. For medical products, the faster we move to bring new medical products to market, the

3 H.B. Ward et al., A Systematic Review of Noninvasive Brain Stimulation for Opioid Use Disorder, 23 Neuromodulation: Technology at the Neural Interface 301 (2020).

4 Id. at 307.

less information regulators will have and the greater the risk that some of those products will turn out to be bad. This risk can arise on the efficacy front, where approved products can come on the market, displacing the standard of care and sucking billions of dollars out of the health care system, only to turn out to be useless. Epstein focuses on the more worrisome problem that a product comes onto the market, but ultimately does more harm than good.

Together these chapters contribute to our understanding of how the regulation of medical devices, or the lack thereof, shapes what we do or do not know about them. In the race to help patients, it is necessary to make sure that our new medical products actually help them. As I have written before, it cannot simply be presumed.[5]

[5] Christopher T. Robertson, The FDCA as the Test for the Truth of Promotional Claims, in FDA in the 21st Century: The Challenges of Regulating Drugs and New Technologies (I. Glenn Cohen & Holly Fernandez Lynch eds., 2015).

12

Clouded Judgment

Preventing Conflicts of Interest in Drug Courts

Jody Lyneé Madeira, Barbara Andraka-Christou, Lori Ann Eldridge, and Ross D. Silverman[*]

12.1 THE GROWING RELATIONSHIP BETWEEN PHARMACEUTICAL AND MEDICAL DEVICE MANUFACTURERS AND DRUG COURTS

United States' pharmaceutical companies and medical device manufacturers are marketing their products directly to drug courts – with controversial results.[1] These activities can be associated with court policies and staff beliefs that are anti-agonist – opposed to forms of medications for opioid use disorder (MOUD[2]) containing opioids. Anti-agonist beliefs and policies can harm client outcomes when judges narrow MOUD options to one medication, or partner with providers who prefer one medication.

In the Greenwood City, Indiana, drug court overseen by Judge Lewis Gregory, patients received a neurostimulation medical device called the Bridge to assist them with detoxification before transitioning to Vivitrol. Judge Gregory began using the device in February 2017 after meeting with the manufacturer, Innovative Health Solutions (IHS). His court also only used Vivitrol because he "was certainly not going to do a medication-assisted treatment program with drugs which people used to get high."[3] But IHS did not receive FDA marketing authorization until November 2017, and existing research used controversial methodology and lacked IRB oversight.[4] Were

* This chapter was supported in part by funding for the Indiana Addictions Law and Policy Surveillance Project (Silverman, PI) via the Indiana University Addictions Grand Challenge.

1 Jake Harper, To Grow Market Share, A Drugmaker Pitches Its Product to Judges, NPR (Aug. 3, 2017), www.npr.org/sections/health-shots/2017/08/03/540029500/to-grow-market-share-a-drugmaker-pitches-its-product-to-judges; Jake Harper, Questions Raised about Study of Device to Ease Opioid Withdrawal, NPR (May 2, 2018), www.npr.org/sections/health-shots/2018/05/02/602908208/questions-raised-about-study-of-device-to-ease-opioid-withdrawal.

2 MOUD is sometimes referred to as medication-assisted treatment (MAT).

3 Scott L. Miley, Device Said to Stem Opioid Withdrawal Pain, Tribune Star (Nov. 19, 2017), www.tribstar.com/news/local_news/device-said-to-stem-opioid-withdrawal-pain/article_3d97061f-e8d1-5b6f-ae9b-74965c09a62a.html.

4 Jody Lyneé Madeira, Vulnerable Patients – Easy Targets for Companies Willing to Sacrifice Ethics for Profits, The Hill (May 21, 2018), https://thehill.com/opinion/healthcare/388634-vulnerable-patients-easy-targets-for-companies-willing-to-sacrifice-ethics.

such concerns raised with the decision makers? Perhaps not, given that these decisions were occurring in a court rather than in a clinical setting. In the Hocking County Municipal Vivitrol Drug Court near Athens, Ohio, Judge Fred Moses decided to only allow clients to access the non-agonist medication Vivitrol – a choice he made after meeting Vivitrol's manufacturer, Alkermes, at a professional conference and asking sales representatives to send the court's affiliated clinician free starter doses.[5] This decision ran counter to medical standards and professional guidance supporting client access to all types of MOUD.[6]

Manufacturer relationships with criminal justice institutions and drug courts represent a new frontier. Alkermes sales representatives have marketed Vivitrol to court officials in numerous states, including Missouri, Massachusetts, Ohio, West Virginia, Alaska, and Indiana, and administered injections to parolees in Michigan, Illinois, Wisconsin, Vermont, New Hampshire, and Pennsylvania; it has also lobbied state and national policy makers for laws favoring Vivitrol.[7] As of 2017, Vivitrol was used in 450 publicly funded initiatives, such as court and parole programs, in 39 states.[8] While manufacturer-court relationships are relatively novel, their conventional counterpart, the pharmaceutical sales representative-physician marketing efforts, has generated a robust body of scholarship that is helpful in understanding their potential consequences.

One might assume that effective gatekeepers keep watch over these relationships and their consequences, including the FDA, federal and state legislatures, state court systems, and/or legal and medical professional associations that at least ensure that public officials receive accurate and complete information about MOUD. But these gatekeepers are nonexistent, lack important knowledge, or are susceptible to manufacturer influence. Meanwhile, these industries are attempting – and succeeding – at persuading local communities and states to use limited or less-effective MOUD options.

This chapter examines the growing relationships between medical device and pharmaceutical manufacturers and drug courts, arguing attention must be paid to reveal and interrogate potentially detrimental influences that can harm client outcomes. Section 12.2 describes the manufacturer-drug court relationship, explores treatment team beliefs about MOUD, and explores two examples. Section 12.3 applies a conflict-of-interest framework to assess these relationships and discusses how treatment teams can be "moral entrepreneurs" that make non-evidence-based choices against clients' best interests. Section 12.4 poses potential solutions to this dilemma.

5 Alec MacGillis, The Last Shot, ProPublica (June 27, 2017), www.propublica.org/article/vivitrol-opiate-crisis-and-criminal-justice.

6 See discussion infra Section 12.3.

7 Harper, Drugmaker, supra note 1.

8 MacGillis, supra note 4.

12.2 THE RELATIONSHIP BETWEEN DRUG COURTS AND MEDICAL MANUFACTURERS

States have created drug courts as a therapeutic alternative to incarceration in cases involving nonviolent, low-level criminal charges.[9] Instead of incarceration, drug court clients can live and work in the community if they follow drug court requirements, including treatment policies. Studies suggest that, on balance, drug court program participation is more effective than incarceration at preventing drug use relapse and reincarceration.[10] The Trump Opioid Crisis Commission commended drug courts as a "central component of the pretrial diversion process,"[11] encouraging their implementation in all ninety-three Federal district courts and every US county.[12]

12.2.1 *Drug Court Staff Beliefs Regarding Treatment for Substance Use Disorder*

Drug courts typically do not provide treatment directly, but rather set treatment policies, establish relationships with community substance use disorder (SUD) treatment providers to whom they refer clients, and monitor treatment adherence. Participant noncompliance with drug court policies can result in program expulsion and incarceration. Drug courts are operated by teams headed by a judge.[13] Court teams may also include a program coordinator, court case manager, prosecutor, probation/parole officer, law enforcement official, counselor, and clinical case manager.[14] Most team members lack medical training, most teams lack physicians, and counselors and clinical case managers engaged on treatment teams typically are employed by a partnering health care organization, and not the court. To date, little is known about how drug court teams set treatment policies, especially with respect to opioid use disorder (OUD) treatment.

The gold standard of care for OUD is MOUD with methadone, buprenorphine, or naltrexone.[15] Methadone and buprenorphine (including but not limited to Suboxone) are opioid agonists that activate the brain's mu opioid receptors,

9 Celinda Franco, Drug Courts: Background, Effectiveness, and Policy Issues for Congress (2010), https://fas.org/sgp/crs/misc/R41448.pdf.

10 Ojmarrh Mitchell et al., Assessing the Effectiveness of Drug Courts on Recidivism: A Meta-Analytic Review of Traditional and Non-Traditional Drug Courts, 40 J. of Crim. Justice 60–71 (2012).

11 The President's Commission on Combating Drug Addiction and the Opioid Crisis, Final Report, at 73, www.whitehouse.gov/sites/whitehouse.gov/files/images/Final_Report_Draft_11-1-2017.pdf.

12 Id. at 10.

13 Barbara Andraka-Christou, What is Treatment For Opioid Addiction in Problem-Solving Courts? A Study of 20 Indiana Drug & Veterans Courts, 13 Stan. J. Civ. Rights & Civ. Lib. 189–254 (2017); Nat'l Assoc. of Drug Court Professionals, 2 Adult Drug Court Best Practice Standards (2015).

14 Andraka-Christou, supra note 12; Nat'l Assoc. of Drug Court Professionals, supra note 12.

15 Nat'l Acads. Of Sci., Eng'rs, & Med., Medications for Opioid Use Disorder Save Lives (2019); Substance Abuse & Mental Health Servs. Admin., Treatment Improvement Protocol 63: Medications for Opioid Use Disorder (2018).

decreasing opioid cravings and preventing painful withdrawal symptoms. Agonist treatment is associated with as much as a 50 percent decrease in mortality from overdose.[16] In contrast, naltrexone is a non-opioid antagonist that blocks opioids from activating the brain's mu opioid receptors. Vivitrol, approved for OUD treatment in 2010, is an intramuscular injectable extended-release version of naltrexone that is more effective than a placebo at preventing return to drug use, including for criminal justice system participants.[17]

While few studies to date have directly compared the efficacy of buprenorphine or methadone to Vivitrol, buprenorphine and methadone appear more effective at preventing overdose deaths, do not necessitate complete detoxification, and are more cost-effective.[18] Additionally, Vivitrol is harder to start because it requires complete detoxification from opioids.[19] According to one randomized controlled comparative study, it was harder to initiate patients onto Vivitrol than oral buprenorphine, creating a relatively higher rate of return to drug use for patients randomized to Vivitrol as compared to oral buprenorphine; however, patients who successfully initiated onto Vivitrol had comparable rates of return to drug use as those on oral buprenorphine.[20] Therefore, patients may need detoxification support and/or high motivation levels to successfully start Vivitrol.[21] Two more recent studies found that agonists were more protective against opioid overdose than Vivitrol.[22] Lastly, at approximately $1,300 per thirty-day dose, Vivitrol is significantly more expensive, and far less cost-effective, than other OUD medications.[23]

16 Marc R. Larochelle et al., Medication for Opioid Use Disorder After Nonfatal Opioid Overdose and Association with Mortality, 169 Annals of Int. Med. 137 (2018); Thomas Santo Jr. et al, Association of Opioid Agonist Treatment with All-Cause Mortality and Specific Causes of Death Among People with Opioid Dependence: A Systematic Review and Meta-analysis, 78 JAMA Psychiatry 979–993 (2021).

17 Donna M. Coviello et al., A Multisite Pilot Study of Extended-Release Injectable Naltrexone Treatment for Previously Opioid-Dependent Parolees and Probationers, 33 Substance Abuse 48–59 (2012); Michael S. Gordon et al., A Phase 4, Pilot, Open-Label Study of VIVITROL® (Extended-Release Naltrexone XR-NTX) for Prisoners, 59 J. Substance Abuse Treatment 52–8 (2015); Brantley P. Jarvis et al., Extended-Release Injectable Naltrexone For Opioid Use Disorder: A Systematic Review, 113 Addiction 1188–209 (2018).

18 Sarah E. Wakeman et al., Comparative Effectiveness of Different Treatment Pathways for Opioid Use Disorder, 3 JAMA Network Open (2020); Jake R. Morgan et al., Overdose Following Initiation of Naltrexone and Buprenorphine Medication Treatment for Opioid Use Disorder in a United States Commercially Insured Cohort, 200 Drug & Alcohol Dependence 34–9 (2019).

19 Joshua D. Lee et al., Comparative Effectiveness of Extended-Release Naltrexone Versus Buprenorphine-Naloxone For Opioid Relapse Prevention (X:BOT): A Multicentre, Open-Label, Randomised Controlled Trial, 391 Lancet 309–18 (2018).

20 Lee et al., supra note 19.

21 Id.

22 Morgan et al., supra note 19; Wakeman et al., supra note 19.

23 Wash. State Institute for Pub. Pol'y, Substance Use Disorders Benefit-Cost Results, http://www.wsipp.wa.gov/BenefitCost/Pdf/7/WSIPP_BenefitCost_Substance-Use-Disorders.

Unfortunately, drug court OUD treatment policies may run contrary to best practices. A 2013 study found that up to 50 percent of adult drug courts prohibit methadone and buprenorphine; and a 2021 study found that judges are more likely to have favourable policies toward Vivitrol as compared to buprenorphine or methadone.[24] The substance and accuracy of court teams' treatment policies relate to program member beliefs about treatment safety, efficacy, and diversion potential.[25] Compared to agonist treatments, court staff appear to have relatively more positive beliefs about Vivitrol,[26] despite emerging data suggesting that agonist treatments are comparatively more effective at preventing overdose death.[27]

Device and pharmaceutical manufacturers (Industry) may directly inform court staff beliefs about MOUD. From 2010 to 2017, as the opioid epidemic exploded, few OUD treatment education options were available to courts beyond industry representatives.[28] Media articles,[29] a qualitative study of Indiana courts,[30] and a quantitative study of Florida courts[31] suggest that many court staff receive information about OUD treatments directly from pharmaceutical companies, especially Alkermes. For example, in a convenience sample of 121 Florida court staff, 36 percent reported receiving training from Alkermes, 24 percent from a buprenorphine manufacturer, and 11 percent from a methadone manufacturer. Among those who received training from a medication manufacturer, 55 percent received training from at least two companies. Another recent study found that, after controlling for opioid overdose deaths in an area, drug courts' location was significantly and positively associated with pharmaceutical payments to physicians for MOUD (tracked under sunshine laws),[32] suggesting that pharmaceutical companies may target physicians in areas where they know drug courts make referrals.

24 Harlan Matusow, Medication Assisted Treatment in US Drug Courts: Results from a Nationwide Survey of Availability, Barriers and Attitudes, 43 J. Substance Abuse Treatment (2012); Barabara Andraka-Christout et al., Criminal Problem-Solving and Civil Dependency Court Policies Regarding Medications for Opioid Use Disorder, Subst Abus. 1–8 (2021).

25 Andraka-Christou, supra note 12; Matusow et al., supra note 24.

26 Andraka-Christou, supra note 12; Barbara Andraka-Christou et al., Court Personnel Attitudes Towards Medication-Assisted Treatment: A State-Wide Survey, 104 J. Substance Abuse Treatment 72–82 (2019); Barbara Andraka-Christou & Danielle Atkins, Beliefs About Medications for Opioid Use Disorder Among Florida Criminal Problem-Solving Court and Dependency Court Staff, 46 Am. J. Drug & Alcohol Abuse 749, 749–60 (2020).

27 Lee et al., supra note 19; Morgan et al., supra note 18; Wakeman et al., supra note 19.

28 The National Judicial Opioid Task Force, a collaboration of representatives from the Conference of Chief Justices and State Court Administrators was formed in 2017 and published its recommendations concerning treatment best practices in November 2019. See Nat'l Judicial Opioid Task Force, Courts as Leaders in the Crisis of Addiction (Nov. 18, 2019), www.ncsc.org/~/media/Files/PDF/Topics/Opioids-and-the-Courts/NJOTF_Final_Report_111819.ashx.

29 Harper, supra note 1.

30 Andraka-Christou, supra note 12.

31 Barbara Andraka-Christou et al., Receipt of Training about Medication for Opioid Use Disorder from Pharmaceutical Manufacturers: A Preliminary Study of Florida Criminal Problem-Solving and Dependency Court Staff, 39 Drug & Alcohol Rev. 583, 583–587 (2020).

32 Id.

Some court staff's understanding of substance use may reflect cultural and personal perspectives about addiction, "viewing it as moral weakness that call[s] for tough paternalism."[33] According to Andraka-Christou, judges have differing conceptions of sobriety, from living life without any substances (including medications) to living life without misusing substances.[34] Some court staff view agonists merely as "trading one drug for another" or "not really quitting."[35] Court staff beliefs about MOUD may also reflect beliefs and practices of the treatment providers with whom they collaborate, with one study of a convenience sample of court staff finding that half felt their collaborating provider did not encourage agonist MOUD.[36]

Despite the effectiveness of agonist MOUD at decreasing overdose death and return to drug use, several studies have documented hostile court staff attitudes towards agonist treatment,[37] particularly methadone,[38] due to its perceived diversion and misuse potential, distrust of methadone providers (often located in high-crime areas), and misunderstandings about medication safety and efficacy.[39] Court staff view buprenorphine slightly more favorably, but may require or strongly encourage clients to transition off upon entering the program[40] despite medical studies indicating that longer-term buprenorphine use is more effective than shorter-term use.[41] As with methadone, court staff appear to distrust providers and worry about potential client misuse or diversion of buprenorphine.[42] One Ohio drug court judge stated, "the Suboxone zombies aren't getting better ... The people who want the Vivitrol are the ones who want to get healthy and get better."[43]

Court staff have more favorable beliefs about Vivitrol because it cannot be misused or diverted and lacks an opioid ingredient.[44] Judges are critical of its cost, however, even though clients can get free samples or discounts through state-funded programs or Alkermes. One judge stated, "we work really closely with the drug rep from Alkermes ... and they 've been very supportive in finding us, giving us discounts for some of our people, even providing a month or two of free doses."[45]

33 MacGillis, supra note 4.

34 Barbara Andraka-Christou, The Opioid Fix: America's Addiction Crisis and the Solution They Don't Want You to Have Ch. 6 (2020).

35 Id.

36 Barbara Andraka-Christou & Danielle N. Atkins, Whose Opinion Matters about Medications for Opioid Use Disorder? A Cross-Sectional Survey of Social Norms Among Court Staff, 42 Substance Abuse (forthcoming 2021), available online at www.tandfonline.com/doi/abs/10.1080/08897077.2020.1846666?journalCode=wsub20.

37 Andraka-Christou, supra note 12; Andraka-Christou et al., supra note 28; Matusow et al., supra note 24.

38 Andraka-Christou et al., supra note 26; Andraka-Christou & Atkins, supra note 26; Matusow et al., supra note 24.

39 Andraka-Christou, supra note 12.

40 Id.

41 Andraka-Christou, supra note 12, at 232–233.

42 Id. at 234.

43 MacGillis, supra note 4.

44 Andraka-Christou, supra note 12, at 235.

45 Id. at 236.

12.2.2 *Examples of Direct-to-Court Marketing: the Bridge and Vivitrol*

Medical device manufacturers market their products directly to drug courts. The National Association of Drug Court Professionals (NADCP) is the primary standard-setting organization for adult drug courts, and heavily influences court staff education. Innovative Health Solutions, the manufacturers of the Bridge, have been a regular presence promoting their product as an adjunct to Vivitrol-based treatment at the NADCP national conference. Even though the device received FDA approval, that status rested solely upon a heavily criticized study that lacked a control group, reported no dropout rate, and lacked IRB oversight. IHS also marketed the Bridge as early as 2016, over a year before receiving FDA approval, engaging in off-label promotion and violating FDA regulations.[46]

As compared to other MOUD manufacturers, Alkermes is most widely known for engaging and "educating" drug court judges. Alkermes initially found that conventional marketing practices were ineffective for Vivitrol[47] and began to cultivate new markets by reaching out to criminal justice officials, drug court judges, and professional associations.[48] In 2014, Alkermes paid $50,000 to become a "champion" sponsor of the NADCP.[49] Alkermes also detailed its strategic targeting of drug court judges and criminal justice institutions at a 2016 analyst and investor event,[50] where CEO Richard Pops described "priming" state "ecosystems" to shape and penetrate markets by aligning messaging to court staff opinions.[51] Alkermes' "road map for future growth" included both a "traditional commercial approach (MD, patient, payer)" and "generat[ing] organic conversations among [a] broad range of stakeholders (criminal justice, policy, caregivers, etc.)"[52] These strategies directly positioned Vivitrol as a novel and superior drug; Alkermes' Vice President of Marketing described "stimulat[ing] organic conversations about 'deserving to know all options' and the potential to end dependence on opioids."[53]

12.3 MORAL ENTREPRENEURSHIP AND CONFLICT OF INTEREST

To understand the potential for bias and conflicts of interest in selecting treatment providers and the associated forms of treatment made available to drug court

46 Harper, Questions, supra note 1.
47 MacGillis, supra note 4.
48 Id. at 71.
49 MacGillis, supra note 4; Harper, Drugmaker, supra note 1; Arlene Weintraub, Alkermes Balks at U.S. Senator's Probe Into "Aggressive" Vivitrol Lobbying and Marketing, FiercePharma (Nov. 7, 2017), www.fiercepharma.com/legal/alkermes-balks-at-u-s-senator-harris-probe-into-vivitrol-marketing.
50 Alkermes, Alkermes Analyst & Investor Event (September 26, 2016), in Harper, Drugmaker, supra note 1.
51 Id. at 44.
52 Id. at 97.
53 Id. at 99.

program enrollees, it is helpful to examine these issues in a related context: the industry sales representative-physician relationship. Some experts believe conflicts arise because business and medical ethics differ: businesses, including medical device and pharmaceutical companies, commonly reward vendors to stimulate sales, while such conduct could be problematic or unethical in medicine.[54] The most controversial practices are industry sponsorship of continuing medical education programs (CME) and "detailing," where industry sales representatives (ISRs) "visit physician offices to discuss the availability and suitability of products."[55]

Advocates of close industry-physician relationships describe them as "a full, honest, fair, and balanced discussion of materials" that gives providers "invaluable assistance" in selecting appropriate medications, and providers reciprocate by giving drugs "preferred status on a hospital's formulary."[56] Because physicians cannot keep up with extensive literature and innovations, the ISR visit is an "extremely effective" encounter, providing essential information in five or ten minutes.[57] Thus, pro-industry advocates assert, marketing communications sell products and facilitate "technology transfer."[58] The potential for bias here is clear; but industry advocates argue that "[a]lthough information coming from a commercial source does present the product in the best possible light, physicians are well aware of this bias and correct for it."[59] Moreover, they contend, visits from competing ISRs "expose[] physicians to multiple biases," allowing them to "make a more informed choice."[60] They concede, however, that physicians make prescription decisions by "relating the decision to a personal value system" to which ISRs can appeal.[61]

A 2019 study found that pharmaceutical manufacturers alone spent more than $20 billion marketing to health care professionals in 2016, including $5.6 billion for prescriber detailing.[62] This study also acknowledged their statistics significantly underestimated the amount industry spent on professional marketing, as the authors were unable to acquire data on marketing related to devices, meetings, and events. While independent firms produce CME programs, they have been found to "skew training material in favor of commercial interests" to retain business.[63]

Critics of close industry-physician relationships describe a conflict between product promotion and education and assert that patients' interests are not best served by

54 Shaili Jain, Understanding Physician-Pharmaceutical Industry Interactions: A Concise Guide (2007).

55 Id. at 12.

56 Erin Albert & Cathleen Sass, The Medical Science Liaison: An A to Z Guide 99 (2007).

57 Mickey C. Smith, Pharmaceutical Marketing: Principles, Environment, and Practice 339 (2002).

58 Id. at 332, 337.

59 Id. at 340.

60 Id.

61 Id. at 276.

62 Lisa M. Schwartz & Steven Woloshin, Medical Marketing in the United States, 1997–2016, 321 J. Am. Med. Assoc. 80–96 (2019).

63 Jim Giles, Drug Firms Accused of Biasing Doctors' Training, Nature (Nov. 20, 2017), www.nature.com/articles/450464a.

industry-influenced prescribing practices.[64] Although physicians often believe they are not influenced by marketing, research clearly shows otherwise.[65] These sophisticated promotional activities exploit the professional's vulnerabilities, often at subconscious levels, to create biases[66] and influence prescribing habits in ways that may not best serve the care recipient.

12.3.1 *Applying a Conflict-of-Interest Framework*

A conflict-of-interest (COI) framework can structure our understanding of relationships between industry and drug court treatment teams, especially since, as shown above, we know: 1) industry representatives already serve either as significant sponsors or appear as vendors at drug court conferences, and 2) industry has been engaged in court team members education and detailing.

As described by Stark,[67] whose work examined COI as it applied to public officials, and has since been applied to health professionals,[68] motivated bias is a process (FN69), and COIs are broken down into three behavioral stages.[69] First, antecedent acts prepare the target of influence's state of mind for partiality or bias, making the target more likely to exercise responsibility for private or personal interests instead of the interests of the public (or patient/program enrolee).[70] Second, antecedent acts influence the target towards certain perspectives, biases, or affinities.[71] Third, the target behaves in ways influenced by antecedent factors.[72] Industry interactions with court team members are, at minimum, antecedent acts toward more favorable arrangements for the industry (in this case prioritizing one MOUD in court treatment referrals or in court policies).

Stark also distinguishes external influences from internal convictions, differentiating between an internal "genuinely subjective belief or commitment" that might become "an encumbrance when its proximate cause lies without, in the importunings of a litigant, the ministrations of a lobbyist or the pressure of a campaign contributor."[73] For example, lobbying is an external attempt to "mobilize the bias," or "strengthen the commitment members have to an already established position on a given question."[74] Internal convictions are difficult or impossible to

64 Jain, supra note 54, at 4.
65 Id. at 9–10. See also Sunita Sah & Adriane Fugh-Berman, Physicians Under the Influence: Social Psychology and Industry Marketing Strategies, 41 J. L, Med. & Ethics 665, 665–72 (2013).
66 See Sah & Fugh-Berman, supra note 65, at 665–666.
67 Andrew Stark, Conflict of Interest in American Public Life (2000).
68 Daniel S. Goldberg, The Shadows of Sunlight: Why Disclosure Should Not Be a Priority in Addressing Conflicts of Interest, 12 Pub. Health Ethics 202–212 (2018).
69 Goldberg, supra note 68.
70 Sheldon Krimsky, Science in the Private Interest: has the Lure of Profits Corrupted Biomedical Research?, 126 (2004); Stark, supra note 67.
71 Krimsky, supra note 70, at 126.
72 Id.
73 Stark, supra note 67, at 149.
74 Id. at 173.

disclose and divest; there is no disclosure form, and disclosure itself only suggests "an irremediable capacity to make an unencumbered decision."[75] Someone who discloses beliefs might "develop an encumbering interest" in maintaining them.[76]

12.3.2 *Judges as Moral Entrepreneurs*

Sociologist Howard Becker coined the term "moral entrepreneurs" to describe individuals in power who work to construct systems that reinforce their beliefs about deviancy (often through criminalization).[77] For example, a moral entrepreneur who believes that all people who use medications with misuse potential are morally deviant would punish and/or exclude people who utilize these products and develop systems that prioritize the use of medications/devices without misuse potential.

For years, judges and drug court treatment teams have been forging ahead in the opioid epidemic, handling massive increases in the proportion of clients with opioid use disorder, including treatment referrals, without much organized guidance. More research must be conducted on the mechanics underlying the selection of treatment providers for drug court teams. That said, our research has found that program managers, as well as judges, are receiving education from industry representatives.[78]

According to Stark, "in law, business, and medicine, the professional (lawyer, manager, doctor) is thought to have fiduciary or 'role-moral' obligations . . . to pursue and protect certain interests possessed by a defined, identifiable set of principles: clients, shareholders, patients."[79] Because drug courts are structured to facilitate opportunities for program enrolees (clients) to access treatment services that effectively address their SUD and help them avoid incarceration and recidivism, judges and treatment team members, as the creators and managers of these systems of care, are charged with the role-moral obligation to act in clients' best interests. This section focuses explicitly on drug court judges because, in the unique setting of the drug court, they lead teams that select and engage treatment providers, are fiduciaries, and must adhere to ethics codes. Even if a manufacturer communicates directly with other team members, such as court program coordinators, judges will have the final say about court policies.

Industry education from antagonist manufacturers and device companies position their products as morally superior to agonist treatments. In this way, antagonist manufacturers motivate bias against the moral entrepreneur – in this case, the judge – and their existing negative beliefs regarding opioids.

75 Id. at 241.
76 Id. at 253; See also Sah & Fugh-Berman, supra note 65.
77 Howard S. Becker, Outsiders: Studies in the Sociology of Deviance (1963).
78 Andraka-Christou, Court Personnel, supra note 12.
79 Stark, supra note 67, at 89.

Some external standards exist to determine clients' best interests as to MOUD, including medical standards of care or best practices and professional guidance.[80]

A judge who supports recovery should follow medical standards for recovery support, rather than engage as moral entrepreneurs. Narrowing treatment options to Vivitrol and/or the Bridge ignores patients for whom these interventions are contraindicated, including pregnant women. Because Vivitrol is costlier, requires detoxification, and is less protective against overdose, judges preferencing Vivitrol in their systems also create a more difficult recovery road for court clients with limited financial means. As the former head of SAMHSA's Center for Substance Abuse Treatment commented, "what we continue to have is a political philosophy colliding with therapeutic strategies, and that political philosophy has less to do with the individual and more to do with moral views about drug abuse."[81]

Because of the unique nature of the relationship between courts and MOUD manufacturers, it would be difficult to regulate these decisions based upon extant judicial conduct rules. American Bar Association Model Code of Judicial Conduct Rule 2.2 requires judges to "uphold the law" when deciding cases; an accompanying comment states, "[a]lthough each judge comes to the bench with a unique background and personal philosophy, a judge must interpret and interpret the law without regard to whether the judge approves or disapproves or the law in question." Yet, there is no law compelling judges to use the highest and best scientific and medical evidence in judicial decision making. In fact, one might argue that this is not the type of "decision making" the model code envisaged.

12.4 IDENTIFYING A RANGE OF POTENTIAL SOLUTIONS

Much can be done to avoid improper influences that may occur in relationships between pharmaceutical manufacturers and drug courts and defuse any potential resulting conflicts. These solutions range from "light" to "heavy." In practice, widespread changes in approaches to court-industry relationships may occur gradually.

An effective "light" solution would be to systematically affirm that a judge's role is overseeing court proceedings as "captain of the ship" and monitoring clients. This role does not, however, include making treatment decisions. Decisions like whether MOUD is appropriate for individual clients, and in which form, must be left to a treatment provider.[82] Judges' comments that they will not allow forms of MOUD that can be diverted or with opioid ingredients reflect inappropriate encroachment on the treatment provider's role. Physicians should receive complementary educational messaging through professional medical associations such as the AMA. Drug

80 Substance Abuse and Mental Health Services Administration, TIP 63: Medications for Opioid Use Disorder (2021).

81 MacGillis, supra note 4.

82 Andraka-Christou, supra note 34, Ch. 6.

courts should also be encouraged to include local physicians on treatment teams or as consultants. Logically, the ideal medical professional would be a practitioner offering holistic treatment options to whom the drug court judge refers clients seeking MOUD. This may be difficult in several areas of the country, however, based on qualified providers' availability and willingness to serve, although new telehealth and expanded methadone rules may extend access to more distant providers. Additionally, since court staff select the health care providers with whom programs partner, they may opt into relationships with providers who have anti-MOUD attitudes.

Another solution would be to provide judges and staff with alternative educational resources free from industry sponsorship. It is not suggested that judges and staff intentionally invited industry representatives to influence court proceedings in earlier years. Rather, courts' eagerness for informational resources were an educational vacuum that pharmaceutical and medical device manufacturers were prepared to fill. Alternative educational content can be provided online and at professional conferences and are currently coordinated through professional associations such as NADCP and NCSC. Some governmental and non-profit organizations have begun offering MOUD-focused education tailored to judges, including information about the appropriate MOUD decision-making role of court team members.[83]

A more involved solution would be to attach restrictions and requirements to court funding, such as conditioning grant monies on court compliance with best practices of allowing all three kinds of MOUD. Recipients of federal Bureau of Justice Assistance (BJA) grants, for example, have to demonstrate that they will not deny clients access to their programs because of MOUD use.[84] This would provide some federal regulatory oversight enforcing best practices; however, this solution has limited reach as only approximately 200 out of 3,000 drug courts nationwide receive BJA funds. State grants could incorporate similar conditions.

A still more comprehensive solution would be to impose state-level certifications mandating that drug courts adhere to certain standards, such as permitting all three forms of MOUD, agreeing to refer clients to certain licensed facilities that must accept Medicaid, etc. For example, Michigan's certification program[85] requires courts to comply with several standards and best practices, including the BJA's *Key Components*[86] and the National Center for DWI Courts' *Ten Guiding Principles of DWI Courts*.[87] These guidelines require drug courts to allow MOUD use "when

83 See, e.g., Florida Courts Substance Abuse Response Opioids and Stimulants Solutions, http://www.courtslearn.com.

84 See, e.g., Bureau of Justice Assistance, Medication Assisted Treatment, https://bja.ojp.gov/sites/g/files/xyckuh186/files/media/document/adc-faq-medication-assisted-treatment.pdf.

85 Mich. Comp. Laws § 600.1062.

86 Nat'l Assoc. of Drug Court Professionals, Defining Drug Courts: The Key Components (Oct. 2004), www.ncjrs.gov/pdffiles1/bja/205621.pdf.

87 Nat'l Center for DWI Courts, The Ten Guiding Principles of DWI Courts, http://www.dwicourts.org/wp-content/uploads/Guiding_Principles_of_DWI_Court_0.pdf.

appropriate, based on a case-specific determination and handle MOUD very similarly to other kinds of treatment" and assert that "the court does not determine the type, dosage, and duration of" MOUD.[88] Similarly, states can pass statutes or regulations prohibiting MOUD bans within courts, as has already occurred in some states.[89]

Finally, a model sunshine law for drug courts could be an integral component of an effective solution scheme. Federal court and employee rules require financial disclosures for gifts and reimbursements above a certain threshold.[90] Federal laws such as the Physician Payments Sunshine Act, passed in 2010, make financial relationships between medical industrial corporations and physicians more transparent and reveal COIs, requiring pharmaceutical, medical device, biological and medical supply manufacturers who are covered by Medicare, Medicaid and the State Children's Health Insurance Program to track financial relationships with teaching hospitals and physicians and report that data to the Centers for Medicare and Medicaid Services. A mandatory disclosure approach acknowledges the role of those seeking to influence system development (the manufacturers) as well as the system participants. A model state sunshine law could encourage states to re-evaluate decisions made years ago, particularly court policies or referral practices prioritizing Vivitrol over agonist treatments.

A sunshine law by itself, however, will have little impact. Disclosure plays a paramount role in avoiding liability for COI but it alone is not a viable solution. If disclosures are made after antecedent acts produce relationships that enable improper influences, the harm has already occurred. An efficacious intervention should take place before acts can lead to partiality.[91] Disclosure alone does not eliminate problematic relationships, thwart influence, or prevent partial behavior.[92] Disclosure of judicial beliefs regarding MOUD would do little but expose easy marks for manufacturers to exploit. Thus, sequestration – prohibition of most industry engagement with drug court team members – may be more effective than disclosure, because eliminating problematic relationships eliminates COIs.[93] Full sequestration need not be imposed due to First Amendment concerns. Instead, state courts administrators could prohibit court team members from meeting with industry representatives, or accepting free lunches or other items from manufacturers.[94] Additionally, state professional licensing boards (e.g., bar associations) could forbid

88 State Court Administrative Office, Mich. Assoc. of Treatment Court Professionals, Adult Drug Court Standards, Best Practices, and Promising Practices 53 (Dec. 2019), https://courts.michigan.gov/Administration/SCAO/Resources/Documents/bestpractice/ADC-BPManual.pdf.

89 See, e.g., 730 ICLS § 166/25 (West 2020) (Illinois).

90 United States Courts, Judiciary Financial Disclosure Regulations § 330, www.uscourts.gov/sites/default/files/guide-vol02d.pdf; 5 U.S.C. § 101–111.

91 Goldberg, supra note 65, at 1.

92 Id.

93 Id.

94 Id.

licensees from applying manufacturer-provided training toward required continuing legal education credits.

Of course, the most effective strategy would be to deploy a web involving many of these proposals. Here, policy makers can follow Alkermes' example, implementing a comprehensive array of educational opportunities and regulatory and oversight measures at local, state, and national levels, in partnership with diverse professional organizations representing law, medicine, and the court system.

13

Disrupting the Market for Ineffective Medical Devices

Wendy Netter Epstein

The current debate over medical device regulation pits safety against innovation. Those in favor of greater regulation point to the need to protect patients from the harms of insufficiently tested devices. Those in favor of less regulation cite the need to promote innovation and move potentially lifesaving devices to market faster.[1] At present, the less regulation, more innovation camp is winning the debate – in part on the argument that postmarket surveillance systems can adequately address safety concerns. But framing the debate this way leaves out key inputs: efficacy and relative effectiveness.

Not all innovation is created equal nor is it equally desirable. The best innovation creates medical devices that are superior to current alternatives, either because they lead to better patient outcomes or because outcomes are just as good, but the care is cheaper. The ideal innovation creates devices that are both clinically better and cheaper. While the potential for devices to significantly improve health outcomes is great – and many devices have had such a positive impact – the prevalence of ineffective devices is nonetheless troubling.[2]

In 2016, the 21st Century Cures Act was signed into law.[3] The Act was designed in large part to accelerate device development and approval. But even under the

[1] See Daniel B. Kramer et al., Ensuring Medical Device Effectiveness and Safety: A Cross-National Comparison of Approaches to Regulation, 69 Food & Drug L. J. 1, 6 (2014); Rita F. Redberg, Improving the Safety of High-Risk Medical Devices, 68 DePaul L. Rev. 327 (2019); US Food & Drug Admin., FDA In Brief: FDA continues Steps to Promote Innovation in Medical Devices that Help Advance Patient Safety Through the Safer Technologies Program (Sept. 18, 2019), www.fda.gov/news-events/fda-brief/fda-brief-fda-continues-steps-promote-innovation-medical-devices-help-advance-patient-safety-through. Compare, e.g., Report Criticized F.D.A. on Device Testing, N.Y. Times (Jan. 15, 2009) (arguing for stricter regulation of devices) with FDA Seeks to Toughen Defibrillator Regulations, N.Y. Times (Mar. 22, 2013) (arguing for looser device regulation).

[2] Debra Jackson et al., Medical Device-Related Pressure Ulcers: A Systematic Review and Meta-Analysis, 92 Int'l J. Nursing Studies (2019); Rushi K.Talati et al., Major FDA Medical Device Recalls in Ophthalmology from 2003 to 2015, 53 Can. J. Ophthalmology 98 (2017), https://doi.org/10.1016/j.jcjo.2017.08.001.

[3] Aaron S. Kesselheim & Jerry Avorn, New "21st Century Cures" Legislation: Speed and Ease vs Science, 317 JAMA 581 (2017).

somewhat stricter regulatory regime that had been in place prior to the Act, there was evidence that ineffective and expensive medical devices were used pervasively. One study identified nearly forty such ineffective medical devices.[4] As shown in Chapter 1, the use of these devices can harm the health of patients and adds significant costs to an already immensely costly system.

Perhaps none of this is surprising given that market mechanisms can be ineffective at promoting ideal device innovation, the regulatory regime is underpowered (even when the Food and Drug Administration (FDA) requires evidence of effectiveness, the bar is low),[5] and the products liability and tort systems do little to force providers to assess relative efficacy.[6] This chapter describes the serious negative consequences that flow from the use of ineffective medical devices and explores some solutions, focusing on the underexplored role that providers and payors might play in beginning to address this problem.

13.1 THE KIND OF INNOVATION WE WANT VERSUS THE MEDICAL DEVICES WE GET

Sometimes medical devices are brand new innovations in that they do not replace anything that came before them. For instance, the stethoscope was first invented in 1816 to improve upon the only method that existed at the time to listen to a patient's heart – placing one's ear on the patient's chest.[7] More often, however, medical devices purport to be improvements to treatments that already exist – an improvement over an existing device (say a next-generation pacemaker) or an alternative to another practice (for example, substituting device technology to control hypertension for pharmaceutical therapy).[8] But how do we evaluate what type of medical device innovation is most desirable?

There are two primary dimensions to consider: the extent to which the device improves patient outcomes[9] and the effect on cost. The best new medical devices simultaneously improve patient outcomes and reduce cost. But we may also be

4 Diana Herrera-Perez et al., Meta-Research: A Comprehensive Review of Randomized Clinical Trials in Three Medical Journals Reveals 396 Medical Reversals, 8 eLife 45183 (2019).

5 Sanket S. Dhruva et al., Strength of Study Evidence Examined by the FDA in Premarket Approval of Cardiovascular Devices, 302 JAMA 2679 (2009); Sarah Y. Zheng et al., Characteristics of Clinical Studies Used for US FDA Approval of High-Risk Medical Supplements, 318 JAMA 619 (2017).

6 Id.; 21 U.S.C. § 360(c) (describing the 510k process). Although note that the US premarket authorization process does contain an effectiveness requirement, whereas the European Union's performance standard is more lenient. See the Official Journal of the European Union for Harmonised European standards for medical devices, https://eur-lex.europa.eu/legal-content/EN/TXT/?uri=OJ:L:2020:090I:TOC.

7 Sherwin B. Nuland, Doctors: The Biography of Medicine 24, 220 (1988).

8 Gregory J. Millman, Medical Devices as Drug Replacements, Wall St. J. (May 28, 2012), https://blogs.wsj.com/source/2012/05/28/medical-devices-as-drug-replacements/?mod=google_news_blog.

9 How to measure improved patient outcomes is a matter of significant controversy. See generally Christopher Buccafusco & Jonathan S. Masur, Drugs, Patents, and Well-Being, 98 Wash U. L. Rev. 1403 (2021).

happy when new devices either improve outcomes or are cheaper. One thing is clear: we do not want devices that score poorly on both patient outcome and cost metrics. To the extent our current system is prompting new devices that simultaneously add cost and do not improve patient outcomes,[10] that is problematic. Yet there is a growing body of evidence showing that such devices are getting approved (or cleared) by the FDA and are being used in practice, without patient knowledge.

When medical devices are determined to be unsafe, it is front page news. Consider the plight of surgical mesh used to repair hernias that had severe side effects,[11] the cement application device used in spinal fusions that grew bone where it was not supposed to,[12] or metal-on-metal replacement hips that caused flesh-rotting metallosis.[13] These devices were recalled, class action lawsuits were filed, and policymakers rightly focused on how these harms could have been avoided.[14] But the same is not true of ineffective medical devices – those that might not be killing people or causing horrendous side effects, but that can nonetheless cause considerable harm when they do not do what they are supposed to do.

Consider the example of the bispectral index monitor (BIS) intended to address anesthesia awareness, which occurs when surgical patients under general anesthesia are aware of events that happened during the surgery after they awaken, sometimes feeling pain.[15] These experiences are associated with posttraumatic stress disorder and anxiety. The BIS monitor was designed to fix the problem by measuring consciousness, allowing the anesthesiologist to titrate anesthesia to avoid awareness.[16] The device was approved by the FDA in 1996. Its use spread so much that BIS monitors were in more than half of all operating rooms.[17] Then, ten years after FDA approval, a large, randomized trial that compared use of the BIS monitor with standardized monitoring procedures found no benefit of the BIS monitor to

10 Device effect on patient outcomes may be highly heterogeneous. Devices may only be effective for a small sliver of the population but used broadly.

11 Sheila Kaplan & Matthew Goldstein, F.D.A. Halts U.S. Sales of Pelvic Mesh, Citing Safety Concerns for Women, N.Y. Times (Apr. 16, 2019), www.nytimes.com/2019/04/16/health/vaginal-pelvic-mesh-fda.html.

12 Joe Carlson & Jim Spencer, Medtronic Agrees to Settlement with Five States in Infuse Case, Star Trib. (Dec. 13, 2017), www.startribune.com/medtronic-agrees-to-settlement-with-five-states-in-infuse-case/463955203/.

13 Jeanne Lenzer, Can Your Hip Replacement Kill You?, N.Y. Times (Jan. 13, 2018), www.nytimes.com/2018/01/13/opinion/sunday/can-your-hip-replacement-kill-you.html.

14 Ralph F. Hall, To Recall or Not to Recall, That Is the Question: The Current Controversy over Medical Device Recalls, 7 Minn. J. L. Sci. & Tech. 161 (2005).

15 Se Woo Park et al., Bispectral Index Versus Standard Monitoring in Sedation for Endoscopic Procedures: A Systematic Review and Meta-Analysis, 61 Digestive Diseases and Sciences 814 (2016); Medical Advisory Secretariat, Bispectral Index Monitor: An Evidence-Based Analysis, 4 Ont. Health Tech. Assessment Series 1 (2004).

16 Id.

17 Vinay Prasad et al., A Decade of Reversal: An Analysis of 146 Contradicted Medical Practices, 88 Mayo Clinic Proceedings 790 (2013).

anesthesia awareness.[18] The monitors were not necessarily unsafe, but they were ineffective and costly.

The story of hip protectors is similar. Hip protectors are devices designed to protect older patients, typically who suffer from osteoporosis, from fracturing their hips in a fall.[19] The FDA has approved a number of different hip protector devices.[20] But now, several postmarket studies have been conducted. None have found evidence that hip protectors are effective in preventing hip fractures.[21] In some studies, patients were more likely to fracture hips when using hip protectors than when not.

Mechanical cardiopulmonary resuscitation (CPR) devices provide a final example. When a patient goes into cardiac arrest, delivering high-quality CPR improves patient outcomes.[22] CPR, however, can be difficult to perform correctly – both to perform chest compressions at the right rate and to compress the chest to the right depth. Mechanical CPR devices ostensibly reduce human error by performing automated CPR at a specified rate and to a specified depth.[23] These devices were originally introduced in the 1960s and have been approved or cleared by the FDA.[24] They are expensive, at an average price of $15,000 each, and are increasingly being used, particularly by EMS agencies.[25]

Counterintuitively, many studies have now shown that mechanical CPR leads to worse patient outcomes than manual CPR, particularly when used outside the hospital.[26] Mechanical CPR is both more costly than manual CPR and also leads to poorer health outcomes. Yet its use persists.

These examples are likely the tip of the iceberg. While these devices were studied after adoption, most do not get the postmarket randomized trial treatment.[27] Nonetheless, the systematic study of medical device effectiveness that has been done provides further reason for concern.

In 2019, authors conducted a comprehensive review of the randomized clinical trials published in three leading medical journals – The Journal of the American Medical Association and the Lancet between 2003 and 2017, and the New England

18 Michael S. Avidan, Anesthesia Awareness and the Bispectral Index, 358 N. Engl. J. Med. 1097 (2008).

19 Douglas P. Kiel et al., Efficacy of a Hip Protector to Prevent Hip Fracture in Nursing Home Residents, 298 JAMA Int'l Med. 413 (2007).

20 Id.

21 Id.

22 Monica E. Kleinman et al., 2015 American Heart Association Guidelines Update for Cardiopulmonary Resuscitation and Emergency Cardiovascular Care, 132 Circulation (2015).

23 Kurtis Poole et al., Mechanical CPR: Who? When? How?, 22 Critical Care 140 (2018).

24 Id.

25 Oren Wacht et al., Mechanical CPR Devices: Where is the Science?, J. Emergency Med. Serv. (2019), www.jems.com/2019/11/12/mechanical-cpr-devices-where-is-the-science/.

26 Poole, supra note 23; Joachim Marti et al., The Cost-Effectiveness of a Mechanical Compression Device in Out-Of-Hospital Cardiac Arrest, 117 Resuscitation 1 (2017).

27 It is not always the case that devices do not work for anyone, but often devices are being deployed in populations for which they are ineffective. See, e.g., Anahad O'Connor, Heart Stents Still Overused, Experts Say, N.Y. Times (Aug. 15. 2013), http://well.blogs.nytimes.com/2013/08/15/heart-stents-continue-to-be-overused/?_r=1.

Journal of Medicine between 2011 and 2017.[28] The study aimed to identify medical reversals, which the authors define as "practices that have been found, through randomized controlled trials, to be no better than a prior or lesser standard of care."[29] BIS monitors, hip protectors, and mechanical CPR devices, are all medical reversals.

The authors' review found close to forty medical reversals involving medical devices.[30] The authors only studied randomized controlled studies that had been published in leading medical journals, but of those studies, a surprisingly high 13 percent of all randomized trials were medical reversals.[31] These findings are consistent with other analyses that have been conducted.[32]

The next section explores why it is likely that many ineffective devices have prevailed in the market despite the fact that they do not work (or work less well) than other less-expensive options.

13.2 WHY INEFFECTIVE MEDICAL DEVICES ARE IN USE

How exactly do we end up with ineffective medical devices? In theory, three protections should prevent or at least minimize the occurrence: markets, the regulatory regime, and tort law.[33] In practice, however, all are flawed.

13.2.1 *Market Insufficiencies*

Well-functioning markets should check false claims of effectiveness. If a vacuum is advertised to pick up pet hair and it turns out that it does a lousy job, word will get out and people will not buy the vacuum. If the vacuum is merely adequate at picking up pet hair, but the model is more costly than similarly effective alternatives, consumers will not buy the vacuum. In the medical device context, if a glucose monitoring system does not accurately read glucose levels, and this fact is discoverable, patients should not buy it. And if the glucose monitoring system is adequate but more expensive than alternatives, people should not buy it.

But several characteristics make the medical device market unique. First, while a consumer can see whether the vacuum does a good job removing pet hair, a patient

28 Diana Herrera-Perez et al., Meta-Research: A Comprehensive Review of Randomized Clinical Trials in Three Medical Journals Reveals 396 Medical Reversals, 8 eLife 45183 (2019), https://elifesciences.org/articles/45183.

29 Id.

30 See also Daniel J. Niven et al., Towards Understanding the De-Adoption of Low-Value Clinical Practices: A Scoping Review, 13 BMC Med. 255 (2015); Desir´ee Sutton et al., Evidence Reversal-When New Evidence Contradicts Current Claims: A Systematic Overview Review of Definitions and Terms, 94 J. Clinical Epidemiology 76 (2018).

31 Herrera-Perez, supra note 28.

32 Id.

33 Patent law is also unhelpful. The USPTO reviews devices for usefulness, but there is no mechanism to assess effectiveness. See 35 U.S.C. § 101.

often cannot tell if the medical device does what it is supposed to do. Most patients are unable to tell if they need the medical device in the first place and are ill-equipped to select the best one even if they have access to necessary information, which they often do not. Second, patients are not making decisions alone. They must rely on doctors and other providers to act as their agents to choose the most effective device. But providers can be swayed by reimbursement rates, conflicts of interest such as side deals with device manufacturers, a desire to experiment with the latest technology, and pressure from patients and advocacy groups. When a device is not effective, it is not necessarily in the best interests of the provider to disclose that information. And even after evidence is shared that a device does not work, providers who have used a device for a long time may be hesitant to change their practices. Finally, another complication is that a third-party payor typically reimburses for device cost, lessening the impact of cost considerations on decision making. So low-value and high-value devices can be profitable just the same.

13.2.2 *Regulatory Failures*

When markets alone are not sufficient, we turn to regulation. One might assume that the FDA only approves devices that are both safe and effective. But that may not be the case.

To start, the FDA classifies devices based on risk to the patient, with Class I devices being low risk (e.g., bandages), Class II being intermediate risk (e.g., wheelchairs), and Class III being highest risk (e.g., implantable pacemakers). As others in this volume have noted, more than 80 percent of devices are exempted from the FDA's premarket approval process based on their classification and either do not require review or are instead permitted to be marketed following clearance through the 510(k)-approval pathway.[34]

Let us start with the 510(k) pathway. Devices subject to its requirements need not provide independent evidence of effectiveness. Manufacturers only need establish that the device is "substantially equivalent" to a predicate device already on the market. Devices have been cleared even if the predicate had been removed from the market or if the predicate had been initially approved without judging effectiveness.[35] While the 510(k) pathway must exist for minor adjustments to approved devices, concerns about the process are well documented.[36]

But even for Class III devices that must submit to the more rigorous premarket review process, where evidence of effectiveness is theoretically required, there is still

34 Institute of Medicine, Medical Devices and the Public's Health: The FDA 510(k) Clearance Process at 35 Years (2011), www.nap.edu/catalog/13150/medical-devices-and-the-publics-health-the-fda-510k-clearance.

35 Gail A. Van Norman, An Overview of Approval Processes: FDA Approval of Medical Devices, 1 JACC 277 (2016).

36 Id.

little guarantee that the device will be effective and even less so that it will be better for patient outcomes and less costly.[37] The Federal Food, Drug & Cosmetic Act is vague about what a showing of effectiveness requires[38] and the federal regulations do not provide much additional guidance, stating:

> There is reasonable assurance that a device is effective when it can be determined, based upon valid scientific evidence, that in a significant portion of the target population, the use of the device for its intended uses and conditions of use, when accompanied by adequate directions for use and warnings against unsafe use, *will provide clinically significant results.*[39]

But the term "clinically significant results" is not defined in the medical device statute or in the regulations. It is nonetheless generally understood that even a study without statistical significance can be enough to gain approval for a device.[40] Often applications are approved based on a single clinical study that might not even be a randomized trial.[41] There has been almost no focus in case law on what it means for a medical device to be "effective," which is consistent with the secondary importance that effectiveness plays relative to safety of medical devices.[42]

To put a sharper point on it, consider the difference in effectiveness approval standards for devices and drugs. For a drug to be approved by the FDA, a manufacturer must submit at least two adequate and well-controlled studies, each convincing on its own, to establish effectiveness.[43]

There might be good reason for not requiring the same level of evidence for medical devices – in that it is more difficult and costly to run trials of sufficient size given heterogeneity of test subjects for at least some medical devices as compared to drugs.[44] And yet, studies that are not blinded and nonrandomized often provide poor evidence.[45] Thus, the regulatory framework does little to prevent ineffective devices from hitting the market.

37 See Neel U. Sukhatme & M. Gregg Bloche, Health Care Costs and the Arc of Innovation, 104 Minn. L. Rev. 955, 982 (2019).

38 21 U.S.C. § 360(c)(a)(2)(A–C).

39 21 C.F.R. § 860.7(e)(1) (emphasis added).

40 Jonathan J. Darrow, Pharmaceutical Efficacy: The Illusory Legal Standard, 70 Wash. & Lee L. Rev. 2073, 2073–4 (2013).

41 Sanket S. Dhruva et al., Strength of Study Evidence Examined by the FDA in Premarket Approval of Cardiovascular Devices, 302 JAMA 2679 (2009); Sarah Y. Zheng et al., Characteristics of Clinical Studies Used for US Food and Drug Administration Approval of High-Risk Medical Device Supplements, 318 JAMA 619 (Aug. 15, 2017).

42 Stephanie P. Fekete, Litigating Medical Device Premarket Classification Decisions for Small Businesses: Have the Courts Given the FDA Too Much Deference? The Case for Taking the Focus Off of Efficacy, 65 Cath. U. L. Rev. 605, 630 (2016).

43 21 C.F.R. § 314.126.

44 Marianne Razavi et al., U.S. Food and Drug Administration Approvals of Drugs and Devices Based on Nonrandomized Clinical Trials: A Systematic Review and Meta-analysis, 2 JAMA Network Open 11 (2019), https://jamanetwork.com/journals/jamanetworkopen/fullarticle/2749563.

45 See Deepak L. Bhatt et al., A Controlled Trial of Renal Denervation for Resistant Hypertension, 370 N. Engl. J. Med. 1393 (2014).

13.2.3 *Limited Role for Products Liability and Tort Law*

Another check that should deter companies from selling – and doctors from using – ineffective medical devices is products liability and tort law. A patient who was harmed by an ineffective device should be able to sue the manufacturer who sold it or the doctor who used it.

But the US Supreme Court in *Riegel v. Medtronic, Inc.*,[46] held that federal law preempts state law products liability claims for devices that were approved through the FDA's premarket approval process. For such devices, the FDA has in theory adjudged effectiveness. Despite the very limited nature of the review in practice, individuals harmed by such ineffective devices cannot sue manufacturers under products liability doctrine.

Claims are preserved for devices cleared through the 510(k) pathway for which there is no effectiveness screen.[47] However, this can be of little help if the patient does not learn of device ineffectiveness and its contribution to poor health outcomes, as is often the case. For this reason, cases that do get brought tend to be based on safety issues rather than effectiveness concerns.

Another potential check on ineffective devices is the right to sue the medical provider who used an ineffective medical device to the detriment of the patient. These types of cases could, in theory, motivate doctors not to use ineffective devices – or to rely on evidence of effectiveness more consistently in making treatment choices. In practice though, there are a number of hurdles. The first is that just mentioned – that patients often will not discover that the device was ineffective. Second, a doctor using a device approved (or cleared) by the FDA for the purpose approved by the FDA will generally not be liable under the custom and practice-based malpractice standards.[48] If a doctor can prove that he or she followed the same course as a reasonable provider would under the same circumstances, the doctor will generally prevail. A doctor could be liable for failure to warn a patient about potential dangers of a device, but if this information is not easily discoverable by the doctor (for instance if randomized controlled trials have not been done that have shown the device to be ineffective), there will be no liability.

As a practical matter then, products liability and tort law are underpowered to deter the use of ineffective medical devices.

13.3 THE HARM CAUSED BY INEFFECTIVE MEDICAL DEVICES

The harm that flows from unsafe devices is clear. But ineffective medical devices also cause harm – in worse health outcomes and the waste of valuable financial

46 Riegel v. Medtronic, Inc., 552 U.S. 312 (2008).

47 See Medtronic, Inc. v. Mirowski Family Ventures, LLC, 571 U.S. 191 (2014).

48 Mark Herrmann & Pearson Bownas, Keeping the Label Out of the Case, 103 Nw. U. L. Rev. Colloquy 477, 480 (2009).

resources. Also, more subtly but still importantly, ineffective devices provide a false sense that problems have been solved, quelling innovation in necessary areas, and engendering mistrust in the health care system.

13.3.1 *Worse Health Outcomes: The Hazy Line Between Safety and Effectiveness*

Perhaps the most famous example of an ineffective medical device concerns stents. For over a decade, in stroke patients, many physicians looked for the narrowing of the smaller vessels in the brain. If they were found, physicians placed stents – small metal mesh tubes – to prop open the vessel for the purpose of reducing future risk of stroke.[49] In 2011, a robust randomized controlled trial was conducted – the first of its kind to test the effectiveness of the stenting procedure, although it had already been approved by the FDA and had been in use for a decade. The study found that stents were not effective in preventing a stroke, and in fact, actually led to worse health outcomes.[50]

This example shows how the line between safety and effectiveness can be a blurry one. Often times, when a choice is made to use a device that is ultimately ineffective, it is to the exclusion of a different device (or medication) that works better. Not all medical reversals will result in worsened health outcomes. But there is a heightened risk.

Relatedly, ineffective medical devices can lead to patient harm by giving a false sense of security. The use of hip protectors may (subconsciously) have led nursing home personnel to do less to prevent falls. And because it does not work to lessen fractures, the result might be an increase in hip fractures. An anesthesiologist who relied on the BIP monitor to prevent anesthesia awareness may have been lulled into not as diligently checking other signals of awareness, resulting in increased patient trauma.

While often times the harm from ineffective medical devices is not as obvious as from devices that are deemed unsafe, ineffective medical devices still make patients worse off.

13.3.2 *Economic Harms*

The other obvious harm that flows from the use of ineffective devices is economic. The US health care system is more expensive than that of all other industrialized nations.[51]

49 See Marc Chimowitz et al., Stenting Versus Aggressive Medical Therapy for Intracranial Arterial Stenosis, 365 N. Engl. J Med. 993 (2011). A similar approach was used in coronary patients.

50 Id.; Vinayak K. Prasad & Adam S. Cifu, Ending Medical Reversal: Improving Outcomes, Savings Lives (2015).

51 See, e.g., Karen Davis et al., Mirror, Mirror on the Wall, 2014 Update: How the Performance of the U.S. Health Care System Compares Internationally, The Commonwealth Fund (June 16, 2014),www.commonwealthfund.org/sites/default/files/documents/___media_files_publications_fund_report_2014_jun_1755_davis_mirror_mirror_2014.pdf.

By some estimates, a third of all US health care spending is unnecessary.[52] That includes spending on ineffective medical devices.

While medical devices currently only account for about 6 percent of health care spending in the United States, the market is growing rapidly.[53] In 2018, the US market was valued at $169 billion,[54] and it is on a strong growth trajectory with revenues expected to double in the next decade.[55]

Additionally, the cost of an ineffective medical device often goes beyond just the cost of the actual device. We pay doctors to place the devices. Sometimes additional scans and diagnostics are ordered because of the medical device.[56] Surgeries may be required to remove ineffective implanted devices.

13.3.3 *Other Harms*

There are other less obvious harms that flow from the use of ineffective medical devices. For one, the appearance that a device exists to solve a problem – when in reality it does not – stifles innovation in that domain. The use of ineffective medical devices also harms public trust in the medical system and specifically in medical providers.

13.4 INCENTIVIZING EFFECTIVENESS

In the current system, ineffective medical devices (and comparatively ineffective ones) are too frequently approved by the FDA and used on patients. Practices concerning these devices are often difficult to stop once they become a part of the standard of care and they can cause both significant patient harm and unnecessary expense. But in order to fix the problem, ineffective medical devices have to be identified, and if they are adopted before identification, there must be a mechanism for discontinuing them. These are not easy problems to solve.

Many scholars promote stricter regulatory standards for ex ante proof of effectiveness.[57] While this would be a logical solution – requiring manufacturers to prove effectiveness before any patients are harmed and any funds are unnecessarily spent – making this change in practice is difficult. There is a strong movement to

52 See Sarah Kliff, We Spend $750 Billion on Unnecessary Health Care. Two Charts Explain Why, Wash. Post (Sept. 7, 2012), www.washingtonpost.com/news/wonk/wp/2012/09/07/we-spend-750-billion-on-unnecessary-health-care-two-charts-explain-why.

53 Martin Wenzl & Elias Mossialos, Prices for Cardiac Implant Devices May Be Up to Six Times Higher in the Us Than in Some European Countries, 37 Health Affairs 1570 (2018).

54 Medical Devices Market Size, Share, and Industry Analysis By Type, Fortune Business Insights (Apr. 2019), www.fortunebusinessinsights.com/industry-reports/medical-devices-market-100085.

55 Id.

56 This was the case with intracranial stents where MRIs were frequently ordered just to search for narrowed arteries in need of stents. Prasad, supra note 17 at 90.

57 See, e.g., Dhruva, supra note 41.

reform the 510(k) process, which might address those devices that are cleared without any effectiveness review at all. But as to the Class III premarket authorization process, the FDA is under pressure to get devices to market quicker and at a lower cost, which is at odds with tightening effectiveness standards.

One way to address the cost concerns would be for the government to fund this research. But that does not do anything to lessen the overall cost of the endeavor, nor does it address the time-to-market concerns.

The other commonly proposed solution is to improve the postmarket surveillance process – which is already underway with the 21st Century Cures Act.[58] There are initiatives like the National Evaluation System for health Technology (NEST) – a public-private partnership intended to conduct active surveillance on postmarket medical devices.[59] And the Patient-Centered Outcomes Research Institute (PCORI) already conducts postmarket comparative effectiveness research on drugs and devices.[60]

The concept is laudable. But as currently conceived, the postmarket surveillance process largely depends on voluntary reporting. The FDA does not have the resources to police and ensure compliance.[61] The postmarket surveillance process is also more likely to identify safety concerns than effectiveness concerns. While the FDA can also order postmarket clinical studies, that is generally only in response to adverse events reports. The process could be improved with a registry that requires reporting of all device-related patient outcomes. The registry would have to be actively monitored and analysed to produce useful information.[62]

PCORI's medical device research intended to aid doctor and patient decision making is also a step in the right direction. But it lacks a mechanism to incentivize using the results of the work. For instance, the law currently forbids government payors from adjusting reimbursement on the basis of PCORI data.[63]

It may be possible to build on these ideas, but the role that both providers and payors play in constraining the use of ineffective devices also deserves more focus.

58 See 21st Century Cures Act, Pub. L. No. 114–255, § 3058(b)(5)(C), 130 Stat. 1033, 1129 (2016).

59 US Food & Drug Administration, Medical Device Safety Action Plan: Protecting Patients, Promoting Public Health, www.fda.gov/media/112497/download.

60 Dave A. Chokshi, A Course in Reversal, 387 The Lancet 1266 (2016), www.healthaffairs.org/do/10.1377/hblog20150403.046100/full/; Lise Rochaix, Incorporating Cost-Effectiveness Analysis Into Comparative-Effectiveness Research: The French Experience, Health Aff. Blog (Apr. 3, 2015), www.healthaffairs.org/do/10.1377/hblog20150403.046100/full/. There may also be an expanded role for independent technology assessment. See Mitchell D. Feldman et al., Who Is Responsible for Evaluating the Safety and Effectiveness of Medical Devices? The Role of Independent Technology Assessment, 23 J. Gen. Internal Med. 57 (2008).

61 Megan C. Andersen, 21st Century Cures Act: The Problem with Preemption in Light of Deregulation, 52 U. Mich. J. L. Reform 801, 817–18 (2019); Corinna Sorenson & Michael Drummond, Improving Medical Device Regulation: The United States and Europe in Perspective, 92 The Milbank Quarterly 114 (2014).

62 Opinion: 80,000 Deaths. 2 Million Injuries. It's Time for a Reckoning on Medical Devices, N.Y. Times (May 4, 2019), www.nytimes.com/2019/05/04/opinion/sunday/medical-devices.html.

63 See Affordable Care Act, Pub. L. No. 111–148, § 6301(c), 124 Stat. 119 (2010).

While providers may not often be held liable when devices are ineffective, they would still benefit from better technology that makes their jobs easier and results in better outcomes for patients. In recognition of this, there are initiatives to involve professional societies in the identification of ineffective devices.[64] For instance, the Choosing Wisely campaign tasked medical societies with preparing lists of ineffective interventions, including medical devices.[65] But Choosing Wisely has to have data on which to base its recommendations. It can be helpful in uprooting ineffective devices when new studies suggest lack of efficacy (or when PCORI data does). But providers are unlikely to run or fund studies of devices themselves. Nonetheless, working to change professional norms can be impactful. More broadly, medical education has started to focus decision making more squarely on evidence and data.[66] If providers can learn to rely less on the imprimatur of FDA approval or clearance and more on reliable studies of devices, it can make a big impact.

Perhaps the most promise, however, lies in an expanded role for private payors – and possibly even for government payors. Payors have the motivation to quell the use of ineffective devices.[67] Profit-motivated insurers, but even government payors, benefit from higher-quality, less-expensive care. Payors could make a huge impact by tying reimbursement decisions to data of effectiveness, as is the practice in most European countries.[68]

Admittedly, there are many reasons we might be leery of US payors playing this role. Insurers may take an overly aggressive stance in denying coverage, motivated more by profit maximization than by the betterment of patient health and the banishment of truly ineffective devices. Also, medical device efficacy may be heterogeneous. Even if a device is not effective for certain patients, it may nonetheless be for others. This can be hard to discern from studies, particularly if the test population is not diverse. Payors might also not have as much leverage as they do in other reimbursement decisions in a world of limited alternatives.

But the biggest impediment to tying reimbursement to effectiveness data is the lack of the data on which these decisions might rely. Payors are already engaging

64 Medical record data is also an under-utilized source of information on medical devices. Alison Callahan et al., Medical Device Surveillance with Electronic Health Records, 2 Npj Digital Med. 1 (2019).

65 Choosing Wisely Campaign, http://www.choosingwisely.org/; Wendy Netter Epstein, Nudging Patient Decision-Making, 92 Wash. L. Rev. 1255 (2017).

66 See Jane P. Gagliardi et al., Innovation in Evidence-Based Medicine Education and Assessment: An Interactive Class for Third- and Fourth-Year Medical Students, 100 J. Med. Library Ass'n 306 (2012).

67 Rebecca S. Eisenberg & W. Nicholson Price II, Promoting Healthcare Innovation on the Demand Side, 4 J. L. & Bioscience 3, 14–23 (2017).

68 Cornelia Henschke & Rita F. Redberg, Medical Device Price Differentials in the U.S. and Europe – Rethinking Price Regulation?, Health Aff. Blog (Dec. 7, 2018), www.healthaffairs.org/do/10.1377/hblog20181206.716970/full/ (discussing how both efficacy and cost-effectiveness data informs reimbursement decisions in many European countries). In the United States, Government payors are constrained by law in how they may make reimbursement decisions. See Rachel E. Sachs, Delinking Reimbursement, 102 Minn. L. Rev. 2307, 2315 (2018).

private technology assessment organizations to do effectiveness analyses, but those assessments are limited by the lack of published data on which to conduct the analyses. So perhaps the better question is what can payors do to incentivize the creation of the necessary data?

Payors may be able to better mine and use their own data to assess effectiveness. Or they could use their bargaining power to incentivize the study of device effectiveness. Payors negotiate with manufacturers over the price the payor is willing to pay for a device. While refusing reimbursement entirely may be impossible, payors can condition reimbursement on manufacturer agreement to fund or participate in a study of device effectiveness. The Government already does this to a limited degree. The Centers for Medicare and Medicare Services (CMS) may conditionally approve reimbursement for a device while requiring that additional evidence be collected about device effectiveness through a clinical trial or device registry.[69]

Payors can also play a more active role in steering providers away from devices that may be ineffective based on the results of those studies.[70] In general, payors have bargaining power that could be better employed to promote the study, not just of device safety, but also of device effectiveness.

69 See James D. Chambers et al., Private Payers Disagree with Medicare Over Medical Device Coverage About Half the Time, 34 Health Affairs (Aug. 2015).

70 See Wendy Netter Epstein, The Health Insurer Nudge, 91 S. Cal. L. Rev. 593 (2018).

14

Preventing Medical Device-Borne Outbreaks

The Case of High-Level Disinfection Policy for Duodenoscopes

Preeti Mehrotra, David J. Weber, and Ameet Sarpatwari

14.1 INTRODUCTION

Multiple outbreaks of antibiotic-resistant bacteria in recent years have been traced to contaminated duodenoscopes in health care facilities in the United States and Europe.[1] These events prompted intensive postmarket surveillance of three large duodenoscope manufacturers, the creation of voluntary hospital-based culturing programs,[2] and US Food and Drug Administration (FDA) safety warnings emphasizing the importance of following manufacturers' instructions for use (IFUs) for performing high-level disinfection (HLD) or sterilization of equipment, also known as reprocessing.[3] However, as outbreaks continued, the US Joint Commission made high-level disinfection or sterilization of all reusable scopes and probes a central component of its 2018 hospital accreditation programming.[4] This chapter highlights the regulations governing medical devices, the etiology of the duodenoscope outbreaks, and the policy measures implemented and regulatory challenges persisting in the wake of the outbreaks. Given the proliferation of scopes and probes in medical care – including outbreak settings of highly infectious diseases such as the Ebola virus disease[5] and carbapenem-resistant Enterobacteriaceae (CRE)[6] – reprocessing cannot and should not remain an abstract part of device regulation. Amplifying the perspective of infection prevention and control in the medical device regulatory landscape is critical to achieve optimal and sustainable reforms.

1 Zachary A. Rubin & Rekha K. Murthy, Outbreaks Associated with Dudoenoscopes: New Challenges and Controversies, 29 Curr. Opin. Infect. Dis. 407 (Aug. 2016).

2 US Food & Drug Admin., Infections Associated with Reprocessed Duodenoscopes, www.fda.gov/medical-devices/reprocessing-reusable-medical-devices/infections-associated-reprocessed-duodenoscopes.

3 Id.

4 The Joint Commission, High Level Disinfection BoosterPak, www.dilon.com/wp-content/uploads/2020/05/Joint-Commision-HLD-and-Sterilization-BoosterPak.pdf.

5 Patricia Henwood, Imaging an Outbreak: Ultrasound in An Ebola Treatment Unit, 381 N. Engl. J. Med. 6 (Jul. 2019).

6 Rubin & Murthy, supra note 1.

14.2 REGULATORY HISTORY AND DUODENOSCOPE OUTBREAKS

Under FDA regulations, devices fall into three classes. Duodenoscopes are categorized as Class II devices, which confer moderate risk and require regulatory controls such as the establishment of performance standards, postmarket surveillance, patient registries, and/or labeling requirements.[7] Class II devices require only premarket notification through the FDA's 510(k) pathway.[8] By contrast, Class III devices such as implantable pacemakers, which "support or sustain human life, are of substantial importance in preventing impairment of human health, or which present a potential, unreasonable risk of illness or injury,"[9] require premarket approval (PMA), the most stringent type of device market application required by the FDA.

Yet despite its classification as a Class II device, duodenoscopes were linked to at least twenty-five outbreaks of CRE between 2012 and 2015.[10] The actual toll was likely far higher, but unknown given gaps in reporting and surveillance.[11] By early 2013, the manufacturer Olympus knew of two independent lab reports, which found that one of their duodenoscope models featuring a difficult-to-access elevator channel could harbor bacteria even after cleaning according to the manufacturer's instructions.[12] Even though the FDA began investigating elevator channels in 2013 in collaboration with the Centers for Disease Control and Prevention (CDC), Olympus did not forward the laboratory reports to the FDA or alert US hospitals, physicians, or patients to the risk of infection until February 2015.[13] Further investigation revealed that two major duodenoscope manufacturers failed to pursue a new 510(k) premarket notification prior to bringing their devices with elevator channels to market. Custom Ultrasonics, the manufacturer of an automated reprocessor that was implicated in some outbreaks, also failed to report critical updates to their device to FDA as required by law.[14] Finally, the FDA was also unaware of manufacturer warnings to European regulators that had occurred as early as 2013.[15]

These events highlighted various inadequacies in manufacturer reporting, hospital investigation, and regulator action, which prompted the CDC and FDA to reexamine reprocessing IFUs. In March 2015, the CDC released an interim duodenoscope surveillance protocol for health care facilities in cooperation with the FDA

7 US Food & Drug Admin., Regulatory Controls, www.fda.gov/medical-devices/overview-device-regulation/regulatory-controls.

8 Id.

9 US Food & Drug Admin., Premarket Approval, www.fda.gov/medical-devices/premarket-submissions/premarket-approval-pma.

10 Health, Education, Labor Pensions Committee, U.S. Senate, Preventable Tragedies: Superbugs and How Ineffective Monitoring of Medical Device Safety Fails Patients (2016).

11 Id.

12 Id.

13 Id.; US Food & Drug Admin., supra note 2.

14 Health, Education, Labor Pensions Committee, supra note 10.

15 Id.

and the American Society for Microbiology (ASM).[16] In October of the same year, the FDA ordered three major duodenoscope manufacturers to conduct postmarket surveillance studies to better understand duodenoscope-transmitted infections.[17]

However, it was not until June 2017 that the FDA promulgated regulations to require manufacturers of certain high-risk reusable Class II medical devices to include validated IFUs regarding cleaning, disinfection, and sterilization in their premarket notification 510(k).[18] These regulations acknowledged that the design of some devices, such as those with lumens or crevices, were higher risk than others.[19] Additionally, the regulations emphasized the importance of the validated instructions not only for automated reprocessors and washing devices, but also for such high-risk devices.[20]

Over the next four years, the FDA released six general updates of reprocessing instructions, twelve general communications on duodenoscopes, and sixteen public correspondences to duodenoscope manufacturers.[21] In November 2015, there was a mandatory recall of Custom Ultrasonics reprocessors and in February 2018, the FDA, CDC, and ASM released voluntary standardized protocols for duodenoscope surveillance culturing.[22] Yet in an August 2019 safety communication, the FDA's postmarket surveillance report noted a continued "elevated rates of contamination, including the presence of high concern organisms" such as E. Coli and Pseudomonas aeruginosa, highlighting persisting concerns of HLD and complex endoscope design.[23]

These concerns have helped fuel a growing market for single-use equipment, with manufacturers of varying scopes and probes developing completely disposable designs. In November 2019, the FDA recommended transitioning to duodenoscopes with disposable components and one month later, gave market clearance for the first fully disposable duodenoscope.[24]

14.3 CHALLENGES

Amid this backdrop, several practical difficulties and regulatory challenges remain. First, although IFUs for reprocessing higher-risk medical devices must now be

16 US Food & Drug Admin., supra note 2.

17 Id.

18 Health, Education, Labor Pensions Committee, supra note 10; infra note 19.

19 Medical Devices: Validated Instructions for Use and Validation Data Requirements for Certain Reusable Medical Devices in Premarket Notifications, 82 Fed. Reg. 26,807 (June 2017).

20 Id.

21 US Food & Drug Admin., supra note 2.

22 Health, Education, Labor Pensions Committee, supra note 10; US Food & Drug Admin., FDA Webinar: Duodenoscope Sampling and Culturing, www.fda.gov/media/112402/download.

23 US Food & Drug Admin., supra note 2.

24 US Food & Drug Admin., FDA recommending transition to duodenoscopes with Innovative Designs to Enhance Safety, www.fda.gov/medical-devices/safety-communications/fda-recommending-transition-duodenoscopes-innovative-designs-enhance-safety-fda-safety-communication; US Food & Drug Admin., New Release: FDA Clears First Fully Disposable Duodenoscope, www.fda.gov/news-events/press-announcements/fda-clears-first-fully-disposable-duodenoscope-eliminating-potential-infections-caused-ineffective.

validated in accordance with FDA regulation, processes for validation are not standardized and are often unclear. Current FDA guidance refers manufacturers to technical information reports (TIRs) developed by the Association for the Advancement of Medical Instrumentation (AAMI), specifically AAMI TIR 2 ("labeling instructions for reusable medical device") and TIR 30 ("compendium of processes, materials, test methods, and acceptance criteria for cleaning reusable medical devices").[25] However, most AAMI TIRs were last published in 2010 and are in critical need of updating.

In 2015, AAMI published the more rigorous "Standard 91: Flexible and semi-rigid endoscope processing in healthcare facilities," which outlines facility-level quality control practices, addresses human factors issues related to reprocessing, and comments on the design and flow of reprocessing departments.[26] Yet full implementation of this standard, including cleaning verification processes, schedules, and tracking and tracing of all related endoscope equipment, remains challenging.[27] Additionally, given rapid advances in disinfection and sterilization science and changes in regulation, this guidance also requires updating.[28] Work on this has been ongoing since early 2019, but a new draft document had not yet been released as of December 2020.[29]

Thus, over the past decade, manufacturers have largely been left to author IFUs without clear guidance as to what is an acceptable or standard cleaning protocol,[30] resulting in widespread variation in how IFUs are structured and written, the methods used to demonstrate that effective disinfection has occurred, and storage and handling practices.[31] For example, there are no agreed-upon standards to assess if proper cleaning (e.g., detection of protein versus blood versus microbial DNA) has occurred,[32] when older equipment should be sent for maintenance, repair, or replacement, or whether borescopes – an optical device – should be used to detect microscopic rips or tears, particularly in otherwise inaccessible cavities.[33]

25 US Food & Drug Admin., Reprocessing Medical Devices in HealthCare Settings: Validation Methods and Labeling Guidance for Industry and Food and Drug Administration Staff Document, www.fda.gov/media/80265/download.

26 Am. Ass'n Med. Instrumentation, ANSI/AAMI ST91:2015 Flexible and semi-rigid endoscope processing in healthcare facilities, www.aami.org/standards/aami-st91.

27 Beyond Clean Podcast, infra note 29; Judie Bringhurst, Special Problems Associated with Reprocessing Instruments in Outpatient Care Facilities: Physical Spaces, Education, Infection Preventionists, Industry Reflections, 47 Am. J. Infect. Control A58 (June 2019).

28 Am. Ass'n Med. Instrumentation, supra note 26; Beyond Clean Podcast, infra note 29.

29 Beyond Clean Podcast, Mary Ann Drosnock: AAMI Overview, ST91 Update, Flexible Scope Reprocessing, https://beyondclean.libsyn.com/mary-ann-drosnock.

30 Ralph Basile, AAMI TIR 12 and the Future of Device Processing Instructions, 53 Biomedical Instrumentation & Tech. 67 (Jan. 2019).

31 Id.; US Food & Drug Admin., Factors Affecting Quality of Reprocessing, www.fda.gov/medical-devices/reprocessing-reusable-medical-devices/factors-affecting-quality-reprocessing.

32 US Food & Drug Admin., FDA Webinar: Duodenoscope Sampling and Culturing, www.fda.gov/media/112402/download; US Food & Drug Admin., supra note 25.

33 Id.; Am. Ass'n Med. Instrumentation, supra note 26; Bringhurst, supra note 27.

Particularly critical to the disinfection process are manual precleaning steps. Although the FDA requires that reprocessing instructions "should be understandable,"[34] many IFUs are dense and difficult to follow (some IFUs exceed 100 pages). In mandated human factors postmarketing surveillance studies conducted by Fujifilm and Olympus, "most participants expressed some difficulty adhering to the reprocessing manual," with one study concluding that the materials "are not sufficient to consistently ensure user adherence in these core reprocessing areas: precleaning, manual cleaning, manual high-level disinfection, rinsing, and storage and disposal."[35]

IFUs can also contradict guidance from professional societies, which can be in conflict with each other. For example, the Society of Gastroenterology Nurses, the Association for Professionals in Infection Control and Epidemiology, and the Association of Perioperative Registered Nurses all have different recommendations on storage and "hang time" – the maximum duration of storage time before the endoscope is processed for next use.[36] Recognizing such variability, the Joint Commission recently released its own clarification for hospitals, outlining that the IFU remains paramount to professional society guidance and consensus documents. Yet, gaps remain when IFUs are nonspecific or do not address key concerns, leaving hospitals in the position of having to reach out to manufacturers directly.[37]

The interplay between IFUs can also be a challenge. While device manufacturers create their own IFUs, they typically do so separately from the manufacturers of automated reprocessors and high-level disinfectants.[38] This creates another layer of complexity for end users in health care facilities, particularly those that use manual methods of disinfection. In reconciling IFUs, a hospital's ability to swiftly recognize concerns and call attention to appropriate leadership can be hampered.[39] Some device manufacturers of scopes create their own reprocessing equipment exclusively for their own devices,[40] which can mitigate the burden of IFU coordination but can

34 Supra note 19; Basile, supra note 30.

35 US Food & Drug Admin., supra note 24; US Food & Drug Admin., Factors Affecting Quality of Reprocessing, www.fda.gov/medical-devices/reprocessing-reusable-medical-devices/factors-affecting-quality-reprocessing; US Food & Drug Admin., 522 Postmarket Surveillance Studies, www.accessdata.fda.gov/scripts/cdrh/cfdocs/cfPMA/pss.cfm.

36 Am. Ass'n Med. Instrumentation, supra note 26.

37 The Joint Commission, Clarifying Infection Control Policy Requirements, 39 Perspectives (Apr. 2019); The Joint Commission, Manufacturer's Instructions for Use- Addressing Conflicts Amongst IFUs for Different Equipment and Products: Frequently Asked Questions, (Apr. 2020), www.jointcommission.org/standards/standard-faqs/hospital-and-hospital-clinics/infection-prevention-and-control-ic/000002252/.

38 Bringhurst, supra note 27; US Food & Drug Admin., Information about Automated Endoscope Reprocessors and FDA's Evaluation, www.fda.gov/medical-devices/reprocessing-reusable-medical-devices/information-about-automated-endoscope-reprocessors-aers-and-fdas-evaluation.

39 Supra note 19; Bringhurst, supra note 27.

40 Olympus, Olympus Investor Day 2017: Medical Business Strategy, www.olympus-global.com/ir/data/pdf/id_2017e_03.pdf.

also result in undue contractual leverage, limiting the ability of hospitals to diversify their inventories.

More broadly, concern exists that HLD may be insufficient for scopes.[41] The decades-old Spaulding criteria outlines the use of HLD for semi-critical devices such as scopes and sterilization for critical devices such as surgical instruments.[42] Performing HLD typically results in a 6-$\log_{10}$ reduction of micro-organisms, whereas sterilization results in at least a 12-$\log_{10}$ reduction.[43] However, flexible endoscopes acquire high levels of microbial contamination or bioburden during each use, and may contain ten[44] enteric micro-organisms after use, with buildup around closed channels.[45] Accordingly, some infection prevention experts refer to HLD as creating a "nonexistent margin of safety" that is unable to achieve disinfection consistently.[46]

Challenges also exist with sterilization. Typical scope materials cannot handle the high temperatures required for the most commonly available and robust methods of sterilization (i.e., steam).[47] Additionally, existing sterilants have notable drawbacks. For example, ethylene oxide, a sterilant for rigid scopes, requires lengthy processing and aeration time.[48] In high quantities, it also poses health hazards, including carcinogen risk.[49] Because of this risk, ethylene oxide is unavailable in many US hospitals. In 2019, two large device facilities were closed by state environmental protection agencies in response to higher than acceptable levels of ethylene oxide in the air, creating abrupt shortages of sterilized devices.[50]

Finally, while the market for single-use equipment may be viewed as a clear path forward, inadequate attention has been given to associated waste streams. Use of disposable duodenoscopes[51] would contribute to the market growth of disposable

41 William A. Rutala & David J. Weber, Disinfection, Sterilization, and Antisepsis: An Overview, 47 Am. J. Infect. Control A3 (June 2019); Rutala & Kanamori, infra note 43; Spaulding, infra note 42.

42 E.H. Spaulding, Chemical Disinfection of Medical and Surgical Materials, in Disinfection, Sterilization and Preservation (C. Lawrence & S.S. Block eds., 1968).

43 William A. Rutala et al., What's New in Reprocessing Endoscopes? Are We Going to Ensure "The Needs of the Patient Come First" by Shifting from Disinfection Sterilization?, 47 Am. J. Infect. Control A62 (June 2019).

44 Health, Education, Labor Pensions Committee, supra note 10; supra note 19; US Food & Drug Admin., supra note 24; US Food & Drug Admin., supra note 32.

45 Rutala et al., supra note 43.

46 Id.; Rutala & Weber, infra note 48.

47 Rutala & Weber, infra note 48; US Envtl. Protection Agency, Ethylene Oxide, https://cfpub.epa.gov/ncea/iris2/chemicalLanding.cfm?substance_nmbr=1025.

48 Willian A. Rutala & David J. Weber, CDC Guideline for Disinfection and Sterilization in Healthcare Facilities, www.cdc.gov/infectioncontrol/pdf/guidelines/disinfection-guidelines-H.pdf.

49 Id.; US Envtl. Protection Agency, supra note 47; Caryn Roni Rabin, To Prevent Deadly Infections, FDA Approves the First Disposable 'Scope', N.Y. Times (Dec. 13, 2019).

50 US Food & Drug Admin., Statement on concerns with medical device availability due to certain sterilization facility closures, www.fda.gov/medical-devices/general-hospital-devices-and-supplies/fda-innovation-challenge-2-reduce-ethylene-oxide-emissions (last visited July 6, 2020).

51 V. Raman Muthusamy et al., Clinical Evaluation of a Single-Use Duodenoscope for Endoscopic Retrograde Cholangiopancreatography, 18 Clin. Gastroenterol. Hepatol. 2108 (Nov. 2019).

designs for other scopes and probes, but the environmental footprint of single-use equipment has yet to be modeled nationally and internationally.[52] In one study, single-use laryngoscope handles generated an estimated sixteen to eighteen times more lifecycle carbon dioxide equivalents (CO_2-eq) than traditional low-level disinfection of the reusable steel handle, and single-use plastic tongue blades generated an estimated five to six times more CO_2-eq than the reusable steel blade treated with high-level disinfection.[53] However, some studies suggest higher emissions of Co_2-eq may be offset by the cost of personal protective equipment (PPE), and that the energy consumption of reprocessing equipment also needs to be considered.[54] These comments underscore the need for further data points to build comprehensive models.

14.4 SOLUTIONS AND FUTURE DISCUSSION

Addressing the above challenges requires engagement between manufacturers, clinicians, regulators, central processing departments, infection prevention and control leadership, and health care administrators. Inconsistencies between IFUs and the lack of transparency and standardization around validation in all domains – precleaning, disinfection, storage, maintenance, and repair – should be key priorities for the FDA and AAMI. Encouragingly, updates to key TIRs are in progress.[55] While working groups developing these documents include diverse stakeholders, including key manufacturers, regulators, and infection prevention experts, TIRs are not made available for public comment.[56] The AAMI standards are made available for public comment, but are solicited by notice in "appropriate AAMI publications or on the AAMI website."[57] Making drafts of TIRs under review publicly available for comment, and making AAMI standards more widely available for review may present opportunities for improvement and promote swifter uptake by manufacturers and health care facilities.[58] Additionally, ensuring timely and concordant adoption of TIRs by the CMS could help ensure that health care facilities and manufacturers keep up to date.

52 Sherman, infra note 53; Niall F. Davis et al., Carbon Footprint in Flexible Ureteroscopy: A Comparative Study on the Environmental Impact of Reusable and Single Use Ureteroscopes, 32 J. Endourology 214 (Mar. 2018); Sorenson & Gruttner, infra note 54.

53 Jodi D. Sherman et al., Life Cycle Assessment and Costing Methods for Device Procurement: Comparing Reusable and Single Use Disposable Laryngoscopes, 127 Crit. Care & Resuscitation 434 (Aug. 2018).

54 Birgitte L. Sorenson & Henrik Gruttner, Comparative Study on Environmental Impacts of Reusable and Single Use Bronchoscopes, 7 Am. J. Envtl. Protection 55 (2018).

55 Beyond Clean Podcast, supra note 29; Basile, supra note 30.

56 Am. Ass'n Med. Instrumentation, Development of Consensus Standards and TIRs, www.aami.org/standards/how-are-standards-developed/standards-policies-and-procedures-intro/development-of-standards-and-tirs.

57 Id.

58 Bringhurst, supra note 27; Basile, supra note 30.

Even with updated AAMI standards, however, implementation will remain a challenge. To facilitate optimal execution, health care administrators should seek to invest in competency and training programs for reprocessing staff and consider including them in contracted services with manufacturers and vendors.[59] Coordination of IFUs across vendors requires close coordination of health care facility infection prevention and control, biomedical/clinical engineering, supply chain, and contracting departments. While committees comprised of representatives from these groups may be found at many large acute care inpatient centers, they may not exist in ambulatory settings or surgical centers, where procedures are common.[60] The absence of such committees should be considered in a facility's gap analysis and should be examined as part of regulatory and reaccreditation requirements.[61]

Since the outbreaks began in 2012, the FDA has expanded its ability to examine the regulatory controls for medical device regulation. The Medical Device Innovation Consortium (MDIC) is a 501(c)(3) public-private partnership with the objective of advancing approaches that "promote patient access to innovative medical technologies and the use of real world evidence in guiding the needs for all stakeholders."[36] As part of the MDIC, the National Evaluation System for Health Technology coordinating center (NESTcc) aims to conduct "efficient and real-world evidence studies throughout the total product life cycle," to "develop, verify, and operationalize methods of evidence generation" and data use in both the pre and postmarket space, and to bring together stakeholders, including the voice and preferences of the patient.[62] The MDIC patient-centered benefit-risk framework creates decision analysis models that evaluate tradeoffs such as risk of infection or associated length of stay associated with a device that a patient may consider.[63] However, the MDIC and NESTcc should ensure the completeness of data to inform such metrics. For example, the risks of device-associated infection cannot be properly quantified without understanding real-world gaps in IFUs related to disinfection and sterilization.

The NESTcc could also elevate its voice in the postmarket space. In partnership with the FDA, the MDIC should continue to support and use evidence from medical device safety reporting by hospitals and device manufacturers through portals like the MedWatch and MedSun.[64] The MDIC and the NESTcc could also offer support in the design and development of postmarket surveillance studies.

59 Basile, supra note 30.

60 Bringhurst, supra note 27.

61 Id.; Rose Seavey, Using a Systematic Approach for Adopting New Technologies in Sterile Processing Departments and Operating Rooms, 47 Am. J. Infect. Control A67 (June 2019).

62 Med. Device Innovation Ctr., National Evaluation System for health Technology Coordinating Center, Overview, https://nestcc.org/about/about-us/.

63 Med. Device Innovation Ctr., Medical Device Innovation Consortium (MDIC) Patient Centered Benefit-Risk Project Report, www.fda.gov/media/95591/download.

64 Med. Device Innovation Ctr., supra note 62.

Though small, the human factors studies mandated by the FDA for Fujifilm and Olympus manufacturers in postmarket surveillance were revealing.[65] In particular, they plainly demonstrated the difficulty in adhering to complex IFUs.[66] If these studies were part of active surveillance in the postmarket period, they could offer critical and earlier insight for manufacturers, health care personnel, and the FDA.

In appreciating the pitfalls of complex IFUs, many infection prevention and control experts have called for the reclassification of scopes as critical devices that require sterilization.[67] There is regulatory precedent for such action. In 1992, the FDA mandated a shift from disinfection to sterilization for dental handpieces, even though there were no documented cases of disease transmission associated with dental hand pieces.[68] Professional societies should support this transition, and accreditation agencies should start developing standards to facilitate institutional accountability.[69]

Incentives will likely be needed to encourage further development of sterilization options, including low temperature sterilization technologies (LTSTs). The FDA recently started this process, announcing in November 2019 four participants in an "innovation challenge" to identify disinfection and sterilization alternatives that can be implemented at a large scale and maintain high throughput.[70] Two of these participants will focus on the use of vaporized hydrogen peroxide technology that is currently being used on a large scale to disinfect respirators during the COVID-19 pandemic.[71] While participation does not constitute "regulatory acceptance," manufacturers should expect that the FDA remains committed to expeditiously clearing LTSTs as they are developed if safety and effectiveness standards are met.[38] In turn, manufacturers should commit to the FDA's endorsement of creating scopes with innovative designs, including manufacturing scopes with materials that are compatible with LTSTs.[72]

More recently, the FDA announced a second innovation challenge to decrease ethylene oxide emissions.[73] In parallel and in light of closures of sterilization facilities due to high ethylene oxide emissions, the US Environmental Protection

65 US Food & Drug Admin., supra note 35.

66 US Food & Drug Admin., supra note 24; US Food & Drug Admin., supra note 35.

67 Rutala & Weber, supra note 41; Rutala et al., supra note 43; Rutala & Weber, supra note 48.

68 Rutala et al., supra note 43.

69 Id.

70 US Food & Drug Admin., FDA Innovation Challenge 1: Identify New Sterilization Methods and Technologies, www.fda.gov/medical-devices/general-hospital-devices-and-supplies/fda-innovation-challenge-1-identify-new-sterilization-methods-and-technologies.

71 US Food & Drug Admin., Investigating Decontamination and Reuse of Respirators in Public Health Emergencies, www.fda.gov/emergency-preparedness-and-response/mcm-regulatory-science/investigating-decontamination-and-reuse-respirators-public-health-emergencies.

72 US Food & Drug Admin., New Release: FDA Clears First Fully Disposable Duodenoscope, www.fda.gov/news-events/press-announcements/fda-clears-first-fully-disposable-duodenoscope-eliminating-potential-infections-caused-ineffective; Rutala et al., supra note 43.

73 US Food & Drug Admin., FDA Innovation Challenge 2: Reduce Ethylene Oxide Emissions, www.fda.gov/medical-devices/general-hospital-devices-and-supplies/fda-innovation-challenge-2-reduce-ethylene-oxide-emissions.

Agency (EPA) issued a notice of proposed rulemaking to solicit information from industry and the public on strategies for further reducing ethylene oxide emissions from commercial sterilization and fumigation operations. This includes reviewing and updating regulations for sources that emit ethylene oxide and to better understand and address ethylene oxide emissions at facilities.[74] Such interagency coordination will be needed to more identify the optimal role of ethylene oxide in medical device sterilization, the effects of endoscope sterilization, and the impact on the supply chain and transportation operations.[75]

Finally, hospitals and clinics will need to consider the far-reaching impacts of incorporating disposable equipment, especially as pathogens of high consequence such as CRE, take hold.[76] Hospitals and clinics will need to partner and engage early with major biomedical waste companies and recycling vendors both in the United States and globally to create a regulated, functional waste stream.[77] These groups will need to understand large throughput hospital- and clinic-based workflows, calculate new labor costs, and consider implications for their supply chains. Corporate social responsibility platforms should expand to account for the impact of such activities and integrate this work into ongoing sustainability efforts, including tracking fleet and incinerator emissions.[78] To more fully weigh complete environmental impact, cradle-to-grave lifecycle assessment and lifecycle costing methods should be used.[79] For example, the EPA's Tool for the Reduction and Assessment of Chemical and other Environmental Impacts can be used to model environmental impacts of greenhouse gases and other pollutant emissions.[80] As is required to examine ethylene oxide impacts, a sustained FDA and EPA partnership can help, facilitating detailed data gathering to inform national and international economic and environmental analyses. This effort should discuss how to weigh energy consumption of reprocessing departments and facilities, human labor costs, and PPE usage.

While the NESTcc represent the FDA's efforts to modernize the 510(k) process, the FDA will need to embed both the perspectives of infection control and environmental sustainability to transform its approach.[81] In particular, understanding the

74 US Envtl. Protection Agency, EPA Seeks Input on Strategies to Reduce Ethylene Oxide Emissions from Commercial Sterilizer Operations, www.epa.gov/newsreleases/epa-seeks-input-strategies-reduce-ethylene-oxide-emissions-commercial-sterilizer.

75 Id.; US Food & Drug Admin., supra note 73.

76 Muthusamy et al., supra note 51; J.Y. Bang et al., Concept of Disposable Duodenoscope: At What Cost?, 68 Gut 1915 (2019).

77 Rabin, supra note 49; Sharps Compliance, infra note 78.

78 Sharps Compliance, Inc., Incineration and Treatment, www.sharpsinc.com/high-temperature-incineration; Stericycle 2019 Corporate Social Responsibility Overview, www.stericycle.com/white-papers/corporate-social-responsibility-2019.

79 Sherman et al., supra note 53; Davis et al., supra note 52; Sorenson & Gruttner, supra note 54.

80 Sherman et al., supra note 53.

81 US Food & Drug Admin., Statement from FDA Commissioner Scott Gottlieb, M.D. and Jeff Shuren, M.D., Director of the Center for Devices and Radiological Health, on transformative new steps to modernize the FDA's 510(k) program to advance the review of the safety and effectiveness of medical

tradeoffs associated with sustainable production and consumptions practices can shift the FDA approach from reactive to proactive.[82]

14.5 CONCLUSIONS

High-level disinfection and sterilization of medical equipment has slowly evolved over the past three decades. The outbreaks of drug-resistant bacteria traced to contaminated duodenoscopes offer a case study in understanding the gaps in medical device regulation. Although the FDA has made strides in closing these gaps, important and critical problems persist; the concerns exposed in the duodenoscope outbreaks expand beyond scopes and spans larger concerns around device design, cleaning, disinfection, management, uptake and care. Together, these experiences call for a greater voice for infection prevention and control in the medical device ecosystem. The NESTcc and the FDA's ongoing private-public partnership consolidate national efforts for medical device safety: minimizing disease transmission and considering environmental harms should be part of that mission.

devices, www.fda.gov/news-events/press-announcements/statement-fda-commissioner-scott-gottlieb-md-and-jeff-shuren-md-director-center-devices-and.

82 Andrea J. MacNeill et al., Transforming the Medical Device Industry: Road Map to a Circular Economy, 39 Health Aff. 2088 (2020).

15

Regulating Devices that Create Life

Katherine L. Kraschel

In vitro fertilization (IVF) led to approximately 74,590 births in 2018.[1] IVF success rates have increased roughly three-fold since the first live birth in 1978. Yet today the chance of giving birth using IVF is barely better than a coin toss, even for the youngest, healthiest patients.[2] Scientists and industry are pursuing methods to improve IVF success rates. However, many clinics seem unconcerned with the effectiveness of new methods. Marketing of these methods, so-called IVF "add-ons," to vulnerable patients seeking to start a family has led to calls for greater regulatory scrutiny.[3]

Add-ons include methods such as selecting the "best" sperm in a semen sample, or artificially "activating" eggs to prepare embryos for transfer to a uterus.[4] They run from a couple hundred dollars to more than ten thousand dollars. Data on their utilization is limited, but one estimate suggests that 74 percent of fertility patients used at least one add-on.[5]

Most notoriously, the practice of preimplantation genetic screening or preimplantation genetic testing for aneuploidies (PGS or PGT-A) is used to identify (and usually discard) embryos that show an abnormal number of chromosomes.[6] Mounting evidence illustrates that the $6,000–$12,000 test is not a good predictor of whether an embryo will develop into a healthy baby; one estimate suggests that approximately 40 percent of healthy embryos may have been unnecessarily discarded based on PGS results.[7] While the test may accurately identify cells exhibiting

1 Society for Assisted Reproductive Technologies, National Summary Report 2018, www.sartcorsonline.com/rptCSR_PublicMultYear.aspx?reportingYear=2018#.

2 Society for Assisted Reproductive Technologies, National Summary Report 2017, www.sartcorsonline.com/rptCSR_PublicMultYear.aspx?ClinicPKID=0#patient-cumulative.

3 Pamela Mahoney Tsigdinos, The Big IVF Add-On Racket, N.Y. Times (Dec. 12, 2019).

4 Alessandra Alteri et al., The IVF Shopping List: To Tick or Not to Tick, 4 EMJ 14 (2019).

5 Human Fertilisation and Embryology Authority, Treatment add-ons (2019), www.hfea.gov.uk/treatments/explore-all-treatments/treatment-add-ons/.

6 Stephen S. Hall, Tens of Thousands of Women Thought They Couldn't Have Babies. But What If They Could, N.Y. Mag. (Sept. 18, 2017).

7 Richard J. Paulson, Preimplantation Genetic Screening: What Is the Clinical Efficacy? 8 Fert. Steril. 228 (2017).

aneuploidies, many questions remain regarding whether and how those results predict the health of a child resulting from the embryos tested. This means that many patients' hopes at biological parenthood may have been squandered due to their reliance on an expensive, erroneous test. To date, there has been no regulatory activity in the United States to stop clinics from making claims about, providing, or charging for PGS testing.

This chapter describes the genesis of the direct-to-consumer nature of the US fertility services market that makes consumers uniquely susceptible to offers of unproven technologies in hopes of increasing their likelihood of pregnancy success. It explores the many modes of regulation in the United States and their shortcomings as well as the limits of the Food and Drug Administration's (FDA's) lack of jurisdiction over embryos and the tests used to select and modify them. In light of these limitations, the chapter concludes by posing a two-pronged path forward to address the most pressing concerns about add-ons: 1) amendments to existing federal law to require fertility clinics and labs to report a list of all services they offer patients and tie their utilization to rates of success and 2) Federal Trade Commission enforcement action against clinics who make deceptive and/or unsupported claims about add-ons and other technologies.

15.1 FERTILITY SERVICES DIRECT-TO-CONSUMER MARKET

Modern assisted reproduction in the United States is a health care anomaly. First, fertility treatments are not consistently covered by private or public insurance, although coverage has increased in recent years. Consumer patients are cost-sensitive and will select providers based upon particular services offered.[8] Patients do not benefit from signals of necessity or quality from insurance companies' coverage decisions. People seeking fertility treatments rely heavily on the Internet and fertility center websites to inform their choices.[9] The resulting direct-to-consumer fertility markets makes the veracity of claims made by clinics critical to ensure consumers make informed choices. Yet, most fertility clinic websites do not comply with the guidelines outlined by the American Medical Association or the industry's own self-regulatory body.[10]

[8] Debora L. Sparr, The Baby Business: How Money, Science, and Politics Drive the Commerce of Conception (2006).

[9] Huang et al., Internet Use by Patients Seeking Fertility Treatment, 83 Int. J. Gynecol. Obstet. 83 (2003); EC Haagen et al., Current Internet Use and Preferences of IVF and ICSI Patients, 18 Hum. Rep. 2073 (2003).

[10] Robert Klitzman et al., Preimplantation Genetic Diagnosis (PGD) on In-Vitro Fertilization Websites: Presentations of Risks, Benefits, and Other Information, 92 Fert. Steril. 1276 (2009); Mary E. Abusief et al., Assessment of United States Fertility Clinic Websites According to the American Society for Reproductive Medicine (ASRM)/Society for Assisted Reproductive Technology (SART) Guidelines, 87 Fert. Steril. 88 (2007).

The medical component of the fertility industry does not act alone. Physician-run clinics interact with other for-profit players including multi-million-dollar sperm banks and agencies that broker provision of sperm, eggs, embryos, and surrogacy services. These transactions take place outside the context of any physician-patient relationship and contribute to the transactional atmosphere of fertility services. The market creates competition for patients and an incentive for providers to distinguish themselves by offering services that could improve patient consumers' likelihood of success.

Second, fertility innovation has been left to rely on private funds due to a ban on government funding.[11] Public funding triggers ethical obligations in developing new technologies, including informed consent requirements. Without public funding, fertility innovation occurs free from restrictions placed on most biomedical research. Coupled with its transactional nature, it is no surprise that fertility clinics offer and sell unproven add-ons in order to attract patients. At best, this means that empowered consumers are knowingly subsidizing the development of unproven technologies in hopes they might be lucky. At worst, vulnerable consumers are being exploited to spend significant funds for futile or harmful services they believe increase their odds of success.

The dangers of add-ons seem to be precisely the type of threat to public health that state medical boards and the FDA are designed to address – to eliminate unsafe or unproven medical interventions from the market or to "assur[e] the safety, effectiveness, quality, and security"[12] of medical interventions. Could the FDA not regulate these new technologies as medical devices applied to the earliest forms of human life? These questions are addressed in the following sections.

15.2 THE US FRAGMENTED PATCHWORK OF ART REGULATION

Federal oversight over the Assisted Reproductive Technology (ART) industry is well discussed within the academic literature and the popular press. Many have called the United States the "wild west";[13] however, as one of the editors of this volume points out, a number of mechanisms moderate behavior in US ART markets, resulting in a fragmented patchwork of regulation.[14] In fact, the American Society for Reproductive Medicine (ASRM) claims that "Assisted Reproductive Technologies are among the most regulated medical procedures in the United States."[15]

11 Omnibus Appropriations Act of 2009, Pub. L. No. 111–118, § 509(a)(2).

12 US Food & Drug Admin., FDA Fundamentals, www.fda.gov/about-fda/fda-basics/fda-fundamentals.

13 Judith Daar, Federalizing Embryo Transfers: Taming the Wild West of Reproductive Medicine?, 23 Colum. J. Gender & L. 257 (2012).

14 I. Glenn Cohen, The Right to Procreate in Assisted Reproductive Technologies in the United States, in Oxford Handbook of Comparative Health Law (Tamara K. Hervey & David Orentlicher eds., forthcoming).

15 American Society for Reproductive Medicine, Oversight of Assisted Reproductive Technology (2010), www.asrm.org/globalassets/asrm/asrm-content/about-us/pdfs/oversiteofart.pdf.

If the United States is the "wild west" of ART, it is not because there are no sheriffs in town. There are multiple sheriffs, mayors, and informally deputized leaders each trying to address their own overlapping concerns. Some of these regulations and private law controls are discussed in this section.

15.2.1 *Federal Regulation of Fertility Industry & Reproductive Medicine*

Within the federal government, four agencies regulate ART: the FDA, the Centers for Medicare and Medicaid Services (CMS), the Department of Health and Human Services, through the Centers for Disease Control (CDC), and the Federal Trade Commission (FTC). The FDA regulates the approval of fertility drugs and requires gamete screening to prevent transmission of communicable diseases. The future of the role of the FDA and FTC will be further discussed in Sections 15.3 and 15.4 respectively.

CMS regulates laboratories through the Clinical Laboratory Improvement Amendment of 1988 (CLIA).[16] However, CLIA applies to tests connected with human diagnoses, such as testing blood or semen for fertility-related issues; it does not extend to testing on embryos.

The Department of Health and Human Services (through the CDC) is explicitly charged with oversight of ART. The Fertility Clinic Success Rate and Certification Act of 1992 (FCSRCA) requires fertility clinics to report their success rates and ART data.[17] The FCSRCA was passed in light of public concern with fertility clinics overstating the likelihood of success to prospective patients. FCSRCA also attempts to step in where CLIA leaves off by issuing model guidance for embryology laboratory certification. However, there is no enforcement mechanism to compel clinics to comply, and the model recommendations create no legal obligation for labs to adopt them.[18]

Finally, the FTC has broad authority to prohibit "unfair or deceptive acts or practices affecting commerce."[19] The billion-dollar fertility industry clearly affects commerce and falls under FTC control. In contrast to FCSRCA, the FTC Act includes enforcement power. The FTC previously exercised its authority in fertility services when it filed charges for deceptive practices against five clinics for misrepresenting their success rates in October 1992.[20] Additionally in July 1995, the FTC authored an editorial in the leading journal of reproductive medicine in which it described its "concerns with advertising pregnancy success rates."[21]

16 42 U.S.C. § 263a (2019).
17 Fertility Clinic Success Rate and Certification Act of 1992, Pub. L. No. 102–493, 106 Stat. 3146.
18 64 Fed. Reg. 39,374.
19 15 U.S.C. § 45 (2019).
20 Robert Pear, Fertility Clinics Face Crackdown, N.Y. Times (Oct. 26, 1992).
21 Michael A. Katz, Federal Trade Commission Staff Concerns with Assisted Reproductive Technology Advertising, 64 Fert. Ster. 10 (1995).

15.2.2 *State Regulation of Fertility Industry and Reproductive Medicine*

State practice of medicine laws, including licensing of medical professionals, facilities, laboratories, and pharmacies, apply to ART. State medical boards could act to suspend or revoke licenses if clinics or providers make false claims about their success or perform procedures that harm their patients. However, reliance on practice of medicine and licensing may be ineffective; state medical boards are reticent to turn against one of their own even in the face of repeated patterns of bad behavior.[22]

Much of the innovation in the space of reproductive medicine is happening in the laboratory, not the clinic, and procedures are performed by embryologists (scientists usually with masters or doctorate level training who create and manipulate embryos), not physicians. States do not license embryologists; like laboratories, embryologist certification is available but optional.[23] IVF clinics rarely require a license of the physical space separate from the professional license held by the providers who practice within it. Without enacting licensing and regulatory authority over labs, clinics, and embryologists, states currently have little ability to intervene. However, there has been some recent legislative action to require licensing of labs that handle embryos.[24]

State law also governs tort claims for medical malpractice or other harms caused by mistakes in the fertility industry. However, the tort system leaves plaintiffs, in cases against fertility clinics and laboratories, empty handed due to its unwillingness or inability to recognize and monetize the types of harms caused by mistakes in reproduction.[25] Finally, similar to the FTC at the federal level, state attorneys general have enforcement power over fraud and unfair trade practices within their state, but none have taken actions similar to the FTC's.

15.2.3 *Professional Self-Regulation*

Professional self-regulation plays an important role in the US fertility market. ASRM is the most influential governing body; its Practice and Ethics Committees issue guidelines and reports on clinical practice and guiding principles, respectively.[26] Compliance with ASRM recommendations is not legally required, nor does ASRM have enforcement power. In addition, ASRM has been criticized for its inherent conflict of interest, since its members are those that have a financial stake in the industry's success.[27]

22 Dov Fox, Birth Rights and Wrongs: How Medicine and Technology are Remaking Reproduction and the Law 27 (2019).

23 American Society for Reproductive Medicine, supra note 15.

24 Assemb. 4605, 218th Leg. (N.J. 2018).

25 Fox, supra note 22.

26 Daar, supra note 13.

27 Andrea Preisler, Assisted Reproductive Technology: The Dangers of an Unregulated Market and the Need for Reform, 15 DePaul J. Health Care L. 213 (2013).

The ASRM Ethics Committee issued an opinion on innovative new techniques in 2015. It stated:

> Consider the consequences of bringing interventions to practice before they have been adequately studied and sufficiently validated ... a new practice becomes commonplace before there is evidence to support its effectiveness ... enthusiasm to address a vexing clinical problem led to the premature adoption of a new treatment. Such enthusiasm can lead to dissemination of an innovative treatment through media reports, lectures, and conferences before adequate data are available and before peer review has been accomplished. Early adoption can be confusing for patients, who may not understand that a treatment they have read about lacks a basis in evidence and may, in fact, do them more harm than good.[28]

The tension between the benevolent desire to help patients and the ethical necessity for patience to first produce robust and reliable data, coupled with the lack of federal funding leaves clinics with three options: 1) subsidize research – bear the cost of innovation and do not charge patients for unproven procedures/new technologies; 2) focus on static clinical care and refuse to offer any innovative treatments to patients; or 3) adopt a problematic hybrid approach by charging patients for unproven innovative treatments. This third scenario – of conflating research (generating generalizable knowledge through a process in which patients understand they may not benefit from participation) and clinical care – is the problematic approach the ASRM guidance seeks to discourage; it is also the behavior that has given rise to the growing number of stories of patients who needlessly lost embryos due to the widespread use of PGS and calls for concern over add-ons.

15.3 FDA REGULATION OF REPRODUCTIVE TECHNOLOGY DEVICES (OR EMBRYOS?)

The FDA's regulation of ART is limited to its authority under the Food Drug and Cosmetic Act (FDCA)[29] and the Public Health Services Act (PHSA).[30] The jurisdictions of the FDA depends upon how a technology is used and how embryos are characterized. Coherently regulating many facets of ART under the FDCA and/or PHSA would require the FDA to decide: if an embryo is legally equivalent to a human warranting protection and the objects of regulation the devices used to manipulate it, or if the gestating human is to be protected and the embryo the object of regulation as a "biological product" or "drug" used to create a pregnancy. The legal, ethical, and political implications of such a determination may be one of many reasons the FDA has not actively exercised enforcement powers over add-ons and why categorization of embryos and ART innovations remains unclear. Since

[28] Ethics Committee of the American Society for Reproductive Medicine, Moving Innovation to Practice: a Committee Opinion, 104 Fert. Steril. 39, 40 (2015).

[29] 21 U.S.C. § 321 (2019).

[30] 42 U.S.C. § 262 (2019).

2015, Congress has signaled annually that it does not want to empower the FDA to make determinations with such vast societal implications.[31]

The FDA has classified one device used to manipulate embryos for implantation. This move implicates its jurisdiction over such devices; it also illustrates that it may be an ineffective regulator even if doing so is a proper exercise of its jurisdiction.

15.3.1 *Are Add-Ons Devices?*

Section 201(h) of the FDCA defines a medical device as "an instrument, apparatus ... or other similar or related article ...

2) intended for use in the diagnosis of disease or other conditions, or in the cure, mitigation, treatment, or prevention of disease, in man or other animals, or
3) intended to affect the structure or any function of the body of man or other animals."[32]

To illustrate, consider lasers used for "assisted hatching." The laser is intended to weaken the outer layer of cells (the structure and function) of the embryo prior to implantation to increase the chances of implantation in the uterine wall. If lasers are medical devices, it would follow that the FDA concluded that the embryo is "body of man or other animals." As discussed below, if the "device" is intended to treat infertility, then the embryo would be the device itself, not the laser that manipulated it.

In 2004, the FDA received a premarket notification and a request for device classification for "Assisted Reproduction Laser Systems."[33] It granted the request and issued guidance to ensure its use is safe and effective.[34] Conversely, the Human Fertilisation and Embryology Authority (HFEA) in the United Kingdom deemed assisted hatching "experimental" and found no evidence of safety and effectiveness, and other researchers agree.[35] Guidance from the FDA identified many of the risks that have come into focus since 2004, including "damages to the embryo" and "ineffective treatment."[36] There have long been concerns about the FDA's ability to effectively compel postmarket surveillance that would be needed in light of the mounting evidence.[37] Taken collectively, FDA regulation of assisted hatching lasers

31 Consolidated Appropriations Act of 2016, Pub. L. No. 113–114, § 749, 129 Stat. 2244; I. Glenn Cohen et al., Gene Editing Sperm and Eggs (not Embryos): Does it Make a Legal or Ethical Difference?, 48 J. L. Med. Ethics 619 (2020).

32 21 U.S.C. § 321(h).

33 21 C.F.R. § 884.6200(a).

34 US Food and Drug Administration Reclassification Order 510k number K040045 (Nov. 4, 2004), www.accessdata.fda.gov/cdrh_docs/pdf4/K040045.pdf.

35 Human Fertilisation & Embryology Authority, Treatment add-ons, www.hfea.gov.uk/treatments/treatment-add-ons/; Alteri et al., supra note 4.

36 Id.

37 Bridget M. Kuehn, IOM Urges FDA to Be More Aggressive in Monitoring Safety of Approved Drugs, 307 JAMA 2475 (2012).

may be a case study to illustrate that even if the FDA appropriately exercised its jurisdiction over medical devices (which is a big if), it is ill-suited to regulate effectively.

Now consider PGS. PGS is used to identify a condition – having an abnormal number of chromosomes. However, PGS tests an embryo, not "man or other animals." The FDA has asserted its enforcement power over genetic tests for human medical conditions;[38] however, FDA guidance regarding in vitro diagnostic testing expressly excludes "pre-implantation embryos," suggesting that a diagnostic device used on an embryo does not trigger the same regulatory attention as the homologous test on a human.[39]

15.3.2 *Are Add-On-Manipulated Embryos Biological Products or Drugs?*

The FDA regulates biological products through the PHSA,[40] and its applicability to the provision of sperm and eggs is often cited as the FDA's "only" role in regulating fertility services.[41] The purpose of the PHSA is to prevent the introduction, transmission, or spread of communicable disease (not ensure safety and efficacy of any clinical interventions).[42] Under the law, a biological product is:

> a virus, therapeutic serum, toxin, antitoxin, vaccine, blood, blood component . . . or analogous product . . . applicable to the prevention, treatment, or cure of a disease or condition of human beings.[43]

It is not clear that an embryo is an "analogous product." The listed products are components of a biological organism while an embryo is an organism in itself.[44] However, the FDA lists embryos as biological products in guidance regarding which types of biological specimens are considered biological products and which are devices.[45] Regulating embryos as biological products does not address the concerns raised by IVF add-ons. The purpose of regulating biological products is to prevent communicable disease transmission, so they do not undergo premarket review.

38 Elizabeth R. Pike & Kayte Spector-Bagdady, Device-ive Maneuvers, FDA's Risk Assessment of Bifurcated Direct-to-Consumer Genetic Testing, in FDA in the 21st Century: The Challenges of Regulating Drugs and New Technologies 470 (Holly Fernandez Lynch & I. Glenn Cohen eds., 2015).

39 Reference to FDA Guidance for Next Generation Sequencing and IVDs, www.fda.gov/media/99208/download.

40 42 U.S.C. § 262.

41 I. Glenn Cohen et al., Losing Embryos, Finding Justice: Life, Liberty, and the Pursuit of Justice, 169 Ann. Internal Med. 800 (2018).

42 42 U.S.C. § 262(i)(1).

43 Id.

44 Elizabeth C. Price, Does the FDA Have Authority to Regulate Human Cloning?, 11 Harv. J. L. & Tech 619 (1998).

45 FDA Regulation of Human Cells, Tissues, and Cellular and Tissue-Based Products (HCT/P's) Product List, www.fda.gov/vaccines-blood-biologics/tissue-tissue-products/fda-regulation-human-cells-tissues-and-cellular-and-tissue-based-products-hctps-product-list.

However, different regulations apply if the product is more than "minimally manipulated."[46] The FDA has concluded that technologies such as human cloning and mitochondrial transfer constitute more than minimal manipulation and make them biologic drugs requiring premarket approval before use.[47] Some, but not all, add-ons would move embryos out of the "biological product" definition. Embryos screened for aneuploidy with PGS might remain biological products if the screening is considered minimal manipulated while others (such as embryos punctured to encourage hatching) would be considered drugs, adding further confusion to the regulatory patchwork.

Assuming an embryo is an analogous biological product or a drug depending upon how manipulated it is, the definition of a drug poses an additional question – is an embryo an article intended to affect the structure of function of the body? Its effect on the gestating person's body is the most compelling jurisdictional hook for FDA regulation of manipulated embryos as drugs. Courts have upheld the FDA's jurisdiction over regenerative medicine for similar biological specimens being (re) implanted into humans for treatment.[48] However, if add-on-manipulated embryos are drugs, every unique, manipulated embryo created could require preapproval. Such a regulatory scheme would likely bring using add-ons and the innovation creating them to a screeching halt.

Perhaps more importantly, such a conclusion, that a human embryo is the object of federal regulation, signals other normative values, which administrative agencies are not empowered to impose.

15.3.3 *Should Congress Expand FDA Jurisdiction to Include Embryos and the Devices Used to Manipulate Them?*

Currently, FDA regulation of manipulated embryos intended for transfer into a uterus to create a pregnancy is unclear at best. At worst, it is incoherent and intentionally obfuscated in order to side-step thorny ethical and political issues or to further particular ethical views. It is impossible for the FDA to regulate add-on-manipulated embryos without signaling their moral status as either worthy of protection like people or as articles to be regulated like devices, and administrative agencies are not the appropriate bodies to make such determinations.

Congress could address the issue by enacting legislation to expand the FDA's power to include regulation of human embryos; however, this is a politically untenable solution. Suppose conservative legislators proposed treating embryos like people, making nearly all add-ons drugs or devices. Such a move would raise questions about the permissibility of all IVF because the majority of cycles result

46 21 C.F.R. § 1271.3(f).

47 Myrisha S. Lewis, Halted Innovation: The Expansion of Federal Control Over Medicine and the Human Body, 5 Utah L. Rev. 1073 (2018).

48 United States v. Regenerative Sciences, LLC, 741 F.3d 1314 (D.C. Cir. 2014).

in discarding one or more embryos, and even conservative constituencies want access to IVF. Second, more liberal lawmakers are unlikely to favor federal oversight of ART. Many might fear that any federal regulation of reproduction, particularly one that implicates the legal status of embryos, could jeopardize reproductive justice by inviting restrictive regulations such as restricting access to abortion.

In sum, trying to twist the FDA's mandate into a mechanism to regulate add-ons or attempting to pass new legislation to expand its mandate are not feasible options. Even if either was successful, expanding the FDA's jurisdiction would only create an incomplete method to address the mounting concerns raised by information provided to patients about the value of add-ons in improving the likelihood of achieving a healthy, successful pregnancy.

15.4 MOVING CONSUMER PROTECTION (AND INNOVATION) FORWARD

In many ways, the HFEA in the United Kingdom provides the ideal example for the United States to adopt.[49] It would consolidate oversight into a central, federal agency and provide consumer-centric information to inform decision making. However, federal action to create a new agency charged with overseeing embryos and the fertility industry is not a pragmatic resolution for many of the same reasons a change to the FDA's charge is unlikely.[50]

Similarly, state action to regulate in this space may be difficult. Even if state action is plausible, forum-shopping lessons learned from areas related to ART governed by state law (such as surrogacy) teach us that national-level control is desirable. In light of these limitations, I propose a two-pronged solution: 1) amendments to FCSRCA to require fertility clinics and labs to report a list of all services it offers patients, and 2) enforcement by the FTC. In sum, the approach taken almost thirty years ago to rein in fertility clinics overstating their success rates should be similarly utilized to protect consumers from unproven add-ons that claim to improve success.

First, Congress should amend the FCSRCA to require clinics and labs to report a list of services it offers to its patients, particularly those it lists on its website and in promotional materials. In addition, it should expand reporting to link utilization of those technologies with the success rate reporting already required such as confirmed pregnancy and live births. While such a system would not offer the gold standard of randomized controlled trials for new technologies, it would generate retrospective studies to provide indicators of effectiveness. The additional reporting could provide an imperfect postmarket surveillance mechanism. As noted above, the FDA has underperformed in postmarket activity even in areas in which its regulatory power is clear. If a clinic is consistently selling its patients laser-assisted hatching but

49 Gladys B. White, Crisis in Assisted Conception: The British Approach to an American Dilemma, 7 J. Women's Health 321, 327 (1998).

50 Alicia Oullette et al., Lessons Across the Pond: Assisted Reproductive Technology in the United Kingdom and the United States, 31 Am. J. L. & Med. 419 (2005).

there is no evidence that it improved rates of success, clinics could be held accountable for representations made to patients about the value of assisted hatching.

Revisions to the FCSRCA could also include a mechanism by which the CDC, much like the United Kingdom's HFEA, could grade innovations based upon the data collected, and disseminate the evaluation publicly. This proxy for necessity/value addresses one of the unique problems posed by the direct-to-consumer nature of fertility services and could fill the void left by the lack of insurance providers' coverage decisions. Fertility market consumers' propensity to turn to the internet for guidance regarding fertility treatments suggests this could be an effective way to protect them from paying for unproven services. In addition, the data could be used by the FTC to trigger disclamatory language requirements or limit the types of representations that players in the ART market can make to consumers.

Amendments to the FCSRCA are politically feasible. Expanded reporting requirements do not involve governmental judgments regarding when life morally and legally begins. Moreover, the current political moment resembles the conditions that gave rise to the FCSRCA in 1992 – there is growing concern with new technologies thanks to popular press coverage.

To address pushback from the industry due to the cost of additional reporting requirements, Congress could make the legislation more attractive by limiting the FDA's role as it did regarding in the original FCSRCA, and explicitly place embryos and the devices used to manipulate them outside of the FDA's wheelhouse. Reporting requirements may seem like an inexpensive price to pay for protection from a more cumbersome regulatory scheme like premarket FDA approval.

Second, the FTC should exercise its enforcement power against clinics and labs that make unsubstantiated claims about the efficacy of add-ons. Given previous FTC activity on the heels of FCSRCA's passage, amendments to the FCSRCA and the public attention that could follow may be a good catalyst to motivate FTC enforcement. Expending federal funds is justified in light of the size of the fertility market. This work undertaken in conjunction with an updated FCSRCA would allow the FTC to gauge the veracity of claims clinics make about the ways the services they provide improve the likelihood of success. This is strikingly similar to the claims the FTC brought in the 1990s when clinics inflated or used deceptive methods of calculation to inflate about their IVF success rates.

As for those claims that may not go so far as to be deceptive but raise concerns given the consumer reliance on the clinic's expertise, FTC regulation of over-the-counter drugs and cosmetics advertising may be a helpful analogy to consider; it requires advertising to be truthful and substantiated by evidence.

In addition, FTC enforcement could apply across other parts of the fertility industry, including sperm, egg, and surrogacy brokers, and could be a centralized "sheriff." For example, sperm and egg banks make problematic representations regarding the traits and anonymity of sperm and egg providers. The FTC could provide an effective mechanism to address these concerns.

15.5 CONCLUSION

Consumers are willing to pay an unusually high emotional, physical, and financial price to have a chance at becoming a genetic parent. The evolution of the consumer-centric US fertility market and inefficient patchwork of overlapping regulatory bodies and legal systems has left them without sufficient safeguards against purchasing unproven interventions to increase their likelihood of success. The FDA is the familiar actor to protect patient consumers from unproven treatments; however, it is not clear if it is legally empowered to exercise jurisdiction, and it is undesirable and infeasible for Congress to expand its purview.

Greater FTC enforcement and legislation to expand reporting requirements represent politically feasible, appropriately consumer-protective, and innovation-preserving options to address the challenges posed by innovation in this unique industry. Hopefully, these changes will avoid a repeat of the devastating reality faced by many patients whose embryos were perhaps prematurely discarded and protect intended parents from harmful or opportunistic behavior in an already physically, emotionally, and financially draining process.

PART V

Medical and Legal Oversight of Medical Devices

Introduction

Carmel Shachar

Part V of our volume, "Medical and Legal Oversight of Medical Devices," can be thought of as the part that tries to address the question of "what now?" Previous parts have grappled with the regulation of medical devices as they are developed and come onto the market. Part IV considered the impact that devices may have on patients and family members once they are approved for us. Part V takes that focus a step further to consider how we should monitor, evaluate, and regulate medical devices once they are approved and on the market.

This is an important question because, despite the best efforts of regulators to evaluate products before they reach patients, not all medical devices will prove themselves entirely safe. Sometimes, flaws or challenges in a medical device will only be revealed when there are a wider number of users, beyond the scope of any clinical trial. Therefore, it is critical that the medical system develop methods of flagging concerns with approved devices, and that the legal and regulatory system be able to respond to these concerns. This is a challenging task for both the medical and legal systems, however. It essentially asks how we put the rabbit back in the hat. The rabbit, in this case, being the approval and availability of medical devices post-initial approval.

The authors of the chapters in Part V consider the challenge of monitoring the "rabbit," following up on concerns regarding the rabbit, and regulating the rabbit from different perspectives. Some chapters focus on the regulatory system as the actor who can properly supervise and deal with the rabbit. Sanket Dhruva, Jonathan Darrow, Aaron Kesselheim, and Rita Redberg open the part with "Ensuring Patient Safety and Benefit in Use of Medical Devices Granted Expedited Approval." They flag that with a more flexible and streamlined approval process comes an increased chance of unforeseen risks to patients. Therefore, it is necessary to update postmarket requirements to require fuller studies. Efthimios Parasidis and Daniel Kramer likewise turn to the regulatory system to provide sufficient postapproval oversight in their chapter, "Compulsory Medical Device Registries: Legal and Regulatory Issues." While Dhruva et al. argue for postmarket studies, Parasidis and Kramer support the use of registries to track patient experiences with approved medical devices. They note that registries are perhaps underdeveloped as a tool to monitor medical devices, especially around data governance.

David Rosenberg and Adeyemi Adediran close Part V by considering the interplay of the regulatory system and market pressures in their chapter, "Strengthening the Power of Health Care Insurers to Regulate Medical Device Risks." Similar to the Dhruva and Parasidis chapters, this piece turns to regulatory solutions to solve postapproval problems. This chapter is different, however, in that it focuses on using regulatory solutions to harness the market power wielded by insurers to adopt or avoid certain medical devices. This chapter highlights for the reader that once medical devices are approved by regulatory agencies, we move beyond a relationship focused tightly on the manufacturer and the regulator, to add in payors and patients.

The other two chapters in Part V are less focused on putting the rabbit back in the hat and more focused on the role of the medical system in monitoring and responding to postapproval issues. Anthony Weiss and Barak Richman look to how the medical profession can incorporate medical technology into physician self-regulation mechanisms, namely peer review. Their chapter, "Professional Self-Regulation in Medicine: Will the Rise of Intelligent Tools Mean the End of Peer Review," flips the focus in the part. From considering how we can continue to supervise and regulate medical devices, Weiss and Richman instead ask how can we use medical devices to supervise and regulate human practitioners of medicine? Megan Wright and Joseph Fins, in their chapter, "Regulating Post-Trial Access to In-Dwelling Class III Devices," consider the ethics of risky medical devices embedded in the human body. While Wright and Fins touch on regulatory best practices for following up on study subjects with these implanted devices, they focus strongly on the ethical implications of leaving or removing these devices posttrial.

Overall, the authors of Part V remind us that regulatory approval to bring a medical device to market is not a "happily ever after" or even a final chapter in a story. Instead, approval can be considered a midpoint or inflection point. The subsequent story, of how to monitor, identify problems, and address challenges in approved medical devices, raises significant questions. Our authors grapple with the right mechanisms to tackle these challenges, including the legal and medical systems.

16

Ensuring Patient Safety and Benefit in Use of Medical Devices Granted Expedited Approval

Sanket S. Dhruva, Jonathan J. Darrow, Aaron S. Kesselheim, and Rita F. Redberg

In recent years, legislative mandates and regulatory policy in the United States have sought to streamline testing and approval requirements for novel medical devices with the goal of lowering development costs and accelerating market entry. But increasingly flexible approval requirements mean greater uncertainty as to the extent to which authorized medical devices will benefit patients without unforeseen risks. Some authorized medical devices have later been found to have safety or effectiveness concerns, but once a product is marketed it can be difficult for regulators to take remedial action. There are several reasons for this, including a reluctance to engage in regulatory self-reversal; physician and patient enthusiasm for novel technologies; generous payor coverage that provides higher margins; the challenges of conducting randomized postmarket clinical trials; and the effectiveness of devices in some, but not necessarily most or all, clinical settings. To address these reasons for inadequate regulatory response and better ensure that patients benefit from medical devices approved through special development pathways, we recommend that current expedited development or approval programs be contingent upon 1) timely progress of mandatory postmarket studies and 2) clinical data from these postmarket studies demonstrating that the threshold of reasonable assurance of safety and effectiveness is met for the primary endpoints. Until postmarket studies are completed, improved disclosure to patients is necessary to ensure they are able to provide informed consent.

16.1 BACKGROUND

The availability of medical devices in the United States is overseen by the Food and Drug Administration (FDA), which evaluates new devices under a framework established by the 1976 Medical Device Amendments.[1] Under this law, devices are classified into three tiers, with the rigor of regulatory review commensurate with anticipated risk to patients. The highest-risk devices (Class III) are subject to the

[1] Medical Device Regulation Act, Pub. L. No. 94–295, 90 Stat. 539 (1976).

FDA's most stringent review process, called Premarket Approval (PMA),[2] and are required to demonstrate a reasonable assurance of safety and effectiveness to receive marketing authorization. More flexible standards are applied to lower-tier devices (Class I and II), many of which are exempt from review altogether. Since the FDA Modernization Act of 1997, the FDA must consider the "least burdensome" means of evaluating medical devices, defined in FDA guidance as "the minimum amount of information necessary to adequately address a relevant regulatory question."[3]

While this regulatory framework has helped steward new devices that benefit patients onto the market, it has also allowed for the marketing of unsafe and ineffective medical devices, some of which have remained on the market for years. Even for devices subject to PMA, rigorous high-quality evidence is not necessarily required.[4] Studies have found low rates of randomization and blinding (i.e. allocation concealment among involved individuals) among clinical trials supporting approval of such devices.[5] Trials are often single-arm, with comparison to historical (instead of active) controls, which can lead to biased estimates of treatment effects.[6] Surrogate measures used in pivotal trials often do not translate to meaningful clinical improvements.[7] "Training patients," which allow clinicians to gain experience using or implanting a device, are often excluded from reported clinical trial results, widening the gap between labeled efficacy and real-world

[2] US Food & Drug Admin., Premarket Approval (PMA), https://www.fda.gov/medical-devices/premarket-submissions/premarket-approval-pma.

[3] US Food & Drug Admin., The Least Burdensome Provisions: Concept and Principles; Guidance for Industry and Food and Drug Administration Staff, https://www.fda.gov/media/73188/download.

[4] Sanket S. Dhruva et al., Strength of Study Evidence Examined by the FDA in Premarket Approval of Cardiovascular Devices, 302 JAMA 2679 (2009); Connie E. Chen et al., Inclusion of Training Patients in US Food and Drug Administration Premarket Approval Cardiovascular Device Studies, 171 Arch. Intern. Med. 534 (2011); Sanket S. Dhruva et al., Gender Bias in Studies for Food and Drug Administration Premarket Approval of Cardiovascular Devices, 4 Circ. Cardiovasc. Qual. Outcomes 165 (2011); Connie E. Chen et al., Inclusion of Comparative Effectiveness Data In High-Risk Cardiovascular Device Studies at the Time of Premarket Approval, 308 JAMA 1740 (2012); Vinay K. Rathi et al., Characteristics of Clinical Studies Conducted Over the Total Product Life Cycle of High-Risk Therapeutic Medical Devices Receiving FDA Premarket Approval in 2010 and 2011, 314 JAMA 604 (2015); Benjamin N. Rome et al., FDA Approval of Cardiac Implantable Electronic Devices Via Original and Supplement Premarket Approval Pathways, 1979–2012, 311 JAMA 385 (2014); Sanket S. Dhruva et al., Revisiting Essure–Toward Safe and Effective Sterilization, 373 N. Engl. J. Med. (2015); Rita F. Redberg, Sham Controls in Medical Device Trials, 371 N. Engl. J. Med. 892 (2014); Sarah Y. Zheng et al., Characteristics of Clinical Studies Used for US Food and Drug Administration Approval of High-Risk Medical Device Supplements, 318 JAMA 619 (2017); Rita F. Redberg & Sanket S. Dhruva, The F.D.A.'s Medical Device Problem [Op-Ed], N.Y. Times (July 17, 2015), https://www.nytimes.com/2015/07/17/opinion/the-fdas-medical-device-problem.html; L. Camille Jones et al., Assessment of Clinical Trial Evidence for High-Risk Cardiovascular Devices Approved Under the Food and Drug Administration Priority Review Program, 178 JAMA Intern. Med. 1418 (2018).

[5] Dhruva et al., supra note 4; Zheng et al., supra note 4; L. Camille Jones et al., supra note 4.

[6] H. Sacks et al., Randomized Versus Historical Controls for Clinical Trials, 72 Am. J. Med. 233 (1982).

[7] William S. Weintraub et al., The Perils of Surrogate Endpoints, 36 Eur. Heart J. 2212 (2015).

effectiveness.[8] Trials often include small numbers of selected patients that may not represent the diversity of real-world patients, for example, due to the exclusion of older adults, women, or those with co-morbidities.[9] Trial followup is commonly short – an important limitation because many of these devices are permanently implanted, but safety concerns may not be apparent until years after approval.

Evidence limitations for 510(k) cleared devices are even greater.[10] This commonly used process is based on "substantial equivalence" to one or more predicate (i.e. previously available) medical devices.[11] Aware that the predicates on which equivalence was based had no requirement for safety or effectiveness, Congress recognized early on that the substantial equivalence requirement of the 510(k) clearance process did not provide full assurance of safety and effectiveness.[12] In 2011, the Institute of Medicine drew attention to this concern and recommended replacing the pathway,[13] which has been responsible for the highest proportion of medical device recalls.[14]

Given the limitations in clinical evidence leading to uncertainties of benefit and risk at the time of approval, medical devices might be expected to undergo timely and rigorous postapproval evaluation. Yet only 54 out of 792 (or 7 percent) postapproval studies ordered between 1991 and 2020 were randomized clinical trials,[15] and of 28 PMA devices approved from 2010–2011, only 13 percent of 204 FDA-required or manufacturer/investigator-initiated postapproval studies were completed between three and five years after FDA approval.[16] Even eight to ten years after approval, only one-third were completed with final results reported on clinicaltrials.gov or in peer-reviewed publications.[17] The FDA has never issued a warning letter or penalty because of study delays or inadequate progress of a medical device postapproval study.[18]

8 Connie E. Chen et al., supra note 4.
9 Dhruva et al. (2011), supra note 4.
10 Rita F. Redberg & Sanket S. Dhruva, Moving from Substantial Equivalence to Substantial Improvement for 510(k) Devices, 322 JAMA 927 (2019).
11 Supra note 1.
12 H. Comm. Energy & Commerce, Subcommittee on Oversight and Investigations, Medical Device Regulation: the FDA's Neglected Stepchild: an Oversight Report on FDA Implementation of the Medical Device Amendments of 1976 (1983).
13 Institute of Medicine, Medical Devices and the Public's Health: The FDA 510(k) Clearance Process at 35 Years (2011), https://www.nap.edu/catalog/13150/medical-devices-and-the-publics-health-the-fda-510k-clearance.
14 Diana M. Zuckerman et al., Medical Device Recalls and the FDA Approval Process, 171 Arch. Intern. Med. 1006 (2011).
15 Jonathan J. Darrow et al., 326 FDA Regulation and Approval of Medical Devices: 1976–2019 420 (2021).
16 Rathi et al., supra note 4.
17 Vinay K. Rathi et al., Postmarket Clinical Evidence for High-Risk Therapeutic Medical Devices Receiving Food and Drug Administration Premarket Approval in 2010 and 2011, 3 JAMA Netw. Open (2020).
18 Ian S. Reynolds et al., Assessing the Safety and Effectiveness of Devices after US Food and Drug Administration Approval: FDA-mandated Postapproval Studies, 174 JAMA Intern. Med. 1773 (2014).

Limited pre and postmarket evidence can expose patients to unnecessary harm by allowing the availability of unsafe and/or ineffective medical devices. For example, in 2002 the Essure hysteroscopic sterilization device received premarket approval based on surrogate measures with short (up to two years) followup duration in just 926 women and was subsequently implanted in approximately 750,000 women. Postapproval studies were either not completed or terminated early.[19] Serious adverse events, including bleeding, pain, and unintended pregnancies were reported by thousands of women. The FDA responded by requiring new studies, and the device was eventually voluntarily removed from the market by its manufacturer in 2018 – sixteen years after FDA approval and just months after the Netflix documentary, *The Bleeding Edge*, documented the dangers of Essure and other currently used medical devices.[20]

16.2 INCREASING UNCERTAINTY ABOUT RISKS AND BENEFITS OF MARKETED MEDICAL DEVICES AT THE TIME OF CLEARANCE OR APPROVAL

Despite the limited clinical evidence supporting medical device clearance and approvals, legislative mandates, such as the 2016 21st Century Cures Act's codification of the Breakthrough Devices Program,[21] increase the potential for uncertainty of risks and benefits. These new flexibilities represent Congressional responses to concerns that device availability in the United States sometimes lags behind access abroad.[22]

But new legislation has not been accompanied by rigorous eligibility requirements that would protect patients. For example, devices may qualify for Breakthrough status if "availability is in the best interest of patients," providing the FDA with virtually unbounded discretion.[23] The agency has explicitly acknowledged that accelerating device approvals can reduce certainty of benefit. Agency guidance for the Breakthrough Devices Program, for example, states that the FDA "may accept a greater extent of uncertainty of the benefit-risk profile for these devices if appropriate under the circumstances."[24] Devices approved through expedited pathways are more likely to be approved based on lower-quality evidence, such as trials that lack randomization or blinding, use surrogate measures, or are of limited

19 Sanket S. Dhruva et al., supra note 4.

20 Akshay Pendyal & Joseph R. Ross, The Bleeding Edge: Documenting Innovation and Injury in the Medical Device Industry, 322 JAMA 190 (2019).

21 21st Century Cures Act, PL 114–255 (Dec. 13, 2016); Aaron S. Kesselheim & Thomas J. Hwang, Breakthrough Medical Devices and the 21st Century Cures Act, 164 Ann. Intern. Med. 500 (2016); US Food & Drug Admin., Breakthrough Devices Program: Guidance for Industry and Food and Drug Administration Staff, https://www.fda.gov/media/108135/download.

22 David R. Holmes et al., Clinical Perspective–Early Feasibility Device Medical Studies in the United States: Time for More Than Regulatory Reform, 9 JACC Cardiovasc. Interv. 626 (2016).

23 21st Century Cures Act, supra note 21.

24 US Food & Drug Admin., supra note 21.

duration.[25] A recent study of fifteen "breakthrough" devices found that two of these had been cleared under the 510(k) pathway,[26] a seemingly incongruous designation given that this pathway requires the 510(k) cleared device to be "substantially equivalent" to its previously marketed predicate. The paradox may be explained, if not necessarily justified, by the low and flexible bar to breakthrough designation and the generous definition of "substantial equivalence," which encompasses devices with "significant changes" in materials, design, energy source, or other features as compared to the predicate, so long as they do not raise different questions of safety or effectiveness.[27]

Due to the high costs of some devices, payor coverage must follow FDA authorization before widespread use is feasible. Payors can therefore serve as important gatekeepers against potentially unsafe or ineffective devices by restricting coverage until higher-quality evidence of benefit is generated. But payor oversight has been scaled back as well. Since late 2019, the Centers for Medicare and Medicaid Services (CMS) has been providing New Technology Add-On Payments for all FDA-designated Breakthrough Devices and increased reimbursement,[28] while waiving its longstanding (nineteen years) criterion that devices eligible for such add-on payments actually provide "substantial clinical improvement."[29] Increasing reimbursement without high-quality evidence of patient benefit means that such data are not likely to ever be generated, as FDA approval and insurer coverage are strong incentives for conducting new high-quality trials.

The COVID-19 pandemic has accelerated the trend toward lower evidentiary thresholds. For example, in August 2020, the Impella® (Abiomed, Danvers, MA), a mechanical circulatory support device, received Emergency Use Authorization (EUA) for patients who experience complications while receiving extracorporeal membrane oxygenation,[30] despite limited established efficacy for this indication. EUA is a mechanism authorized by Congress in 2004 that allows widespread preapproval access for drugs or medical devices that "may be effective" in case of

25 Jones et al., supra note 5; Early Experience with the FDA's Breakthrough Devices Program, 38 Nat. Biotechnol. 933 (2020).

26 James L. Johnston et al., infra note 25.

27 US Food & Drug Admin., The 510(k) Program: Evaluating Substantial Equivalence in Premarket Notifications [510(k)]; Guidance for Industry and Food and Drug Administration Staff, https://www.fda.gov/media/82395/download.

28 Centers for Medicare & Medicaid Services, Medicare Program; Hospital Inpatient Prospective Payment Systems for Acute Care Hospitals and the Long-Term Care Hospital Prospective Payment System and Policy Changes and Fiscal Year 2020 Rates; Quality Reporting Requirements for Specific Providers; Medicare and Medicaid Promoting Interoperability Programs Requirements for Eligible Hospitals and Critical Access Hospitals (2019), https://www.federalregister.gov/documents/2019/08/16/2019-16762/medicare-program-hospital-inpatient-prospective-payment-systems-for-acute-care-hospitals-and-the.

29 Timothy J. Judson et al., Evaluation of Technologies Approved for Supplemental Payments in the United States, 365 BMJ (Clinical research ed). (2019).

30 Abiomed, FDA Issues Emergency Use Authorization for Impella Heart Pumps to Provide Unloading Therapy to COVID-19 Patients, https://investors.abiomed.com/investors/press-releases/news-details/2020/FDA-Issues-Emergency-Use-Authorization-for-Impella-Heart-Pumps-to-Provide-Unloading-Therapy-to-COVID-19-Patients-08-04-2020/default.aspx.

declared emergencies associated with chemical, biological, radiological, or nuclear threats. Another similar device, the Impella RP®, received EUA in June 2020 for patients with COVID-19-related right-sided heart failure.[31] Emergency use was authorized even though a May 2019 "Dear Doctor" letter advised that fewer than 30 percent of patients receiving the device in a postapproval trial for a different indication lived to thirty days, hospital discharge, or to the start of next longer term therapy (this proportion of real-world survival was much lower than in premarket clinical studies, which had demonstrated that 73.3 percent survived to thirty days, hospital discharge, or the start of longterm therapy).[32] It was subsequently determined that lower survival was among patients who would not have qualified for premarket clinical studies.

16.3 LACK OF REGULATORY ACTION FOR UNSAFE DEVICES

While the FDA has the authority to revoke device approval, the agency has generally chosen to regulate with a lighter touch. In the rare cases when unsafe or ineffective devices have been removed from the market, manufacturers have done so voluntarily in the shadow of mandatory FDA recall authority, sometimes citing declining sales and possibly motivated by litigation concerns. The previously mentioned discontinuation of the Essure hysteroscopic sterilization device by its manufacturer in 2018 is one example.[33] In other cases, the FDA has imposed new evidence requirements that may have contributed to voluntary withdrawal. For example, after metal-on-metal orthopedic hips were found to have serious adverse events, including the release of metal ions into the bloodstream and adverse local tissue reactions that can lead to pain and device failure,[34] the FDA issued a final order in 2016 that required removal from market within ninety days if a PMA had not been filed for metal-on-metal hips marketed at that time.[35] All manufacturers have voluntarily stopped marketing these devices.[36]

31 Abiomed, FDA Issues Emergency Use Authorization for Impella RP as Therapy for COVID-19 Patients with Right Heart Failure, https://investors.abiomed.com/investors/press-releases/news-details/2020/FDA-Issues-Emergency-Use-Authorization-for-Impella-RP-as-Therapy-for-COVID-19-Patients-with-Right-Heart-Failure-06-01-2020/default.aspx.

32 US Food & Drug Admin., Increased Rate of Mortality in Patients Receiving Abiomed Impella RP System – Letter to Health Care Providers,https://www.fda.gov/medical-devices/letters-health-care-providers/update-increased-rate-mortality-patients-receiving-abiomed-impella-rp-system-letter-health-care.

33 US Food & Drug Admin., Statement from FDA Commissioner Scott Gottlieb, M.D., on manufacturer announcement to halt Essure sales in the US; agency's continued commitment to postmarket review of Essure and keeping women informed, https://www.fda.gov/news-events/press-announcements/statement-fda-commissioner-scott-gottlieb-md-manufacturer-announcement-halt-essure-sales-us-agencys.

34 US Food & Drug Admin., Concerns about Metal-on-Metal Hip Implants, https://www.fda.gov/medical-devices/metal-metal-hip-implants/concerns-about-metal-metal-hip-implants.

35 Effective date of requirement for Premarket Approval for total metal-on-metal semi-constrained hip joint systems, 21 C.F.R. § 888 (2016).

36 US Food & Drug Admin., Metal-on-Metal Hip Implants: The FDA's Activities, https://www.fda.gov/medical-devices/metal-metal-hip-implants/metal-metal-hip-implants-fdas-activities.

In other cases, the agency has not taken regulatory action even when studies with FDA involvement showed that the devices were associated with increased mortality. For example, paclitaxel-coated balloons and stents are sometimes used during endovascular intervention among patients with femoropopliteal peripheral artery disease. A meta-analysis using individual patient data, which followed FDA guidance and had a statistical analysis plan "based on formal discussions with the US Food and Drug Administration with review and approval by industry members," found these devices were associated with a 4.6 percent absolute increase in in-hospital mortality compared to patients receiving standard balloon angioplasty.[37] The FDA concluded that additional clarification was needed,[38] but has not yet taken any regulatory action to restrict use.

The FDA has, at times, revised device labeling or recommended narrower indications in an effort to address safety issues while also minimizing disruptions to the market. For the Essure hysteroscopic sterilization device, the FDA promulgated guidance that included a "patient decision checklist" intended for both patient and physician signature that contained specific information about risks and benefits[39]. Measures such as this are intended to bolster informed consent so that patients are able to exercise appropriate autonomy when deciding whether to have the device implanted. The Wingspan intracranial stent system (Stryker Neurovascular, Kalamazoo, MI) received a Humanitarian Device Exemption approval by the FDA in 2005 based on a single-arm study that enrolled forty-five patients, with outcomes compared to historical controls at thirty days.[40] However, a subsequent randomized trial found that the Wingspan device had an increased risk of the composite endpoint of stroke or death in comparison to medical therapy.[41] Despite these findings, the FDA did not rescind the Humanitarian Device Exemption approval. Instead, the agency left the device on the market so that it would be available as an option for patients similar to those in the initial single-arm study of forty-five patients,[42] even though that study had significant limitations in rigor. Because the FDA does not regulate the practice of medicine, physicians can continue to use these medical devices off-label for patients who do not meet FDA-recommended criteria. To address safety concerns, the FDA issued a Safety

[37] Krishna J. Rocha-Singh et al., Mortality and Paclitaxel-Coated Devices: An Individual Patient Data Meta-Analysis, 141 Circulation 1859 (2020).

[38] Sara Royce et al., US Food and Drug Administration Perspective on "Mortality and Paclitaxel-Coated Devices: An Individual Patient Data Meta-Analysis," 141 Circulation 1870 (2020).

[39] US Food & Drug Admin., supra note 31; US Food & Drug Admin., Labeling for Permanent Hysteroscopically-Placed Tubal Implants Intended for Sterilization; Guidance for Industry and Food and Drug Administration Staff, https://www.fda.gov/media/96315/download.

[40] Ari J. Gartenberg et al., Presumed Safe No More: Lessons from the Wingspan Saga on Regulation of Devices, 348 BMJ (Clinical research ed). (2014).

[41] Marc I. Chimowitz et al., Stenting Versus Aggressive Medical Therapy for Intracranial Arterial Stenosis, 365 N. Engl. J. Med. 993 (2011).

[42] Gartenberg et al., supra note 40.

Communication in 2019 (fourteen years after approval) warning of the increased risk of stroke or death when used outside of approved indications.[43]

16.4 MANAGING POSTAPPROVAL SAFETY OF DEVICES

There are numerous reasons why it is challenging for regulators to reverse their decisions for approved medical devices, even in the face of mounting evidence that calls a device's safety and effectiveness into question. First is a reluctance to engage in regulatory self-reversal. If devices that the FDA determined to meet statutory criteria are later found to be unsafe or ineffective, it can be uncomfortable for the agency to admit that its previous conclusion is no longer valid. This awkward situation can sometimes be avoided while still protecting patients by narrowing the scope of conditions or populations that fall within the labeled indication. Additionally, revoking approval also risks loss of public confidence in initial approvals, potentially deterring the use of unrelated beneficial treatments. The decision to narrow an indication is an acknowledgement that benefits are no longer believed to exceed risks for certain populations or indications and might logically be expected to lead to similar losses of public confidence, but modified labeling tends to draw less attention and is more likely to be perceived as a refinement rather than a reversal.

Similar psychology is at play with patients and physicians, who may have come to rely on the availability of a new device or who are reluctant to believe that a device that they implanted or that is implanted in them could actually do more harm than good. Research in the social sciences on loss aversion suggests that takebacks can be met with greater resistance than refraining from taking an action (in this case, clearing or approving a device) in the first place.[44] Patients may feel that a potentially beneficial therapy is being withheld from them if it is taken off the market. For physicians, intervention bias in medicine leads to the desire to "do something," even if doing nothing may result in improved clinical outcomes.[45] Physicians may think that they are able to selectively use medical devices in patients who will derive clinical benefit, and professional societies may offer such guidance. However, there are important limitations in patients' and physicians' understanding of regulatory approvals, and they may not recognize that FDA approval still leaves important uncertainty.[46]

43 US Food & Drug Admin., Use of the Stryker Wingspan Stent System Outside of Approved Indications Leads to an Increased Risk of Stroke or Death: FDA Safety Communication, https://www.fda.gov/medical-devices/medical-device-safety/use-stryker-wingspan-stent-system-outside-approved-indications-leads-increased-risk-stroke-or-death.

44 Amos Tversky & Daniel Kahneman, Loss Aversion in Riskless Choice: A Reference-Dependent Model*, 106 Quarterly J. Econ. 1039 (1991).

45 Andrew J. Foy & Edward J. Filippone, The Case for Intervention Bias in the Practice of Medicine, 86 Yale J. Biol. Med. 271 (2013).

46 Aaron S. Kesselheim et al., Physicians' Knowledge About FDA Approval Standards and Perceptions of the "Breakthrough Therapy" Designation, 315 JAMA 1516 (2016); Tamar Krishnamurti et al.,

To address this challenge, the FDA could publish guidance documents about benchmarks that must be achieved for a medical device to maintain approval after twelve months on the market. For example, the FDA could mandate that a postapproval clinical trial enroll a certain number of patients and meet specific safety and effectiveness endpoints to remain on the market. Devices that do not meet these parameters could then be withdrawn based upon prespecified, published criteria. As medical devices are often modified through PMA supplements,[47] or through the 510(k) pathway,[48] the expectation would be that all new device iterations would also meet these criteria.

A second challenge is that it can be difficult in the postmarket environment to generate high-quality data sufficient to demonstrate that earlier conclusions were wrong. Although randomized controlled trials remain the gold standard for clinical evidence, once a medical device is widely available, regulators rely primarily on observational data. For example, randomized clinical trials of patent foramen ovale occluders studying device ability to reduce the risk of stroke were delayed for several years because there was no incentive to enroll in a randomized trial when the devices were widely available off-trial.[49] Improved analytical tools have emerged to allow more reliable causal inference from observational data, such as propensity score matching,[50] instrumental variable analyses,[51] and the use of falsification hypotheses,[52] but more may be needed. As the granularity of data and the methods of analysis improve, confidence in observational results can be expected to increase.

Third, outcomes may improve as clinicians gain experience with both the device and its associated procedure, as studies show improved outcomes among patients who receive procedures at hospitals with higher versus lower procedural volume.[53] However, because training patients are often excluded from pivotal trial data, the "experience factor" has already been at least partially captured at the time of authorization. Making the data from the training patients available and included in premarket authorization would provide a more accurate assessment of expected

A Randomized Trial Testing US Food and Drug Administration "Breakthrough" Language, 175 JAMA Intern. Med. 1856 (2015).

47 Rome et al., supra note 4.

48 Brent M. Ardaugh et al., The 510(k) Ancestry of a Metal-On-Metal Hip Implant, 368 N. Engl. J. Med. 97 (2013).

49 Patrick T. O'Gara et al., Percutaneous Device Closure of Patent Foramen Ovale for Secondary Stroke Prevention: a Call for Completion of Randomized Clinical Trials: a Science Advisory from the American Heart Association/American Stroke Association and the American College of Cardiology Foundation, 119 Circulation 2743 (2009).

50 Jason S. Haukoos & Roger J. Lewis, The Propensity Score, 314 JAMA 1637 (2015).

51 Matthew L. Maciejewski & M. Alan Brookhart, Using Instrumental Variables to Address Bias from Unobserved Confounders, 321 JAMA 2124 (2019).

52 Vinay Prasad & Anupam B. Jena, Prespecified Falsification End Points: Can They Validate True Observational Associations?, 309 JAMA 241 (2013).

53 Sreekanth Vemulapalli et al., Procedural Volume and Outcomes for Transcatheter Aortic-Valve Replacement, 380 N. Engl. J. Med. 2541 (2019).

initial outcomes in clinical practice,[54] and is necessary to allow patients and clinicians to make adequately informed decisions. Another possibility is for payors to limit reimbursement for certain medical devices to specific hospitals or physicians that have demonstrated expertise and successful outcomes. To protect patients, health systems could implement privileging requirements that require measurable demonstrations of proficiency with such devices, or medical specialty boards could authorize device- or device/procedure-specific certifications. In addition to these private efforts, Congress could expand existing Risk Evaluation and Mitigation Strategies programs to include devices as well as drugs.

A fourth reason is that devices may turn out to be unsafe or ineffective in some clinical circumstances, but still have benefits that outweigh their risks among other indications. For example, coronary stent placement has been shown to improve outcomes in the setting of patients with ST-segment elevation myocardial infarction. However, studies have shown that there is no benefit from coronary stent placement for patients with stable ischemic heart disease.[55] One way to address this scenario is to broaden use of patient decision checklists, such as with the Essure hysteroscopic sterilization device, to ensure that patients are adequately informed of the FDA-approved indications and the current status of data supporting safety and effectiveness prior to providing consent. Informed consent documents could also include clear FDA-required text, for example, that safety and effectiveness have not been demonstrated for particular indications.

Although the FDA formally has the authority to withdraw products when necessary to protect public health, regardless of manufacturer cooperation, it has rarely exercised this power. In one notorious case, the agency withdrew the metastatic breast cancer indication of bevacizumab (Avastin®) after a confirmatory trial failed to show a benefit in overall survival, leaving the drug itself on the market.[56] Even though the withdrawal was in reality only a labeling change, the FDA's decision was extremely unpopular and faced substantial resistance from the manufacturer and public, which led to delays in its implementation despite the recommendation of the FDA's Oncologic Drugs Advisory Panel.[57] CMS even stated that it would continue to cover the drug for the breast cancer indication. Use of bevacizumab

[54] Chen et al. (2011), supra note 4.

[55] David J. Maron et al., Initial Invasive or Conservative Strategy for Stable Coronary Disease, 382 N. Engl. J. Med. 1395 (2020); William E. Boden et al., Optimal Medical Therapy With or Without PCI for Stable Coronary Disease, 356 N. Engl. J. Med. 1503 (2007); Rasha Al-Lamee et al., Percutaneous Coronary Intervention in Stable Angina (ORBITA): a Double-Blind, Randomised Controlled Trial, 391 Lancet 31 (2018).

[56] Julia A. Beaver et al., A 25-Year Experience of US Food and Drug Administration Accelerated Approval of Malignant Hematology and Oncology Drugs and Biologics: A Review, 4 JAMA Oncol. 849 (2018); Daniel Carpenter et al., Reputation and Precedent in the Bevacizumab Decision, 365 N. Engl. J. Med. (2011).

[57] Sanket S. Dhruva & Rita F. Redberg, Withdrawing Unsafe Drugs from the Market, 30 Health Aff. (Millwood) 2218 (2011).

decreased,[58] but the experience may have dissuaded the agency from taking similar regulatory actions in the future.

16.5 MANAGING ONGOING POSTAPPROVAL UNCERTAINTY OF EVIDENCE

The FDA's growing enthusiasm for expedited approvals increases the need to rely on postapproval medical device studies to better characterize safety and effectiveness. However, such studies may not be completed in a timely manner (or at all).[59] Noncompletion of postmarket studies within requisite timeframes could also be a basis for revoking FDA approval to better protect public health.

Revoking approval based on lack of study completion is even more challenging than revoking approval based on trial results, since withdrawal for noncompletion of studies necessarily occurs in the absence of required study results and thereby allows hope and belief to override evidence-based practice. If devices are nevertheless withdrawn, patients and physicians may understandably be confused about the meaning of FDA approval: if more evidence was needed to demonstrate safety and effectiveness, then why was the device approved? Once devices are available on the market, generous payments for newer procedures can create a financial incentive for their use. Medical device manufacturers are likely to provide reasonable explanations for why clinical studies have been delayed, such as slow enrolment, and optimistically predict that confirmatory evidence will soon be available. In some cases, manufacturers may have incentives to delay postapproval trials, for example, if concerns remain that confirmatory trials will demonstrate a smaller effect size than in premarket data, or if visible enrolment efforts might engender a perception that a device's benefit is uncertain.[60]

To promote more timely development of evidence for the effectiveness of medical devices after expedited approval, Congress could ensure that devices have their expedited approvals automatically lapse if postapproval clinical trials are not completed or making adequate progress by FDA-imposed deadlines. For example, if a prespecified number of patients are not enrolled into a trial by a certain date, approval would lapse, and future potential patients would need to be enrolled in a clinical trial (as in a preapproval setting). Similarly, the FDA and other stakeholders would need to make clear through public messaging that timely postmarket evidence generation is necessary to prevent lapse of approval of a medical device. There is international precedent for similar regulatory

58 Rena M. Conti et al., The Impact of Emerging Safety and Effectiveness Evidence on the Use of Physician-Administered Drugs: the Case of Bevacizumab for Breast Cancer, 51 Med. Care 622 (2013).
59 Rathi et al., supra note 4; Rathi et al., supra note 16; Reynolds et al., supra note 17.
60 Joseph S. Ross et al., Post-market Clinical Research Conducted by Medical Device Manufacturers: a Cross-Sectional Survey, 8 Med. Devices (Auckl). 241 (2015).

action: in Japan, manufacturers of some devices must refile for approval with updated data from clinicians, clinical trials, and publications after a requisite time period to ensure that the data continue to demonstrate safety and effectiveness of the device.[61] If such a measure is implemented, it will be important to provide clear notice to patients of the limited evidence of benefits and risks to ensure that consent to treatment is truly informed.

[61] Daniel B. Kramer et al., Postmarket Surveillance of Medical Devices: a Comparison of Strategies in the US, EU, Japan, and China, 10 PLoS Med. (2013).

17

Compulsory Medical Device Registries

Legal and Regulatory Issues

Efthimios Parasidis and Daniel B. Kramer

17.1 INTRODUCTION

The Food and Drug Administration's (FDA's) strategic vision for monitoring high-risk medical devices emphasizes the role of postmarket registries, which are databases that actively collect and maintain information about individual patient exposures.[1] Registries are cost-effective relative to traditional clinical trials and can enroll large numbers of patients to provide generalizable observations and identification of rare safety events.[2] Although they differ in their structure, study goals, and stewardship – with varying involvement of professional societies, industry, academic centers, and regulators – registries in general may facilitate advancements in device use, manufacture, and design.

Registries are particularly useful for cardiovascular devices, which make up a large proportion of novel device approvals but also are commonly implicated in recalls and adverse event reports.[3] The FDA and the Centers for Medicare and Medicaid Services (CMS) can mandate postmarket registries as a condition of marketing approval or reimbursement, respectively. To help generate timely information on device safety and effectiveness, the FDA and the CMS sometimes require compulsory enrollment with no opt-out mechanism. Although regulators provide guidance and oversight on registry design and use, there has been little evaluation of the legal and ethical implications of compulsory medical device registries. In particular, questions remain regarding the extent to which compulsory registries accord with health privacy laws and ethical standards for human subjects research.

This chapter proceeds in three parts. First, we begin by discussing the emerging and integral role of registries in the FDA's medical device postmarket repertoire,

[1] Prashant V. Rajan et al., Landscape of Cardiovascular Device Registries in the United States, 8 J. Am. Heart Assoc. e012756 (2019).

[2] Mitchell W. Krucoff et al., Bridging Unmet Medical Device Ecosystem Needs with Strategically Coordinated Registries Networks, 314 JAMA 1691 (2015); The Pew Charitable Trusts, Medical Device Registries: Recommendations for Advancing Safety and Public Health (2014).

[3] Prashant V. Rajan et al., Medical Device Postapproval Safety Monitoring: Where Does the United States Stand?, 8 Circ. Cardiovasc. Qual. Outcomes 124 (2015).

with a focus on cardiovascular medical devices. Second, we evaluate the applicability of the Health Insurance Portability and Accountability Act (HIPAA), the Common Rule, and state laws to compulsory registries. Third, we propose additional guidance for registry development, including rules for enrolment, consent, data use, and access to data.

17.2 THE ROLE OF REGISTRIES IN POSTMARKET ANALYSIS OF MEDICAL DEVICES

17.2.1 *Limitations in the FDA's Evaluation and Monitoring of Devices*

The FDA employs a risk-based regulatory framework that classifies medical devices into three categories: Class I (low risk) devices are those that pose a minimal potential for harm, such as tongue depressors and stethoscopes; Class II (medium risk) devices have a higher potential for harm, such as syringes and electrocardiograph machines; and Class III (high risk) devices have the highest potential for harm, such as pacemakers and defibrillators.[4]

All three classes of medical devices are subject to "general controls," which include, inter alia, registration, prohibitions against misbranding and adulteration, and adherence to good manufacturing practices.[5] For Class I and Class II devices where general controls are insufficient to provide a reasonable assurance of safety and efficacy, "special controls" are required, which may include, inter alia, postmarket surveillance, patient registries, and 510(k) premarket notification.[6] For Class III devices where special controls are insufficient to provide a reasonable assurance of safety and efficacy, a premarket approval (PMA) application is required.[7]

The 510(k) pathway principally seeks to establish that a new device is "substantially equivalent" to a device that the FDA has already cleared for marketing. As the FDA explains, the 510(k) pathway "is comparative" whereas the PMA pathway involves "an independent demonstration of safety and effectiveness."[8] The 510(k) process "was specifically intended for devices with less need for scientific scrutiny, such as surgical gloves and hearing aids."[9] Over the years, however, the breadth of devices eligible for the expedited review mechanism has been expanded

[4] US Food & Drug Admin., Premarket Approval (PMA), https://www.fda.gov/medical-devices/premarket-submissions/premarket-approval-pma; US Food & Drug Admin., Premarket Application Review Process, https://www.fda.gov/medical-devices/premarket-approval-pma/pma-review-process; William H. Maisel, Medical Device Regulation: An Introduction for the Practicing Physician, 140 Ann. Intern. Med. 296 (2004).

[5] US Food & Drug Admin., The 510(k) Program: Evaluating Substantial Equivalence in Premarket Notifications, (2014).

[6] Id.

[7] Id.

[8] Id.

[9] Diana M. Zuckerman et al., Medical Device Recalls and the FDA Approval Process, 13 Arch. Intern. Med. 1006 (2011).

significantly, and only 1 percent of medical devices utilize the more rigorous PMA pathway.[10]

Apart from utilization of the 510(k) pathway for some high-risk devices, other high-risk devices come to market as PMA supplements – a subset available where a new device contains changes to an already approved device.[11] PMA Supplements may be required when changes impact the safety or effectiveness of a device, including but not limited to new device indications, labeling changes, use of new manufacturing processes or facilities, changes in sterilization procedures, packaging changes, or changes in design specifications or components.[12] For devices that come to market as PMA supplements, the FDA generally does not require clinical trial data.[13] In recent years, several high-risk cardiac devices approved as PMA supplements – some of which were implanted into hundreds of thousands of patients – have been recalled due to serious safety concerns.[14]

We summarize the distinctions between the 510(k) and PMA pathways here to highlight the fact that it is common for high-risk medical devices to come to market without providing the FDA with clinical trial data that demonstrates the device's safety and effectiveness. In part these accelerated pathways to market are due to budgetary constraints – specifically, Congress has not allocated sufficient funds so that regulators have the resources to oversee and review clinical trial data. A second relevant factor is that there are significant budgetary and scientific barriers to applying robust scrutiny to a large number of devices from conception through real-world utilization (often referred to as the "total product life cycle").[15] In other words, the cost and time to provide meaningful safety and efficacy data would translate to longer periods of time before which a new device could come to market.

These resource constraints are exacerbated by statutory requirements that the FDA utilize "the least burdensome appropriate means of evaluating device effectiveness that would have a reasonable likelihood of resulting in approval."[16] This legal requirement – which is not found in regulations governing FDA review of pharmaceuticals or vaccines – was enacted by Congress, largely at the request of lobbyists and medical device manufacturers.[17] It forces the FDA's hands by requiring that the agency think creatively on how to solicit the least amount of information that can illustrate device safety and efficacy. As a practical matter it translates to device

10 Id.

11 US Food & Drug Admin., Modifications to Devices Subject to Premarket Approval (PMA) – The PMA Supplemental Decision-Making Process: Guidance for Industry and FDA Staff (2018).

12 Id.

13 Benjamin N. Rome et al., Approval of High-Risk Medical Devices in the US: Implications for Clinical Cardiology, 16 Curr. Cardiol. Rep. 489 (2014).

14 Id.

15 See, e.g., Efthimios Parasidis, Patients Over Politics: Addressing Legislative Failure in the Regulation of Medical Products, 2011 Wisc. L. Rev. 929 (2011).

16 US Food & Drug Admin., The Least Burdensome Provisions: Concept and Principles (2019).

17 John J. Smith & Anne M. Shyjan, Defining "Least Burdensome Means" Under the Food and Drug Administration Modernization Act of 1997, 55 Food & Drug L. J. 435 (2000).

approvals that, for the most part, do not require clinical trial data. The least burdensome standard applies even for high-risk medical devices such as implantable cardioverter-defibrillators (ICDs), pacemakers, and artificial heart valves.

Several observers have highlighted limitations in the current legal and regulatory framework, particularly in premarket review.[18] These critiques also extend to the postmarket surveillance scheme which, despite evolving emphasis on new strategies,[19] continues to rely significantly on passive surveillance of marketed medical devices, a mechanism that fails to adequately capture postmarket safety and efficacy concerns.[20] While passive surveillance has been able to capture some instances of patient harms due to faulty devices, underreporting is widespread, and reports submitted to the FDA's passive surveillance database are often submitted late and lack critical information on adverse events.[21] In instances where the FDA mandates postapproval studies, studies have found that progress is often inadequate and many requirements go uncompleted.[22] Inadequate postmarket surveillance is not limited to medical devices, but also plagues postmarket evaluation of pharmaceuticals and vaccines.[23] For truly novel, transformative, and influential therapeutics, then, a robust postmarket surveillance strategy is of great importance to regulators, payors, and the public because it helps produce meaningful evidence to continuously evaluate the safety and efficacy of marketed medical products.

17.2.2 *General Structure and Function of Regulatory Registries*

When structured and utilized properly, registries can provide valuable information to support postmarket analysis on safety and efficacy. As noted above, the FDA can mandate registries either as a condition of approval for high-risk device (a so-called postapproval study) or as a "522 study," which can be applied at any point in a product lifecycle.[24] Timely completion of these studies is the responsibility of device sponsors and, in theory, the FDA can withdraw marketing approval or clearance for failure to do so.

Registries defined by exposure to a specific device or procedure can generate datasets with large sample sizes that include a more diverse set of patients than those in premarket studies. Registries can include or be linked to additional clinical data, which allows for identification of information related to disease severity and

18 Rita F. Redberg & Sanket S. Dhruva, Moving From Substantial Equivalence to Substantial Improvement for 510(k) Devices, 322 JAMA 927 (2019); L. Camille Jones et al., Assessment of Clinical Trial Evidence for High-Risk Cardiovascular Devices Approved Under the Food and Drug Administration Priority Review Program, 178 JAMA Intern. Med. 1418 (2018); Parasidis, supra note 15.

19 US Food & Drug Admin., Strengthening our National System for Medical Device Postmarket Surveillance (2013).

20 Rajan et al., supra note 3; Parasidis, supra note 15.

21 Rajan et al., supra note 3.

22 Id.

23 Parasidis, supra note 15.

24 Rajan et al., supra note 3.

comorbidities and may provide information on the device utilization outside the context of pivotal clinical trials or established guidelines. For example, studies have uncovered divergence from guidelines-based indications for ICDs and cardiac resynchronization therapy.[25] Registries can provide important insights regarding off-label use of devices, such as transcatheter aortic valve replacement (TAVR), that may guide future regulatory decisions about expanded indications.[26]

Registries also play an important role in coverage decisions and subsequent requirements for evidence generation. Once FDA approval is earned, sponsors of new devices typically submit applications to the CMS to determine whether the product meets the statutory requirement of "reasonable and necessary" for reimbursement.[27] Both terms remain somewhat nebulous but together are generally understood to reflect a totality of evidence supportive of clinically meaningful benefits with an acceptable safety profile.[28]

While many services (including use of new devices) are covered by the CMS automatically, in select cases, manufacturers, clinicians, or the CMS request a national coverage determination, which grants, limits, or excludes Medicare coverage nationwide.[29] A small proportion of services thought to be particularly novel, influential for Medicare beneficiaries, or otherwise identified as important from the CMS's perspective are provided conditional reimbursement – "coverage with evidence development."[30] In these cases, payment for services occurs only in concert with a prospective study approved by the CMS as meeting specific scientific goals relevant to safety, effectiveness, or utilization among its beneficiaries. Over the past fifteen years, more than two dozen devices or services have been subject to coverage with evidence development decisions. This includes truly novel and (for Medicare patients in particular, most of whom are aged greater than sixty-five)

25 Sana M. Al-Khatib et al., Non-Evidence-Based ICD Implantations in the United States, 305 JAMA 43 (2011); Adam S. Fein et al., Prevalence and Predictors of Off-label Use of Cardiac Resynchronization Therapy in Patients Enrolled in the National Cardiovascular Data Registry Implantable Cardiac-Defibrillator Registry, 31 J. Am. C. Cardiol. 766 (2010).

26 Ravi S. Hira et al., Trends and Outcomes of Off-label Use of Transcatheter Aortic Valve Replacement: Insights from the NCDR STS/ACC TVT Registry, 2 JAMA Cardiol. 846 (2017).

27 Peter J. Neumann et al., Medicare's National Coverage Decisions for Technologies, 1999–2007, 27 Health Affairs 1620 (2008).

28 Jessica N. Holtzman & Daniel B. Kramer, Harmonizing Standards and Incentives in Medical Device Regulation: Lessons Learned from the Parallel Review Pathway, 46 J. L. Med. Ethics 1034 (2018); Peter J. Neumann & James D. Chambers, Medicare's Enduring Struggle to Define "Reasonable and Necessary" Care, 367 N. Engl. J. Med. 1775 (2012).

29 Daniel B. Kramer et al., Implications of Medicare Coverage for Magnetic Resonance Imaging in Patients with Capped or Epicardial Leads, 1 JAMA Cardiol. 1139 (2018); Peter J. Neumann & James D. Chambers, Medicare's Reset on "Coverage with Evidence Determination," Health Affairs Blog (Apr. 1, 2013).

30 Neumann & Chambers, supra note 28; Daniel B. Kramer & Aaron S. Kesselheim, Coverage of Magnetic Resonance Imaging for Patients with Cardiac Devices: Improving the Coverage with Evidence Development Program, 1 JAMA Cardiol. 711 (2017).

clinically impactful transcatheter treatments for valvular heart disease, devices for stroke prevention, and new "leadless" designs for implantable pacemakers.

17.2.3 *Compulsory Registries for Cardiovascular Devices*

FDA review and CMS reimbursement have brought together agencies with overlapping public health mandates to help establish several pivotal cardiovascular devices registries.[31] While the individual details and methods vary, in general these registries have met the needs of regulatory agencies to develop additional evidence specific to its intended patient population, while also providing a platform for postmarket surveillance studies assessing safety, off-label utilization, real-world outcomes, and potential expansion of indications. The exact purpose, structure, and stewardship of "regulatory registries" – that is, those created primarily to meet requirements of the FDA, CMS, or both – varies according to device. Here we describe two influential cardiovascular device regulatory registries that share the feature of compulsory enrollment.

The National Cardiovascular Data Registry (NCDR) ICD Registry was created in 2005 in concert with expansion of CMS coverage guidelines for primary prevention ICDs, which are ICDs implanted in patients without a history of cardiac arrest or sustained ventricular arrhythmias.[32] A clinical trial published in 2004 demonstrated a survival advantage for ICD implantation in patients with heart failure from left ventricular systolic dysfunction regardless of etiology, widely expanding the pool of patients eligible for an effective but expensive intervention.[33] The ICD Registry was developed by the American College of Cardiology (ACC), which manages a suite of registries under the NCDR umbrella, and the Heart Rhythm Society (HRS), a professional society for cardiac electrophysiology, with guidance from the CMS and FDA. Notably, the CMS coverage memo requires only that data be collected for Medicare beneficiaries. However, the majority of the approximately 1,500 participating sites submit data on all patients who receive ICD implants, and thus the ICD Registry serves as an excellent storehouse of postmarket information.

Several specific analytic questions were posed by the CMS as the guiding scientific goals for the ICD Registry. The overall principle was summarized in the original

31 Holtzman & Kramer, supra note 28.

32 Mark S. Kremers et al., The National ICD Registry Report: Version 2.1 Including Leads and Pediatrics for Years 2010 and 2011, 10 Heart Rhythm e59 (2013); Stephen C. Hammill et al., The National ICD Registry: Now and Into the Future, 3 Heart Rhythm 470 (2006); Stephen C. Hammill et al., Review of the Registry's Second Year, Data Collected, and Plans to Add Lead and Pediatric ICD Procedures, 5 Heart Rhythm 1359 (2008); Stephen C. Hammill et al., Review of the ICD Registry's Third Year, Expansion to Include Lead Data and Pediatric ICD Procedures, and Role for Measuring Performance, 6 Heart Rhythm 1397 (2009); Stephen C. Hammill et al., Review of the Registry's Fourth Year, Incorporating Lead Data and Pediatric ICD Procedures, and Use as a National Performance Measure, 7 Heart Rhythm 1340 (2010).

33 Gust H. Bardy et al., Amiodarone or an Implantable Cardioverter-Defibrillator for Congestive Heart Failure, 352 N. Engl. J. Med. 225 (2005).

2005 memo from the CMS, which indicated: "We are concerned that the available evidence does not provide a high degree of guidance to providers to target these devices to patients who will clearly derive benefit."[34] Specific hypotheses posited to refine that position through the ICD Registry include Table 17.1:[35]

Data collection is performed for over 100 data elements incorporating patient characteristics, procedural details, laboratory tests, and complications that occur within the index hospitalization. These data include multiple individual identifiers, which have facilitated linkages to other datasets such as administrative claims data as well as industry data.[36] Over one million patients have had data entered into the registry, including hundreds of thousands of patients who are not Medicare beneficiaries. There is no consent obtained and no mechanism for patients to opt-out or to

TABLE 17.1 *Hypotheses*

1. The clinical characteristics of the patients receiving ICDs are similar to those of patients involved in the primary prevention randomized clinical trials.
2. The indications for ICD implantation in patients are similar to those in the primary prevention randomized clinical trials.
3. The in-hospital procedure-related complications for patients are similar to those in the primary prevention randomized clinical trials.
4. Certified providers competent in ICD implantation are implanting ICD devices in patients.
5. Patients who receive an ICD represent patients for which current clinical guidelines and the evidence base recommend implantation.
6. The clinical characteristics and indications for ICD implantation do not differ significantly among facilities.
7. The clinical characteristics and indications for ICD implantation do not differ significantly among providers.
8. The in-hospital procedure-related complications for ICD implantation do not differ significantly among facilities.
9. The in-hospital procedure-related complications for ICD implantation do not differ significantly among providers.
10. The in-hospital procedure-related complications for ICD implantation do not differ significantly among device manufacturer, types, and/or programming.

[34] Centers for Medicare and Medicaid Services, CAG-00157R3, Decision Memo for Implantable Defibrillators (2005).

[35] Id. This list is identified in the CMS 2005 Decision Memo.

[36] Joseph G. Akar et al., Use of Remote Monitoring of Newly Implanted Cardioverter-Defibrillators: Insights from the Patient Related Determinants of ICD Remote Monitoring (PREDICT RM) Study, 128 Circulation 2372 (2013); Joseph G. Akar et al., Use of Remote Monitoring Is Associated with Lower Risk of Adverse Outcomes Among Patients with Implanted Cardiac Defibrillators, 8 Circ. Arrhythm. Electrophysiol. 1173 (2015); Daniel B. Kramer et al., Hospice Use Following Implantable Cardioverter-Defibrillator Implantation in Older Patients: Results from the National Cardiovascular Data Registry, 24 Circulation 2030 (2016).

TABLE 17.2 *Specifications and study goals*

1. The heart team and hospital are participating in a prospective, national, audited registry that: 1) consecutively enrolls TAVR patients; 2) accepts all manufactured devices; 3) follows the patient for at least one year; and 4) complies with relevant regulations relating to protecting human research subjects, including 45 CFR Part 46 and 21 CFR Parts 50 and 56.
2. The following outcomes must be tracked by the registry: and the registry must be designed to permit identification and analysis of patient, practitioner, and facility level variables that predict each of these outcomes:
   a. Stroke;
   b. All cause mortality;
   c. Transient Ischemic Attacks (TIAs);
   d. Major vascular events;
   e. Acute kidney injury;
   f. Repeat aortic valve procedures;
   g Quality of Life (QoL).
3. The registry should collect all data necessary and have a written executable analysis plan in place to address the following questions (to appropriately address some questions. Medicare claims or other outside data may be necessary):
   a. When performed outside a controlled clinical study, how do outcomes and adverse events compare to the pivotal clinical studies?
   b. How do outcomes and adverse events in subpopulations compare to patients in the pivotal clinical studies?
   c. What is the longterm (> five-year) durability of the device?
   d. What are the longterm (> five-year) outcomes and adverse events?
   e. How do the demographics of registry patients compare to the pivotal studies

view their own data. Of note, an updated Medicare coverage memo issued in 2018 ended the requirement for entry into the ICD registry as a condition of reimbursement.[37] Data from the ICD Registry has been relied upon in several publications that have analyzed safety and efficacy of ICDs, though the impact of the ICD Registry on CMS reimbursement has been less clear.

Similar motivation supports the Transvalvular Therapeutics (TVT) Registry, a partnership between the Society of Thoracic Surgeons (STS) and ACC that has been approved by the CMS to meet coverage requirements related to TAVR and transcatheter mitral valve repair. These two device types have been transformative therapies over the past several years, bringing minimally invasive options to patients previously considered prohibitive or high risk for surgical intervention and increasingly extending towards wider populations of potential recipients. The FDA worked with the CMS to structure the registry. The CMS coverage memo for TAVR echoed

37 Centers for Medicare and Medicaid Services, CAG-00157R4, Decision Memo for Implantable Cardioverter Defibrillators (2018).

elements of that issued for ICDs, including the following specifications (among others) and articulated study goals Table 17.2:[38]

Again, patients must be enrolled, or the facility risks nonreimbursement. In practice, this means that device recipients are automatically enrolled without consent or an opt-out mechanism. Notably, the ICD registry case report forms can generally be completed entirely from electronic or similar data sources, without the need to speak with patients. The TVT Registry form includes many of the same demographic, clinical, and procedural details as the ICD registry but also captures quality of life information. These additional data points require a brief interview with patients.

17.3 LEGAL FRAMEWORK GOVERNING COMPULSORY MEDICAL DEVICE REGISTRIES

There is no uniform legal framework applicable to all registries. Rather, the reach of the law – including health privacy laws and regulations governing research with human subjects – depends on the structure and function of a registry, as well as the registry steward. This is problematic, since a wide range of stakeholders creates and uses registries, including academic medical centers, not-for-profit entities, professional societies and organizations, private companies, health care payors, provider organizations, and medical device companies.[39] Divergent protections can result in use of health data in ways that contradict the expectations or interests of patients, which may exacerbate lack of trust in data use and the health care system.

17.3.1 *The Scope of HIPAA Protections for Registry Data*

HIPAA protections apply solely to covered entities (i.e., health care providers, health plans, and health care clearinghouses) and the business associates of these entities.[40] Several registry stewards fall outside of HIPAA's reach entirely, so long as they do not collaborate with a covered entity, including medical device companies, patient advocacy groups, and professional societies. Registry data submitted directly from a patient to a registry steward is also not encompassed by HIPAA's protections.[41] And, HIPAA's limitations apply solely to protected health information, not to the collection and use of deidentified data.[42]

For entities that fall under the HIPAA umbrella, the HIPAA security rule requires implementation of a reasonable security plan and security risk assessments.[43] In

38 Centers for Medicare and Medicaid Services, CAG-00430R, Decision Memo for Transcatheter Aortic Valve Replacement (TAVR) (2019).
39 Leslie P. Francis & Michael Squires, Patient Registries and Their Governance: A Pilot Study and Recommendations, 19 Ind. Health L. Rev. 43 (2019).
40 45 C.F.R. § 160.102.
41 45 C.F.R. § 164.514.
42 Id.
43 45 C.F.R. § 164.306.

addition to the protections mandated under the HIPAA security rule, the HIPAA privacy rule affords protections to individuals whose health information is handled by an entity bound by HIPAA. The privacy rule requires patient authorization if health information is to be used in research, but authorization is not required if the information is to be used for public health activities.[44] Via this exception, patient authorization is not necessary for public health surveillance registries that do not include research.[45] This includes registries created to track the quality, safety, or effectiveness of FDA-regulated products.[46] Overall, HIPAA allows covered entities and their business associates to disclose identifiable patient information without patient authorization in cases where a registry: 1) furthers public health activities, including public health surveillance and review of an FDA-regulated device; 2) supports health care operations; or 3) is created pursuant to a legal mandate of health oversight officials, such as for CMS reimbursement.

If public health research is conducted using registry data assembled for public health practice, HIPAA permits disclosure of identifiable patient information without consent for a limited dataset, so long as an institutional review board (IRB) or privacy board issues a waiver of consent and the data source and registry steward enter into a data-use agreement.[47] In considering whether a waiver of consent is appropriate, relevant factors include whether 1) the research involves more than minimal risk, 2) adequate data protections are in place, 3) the research could not practically be conducted if patient authorization is required, and 4) the research could not practically be conducted without identifiable information.[48] Notably, a limited dataset cannot contain certain data points, such as names, device identifiers, and biometric identifiers; accordingly, limited datasets may be of diminished relevance to device registries, and particularly for cardiac device registries where device and biometric identifiers are essential.

Under HIPAA, patient authorization is also not required for health care treatment, payment processing, or health care operations.[49] Accordingly, registries used solely to tailor treatments for patients would not need patient authorization, nor would registries that facilitate health care quality improvement, outcomes evaluation, and development of clinical guidelines.[50] This includes registries created by hospitals or health care providers to track patient outcomes against clinical care standards.[51]

44 45 C.F.R. § 164.508; 45 C.F.R. § 164.512.
45 45 C.F.R. § 164.512.
46 Id.
47 AHRQ, Registries for Evaluating Patient Outcomes: A User's Guide (Gliklich & Leavy eds., 2014) [hereinafter AHRQ Registries User's Guide].
48 45 C.F.R. § 46.116.
49 45 C.F.R. § 164.502.
50 AHRQ Registries User's Guide, supra note 47.
51 Id.

Taken together, HIPAA allows covered entities and their business associates to disclose identifiable patient information without patient authorization in cases where a registry: furthers public health activities, including public health surveillance and review of an FDA-regulated device; supports health care operations; or is created pursuant to a legal mandate of health oversight officials, such as for CMS reimbursement. The public health surveillance exception is particularly relevant in the context of compulsory regulatory registries. Also relevant is the exception whereby identifiable patient data can be disclosed for research purposes if the research could not reasonably be achieved if patient authorization is required. As to the latter, such an argument in the context of a compulsory registry may not withstand scrutiny in cases where direct patient contact in a clinical setting could be expanded to include, for example, verbal or written consent to use of patient data in a registry. The lack of a uniform legal framework to apply across all medical device registries leaves registry stewards to act on an ad hoc basis, which may lead to inconsistent protections across the population.

17.3.2 *Applicability of the Common Rule to Registries*

In instances involving research based on registry information, federal protections governing research with human participants may apply. As a threshold matter, the Common Rule applies to 1) federally funded research sponsored by one of the seventeen federal agencies that have adopted the Common Rule or 2) studies that will be submitted to the FDA in the context of device approval or monitoring. Some institutions – such as academic medical centers – have adopted the Common Rule to all research conducted at the institution, regardless of funding source. Given the breadth of registry stewards, however, there may be instances where a registry steward or data user is not legally bound by the Common Rule. In such instances the steward or data user has the discretion as to whether, and to what extent, to follow the federal guidelines.

The Common Rule's protections apply solely to research, which is defined as a systematic investigation that is designed or developed to contribute to generalizable knowledge.[52] At the outset, it is important to note that the Common Rule does not apply to registries that do not include individually-identifiable information.[53] Moreover, under the statute, research does not include public health surveillance and the provision of health care.[54] These exceptions are particularly relevant in the context of regulatory registries, since registries are often created to monitor public health or comply with FDA postmarket requirements.

At the same time, if identifiable information is used for public health research – rather than public health surveillance – the Common Rule would apply and patient

[52] 45 C.F.R. § 46.102.
[53] 45 C.F.R. § 46.101.
[54] 45 C.F.R. § 46.102.

consent would be required, unless an IRB or privacy board determines that a waiver of consent is applicable.[55] Along these lines, the Common Rule's protections apply to registry research in the context of an FDA-regulated device; as with public health research, the Common Rule would apply and patient consent would be required, unless an IRB or privacy board determines that a waiver of consent is applicable.[56]

For registries that fall within the purview of the Common Rule, regulations require that the registry steward and registry data user obtain informed consent from identifiable individuals who are included in the registry.[57] A waiver of informed consent may apply if the research poses a minimal risk to the research subjects, cannot be practically conducted without a waiver, does not use registry data in identifiable form, and will not adversely affect the rights and welfare of the research subjects.[58]

In instances where informed consent is required, the research participant must be informed of the risks and benefits of the research. This includes information related to privacy protections and the risks of loss of confidentiality.[59] However, pursuant to revisions to the Common Rule enacted in 2016, "broad consent" is now permitted in instances where researchers are conducting downstream research using identifiable personal information. Under the broad consent principle, at the point of initial consent, all that is required is a general description of the type of research that may be conducted, the identifiable information that may be used, timeframe for research, any plans to share information, and contact information for the researchers.[60] Thus, at the time of initial collection, the registry steward can utilize a broad consent document that covers future uses of the patient's information which, as a practical matter, provides little guidance to the patient on how, precisely, their information will be utilized.[61]

The Office for Human Research Protections explains that primary and secondary purposes of an activity are relevant factors to consider in determining whether a project qualifies as research under the Common Rule.[62] As such, registries created for research purposes, in whole or in part, would fall under the Common Rule if the entity creating the registry is bound by the Common Rule's protections.[63] This is distinct from the HIPAA privacy rule, which indicates that the protections apply only if research is the primary purpose behind use of patient information; otherwise, HIPAA classifies the data use as health care operations.

55 AHRQ Registries User's Guide, supra note 47.
56 Id.
57 45 C.F.R. § 46.111.
58 45 C.F.R. § 46.116.
59 Id.
60 Id.
61 AHRQ Registries User's Guide, supra note 47.
62 Id.
63 Id.

IRB review of the registry protocol would include the research purpose of the registry, informed consent arrangements (or an explanation of why informed consent is not necessary), and privacy and confidentiality safeguards.[64] Compulsory registries that are required by law fall under the Common Rule's umbrella only if the registry is used for research. In such cases, consent would be required unless a waiver has been authorized by a governing IRB.[65] Taken together, although the Common Rule affords protections for research that utilizes registry data, registry stewards and downstream data users must be mindful of the ethical implications of consent waivers and other exceptions to the research guidelines. Just because use of registry data without patient consent may be legal, it does not mean that such use is ethically appropriate.

17.3.3 *Additional Laws*

Apart from HIPAA and the Common Rule, we also note briefly that several other laws may apply to the creation and use of registries. The additional laws include federal statutes, state statutes, state common law, and, in the case of registries incorporating data derived from patients outside the United States, laws from other nations. For example, coupled with the Common Rule's application to research involving registries, there are supplemental federal protections and guidelines for research involving prisoners, pregnant women, children, and patients in federally funded substance abuse programs. In addition, the NIH can issue a certificate of confidentiality for a specific project that requires confidentiality beyond the general legal requirements.[66]

Also relevant is the Federal Trade Commission (FTC) Act, which prohibits unfair or deceptive trade practices.[67] Registries fall within the FTC Act's reach, and it would be a deceptive trade practice to provide individuals with false or misleading information regarding data collection or use.[68] State laws, such as California's Consumer Privacy Act, may also dictate rights to bearing on registry design, as will the laws of other nations, such as the European Union's General Data Protection Regulation, if data are collected from or shared within its jurisdiction.

17.4 PROPOSED GUIDELINES FOR DEVELOPMENT AND USE OF COMPULSORY REGISTRIES

The benefits of compulsory registries are tangible and significant. In light of the significant evidence gaps in premarket review, we believe that the potential benefits

64 Id.
65 Id.
66 15 U.S.C. § 45.
67 Id.
68 Francis & Squires, supra note 39.

to be gained from compulsory registries likely outweigh the risks to participating subjects. Yet we are mindful of the implications of compulsory registries on patient autonomy and respect for persons, and thus recommend that a robust informational-disclosure dialogue be implemented as a component of informed consent for clinical care where enrollment in a registry is a requirement for use of the medical device.

Insofar as all patients will have procedural consent obtained prior to device implant, there is an existing mechanism for clinical contact. Moreover, some registries already incorporate detailed patient interviews purely for research purposes, such as the collection of patient-reported outcome measures for key variables such as quality of life. Incorporating a verbal or written consent into the clinical point of care or patient interview would not pose an unreasonable burden on physicians or investigators.

In addition to robust consent and data-linkage protocols, we likewise recommend that registry stewards and data users be held legally accountable for maintaining the security of patient data and providing patients with clear information on data collection and use. This includes providing detailed information on registry sponsorship and specific uses of registry data prior to patient authorization to clinical use of a device. Accountability also includes a privacy-by-design feature whereby registry stewards must affirmatively obtain consent from patients if patient data is to be used beyond the original scope, allowing patients to opt-out of such downstream uses. To further accountability, patients should have easy access to a tracking system that details data use and downstream research.

To promote public trust in compulsory registries, stewards should task a standing advisory committee to track operational and ethical issues. At least one member of the committee should be trained as an ethicist and not have a relationship with the registry steward or downstream data users. The committee should also be a forum whereby patients can raise questions or concerns about the registry. To the extent these criteria are met by an existing institutional review board, there may not be a need to create a separate committee.

17.5 CONCLUSION

Compulsory registries promote patient outcomes and facilitate robust lifecycle analysis of medical devices. Insofar as laws and regulations have significant gaps in instances where patient authorization is required prior to collection and use of patient data, providers and registry stewards have an ethical obligation to inform patients about data collection and use. Contemporary data protection and research laws afford limited protections for individuals, but these existing laws need not dictate ethical guidance. This is particularly true in the context of health information, which is widely viewed as one of the most sensitive informational areas. Instilling supplemental privacy safeguards and data-use limits may be appropriate when patients are compelled to include their personal information into a registry as a condition of receiving medical care.

18

Professional Self-Regulation in Medicine

Will the Rise of Intelligent Tools Mean the End of Peer Review?

Anthony P. Weiss and Barak D. Richman

18.1 INTRODUCTION

Medicine has a longstanding compact with society to prioritize the needs of patients above other aims, a concept as old as the Hippocratic Oath. As an extension of this professional commitment, physicians have been granted the discretion and authority to police their own – to establish professional standards of conduct and to enforce those standards in the practice of medicine against fellow professionals.

Peer review is the culmination of this social compact. Peer review is a decentralized process in which the formal medical staff structures across the country assess adverse medical events, determine whether a colleague's conduct fell short of a professional standard of care, and, when necessary, discipline errant physicians. It is led by physicians, and though the objective is to learn from all errors and improve care throughout the delivery system, its primary focus is on physician conduct. It is so central to the modern practice of medicine that it has shaped the organization of hospitals and embodies the central values of being a medical professional.

However, the contours of peer review are products of – and are thus sensitive to – medical technology. Physician self-regulation and its prevailing current structures are largely driven by the realities of knowledge. Historically, it was held that only physicians had the expertise to distinguish proper from improper care, and thus should be the sole authorities to assess the competence of any individual member of the profession.[1] But modern medicine is now guided by sources of knowledge that no longer lie in the sole possession of physicians. Shifts toward team-based care models rely on the expertise of nonphysicians and skills that lie beyond physician capabilities. Electronic medical records are now the primary repositories of patient medical information and are becoming more capable than physicians at detecting and correcting errors or deviations in practice. And digital technologies increasingly have the capacity to synthesize data to generate diagnoses and medical recommendations, which compare favorably to human experts. These new technologies

[1] Edward H. Livingston & John D. Harwell, Peer Review, 182 Am. J. Surgery 103 (2001).

and systems are challenging the supremacy of physician expertise in medicine, and consequently are eroding the underlying justifications for peer review.

And true disruption might be at hand. Artificial intelligence (AI) and machine learning (ML) algorithms are slowly enabling computer-driven medicine to perform the core functions of peer review: identifying medical errors, learning from adverse outcomes, and instituting reforms.

Even though it is widely known that new capabilities and skills from nonphysicians are playing an increasingly significant role in the practice of medicine, there has been little thought to whether these technological disruptions will necessitate broader changes in the organization and delivery of medicine. This chapter begins that inquiry by exploring the implications that AI and digital technologies have for peer review. We suggest that these technologies do much more than supplement the medical staff's ability to evaluate and improve medical practice. They have the capacity to disrupt traditional centers of authority that underlie peer review and may thereby force a reorganization of medicine and a recalibration of health care regulation.

18.2 PEER REVIEW EXPLAINED

The governance relationship between so-called learned professions and the rest of society has been likened to a social contract. In exchange for professionals investing in valuable expertise, inculcating a commitment to, and offering guidance to state officials, the state defers to professional expertise in both substance and practice.[2] Professionals thus are tasked by the state to define standards of conduct and to discipline themselves accordingly. Economists typically describe this arrangement as a product of information asymmetries – that lay people, even elected officials, have inadequate knowledge to scrutinize the conduct of scientific experts[3] – and sociologists observe that this social arrangement reserves for professionals a privileged status and fierce autonomy that few other laborers enjoy.

Physicians historically have been the archetype of the learned professions, enjoying greater autonomy and self-governance privileges than that afforded to other professional societies, and the expanse of physician self-governance is reflected across numerous public and private mechanisms. States authorize medical societies to establish state licensure regimes and malpractice standards, thereby allowing the profession to define qualifications and minimal standards. States also provide their plenary powers to both licensure boards (thereby prohibiting nonphysicians from engaging in "the practice of medicine") and courts (thereby disciplining those who fail to meet medical board standards). The incorporation of professional standards

[2] William J. Goode, Community Within a Community: The Professions, 22 Am. Sociological Rev. 194 (1957).

[3] Kenneth J. Arrow, Uncertainty and the Welfare Economics of Medical Care, 53 Am. Econ. Rev. 141 (Dec. 1963).

into the law, and the use of the state's police power to enforce those standards, allow medical professionals to maintain a robust and self-sustaining system of self-regulation.

But it might be said that the cornerstone of physician self-governance – and the pinnacle of collaboration between medical professionals and the state – lies in peer review. Both medical boards and state authority defer to institutional peer reviews, and numerous laws cloak the peer review process both to secure its sanctity and reinforce its authority.

This legal arrangement has been described as a unique reflection of successive "devolutions" of medical authority, from federal government to state government, from state government to physician-led state licensing boards, and from these boards to the local medical staff structures within individual hospitals.[4] In many respects, it is a historical compromise reflecting the need to protect the public from deviant medical practice, while recognizing that medicine is an imperfect science with significant regional variation. It is also a means to achieve the end of public safety while avoiding nonphysician (government) intrusion in the doctor-patient relationship, a politically challenging issue.

While voluntary and informal review of physician practice by peers may occur in a number of settings, formal peer review as considered in this chapter is largely a hospital-based function, conducted to meet accreditation requirements specified by the Joint Commission (TJC). Despite some guidance put forward by TJC for medical staff practice, peer review remains highly variable in its structure and process, with relatively little standardization across the country. Peer review is typically conducted by a multi-disciplinary committee of physicians, and supported by hospital personnel, including nurses, safety experts, and attorneys. The peer review committee reports to a physician-led medical executive committee (MEC), which has local responsibility for the oversight of medical practice at a hospital. The committee may serve a number of roles, including initial review of physician qualifications for inclusion on the medical staff. But the committee primarily reviews adverse patient outcomes for evidence of physician negligence or incompetence, typically comparing the actions of the responsible physician to a community standard, looking for gross deviation from usual practice. In some cases, the committee will undertake an exercise, known as root cause analysis, meant to uncover the specific factors which resulted in the adverse patient outcome. The work product of the committee may range from recommendations to the hospital's governing body (via the MEC) to rescind physician privileges, to dismissal of any concern related to the adverse incident.

Peer review is much more than a political compromise or a social compact of convenience. There are benefits that justify empowering local inquiry, by and for

[4] Theodore W. Ruger, Plural Constitutionalism and the Pathologies of American Healthcare, 120 Yale L. J. 347 (2011).

professionals, in assessing medical error. First, because of the complexity of medicine, inquiries into errors are best done by physicians most familiar with the context in which the error took place. In addition to the natural complexity of medicine, which justifies deferring to the expertise of practitioners over the judgment of regulators, there is further reason to defer to physicians who are best acquainted with the surrounding environment, facilities, and personnel in which scrutinized care took place. For this reason, many applications of medical malpractice law recognize regional variations in the practice of medicine and apply locally determined standards of care.

Second, and more significant, local peer review is designed to enhance the benefits of scrutinizing adverse outcomes. Since the ultimate objective is to learn from mistakes and improve the quality of care, the priority of any review process is to acquire accurate information, which plausibly is best done between colleagues within a cloak of trust, reciprocity, and collective learning. The tacit nature of information, the sensitivity of disclosing information related to potential errors, and the formal and informal support structures that embed the disclosure of this information all counsel towards providing discretion and authority to local medical boards.

These purported benefits of peer review are also reflected in the law, as many doctrines explicitly protect the peer review process. For example, any materials generated during the peer review process, including admissions of error, are shielded from discovery in any subsequent malpractice suit. Moreover, if internal documents or materials related to a medical error are not part of a peer review, they then do become subject to discovery. Perhaps most important, the association of peer review with high-quality medicine is enshrined in state licensure law and accreditation standards. A hospital needs to institute a peer review process, administered by a physician-led medical board, to be permitted to care for patients and receive Medicare funds. Peer review is not just thought to be important for maintaining high-quality medical care, it is deemed to be an essential feature of quality assurance for medical facilities.

18.3 CRITICISMS AND SHORTCOMINGS OF PEER REVIEW

Peer review is not without its detractors, however, both within and outside the field of medicine. There are three broad categories of criticism: 1) It promotes a singular societal aim (safety) over other health care ends of importance to the public (like innovation, cost, and access); 2) Like all human processes, it is liable to bias, self-preservation, and abuse; 3) It is ineffective in achieving its primary aim of promoting safe care.

Perhaps owing to the ancient dictum, *primum non nocere*, peer review almost solely focuses on safety of health care to the exclusion of other valuable aims. While nominally, peer review purports to drive learning and improvement, reviews of its success in this area have been disappointing.[5] This is, in part, inherent to the nature of the process – the widespread dissemination of lessons learned (needed for innovation) stands in opposition to the privacy needed to maintain a trusting arrangement for local review. Furthermore, peer review has limited impact on other aspects of the "iron triangle" of health care, including cost containment and access.[6] Given the increasing importance of these parameters in promoting both affordability and public health, the local self-regulatory nature of peer review may be insufficient.

The process of peer review itself has been criticized as being biased,[7] with concerns of both underreporting and overreporting of poor physician practice. Peer review requires physician colleagues to assess each other's work product (patient care) in a reciprocal manner. Despite best intentions, policing one's peers can prove difficult, with a variety of conflicts of interest and social connections serving as barriers to even the most well-meaning and thoughtful peer review committees. Underreporting is an unsurprising result of a process in which unpaid physician committee members are asked to make potential career-ending calls on classmates, friends, and patient-referral sources.[8] On the other hand, peer review has also been used in an overaggressive manner, as one group of physicians attempts to drive out a competing member of another group. Indeed, this anticompetitive practice (sometimes known as "sham" peer review) was the basis for a $2.2 million settlement for the plaintiff in the 1986 antitrust lawsuit brought by Dr. Timothy Patrick against Dr. William Burget and the Astoria Clinic. This settlement sent a strong message to curtail the practice of sham peer review, but further dampened physician interest in participating in peer review, for fear of legal downsides. This led to the passage of the Health Care Quality Improvement Act (HCQIA), which attempted to rectify this by providing legal immunity to those physicians who participate in peer review in good faith.

The efficacy of peer review in evaluating the adequacy of medical care has also come under criticism. Despite the push toward evidence-based medicine, large swaths of care remain outside the evidence-based map, leaving ample room for variation in practice. In addition, many medical errors are the result of cognitive biases that are challenging to elucidate and difficult to mitigate.[9] Indeed, this point highlights the real challenge of the peer review process. To work well, peer review requires: self-reflection and insight, accurate recollection, capacity for thoughtful

5 Mohammad Farhad Peerally et al., The Problem with Root Cause Analysis, 26 BMJ Quality & Safety 417 (2017); Albert W. Wu et al., Effectiveness and Efficiency of Root Cause Analysis in Medicine, 299 JAMA 685 (2008).

6 William L. Kissick, Medicine's Dilemmas: Infinite Needs versus Finite Resources (Yale Univ. Press ed., 1994).

7 Dinesh Vyas & Ahmed E. Hozain, Clinical Peer Review in the United States: History, Legal Development and Subsequent Abuse, 20 World J. Gastroenterology 6357 (2014).

8 George E. Newton, Maintaining the Balance: Reconciling the Social and Judicial Costs of Medical Peer Review Protection, 723 Ala. L. Rev. 723 (2001).

9 Jerome P. Kassirer, Diagnostic Reasoning, 110 Annals of Internal Med. 893 (1989); Geoffrey R. Norman & Kevin W. Eva, Diagnostic Error and Clinical Reasoning, 44. Med. Educ. 94 (2010).

interrogation, cooperativity, and clear communication within a trustworthy circle of colleagues. Deficiencies in any aspect of this set of conditions may limit the adequacy of the evaluation and diminish its impact of provision of safe care.

18.4 THE PROMISE AND CHALLENGES OF ARTIFICIAL INTELLIGENCE (AI)

Against this backdrop, a new era of intelligent tools, including advanced decision support with artificial intelligence, pose an attractive alternative to the peer review process. Artificial intelligence (AI) and machine learning (ML) are predictive modeling approaches which combine data in unique ways, via algorithms, to identify optimal solutions.[10] With improvements in programming, massive increases in computing power, and digitization of nearly all aspects of health care delivery, AI/ML has achieved a series of impressive results, now surpassing human capabilities in many domains, including image recognition. The latest iteration of this type of technology, known as deep learning, shows the capacity for perpetual enhancement in accuracy, self-modifying the algorithms it uses based on the relation of outputs to inputted data.

There is significant enthusiasm for the use of AI/ML within health care. The myriad of potential applications currently fall largely into two domains: image analysis and clinical decision support. The former application has multiple use-cases within health care, from visual analysis of radiographic images,[11] to pathologic tissue diagnosis,[12] to interpretation of retinal scans.[13] These solutions are focused primarily on the diagnostic aspect of health care – distinguishing normal from abnormal and applying the taxonomy of human pathology to abnormal findings.

AI is also being explored to assist with the cognitive decision making so critical to the work of many physicians. Taking disparate bits of information from multiple sources (e.g., patient history, physical exam, diagnostic tests) and determining a diagnosis, prognosis, and therapeutic plan. The range of potential decision-support applications is as broad as the expanse of all of medical practice, and includes recent examples, including early warning prediction of intraoperative hypotension,[14] mortality after heart failure,[15] and suicidal behavior after hospital

[10] Michael D. Howell & Jennifer P. Stevens, Chapter 17: Predictive Modelling 3.0: Machine Learning, in Understanding Healthcare Delivery Science 341 (McGraw Hill eds., 2020).

[11] Liu et al., (2018).

[12] Yahui Jiang et al., Emerging Role of Deep Learning-Based Artificial Intelligence in Tumor Pathology, 40 Cancer Comm. 154 (2020).

[13] Ting et al., (2017).

[14] Marije Wijnberge et al., Effect of a Machine Learning-Derived Early Warning System for Intraoperative Hypotension vs. Standard Care on Depth and Duration of Intraoperative Hypotension During Elective Noncardiac Surgery, 323 JAMA 1052 (2020).

[15] Joon-myoung Kwon et al., Artificial Intelligence Algorithm for Predicting Mortality of Patients with Acute Heart Failure, PLOS One (2019), https://journals.plos.org/plosone/article?id=10.1371/journal.pone.0219302.

discharge.[16] Increasingly, applications are moving beyond diagnosis or prediction, to autonomously enacting therapeutic decisions. For example, closed-loop neurostimulatory devices are being designed to both identify epileptic signals in the brain and immediately treat them via electrical stimulation.[17] Chatbots powered by AI are also now being deployed, to field patient chief complaints and triage them, in some cases recommending basic treatments.[18]

Despite this potential, AI and other digital diagnostics are largely kept out of the peer review process. One reason for this is the traditional structure of peer review. Peer review is focused on physician conduct, more than systems-centered care, and is by design reactive to significant adverse outcomes. Of the many errant and potentially harmful actions that take place regularly in a large and complex hospital, very few attract the attention of peer review scrutiny. Those that do are examined by fellow physicians through traditional means of physician judgment, without the deep computational support that is more commonplace in advanced analytics.

Another reason is that digital monitoring, the foundation on which AI technology is built, has developed around a quality assurance infrastructure that is largely parallel to physician-centric peer review. Modern hospitals institute software that monitors the administration of patientcare that contain safeguards against predictable errors. For example, when medication orders are entered into most hospital computer systems, software reviews these orders for obvious deviations or harmful interactions. This electronic monitoring occurs downstream of most physician conduct and has the capacity to scrutinize daily conduct that usually is outside the domain of peer review.

The real-time digital quality assurance alerts and the retrospective human-led peer review represent largely parallel solutions to improving patient safety, both required for Joint Commission accreditation. Even now, digital monitoring exhibits capabilities that reach much deeper and more objectively into the practice of medicine. Whereas peer review examines perhaps a few dozen adverse outcomes per month, order alert software monitors thousands of inputs daily. Moreover, these software systems can collate and analyze these events to identify common sources of error.

The superimposition of AI offers enormous opportunity for deeper analysis and more sophisticated monitoring that could improve quality assurance. First, AI and data analytics could do more than provide simple alerts to known errors. Deep learning algorithms could examine population health data and tailor recommendations to an individual patient's needs, identify improvements to accepted medical protocols, or anticipate systemic sources of provider error. Second, AI algorithms

16 Trehani M. Fonseka et al., The Utility of Artificial Intelligence in Suicide Risk Prediction and the Management of Suicidal Behaviors, 53 Austl. & N.Z. J. Psychiatry 954 (2019).

17 Urvish Patel et al., Artificial Intelligence as an Emerging Technology in the Current Care of Neurological Disorders, J. of Neurology (2019), https://www.researchgate.net/publication/335406868.

18 Mary Bates, Health Care Chatbots are Here to Help, 10 IEEE Pulse 12 (2019).

could institute real-time guidance to providers at the point of care, both anticipating moments of likely errors and interjecting with medical treatments that data analysis determines is superior to a human's judgment. Perhaps ultimately, such deep learning algorithms could remove the role of human judgment and human implementation altogether. AI could, on its own, identify and implement a tailored treatment, assess preliminary results, change course to alternatives if necessary, and integrate data from a patient's progress to a broader body of knowledge. The role of humans would be to peripherally monitor the AI's implementation, perhaps play some supervisory role, and ensure that the algorithms have the data and resources they need to operate effectively.

18.5 PEER REVIEW AND ARTIFICIAL INTELLIGENCE

The very aspects of AI that make it an exciting adjunct or alternative within health care are those that pose the greatest challenges to peer review. As much as software and digital capabilities can enhance and improve the quality assurance mechanisms that culminate in peer review, those same technologies might also prove to undermine peer review.

The self-learning, black-box nature of AI makes it difficult to interrogate to human knowledge, even if one has expertise in computer technology. As AI puts together information in novel and unique ways, the resulting algorithms may in fact be more accurate. But this reliance on alternative models makes it impenetrable to the physician review process which is framed by longstanding medical Western Medical tradition of the factors to be incorporated in diagnosis, prognosis, and treatment. Physicians simply do not have an understanding of the algorithms used to generate these decisions; decisions that may be swayed by information a physician may not have considered prima facie relevant. Whereas peer review is designed to be by physicians and for physicians, the skillset required to monitor AI-guided medicine would more likely involve computer scientists and software engineers.

In addition, since AI may identify patterns in existing data that will guide treatments where there is current clinical equipoise, the best course of treatment may no longer be determined solely on the basis of published literature. A peer review committee determining if an error occurred will have less information than the machine that directed treatment. Since AI will constantly be at the forefront of medical practice, any human oversight of AI and deep learning algorithms will be, by definition, deficient.

Therefore, however helpful AI might be, it is critical to recognize it contains qualities that are starkly different from human physicians (to state the obvious, machines are different from humans). In some ways, AI is like an uncooperative physician, one whose logic is impenetrable, and speaks another language entirely. To the degree that this new member of the medical staff is guiding care which may in some cases be harmful, it will fall upon local peer review processes to mitigate their impact on other patients. It is uncertain how the traditional approach to reciprocal peer review can effectively manage this task.

18.6 IMPLEMENTING AI INTO HOSPITAL QUALITY ASSURANCE

In short, while the hype and promise surrounding AI is clear, it is also clear that health care AI will not readily fit into existing hospital governance. The oversight of AI will depend heavily on the nature of its use, whether AI is a tool used by providers or whether it becomes a provider in and of itself.[19]

The introduction of AI processes could be maintained and modified to become safely incorporated into the current delivery system. For example, local medical staff policies could be implemented to limit the use of AI, by precluding its use in making immediate patient-facing decisions or requiring physician signoff on all diagnostic or therapeutic decisions. In so doing, human physicians would retain their current authority over medical care and buffer patients from harm related to aberrant AI decisions. The medical staff could also monitor the novel use of AI for a period of time until deemed safe, akin to the Joint Commission-mandated initial focused professional peer evaluations (FPPE) used to evaluate a new member of the medical staff. Furthermore, the medical staff could invite assistance from outside technical experts, such as computer programmers, to assist in interrogating the algorithm used in association with a medical error. This would be akin to the common practice of asking a biomedical engineer to inspect a machine (like an intravenous pump) after a serious event, to help distinguish operator error from device failure. These are not mutually exclusive – some combination of these solutions (and more) could be deployed while still maintaining local regulatory control through the classical peer review process.

A scenario that we think is more likely is that AI applications will chip away at traditional physician-centered medical care and even physician self-governance. The entry of AI, eventually, is likely to surpass the capabilities of local-level provider control, and the physician's primacy in the delivery of health care will wane. One might say that this trend has already begun with greater corporatization in health care and the expansion of nonphysician health care providers. Uptake of AI adds a degree of technical complexity that likely lies outside the physician's expertise, and the logic underlying physician self-governance will collapse. More immediately, AI would spell the end for peer review as a practice. The complexities of an autonomous intelligent health care machine may simply be too challenging for a quaint process from the late-nineteenth century.

[19] Anthony Weiss et al., How AI Will Change the Regulation and Organization of Medicine, Health Affairs Blog (May 3, 2020), https://www.healthaffairs.org/do/10.1377/hblog20200430.833066/full/.

A related challenge will confront the traditional powers that now govern peer review. What is now a physician-dominated process – often exclusively so – must also be able to handle AI-based approaches to health care. A hospital's most critical personnel decisions, including the allocation of admission privileges, remains (by tradition, law, and otherwise) under the control of the physician-led hospital medical staff. If AI and the peer review process become at odds, the continued use of either one will be determined ultimately by the medical staff. The medical staff would have to prove it was capable of managing the growing significance of AI, or it would have to narrow its authority over hospital operations.

This in turn begs the broader question of whether AI will force a change in the organization of the hospital. Peer review is central to a hospital's governance structure precisely because it is a window into the hospital's authority structure. If the locus of control changes in reviewing patient care and scrutinizing provider conduct, the locus of authority will also change in health care delivery. It certainly is hard to imagine that the superiority of AI (if, indeed it earns that superiority) over human-governed quality assurance is compatible with an American hospital's traditional governance structure. If AI changes peer review, it stands to reason that it will require changes to the hospital as well. The power to define standards and determine when those standards are not met – and by whom – is the power that controls the care delivered within the hospital.

A reallocation and reorganization of power in the hospital would certainly signal broader changes in health care delivery. A hospital system would have little trouble leveraging its AI capabilities to reach a broader scale of patients, and hospital administrators untethered to physician limits might reconfigure delivery. Although removing the human element from medicine will introduce meaningful drawbacks – and presumably, AI and digital services will never duplicate human wisdom of physicians – one could imagine how an operations-centric, AI-centric delivery system could advance the aims of population health. An AI-focused health system might monitor and sustain the health of a large population better than one that services patients with physician visits and hospital-based procedures.

18.7 LEGAL AND POLICY IMPLICATIONS

Just as AI might change the operation and governance of the hospital, it will also likely demand changes to health care regulation. The nation's current angst over increased health insecurity, political demands for distributive justice, and the fiscal strain of health care expenditures already fuel public demands for delivery reform. There may be an acute need to develop policies that thoughtfully usher in AI medicine while assuring a worrying public.

Even as AI grows to replace human roles, it will be treated as a device or product and thus will receive the same legal treatment as other technologies currently in use. For example, AI tools are likely to be subject to product liability law, unlike malpractice law that governs physicians. Moreover, even when physicians maintain responsibility for the care provided by AI tools, the law will have difficulty navigating between the two tort regimes.[20] This might also mean a greater regulatory focus on the corporations providing health care, rather than on individual providers or specific tools, and thus might stimulate demand for enterprise liability regimes that will feature employed, rather than independent, physicians.

The shift to product liability or enterprise liability, and an erosion of individual professional liability, could be further fueled by a need to scrutinize the core of malpractice law. If malpractice liability law evolved under a professionalism paradigm – one that nurtured and protected peer review and deferred to professional sources of authority – then the supremacy of AI and the inadequacies of human knowledge will require a rethinking of medical malpractice law. Specifically, if expertise lies more within the domain of the computer engineer than the physician, and if general standards of practice succumb to deep learning algorithms, then the malpractice law's deference to professional standards would be inapposite. Changes would include altering Daubert rules that define expertise, discovery rules that determine what evidence is authoritative and what is not, and substantive rules of tortious negligence and the sources of knowledge from which they are derived.

There would also be a shift towards federal medical device regulation, governed under FDA and intellectual property laws, and away from local regimes that govern the practice of medicine. And because digital products will naturally disseminate in a national (and international) market, there will be diminished tolerance for localities with their own rules and quality standards. We should expect to see a continued loss of local control over medicine, both in law and in practice, and a corresponding shift from local to state and from state to federal oversite of health care delivery.

Licensure regimes might change as well. Instead of licensing boards scrutinizing which humans warrant credentials, the FDA would approve machines and algorithms, and AI certifications would emerge in a to-be-developed federal product approval process. This could both dilute the effect of state medical boards, perhaps the longest surviving institution in modern medicine, and usher in the rise of health care corporations with national reach. Health care systems, insurance companies, and technology companies are the most likely to deploy AI tools, and these providers would be responsible for the outcomes, including safety, cost, and access, much as Ford is responsible for the cars they sell nationwide.

And even if peer review continues, the specific laws surrounding it will be ripe for reform. For example, discovery rules include immunities that protect disclosure during the peer review process, under the logic that peer review requires that immunity. But if quality review relies on digital analytics, which in turn requires the exchange of data across hospital systems, then the logic of limiting discovery is

[20] W. Nicholson Price et al., Potential Liability for Physicians Using Artificial Intelligence, 322 JAMA 1765 (2019).

undermined. In fact, even without the presence of malpractice suits, AI would function best with vigorous reporting requirements, subject to appropriate privacy rules. The laws originally designed to nurture peer review will be redesigned to nurture alternative mechanisms to assure medical quality.

This might suggest a broader need to rethink health care regulation more generally. Regulators should be receptive to the possibility that health care regulation should accommodate the needs of AI, rather than the reverse, and deem the emergence of AI as an occasion for a broader reframing of medical regulation.[21] If AI genuinely represents a potential to improve the quality of medical care, provide the digital products that can achieve population health, and avoid the shortcomings of physician self-governance, then policymakers and medical leaders should plot out the legal rules that would support the growth, improvement, and accessibility of new digital products.

At the same time, there will be significant hesitation to move both the delivery of health care and the regulation of health care away from a professional paradigm. Despite its imperfections, locally controlled, physician-led peer review is a process that has served an important role in ensuring patient safety for more than a century, adapting to innumerable changes in health care practice over that time.

In the end, these questions might be answered by political intuitions and popular perceptions. Peer review has remained a pillar of medical practice because it has succeeded in maintaining the trust of the public, and a move to algorithms could undermine that trust. But the integrity of peer review has been showing cracks of its own and may not continue to win the confidence of a digitally connected public. Perhaps the incorporation of AI tools will require a very different set of rules to maintain public trust.

[21] Barak Richman, Health Regulation for the Digital Age, 379 N. Eng. J. Med. 1694 (Nov. 1, 2018).

19

Regulating Posttrial Access to In-Dwelling Class III Neural Devices

Megan S. Wright and Joseph J. Fins

The authors acknowledge the support of the NIH BRAIN Initiative project, "Cognitive Restoration: Neuroethics and Disability Rights," 1RF1MH12378-01. The views expressed herein are the authors' own and not necessarily those of their institutions or the NIH.

19.1 INTRODUCTION

Research participants in clinical trials often have an interest in maintaining access to a drug or device after the trial has concluded. In the case of clinical trials of in-dwelling Class III medical devices, which are life-sustaining or risky devices that are implanted in the body, participants' interest in posttrial access is considerable. Such devices can be harmful to the participant if not properly maintained or removed, and if the device is beneficial to the participant, they may desire surveillance and maintenance to ensure proper device functioning, as well as access to replacement devices.

To date, the Food and Drug Administration (FDA) has not provided clear guidance about the posttrial access obligations clinical trial sponsors and investigators have to research participants. And while litigation about posttrial access in the case of investigational drugs has resulted in courts finding that there is no legal duty for pharmaceutical companies to continue to provide access to the tested drug to study participants, it is not clear how this body of law would apply to in-dwelling Class III medical devices or what normative obligations sponsors and investigators of such device trials have.

Legal and ethical clarity on this issue is of critical importance, given that such devices, unlike drugs, will remain in a participant's body and may require ongoing maintenance, surveillance, replacement, or explanation.[1] Further, prospective research participants may decline to enroll in studies assessing the safety and efficacy

[1] Saskia Hendriks et al., Ethical Challenges of Risk, Informed Consent, and Posttrial Responsibilities in Human Subject Research with Neural Devices: A Review, 76 JAMA Neurology 1506 (2019); Joseph J. Fins, Deep Brain Stimulation, Deontology and Duty: The Moral Obligation of Non-Abandonment at the Neural Interface, 6 J. Neural Eng. (2009).

of embedded Class III medical devices if they are not guaranteed posttrial access. Such recruitment problems could inhibit production of scientific knowledge and delay effective medical devices from making it to the market, thus harming innovation.

This chapter first explains the FDA approval process for Class III medical devices and the resulting issue of posttrial access to in-dwelling devices. The chapter then explores the law and ethics of posttrial access for drugs, devices, and biologics, highlighting the dearth of legal guidance. The chapter then discusses the case of posttrial access to deep brain stimulation (DBS) and patient perspectives on this issue. We conclude with a call for transparency about the type and degree of posttrial access as part of the preimplantation informed consent process as well as mandating that sponsors fund device maintenance or explantation after the conclusion of the trial.

19.2 POSTTRIAL ACCESS TO IN-DWELLING CLASS III MEDICAL DEVICES?

The FDA categorizes medical devices based on the type and degree of risk from the device. Class III medical devices, such as pacemakers or deep brain stimulation (DBS), are the highest-risk category, and thus receive more scrutiny from the FDA. Class III medical devices are defined as those that are "life-supporting or life-sustaining, or for a use which is of substantial importance in preventing impairment of human health, or … present a potential unreasonable risk of illness or injury."[2] Such devices must, through scientific evidence, demonstrate "reasonable assurance" of safety and efficacy prior to FDA approval.[3]

Not all clinical trials of Class III medical devices will successfully demonstrate safety and efficacy, necessary conditions for receiving FDA approval.[4] Other clinical trials may be successful on these measures, but the study sponsor and investigators may ultimately decide not to bring the device in question to market.[5] Both scenarios can strand research participants who may have an interest in maintaining access to the device if the intervention is or perceived to be efficacious, especially if the device is implanted in the research participant's body (also referred to as invasive or in-dwelling devices).[6] Posttrial access may include routine device maintenance, repair or replacement if the device malfunctions, or device removal, all of which often require specialized skills that only study investigators have. Uncertainty about

2 21 C.F.R. § 860.3(c)(3).

3 Id. at 860.7. The Food and Drug Administration is responsible for "ensuring the safety, efficacy, and security of … drugs, biological products, and medical devices." Food & Drug Admin., What We Do, https://www.fda.gov/about-fda/what-we-do.

4 Hendriks et al., supra note 1, at 1510 (demonstrating development path for neural devices).

5 Even if the device is marketed, the manufacturer may discontinue the device. Id.

6 "Invasive neural devices require an incision or insertion to place or implant the device in a person." Id. at 1506. See also Joseph J. Fins et al., Being Open Minded about Neuromodulation Trials: Finding Success in our "Failures," 10 Brain Stimulation 181 (2017).

posttrial access to in-dwelling devices may dissuade prospective participants from trial enrollment, potentially thwarting the progression of device development from bench to bedside.

As the next section demonstrates, there has been little regulatory guidance from the FDA about the posttrial obligations owed to participants by device or drug sponsors and little case law clarifying this issue.[7] Furthermore, while industry norms tend to govern posttrial access to pharmaceuticals – often offering limited posttrial access[8] – these norms are neither established nor directly analogous to questions of posttrial access to in-dwelling Class III medical devices, such as DBS.

19.3 LAW OF POSTTRIAL ACCESS

Statutory and regulatory guidance for posttrial access to drugs, biologics, and devices is sparse. Most of the attention has instead focused on the passage of state and federal right-to-try laws and expanded access (i.e., compassionate use) to investigational drugs and devices through the 21st Century Cures Act.[9] Conceivably, a former study participant could seek posttrial access through one of these other routes,[10] but the legal and ethical rationales for permitting or prohibiting such access will differ. Right-to-try laws allow terminally ill patients and their physicians to request access to early-stage drug trials, although the study sponsor does not have to grant access.[11] Right-to-try laws exclude medical devices.[12] The FDA also has an expanded access program for seriously ill patients who have no other treatment options to access investigational medical products, including medical devices, that have not yet demonstrated safety or efficacy.[13]

7 Richard S. Saver, At the End of the Clinical Trial: Does Access to Investigational Technology End as Well?, 31 W. N. Eng. L. Rev. 411 (2009).

8 Id.; Christine Grady, The Challenge of Assuring Continued Post-Trial Access to Beneficial Treatment, 5 Yale J. Health Pol'y L. & Ethics 425 (2005).

9 21st Century Cures Act, Pub. L. No. 114-255, 130 Stat. 1033 (2016). See also Jordan Paradise, Three Framings of "Faster" at the FDA and the Federal Right to Try, Wake Forest J. L. & Pol'y (forthcoming).

10 Although with the right-to-try route, they will likely be unsuccessful as industry grants very few of these requests. Paradise, supra note 9. And even if industry were to grant more requests, patients may not have the means to pay for the drugs or devices because their health insurance likely will not cover experimental medication. Id.

11 Right to Try Act, Food, Drug, and Cosmetic Act § 561B (2018); see also Paradise, supra note 9.

12 Only investigational drugs and biologics are included. US Food & Drug Admin., Right to Try, https://www.fda.gov/patients/learn-about-expanded-access-and-other-treatment-options/right-try; see also Paradise, supra note 9.

13 Id.; US Food & Drug Admin., Expanded Access for Medical Devices, https://www.fda.gov/medical-devices/investigational-device-exemption-ide/expanded-access-medical-devices. There are other pathways to access medical devices that have not demonstrated effectiveness, such as the Humanitarian Device Exemption (HDE), which permits patients with rare diseases to access medical devices meant to benefit them. Food & Drug Admin., Humanitarian Device Exemption, https://www.fda.gov/medical-devices/premarket-submissions/humanitarian-device-exemption. The

While accessing investigational drugs and devices outside of enrollment in a clinical trial may be possible through right-to-try laws and expanded access FDA pathways, these options do not directly address the situation of someone who formerly had access to an investigational drug because of their participation in a safety or efficacy study and desires continued access. Moreover, if the device has already made it to market, the expanded access pathway is no longer relevant.

Case law provides some insight into the responsibilities study sponsors and investigators have to provide posttrial access to pharmaceuticals to clinical trial participants. In the mid-2000s, in two well-known court cases,[14] participants in a study testing a new drug for Parkinson's disease wanted continued access to the drugs that they believed were beneficial, but the study sponsor ended the trial because there were safety concerns and limited evidence of efficacy. The study sponsor also refused to provide posttrial access even under the compassionate use option.[15] The study participants argued that there was a contractual duty for the sponsor to provide posttrial access, that they relied on the sponsor's promise to provide the drugs post trial, and that the study sponsor had a fiduciary duty to participants that required posttrial access.[16] Their breach of contract claim failed because the agreement study participants had was with investigators (i.e., the informed consent document) rather than the study sponsors; their promissory estoppel claim failed because again, there was no promise made by the study sponsor to study participants; and the breach of fiduciary duty claim failed because the court declined to find the study sponsor to be a fiduciary, or a person who is expected to act in the best interest of another. The court also considered policy reasons for providing posttrial access, namely that patient enrollment will decline if this is not ensured, but also considered policy reasons against a mandate for sponsors to provide posttrial access, namely that companies would be less inclined to sponsor drug trials in the future.

Posttrial access continues to be governed by private agreement rather than public regulation,[17] which means that study participants are only entitled to what study

HDE pathway to medical devices has unintended negative consequences for scientific advancement because persons requesting access to the device may not enroll in clinical trials assessing the devices' efficacy. Joseph J. Fins et al., Neuropsychiatric Deep Brain Stimulation Research and the Misuse of the Humanitarian Device Exemption, 30 Health Aff. 302 (2011).

14 Abney v. Amgen, Inc., 443 F.3d 540 (6th Cir. 2006); Suthers v. Amgen, Inc., 441 F. Supp. 2d 478 (S.D. N.Y. 2006); see also Saver, supra note 7 (describing these cases); Michelle M. Mello & Steven Joffe, Compact versus Contract – Industry Sponsors' Obligations to Their Research Subjects, 356 N. Eng. J. Med. 2737 (2007) (describing these cases); Vinion v. Amgen Inc., 272 Fed.Appx. 582 (9th Cir. 2008).

15 The study participants argued that the study sponsor was motivated by financial concerns rather than safety and efficacy concerns.

16 The Vinion cases argued for breach of contract, but also various tort claims such as "negligence, misrepresentation, and infliction of emotional distress," all of which failed.

17 See Hendriks et al., supra note 1, at 1511 (describing this in the case of clinical trials for invasive neural devices); Emily Underwood, Researchers Grapple with the Ethics of Testing Brain Implants, Science Magazine (Oct. 31, 2017), https://www.sciencemag.org/news/2017/10/researchers-grapple-ethics-testing-brain-implants.

sponsors and investigators are willing to explicitly agree to, which may not accord with participant preferences or ethical principles such as benevolence, nonmaleficence, and justice. For example, prior to one study of DBS for severe depression, the study sponsor, a medical device company, agreed to pay for the surgery to remove the device and continue supplying batteries.[18] While many participants reported experiencing a benefit from the device, the trial was unsuccessful, and participants who wished to retain the device were left to cover the costs of future maintenance and care themselves, a situation that raised many ethical issues.[19] Given the absence of legal guidance, ethical practice becomes more important. The next section addresses normative dimensions of posttrial access.

19.4 ETHICS OF POSTTRIAL ACCESS

There has been extensive academic commentary about what, if any, ethical duties are owed to clinical trial research participants. Multiple commentators have argued that if participants have experienced a benefit from an investigational intervention during a trial, the principles of nonmaleficence and beneficence demand that they should continue to have access after the trial concludes.[20] Similar arguments for access to trial benefits using the principle of reciprocity have been made given that participants have undergone risk to advance scientific understanding and benefit future patients.[21] These two arguments are embedded in an earlier version of the Declaration of Helsinki, adopted by the World Medical Association: "[a]t the conclusion of the study, patients entered into the study are entitled … to share any benefits that result from it, for example, access to interventions identified as beneficial in the study or to other appropriate care or benefits."[22] Finally, some have argued in the case of DBS trials, the principle of nonabandonment brings with it "a longitudinal fiduciary obligation to provide [research participants] with support," specifically "a responsibility to provide on-going care and a fiscal responsibility for any associated costs" on the part of study investigators and sponsors.[23]

Some argue that determinations about posttrial access should be left to the discretion of investigators and sponsors because there may be uncertainty about whether there is true efficacy of the intervention or whether the benefits outweigh the harms for individual clinical trial participants and for the population at large.[24]

18 Underwood, supra note 17.

19 Id.

20 Grady, supra note 8; Saver, supra note 7; Tom L. Beauchamp & James F. Childress, Principles of Biomedical Ethics (7th ed. 2013).

21 Grady, supra note 8; Saver, supra note 7; Beauchamp & Childress, supra note 20.

22 WMA Declaration of Helsinki, Ethical Principles for Medical Research Involving Human Subjects (1964), https://www.wma.net/policies-post/wma-declaration-of-helsinki-ethical-principles-for-medical-research-involving-human-subjects/; see also Grady, supra note 8; Saver, supra note 7.

23 Fins, supra note 1, at 2.

24 Beauchamp & Childress, supra note 20; Saver, supra note 7. Courts have also addressed the concern that requiring posttrial access may "deter pharmaceutical companies from sponsoring clinical trials as

Some also contend that research participants may have already received benefits from study participation, addressing reciprocity obligations.[25] Offsetting this argument in the case of Class III devices, any benefits may also be accompanied by potential burdens or complications associated with in-dwelling devices or their removal.[26] Furthermore, while participants likely expect posttrial access to the investigatory technology in part because of a therapeutic misconception,[27] the appropriate remedy to this problem is not posttrial access.[28] Instead, scholars have generally called for greater planning and transparency about posttrial access.[29] Finally, mandating posttrial access may raise research costs, ultimately disincentivizing research, resulting in collective societal harm.[30]

While scholars have engaged in the above-described debates, there have been many fewer studies of the viewpoints of participants about duties owed to them stemming from trial participation, especially in the context of in-dwelling devices. Existing empirical research of clinical trial participant attitudes about duties owed to them by investigators, research sponsors, drug and device manufacturers, and regulators has found that many, although not all, participants think there is a duty to provide posttrial access to a drug (or its equivalent) that provided them with benefits after the trial and until approval,[31] and after approval at a fair market or reduced price, for an indefinite period of time.[32] This small body of empirical research about posttrial expectations focused on reports from drug trial participants. It is unknown how device trial participants view these questions.

19.5 DEEP BRAIN STIMULATION AND POSTTRIAL ACCESS

Posttrial access to DBS, which is classified by the FDA as a Class III medical device[33] because it has a greater level of risk to patients,[34] is a particularly pressing issue. DBS is a "programmable and adjustable implant of electrodes into specific deep brain structures that delivers electrical impulses to alter circuit function and overcome

clinical trial sponsors might be required to continue to produce and distribute a drug they believed to be dangerous." Abney v. Amgen, Inc., 443 F.3d 540, 553 (6th Cir. 2006).

25 Saver, supra note 7.

26 Fins, supra note 1.

27 Paul S. Appelbaum et al., The Therapeutic Misconception: Informed Consent in Psychiatric Research, 5 Int'l J. L. & Psychiatry 319 (1982).

28 Saver, supra note 7.

29 Id.; Mello & Joffe, supra note 14.

30 Grady, supra note 8; Saver, supra note 7.

31 This period of time can be lengthy. Grady, supra note 8.

32 Neema Sofaer et al., Subjects' Views of Obligations to Ensure Post-Trial Access to Drugs, Care, and Information: Qualitative Results from the Experiences of Participants in Clinical Trials (epic) Study, 35 J. Med. Ethics 183 (2009).

33 21 C.F.R. § 882.

34 See Hendriks et al., supra note 1, at 1507–8 (describing risks from invasive neural devices, including risks from the surgery to implant the device, risks from the device itself, adverse side effects, privacy and security risks, and financial risks).

abnormal activity."[35] Once properly implanted, the electrodes can be stimulated with varying levels of voltage to produce desired cognitive, emotional, and physical effects. A battery for the electrodes is placed in a patient or research participant's chest. DBS has been shown to be effective and is approved by the FDA for Parkinson's disease[36] and has been tested for treatment-resistant neuropsychological disorders, such as depression.[37] The application of DBS for traumatic brain injuries is currently being explored.[38]

While all research participants have interests in posttrial access to investigational drugs or devices, the stakes are higher for persons enrolled in trials of invasive Class III medical devices, such as DBS, given the higher level of risk of the device coupled with the reality that participants cannot remove the devices. So unlike in clinical drug trials in which the participant can discontinue use of the study drug after the conclusion of the trial, participants in in-dwelling medical device trials have a device permanently embedded, barring a procedure to remove it.[39] Participants in such trials thus have a pressing interest in the device's safety, and if efficacious, ensuring that it remains available to them. This is especially the case for invasive neural technologies. Not only do implanted neural devices share the features of risk and permanence of other in-dwelling medical devices such as cardiac pacemakers, but they affect the brain, and implicate cognitive abilities, personality, identity, and agency in a way that other investigational devices and drugs may not,[40] which again raises the stakes of posttrial access.

Because both electrodes and the battery are implanted devices that cannot be removed by the participant, questions arise about how these devices will be surveilled, maintained, replaced, or removed after the clinical trial assessing their safety and efficacy concludes, especially if the device never receives FDA approval, never makes it to the market, or the device manufacturer stops making the device.[41]

35 Id. at 1507.

36 Günther Deuschl et al., A Randomized Trial of Deep Brain Stimulation for Parkinson's Disease, 355 N. Eng. J. Med. 896 (2006); Hendriks et al., supra note 1, at 1507.

37 See, e.g., Helen S. Mayberg et al., Deep Brain Stimulation for Treatment-Resistant Depression, 45 Neuron 651 (2005); see also Hendriks et al., supra note 1, at 1507 (describing state of DBS research applications).

38 Nicholas D. Schiff et al., Behavioral Improvements with Thalamic Stimulation after Severe Traumatic Brain Injury, 448 Nature 600 (2007); Hendriks et al., supra note 1, at 1507; Central Thalamic Stimulation for Traumatic Brain Injury, 1UH3 NS095554-01, PI Schiff.

39 Devices may have to be removed if there is an infection subsequent to implantation, a complication that occurs for about 5 percent of patients who undergo DBS, or for other complications such as device malfunctioning or lead migration. Onanong Jitkritsadakul et al., Systematic Review of Hardware-Related Complications of Deep Brain Stimulation: Do New Indications Pose an Increased Risk?, 10 Brain Stimulation 697 (2017). There may also be infections from battery placement or replacement. Jonathan Dennis Carlson et al., Deep Brain Stimulation Generator Replacement in End-Stage Parkinson Disease, 128 World Neurosurgery 683 (2019).

40 Hendriks et al., supra note 1, at 1511. Investigational drugs that target neuropsychiatric disorders may also implicate similar issues of identity and agency.

41 Id. at 1510 (depicting lifecycle of device from the start of a clinical trial).

Indeed, there are significant hardware risks with DBS "including infection, malfunction, erosion, and migration or fracture of leads, which may require additional surgery or explantation."[42] Furthermore, many persons implanted with DBS need access to specialized neurosurgeons and neurologists for battery replacement and device programming, which they may not have access to once the study concludes.[43] Even if DBS research participants have continued access to study investigators, "they may be left with costs for device maintenance, continued access, or explantation,"[44] which often are not budgeted for in grants that fund this research and which health insurance likely will not cover.[45] As one of us asked over a decade ago when writing about research participants in trials of investigational neuromodulation technology, "What is their fate? What happens to these patients when the trial ends? Who provides on-going care? Who pays for battery replacement? Who removes a broken device? Who adjusts stimulation parameters . . . in perpetuity?"[46]

Recent ethical guidance from the NIH BRAIN Initiative Neuroethics Working Group, of which one of us (JJF) is a member, about posttrial access to neural devices such as DBS addresses some of these questions. The guidance includes the following recommendations: planning in advance of a study for research participants' posttrial access needs, regardless of whether the device is safe and effective, including planning for cost; ensuring that posttrial access issues are addressed in the process of obtaining institutional review board approval for the study and that plans are communicated to research participants in the informed consent process; and requiring greater obligations posttrial from study sponsors and investigators if the device is beneficial or risky, the study participants are vulnerable, the provision of access would not be costly, the device is too complex for general health care professionals to manage, or the device contains "built-in obsolescence and proprietary hardware and software, effectively locking patients and clinicians into ongoing relationships with a manufacturer."[47]

While the Working Group offered ethical guidance about posttrial access to neural devices, their suggestions do not have the force of law and it is unclear to what extent study sponsors and investigators are heeding these suggestions. Indeed, the Working Group notes that the "locus of posttrial responsibilities is currently determined on a case-by-case basis."[48] And importantly, the views of research

42 Id. at 1507.

43 Fins, supra note 1, at 2 (describing the problem and arguing that engineers should make simpler devices that primary care physicians could operate and create better, longer-lasting batteries).

44 Hendriks, supra note 1, at 1508.

45 Id. at 1511. MedPac, An Overview of the Medical Device Industry, in Report to the Congress: Medicare and the Healthcare Delivery System 220 (2017), http://www.medpac.gov/docs/default-source/reports/jun17_ch7.pdf?sfvrsn=0.

46 Fins, supra note 1, at 2.

47 Hendriks et al., supra note 1, at 1511. Because many medical devices are modified slightly from earlier versions, the lifecycle of a typical device is less than two years. MedPac, supra note 45, at 211.

48 Hendriks et al., supra note 1, at 1511.

participants enrolled in clinical trials of invasive neural devices such as DBS regarding posttrial access remain unclear.[49]

Presently, as part of an ongoing larger study, we are studying the perspectives and experiences of research participants in a DBS clinical trial for patients with moderate to severe traumatic brain injury,[50] and one question we ask is about participants' concerns about posttrial access to the investigational device.[51] Preliminary results from research participants provide a window into the posttrial access hopes and concerns of those enrolled in invasive neural device clinical trials.

Study participants have questions and concerns about posttrial access. Some participants ask about device support and maintenance prior to agreeing to participate in the trial. One participant described proactively engaging their health insurer to determine whether their insurance policy would cover the cost of battery replacement, for example, and also asking investigators about the length and degree of posttrial support. While he understood budgetary constraints of guaranteeing posttrial access in perpetuity, he thought that if there was a benefit from the device, participants should have ongoing access to support and maintenance.

Another study participant became concerned about posttrial access after they had already been implanted. The participant indicated a desire that the device be turned up, and that it never be turned off because it provided such a benefit. The study participant did not want to go back to a time when the device was not available. In fact, the participant emphasized that future study enrollees be warned that they may have a negative experience if their device is turned off during or after the study because they will revert to their old self. That is, if participants experience a beneficial change due to DBS, then if they no longer have access to a functioning device (e.g., dead batteries, faulty electrodes, etc.), they may feel harmed. This participant's informal caregiver also echoed the study participant's concerns, emphasizing that the positive effect of DBS on the participant's life has been so profound that they hoped that the device is never turned off.[52]

49 Some research has shown that "patients receiving DBS expect researchers to provide posttrial medical care, expertise, and equipment (batteries)." Id. at 1510.

50 Cognitive Restoration: Neuroethics and Disability Rights, 1RF1MH12378-01, PI Fins; Central Thalamic Stimulation for Traumatic Brain Injury, 1 UH# NS095554-01, PI Schiff; Nicholas D. Schiff et al., Central Thalamic Brain Stimulation Modulates Executive Function and Fatigue in a Patient with Severe to Moderate Traumatic Brain Injury, Annual BRAIN Initiative Investigators Meeting (Apr. 13, 2019).

51 Research on participants' views on invasive investigative medical devices is in its infancy, but some qualitative research on participants enrolled in DBS for depression and OCD trials indicates that participants need DBS adjustments fairly often and also need access to battery maintenance, which implicate posttrial access issues. Eran Klein et al., Brain-Computer Interface-Based Control of Closed Loop Brain Stimulation: Attitudes and Ethical Considerations, 3 Brain-Computer Interfaces 140 (2016).

52 The study participant also expressed concern about changing the battery or knowing whether the device was programmed correctly.

While more data about the views of participants and their informal caregivers is needed, these preliminary insights speak to the need to hear the voices of those most proximate to these trials. As we continue our study, we plan to add more research participant perspectives to the policy and ethical debate over posttrial access to implanted Class III medical devices.

19.6 ADAPTING THE REGULATORY REGIME FOR INNOVATIVE MEDICAL DEVICE TECHNOLOGIES

The FDA recently released draft guidance calling for patient input into clinical trial design for medical devices.[53] The guidance about patient engagement is meant to "mitigate some of the practical challenges to robust clinical investigations, including challenges concerning study/research participant enrollment and retention in the study" through strengthening the informed consent documents and prioritizing clinical endpoints patients care about, for example.[54] Another important part of patient feedback on clinical trial design is what patients/participants and families think investigator and sponsor responsibilities are with respect to posttrial access to a functioning embedded medical device. These data can help inform policy creation.

As data collected from participants in our study has shown, individuals have an interest in maintaining access to a safe and effective device after their participation in a clinical trial ends. But while their perspectives are important, they are just one part of the regulatory puzzle. The views of investigators, sponsors, and manufacturers also need be considered, as the social compact centering around device implantation transcends the narrow purview of informed consent, especially if there are conflicts between participant preferences and the sponsors or manufacturers bringing innovative devices to market given economic constraints.

We argue for a bifurcated conception of responsibility for posttrial access. With respect to investigators, we argue, that at a minimum, they owe a duty of complete transparency to participants and prospective participants about posttrial access to surveillance, maintenance, upgrades, or removal of Class III implanted devices as part of an ongoing informed consent process. Transparency about posttrial access necessitates advance planning. Our argument for planning and transparency is in

53 US Food & Drug Admin., Patient Engagement in the Design and Conduct of Medical Device Clinical Investigations: Draft Guidance for Industry, Food and Drug Administration Staff, and Other Stakeholders (2019), https://www.fda.gov/media/130917/download. This guidance accords with the view that creating policy based in part on participant/patient preferences will increase welfare. Mark A. Hall et al., Rethinking Health Law, 41 Wake Forest L. Rev. 341 (2006); Lois Shepherd & Mark A. Hall, Patient-Centered Health Law and Ethics, 45 Wake Forest L. Rev. 1429 (2010).

54 US Food & Drug Admin., supra note 53. A participant/patient-centered approach also enhances compliance and facilitates embodiment of devices by the participant. Eran Klein et al., Engineering the Brain: Ethical Issues and the Introduction of Neural Devices, 45 Hastings Ctr. Rep. 26 (2015).

line with the recommendations from the NIH BRAIN Initiative Neuroethics Working Group discussed previously.[55]

Duties to plan for and be transparent about posttrial access are not limited to medical device trials. Indeed, these duties apply to all clinical trials, including pharmaceutical trials, because disclosing posttrial access plans to prospective participants is necessary to obtain genuine informed consent. But ensuring ethical clinical trials of Class III implanted devices, especially neural devices, demands more of investigators and sponsors to ensure that study participants are not harmed and are treated justly, given participants' posttrial access preferences and expectations; the greater risk to study participants, many of whom are vulnerable because of their existing medical conditions, from implanting a device; the probable permanence of the device and the need for ongoing access to specialized medical care and device maintenance; and the potential for changed personality and identity with a brain-based medical intervention.

Thus, with respect to study sponsors and the medical device industry, we argue that there is a correlative set of responsibilities to participants and their families to ensure ongoing access to repairs, maintenance, and the costs of explantation (should participants desire device removal) for embedded neural devices. Funds should be put aside at the start of a trial to ensure such access after a trial has concluded. While this requirement may seem financially onerous, these costs would likely be a small fraction of the total expenditures related to research and device development. Indeed, these ongoing costs should be understood as central to maintaining the integrity of this work, as part of the cost of doing business, and a concrete set of ethical obligations given the unique challenges of in-dwelling neural devices.[56] With this recommendation, we move beyond what the NIH BRAIN Initiative Neuroethics Working Group proposes, given the many qualifications contained in their arguments about posttrial access (e.g., conditioning investigator and sponsor responsibility to provide access on criteria such as study participant vulnerability, degree of device benefit, cost of posttrial access, etc.).[57]

These additional responsibilities should be more than an ethical duty – they should also be legally required. But unlike the current norm of leaving matters of posttrial access to private agreements, we argue that posttrial access decisions

55 Hendriks et al., supra note 1.

56 Ensuring posttrial access to implanted neural devices can be considered a "compensatory ethic," which weighs the needs and preferences of study participants over those of investigators and sponsors given the risk the participant has borne and the undesirability of potential benefits only accruing to others if the participant is not ensured posttrial access. See Joseph J. Fins, Pandemics, Protocols, and the Plague of Athens: Insights from Thucydides, 50 Hastings Ctr. Rep. 50 (2020) (describing the compensatory ethic with respect to ventilator allocation guidelines and preference given to health care providers given their service at great risk in the context of the COVID-19 crisis).

57 Hendriks et al., supra note 1.

should be subject to regulatory oversight by the FDA, which can ensure that investigators and sponsors are fulfilling their ethical duties to study participants after balancing the competing interests, if any, of the parties. Additionally, both aspects of this bifurcated set of responsibilities should be approved by an Institutional Review Board prior to the beginning of the clinical trial.[58]

[58] See also Fins, supra note 1, at 2.

20

Strengthening the Power of Health Care Insurers to Regulate Medical Device Risks

David Rosenberg and Adeyemi Adediran[*]

20.1 INTRODUCTION

There is growing concern over the FDA's persistent failure to prevent the marketing of medical devices that subject patients to previously undetected risks of death, disability, and other serious injuries.[1] Departing from the dominant approach to reform calling for expanding FDA authority and resources, state tort law, and other modes of government oversight, we consider harnessing the regulatory power of market forces, particularly those uniquely exerted by health care insurers ("insurers").[2] Essentially, insurers' regulatory power derives from their market-gatekeeping coverage and purchase decisions that determine the economic fate of all FDA-approved devices; capacity to constantly and comprehensively monitor the market for product-related accidents, including manifestations of new and increased risks; and exposure to paying the medical and other expenses of injured insured patients.

Insurers thus can surpass other nongovernmental as well as governmental forms of oversight (for example, academic researchers, physicians, manufacturers, tort lawyers) in enhancing FDA efforts to protect patients from unreasonably risky product designs, warnings, and usage. They can draw on the continuous inflow of insured-patient requests for payment of medical and other expenses resulting from product-related

[*] We thank I. Glenn Cohen, Ethan Gurwitz, Christopher Robertson, Steven Shavell, and Kathryn E. Spier for comments.

[1] See, e.g., 80,000 Deaths. 2 Million Injuries. It's Time for a Reckoning on Medical Devices, N.Y. Times (May 4, 2019), https://www.nytimes.com/2019/05/04/opinion/sunday/medical-devices.html?action=click&module=RelatedLinks&pgtype=Article (attributing significant incidence of medical device accidents to the "combination of dubious regulatory approvals, skimpy post-market surveillance, and faltering responses from regulators").

[2] State tort law generally applies the negligence rule, which holds device manufacturers liable for failing to exercise reasonable care in designing the product and warning of its risks. In Riegel v. Medtronic, Inc., 552 U.S. 312 (2008), the Supreme Court preempted enforcement of any state tort claim involving a medical device that had been marketed in FDA-approved form and manner when the allegations of manufacturer misfeasance contradict specific agency findings that the product was safe and efficacious.

injuries to supply the FDA with both a superior source of reliable postmarket data on product risk and efficacy and virtually instantaneous notice of emerging signs of new or increased risks.[3]

Monitoring for emerging device risk is of vital importance to insurers because they will pay the medical and other product-related accident costs incurred by their insured injured patients. Exposure to bearing product-related accident costs drives insurers to include the implicit price of accidents in coverage and purchase decisions. Therefore, insurers operating in the normal course of business select for safer and more efficacious medical devices and uses.[4]

Insurers' risk-rated coverage and purchase decisions can serve as an unmatched means of fortifying manufacturers' incentives to exercise reasonable precautions in developing, testing, and marketing their products. They also supplement FDA-prescribed warnings and informed physician judgments by curtailing overuse of medical devices, evaluating the comparative safety and efficacy of products and other treatments, and better-fitting product benefits to patients' medical needs. Because insurers bear the accident costs of false positives – that is, of curtailing patient access to a device based on an erroneous finding of undue risk – as well as false negatives, they have incentives to make measured and reliable decisions.

Yet, market impediments may prevent insurers from exercising their regulatory powers for maximum social benefit. Depending on market and other factors, sharp competition can be part of the problem. An insurer might delay or refrain from publicly reporting the discovery of an emergent risk to the FDA for fear of competitors freely capitalizing on proprietary information concerning adjustment of its coverage and purchase decisions. While transmission of product-related risk in insured-patient payment requests may not involve great expense, translating that information into risk-rated coverage and purchase decisions is another matter. Deriving reliable implicit risk-rated prices to incorporate into coverage and purchase decisions can involve expensive AI systems and other private sources and methods of aggregating and analyzing data to discern patterns or even signs of new or increased risks; determine causal mechanisms and associations in the various contexts, practices and behaviors that frequently characterize the heterogeneity of health care provider and patient use of the product; and estimate accident prevalence and costs among the patient population.

Most importantly, insurers lack sufficient financial incentives to exercise their regulatory powers for maximum social benefit because two structural features of all insurance systems, private and public, shield them from bearing the total costs of

3 See Rebecca S. Eisenberg & W. Nicholson Price, Promoting Healthcare Innovation on the Demand Side, 4 J. L. & Biosciences, 3, 12–13 (2017) (describing insurers' wealth of information on product uses, efficacy, and risks).

4 Analysis of the incentives of US and foreign government insurers to effectively monitor the use and risk of medical devices they supply and to make appropriate coverage and purchase adjustments is beyond the scope of this chapter.

product-related accidents. First, because risk-averse individuals are unwilling to pay premiums or taxes for nonmonetary losses (harm that money cannot remedy, such as death), insurance does not provide coverage for it.[5] Nonmonetary loss, however, represents a real and major diminution of individual welfare that must be included in the total amount of product-related accident costs when determining the reasonable amount of resources to expend in securing maximum social benefit from safety precautions. The second structural constraint is insurance subrogation, the contractually or legally created means by which insurers recoup from insured-patient tort recoveries the amount they have paid out in covering medical and other injury-related expenses.[6] In calculating the product-related accident costs they anticipate bearing – to determine coverage and purchase decisions – insurers rationally discount that burden by the amount they expect to be reimbursed from tort recoveries through subrogation. Cumulatively, these structural constraints relieve insurers of well over half of the total product-related accident costs.[7]

We propose two simple and virtually costless federal statutory reforms to correct these market defects. Pursuant to the first, Congress would require insurers to report medical device accidents to the FDA. This would overcome any market competition constraints on insurers' willingness to publicly disclose proprietary information. The second would have Congress establish a federal rule of manufacturer strict tort liability that is predicated on proof of causation alone and pays damages directly and fully to the US Treasury.[8] For the purposes of removing the structural constraints on insurers' financial incentives to reduce risk, the principal virtue of manufacturer strict liability is that tort damages account for both monetary and nonmonetary losses and – because manufacturers will reflect total expected tort damages in their product prices – thus lead insurers to consider the total costs of product-related accidents in monitoring the market for risk and risk-rating their coverage and purchase decisions. Paying recoveries into the US Treasury eliminates the other market defect of subrogation reimbursement.[9] Initiation of strict manufacturer liability actions would first require FDA validation of the causal connection

5 See A. Mitchell Polinsky & Steven Shavell, The Uneasy Case for Product Liability, 123 Harv. L. Rev. 1437, 1462 (2010).

6 For a general discussion of insurance subrogation, see Tom Baker, Insurance Law and Policy 391–407 (2003).

7 This estimate reflects the roughly equal division in tort recoveries between monetary and nonmonetary losses. See Tillinghast-Towers Perrin, U.S. Tort Costs: 2002 Update 17 fig. (2002).

8 This type of strict liability rule was introduced in David Rosenberg, A Sampling-based System of Civil Liability, 15 Theoretical Inquiries L. 635, 659 (2014), and developed in Steven Shavell, On the Redesign of Accident Liability for the World of Autonomous Vehicles (2019), http://ssrn.com/abstract=3437474. The federal strict manufacturer liability rule we propose would replace state tort law to the extent it is not currently preempted from regulating medical device risks. For discussion of the regulatory deficiencies of the negligence rule and comparative advantages of strict liability, see infra, at note 23.

9 Although manufacturers and insurers might address these problems contractually, we know of no such arrangements and do not consider the contractual option here.

between product and injury, and then the decision by the Civil Division of the Department of Justice to litigate claims directly or by auctioning them to private attorneys.

We examine the mandatory reporting proposal in Section 20.2 and the manufacturer strict liability proposal and system for enforcing it in Section 20.3. Section 20.4 concludes.[10]

20.2 MANDATORY REPORTING

Currently, Congress requires only manufacturers (or importers) and device user facilities (end-users) such as hospitals to report medical device accidents. In this section, we address whether insurers should be included.

Driven by financial self-interest and informed by the constant flow of insured-patient payment requests, insurers have the unrivaled capacity to monitor the market continuously and comprehensively for incidents of product-related accidents generally, and signs of emergent danger especially. Insurers are thus uniquely equipped to serve FDA market surveillance objectives, particularly as early warning "watchdogs."

Undoubtedly insurers are motivated to voluntarily report newly detected risks to the FDA. Insurers, like other participants in the health care system, embrace the ethos of "doing no harm." Further, in accelerating FDA investigation and intervention, insurers' reporting will reduce accident risk and hence their outlays for medical and other expenses, and relatedly their costs to analyze risk data and adjust coverage and purchase decisions accordingly. Expedited FDA intervention has the further beneficial effect of preventing insurers from perversely competing for market share by delaying or otherwise manipulating coverage and price responses to newly discovered risks.

Competition gives rise to concern that insurers may lack optimal reporting incentives. Despite benefiting from accelerated FDA intervention, insurers may hesitate to report newly discovered risks in some cases. Doubtless, insurers will not think twice about reporting accidents that directly implicate readily determinable defects or risky features of a widely sold or frequently used product. In such cases, no competitive advantage is likely to accrue from delayed reporting, as other insurers probably would be experiencing similar accidents and making corresponding adjustments in coverage and purchase decisions. A different case arises when accidents are sporadic or the insurer incurs substantial expense in generating proprietary information to discover the risk, determine its nature, estimate product-wide accident incidence and costs, and based on that analysis, make risk-rated coverage and

[10] Many reform proposals call for expanding the scope of FDA surveillance and tort liability. To our knowledge, none consider the basic reforms advanced in this chapter; nor are any designed to strengthen the regulatory power of health care insurers.

purchase decisions. The prospect of competitors free riding on this investment may dull the insurer's incentive to immediately notify the FDA.

Congress can address this problem simply by subjecting insurers at minimum to equivalent investigation and reporting requirements as those presently applied to manufacturers and end-users. That mandate casts a broad discovery net for any information the reporter may have or can reasonably obtain that suggests that use of, or exposure to, a medical device caused, contributed to, or had been a factor in causing or contributing to the injury of a patient (or health care employee, or another person). The source of the risk is also defined capaciously to include product malfunction, failure, manufacturing or labeling defects, or user error. The mandate applies to major product accidents involving death or other serious injuries – defined as posing a threat to patient life, danger of permanent impairment of body function or structure, or need for medical intervention to prevent such fatality or impairment.[11]

Generally, in choosing between voluntary and mandatory reporting of adverse information, the system designer considers the relative social value of the former motivating discovery of more information for private use and the latter motivating discovery of less information for public use.[12] Regarding insurers, both factors point unambiguously in favor of mandatory insurer reporting.

The key variable affecting the quantity of reported information is whether insurers' concerns about adverse effects from public disclosure might lead them to ignore or underinvest in discovering product-related risks. Normally, such perverse incentives arise when the adverse information triggers administrative agency and tort liability sanctions. Contrary to manufacturers and end-users, insurers face no such adverse consequences from reporting product-related risks to the FDA. The only potential cost is competitor free riding, which affects manufacturers to a far greater extent. Moreover, insurers' marginal cost, if any, will likely be negated by the benefits of FDA intervention and the fact that the entire industry is subject to the mandatory disclosure rule. Regardless, insurers will hardly find wilfully reducing monitoring efforts worthwhile, as this increases the chance of paying large, unexpected accident costs and only prevents the possibility of a temporary and usually small competitive disadvantage.

Regarding the second factor, the question is whether greater regulatory benefits accrue from private party use of more discovered information than from public regulator use of less disclosed information. Greater discovery efforts under a voluntary disclosure regime might result in manufacturers detecting product-related risks that they can

[11] In requiring hospitals and other end-users to report product accidents, Congress has implicitly found no administrative difficulty applying the mandate to entities other than device manufacturers, with whom the FDA has a general regulatory relationship. Extending the reporting requirement to insurers – the gatekeepers of the medical device market who purchase the products from manufacturers and provide them to end-users – will significantly improve the efficiency and effectiveness of the agency's postmarket surveillance program.

[12] A. Mitchell Polinsky & Steven Shavell, Mandatory versus Voluntary Disclosure of Product Risks, 28 J. L. Econ. & Org. 360 (2010).

remedy, for example, by recalling the device before anyone else recognizes the problem. Yet, as Congress apparently decided in mandating manufacturer disclosure, the prospect of voluntary recall – which might well be small given the high costs exacted by competitive market forces, including bankrupting a firm with few revenue-generating products – was outweighed by the regulatory benefits from disclosure, including spillover gains in agency knowledge and experience for overseeing similar products and benefits from its independently remedying the problem with the product in question. Extending the mandate to insurers is not a close call, as there is no conflict of interest in the public and private use of product-related risk information. Quite the contrary, their complementary use of the information synergistically enhances joint regulatory benefit.

20.3 STRICT LIABILITY

This section explains the purpose and evaluates the cost-effectiveness of the proposed rule of strict liability and the system for enforcing it.

The regulatory function of civil liability, like that of the FDA and other government and nongovernment modes of controlling medical device risks, is motivating risk-controllers (manufacturers) to invest in reasonable precautions. Reasonable precautions result from manufacturers optimally adjusting two principal interrelated risk-control factors: level of care (for example, improving product design to facilitate sterilization) and level of risky activity (for example, reducing resorts to CT scans). In threatening manufacturers with paying for a patient's total product-related monetary and nonmonetary losses – to the extent measured and monetized in tort – civil liability induces the manufacturer to take reasonable precautions by adjusting the interrelated care and risky activity levels to avoid creating and marketing an unreasonably dangerous product.[13]

Because the straightforward threat of bearing total accident costs motivates manufacturers to exercise reasonable precautions, strict liability achieves this regulatory objective without entangling courts and litigants in a misbegotten fact-finding process of determining what interrelated levels of care and risky activity constitutes reasonable precautions and whether the manufacturer took such precautions in fact. Manufacturers will consider all relevant dimensions of care – from the salient matters of product design to the many less conspicuous but no less critical choices in the scope of research, including the performance of nonmedical devices; methods, types, setup, and management of safety studies; qualifications, training, and compensation of researchers and managers; extent of premarket tests and other efforts to discover the potential for latent risks; and investigation of countless

[13] In other words, strict liability motivates manufacturers to take reasonable precautions against accidents to minimize the sum of their costs of avoiding harm, bearing risk, and, in the event of accident, paying damages and litigation expenses. As such, manufacturers' pursuit of maximum profit vicariously maximizes the social value of their risk-control (regulatory) powers.

scenarios of how, when, and where the product will be used, including consideration of differences in end-user abilities and behavior. Similarly, the manufacturer will make the socially appropriate investment in moderating its risky activity level. For example, it may reduce excessive sales – exposing a sub-group of patients to a risky device for little or no offsetting gain in medical benefit – by toning down advertising and refraining from engaging in problematic promotional tactics. Beyond that, strict liability has the singular activity level-reduction benefit of compelling manufacturers to internalize expected damages and incorporate the anticipated total accident cost in their product prices. Thus, strict liability engenders a "price-signaling" effect that lowers demand, reducing unnecessary use of a risky product, and, ultimately, the incidence of injury.

Health care insurers, functioning as expert buyers with gatekeeping market power, make the medical device market ideal for the use of strict liability to regulate product risks. Strongly motivated to monitor for, and incorporate, the implicit cost of expected product-related accidents into their coverage and purchasing decisions, insurers will be highly attuned to the price signals from strict liability.[14] Far from price takers, insurers would respond to those signals with speedy and deliberate adjustments of coverage and purchase decisions, effectively reducing risky product sales, use, and hence patient injury.[15]

Strict liability and health care insurers mutually reinforce their power to regulate medical device risk. Insurers improve the regulatory coherence of strict liability pricing signals. Risk-neutral, rational, and expert insurers will be free of the risk misperception and demand elasticity problems that may distort the effects of price signals on ordinary consumers.

Regarding insurers, strict liability per se, through its price-signaling effect, closes the major gap in their accident-cost exposure for product-related injuries, in addition to saving them the cost of calculating the implicit price of accident risk. Threatening liability for total expected accident costs, strict liability leads insurers to internalize nonmonetary as well as monetary losses, and to adjust their coverage

[14] Price signals will relieve insurers of much of the burden of determining and incorporating in purchase and coverage decisions the implicit product-related accident cost. Nonetheless, the need will remain for insurers to proactively modify coverage and purchase decisions, given the inevitable delay between the emergence of a new or increased risk from general market use of a product and related changes in FDA regulatory prescriptions and manufacturer prices. Moreover, insurer coverage and price decisions will still be required to fine-tune manufacturer price signals which normally reflect a product's average risk in the relevant patient population. By tailoring a risky product's use to the medical needs of individual or subgroups of patients, these decisions augment the precision medicine effects of FDA warnings and advisories and physician prognoses and judgments.

[15] Patients switching insurance plans might vary the amount of product use and risk among insurers, but it will not diminish or otherwise distort the proposed rule's deterrent effects. The product's aggregate expected accident cost that patients incur will remain unchanged, and hence so will the manufacturer's total, strictly enforced expected liability and the resulting insurance industry-wide price-signaling effect on coverage and purchase decisions.

and purchase decisions accordingly, thereby maximizing the social benefit of their regulatory power.

However, the proposed strict liability rule is needed to fully correct structural market defects. This is because, under conventional strict liability, insurers retain subrogated reimbursement for outlays to cover monetary losses. Subrogation reimbursement substantially reduces insurers' financial incentives to maximize regulatory benefits both by offsetting their coverage exposure and by diluting strict liability's price-signaling effects for monetary losses. The proposed rule corrects this market defect, effectively eliminating subrogated reimbursements, by requiring payment of all recoveries directly and in full to the US Treasury. Ending the prospect of subrogated recoupment will spur insurers to take full account of total expected accident costs – nonmonetary and monetary – when determining the implicit risk-rated price of a device they are considering covering and purchasing.

The system we envision for enforcing the proposed rule of strict manufacturer liability should assure its reliable, measured, and socially appropriate use. Prospective claims would proceed through two stages of merits screening. First, the FDA would, in the normal course of investigating and considering its regulatory response to reported incidents of serious device-related accident, verify the nature, extent, and harmful consequences of the causal connection between product use and patient injury.[16] The manufacturer probably would be notified that the investigation is ongoing and, when needed, required to disclose relevant information and otherwise participate and cooperate fully in the investigatory process. Only positive determinations of causation and harm would send the case to the next stage. At any point in this process, the FDA can exercise its normal regulatory power to control the product risk, including order recalls, curtail marketing, and require new or amplified warnings.

The Civil Division of the Department of Justice would conduct the second stage of merits screening. Division lawyers will formulate and review the merits of the strict liability claim and appraise its expected recovery value net of litigation cost. To avoid wasting government, manufacturer, and court resources, the claim would be dropped (or converted into a fixed fine) unless its expected net recovery value exceeds some minimum threshold amount, best set by Congress. Before litigation commences, the manufacturer may present contradictory or mitigatory evidence and seek settlement.

When the case goes to court, the government could sue directly or auction the claim to private attorneys. If the claim is auctioned, the winning bidder will pay the bid amount to the US Treasury and retain any recovery from successfully litigating the case. To reduce the complications and costs of litigation, Congress could give

16 The real-time availability and quality of information from insurers will enhance the reliability of FDA causation determinations, particularly in augmenting as well as facilitating use of trend analysis. For pertinent FDA oversight authority and process see, e.g., Food, Drug, and Cosmetic Act, 21 U.S.C. § 360i-l; 21 C.F.R. § 810.1, 810.2, 810.10, 822.2, 822.3.

FDA findings of a causal connection the evidentiary force of a rebuttable presumption establishing a prima facie case of liability on the causation element and promulgate a schedule of damages that would replace ad hoc and disputed case-by-case litigation and recoveries.[17]

In sum, the combined effect of strict liability price-signals and, with the elimination of subrogation reimbursements, exposure to paying insured-patient economic losses will lead insurers to optimally risk-rate coverage and purchase decisions. This, in turn, will reinforce manufacturers' incentives to take reasonable precautions in developing, testing, and marketing medical device products. The inflow of insured-patient bills will also enable insurers to inform the FDA of product-related accidents, including those indicating emergence of increased and new risks. Based on their current and comprehensive knowledge and estimates of the therapeutic and accident experience of products on the market, insurers' coverage and purchase decisions can disaggregate the generalizations of FDA warnings and statistical models of academic researchers to supplement physician judgments in fine-tuning the fit between comparative product benefits and patients' medical needs.[18]

Two questions about the cost-effectiveness of the proposed strict liability rule and its enforcement system warrant attention: first, as with any reform proposal, whether expected social benefits exceed administrative and substantive law enforcement costs; and second, more specifically, whether the strict liability rule would better promote social welfare by paying damages as compensation to injured patients, rather than to the government.[19]

20.3.1 *Administrative Costs*

The dispositive answer to this question is that the administrative-cost footprint of our proposal is virtually nil. Enforcing the proposed strict liability rule generally entails no complicated legal and factual issues. All courts, and hence the government and manufacturers, need to know is the causal connection between the patients' product

17 Congress could adapt for use in enforcing strict manufacturer liability a version of the schedule of damages and evidentiary presumptions employed by several federal compensation programs. See Peter H. Meyers, Fixing the Flaws in the Federal Vaccine Injury Compensation Program, 63 Admin. L. Rev. 795 (2011) (comparing the cost-saving benefits of damage scheduling and evidentiary presumptions in the vaccine and other federal compensation programs).

18 The one regulatory gap that the proposed system does not completely close relates to possible insurer investments in affirmative oversight by undertaking postmarket product testing for new or increased product risks. Insurers apparently conduct such evaluations. See Blue Cross Blue Shield Association Works with FDA And Manufacturers To Accelerate Patient Access To New Medical Devices (2016), https://www.bcbs.com/news/press-releases/blue-cross-blue-shield-association-works-fda-and-manufacturers-accelerate; see also Eisenberg & Price, supra note 3(proposing that insurers evaluate device efficacy based on their extensive holdings of claims and other data on product performance). However, given the lack of nonmonetary loss coverage, insurers might not have sufficient financial incentive to invest optimally in product testing.

19 Space limitations prevent comparative assessment of such alternatives as enhancing FDA premarket oversight.

use or exposure and the resulting accident losses. These are straightforward matters in most cases.

This no-cost assessment holds even though our proposal extends civil liability to medical devices that Supreme Court preemption rulings currently shield from state tort law, and could give rise to disputes over causation and nonmonetary loss in some cases.[20] The reason is that the litigation of all strict liability claims hinges on FDA findings of causation, and the FDA (with manufacturers typically participating) will continue to investigate and determine that question exactly as it currently does in carrying out its regulatory function in every case of serious product-related injury for all classes of device.

Disputes will be especially likely to settle quickly and inexpensively in the proposed system. Expecting FDA causation findings to strongly influence the outcome of adjudicated claims and leery of chancing juries awarding high nonmonetary damages, manufacturers will almost surely forgo follow-on litigation in favor of settlement. Moreover, because strict liability damages will be levied and distributed solely for deterrence purposes, and therefore can be assessed on average rather than for individual patients, courts could readily employ collectivized modes of adjudication, such as class actions and sampling, to resolve any causation and nonmonetary loss disputes.[21] Congress could further reduce administrative costs, as noted above, by giving FDA causation findings the force of a rebuttable presumption establishing a prima facie case for strict liability and promulgating a schedule of damages.

Some might think, mistakenly, that strict liability damages will inflate manufacturers' costs of doing business and inhibit their investment in device innovation. The proposed rule merely shifts the burden of bearing accident costs from patients to manufacturers, who would otherwise have borne them but for the defective medical device market. Indeed, manufacturers could never successfully dump such accident costs on well-informed patients purchasing medical devices in a well-functioning market. In correcting the defective medical device market, the proposed strict liability rule thus revokes a subsidy that perversely increases manufacturers' profit margin at the expense of patients' safety.[22]

20 Our proposal avoids problems that led Congress to preempt state tort law claims. By holding manufacturers liable for product-related accident costs on FDA-determined causation grounds alone, the proposed strict liability rule does not implicate or conflict with any FDA findings of safety and efficacy, however specific their nature. Whether Congress should grant federal and state courts concurrent jurisdiction to enforce the rule is a matter beyond the scope of this chapter.

21 See Rosenberg, supra note 8.

22 Even if subsidy were needed to promote innovation, relieving manufacturers of efficient regulatory controls and thereby putting patients at greater unreasonable risk of serious personal injury is a socially dubious means to the end. Many cost-effective options exist for subsidizing innovation without jeopardizing the lives and health of patients, for example encouraging breakthrough discoveries with special patent protections, tax credits, research grants, priority and expedited FDA review, and prizes.

20.3.2 *Substantive Costs*

It would also be a mistake to think the negligence rule is more cost-effective than strict liability. The negligence rule suffers from long-recognized and well-documented fundamental regulatory failings.[23] In requiring courts to determine whether a defendant manufacturer exercised reasonable precautions, the negligence rule entails an enormously expensive regulatory inquiry, one that is inevitably misguided and socially wasteful. Primarily, high-cost barriers prevent courts from obtaining and analyzing evidence of critical relevance regarding multiple dimensions of care and risky activity. Deprived of this evidence, courts cannot reliably make the complicated factual findings on which the basic questions of negligence liability must turn: first, establishing the optimal, interrelated adjustment of levels of care and risky activity that defines the standard of reasonable precautions governing the case; and second, determining whether the manufacturer's actual precautions satisfied the standard. Consequently, enforcement of the negligence rule systematically fails to confront manufacturers with sufficient sanctions – that is, with a threat of liability for damages equaling total accident costs – and hence fails to create optimal legal incentives for them to take all reasonable safety precautions in developing, testing, and marketing their products.[24]

Compared to the negligence rule, strict liability produces superior regulatory results because courts can enforce it without undertaking the costly task of establishing and applying a standard of reasonable precautions and making the resultant complicated factual findings. As Holmes observed in explaining the policy supporting use of strict liability rather than negligence, "as there is a limit to the nicety of inquiry which is possible in a trial, it may be considered that the safest way to secure care is to throw the risk upon the person who decides what precautions shall be taken."[25] The same advantage of strict liability applies with added force to avoiding even greater cost barriers to determining the far more complex questions regarding the reasonable level of risky activity, and ultimately, the reasonable combination of care and risky activity levels.[26]

Many think the negligence rule has a possible litigation-cost advantage because only claims evincing both negligence and causation will be filed compared to strict liability allowing suit on causation alone. The plausibility of this conjecture, however, is undermined because it never accounts for the costs of plaintiff-lawyers necessarily investigating the entire pool of plaintiff device-caused injuries to

[23] The following comparative evaluation of strict liability versus negligence is drawn from Steven Shavell, Economic Analysis of Accident Law (1987).

[24] The significant chance courts will erroneously determine the optimal levels of care and risky activity can also create excessive deterrent effects.

[25] O.W. Holmes, The Common Law 117 (1881).

[26] Holmes also intuited strict liability's use in moderating (including through price-signaling) the level of risky activity. See David Rosenberg, The Hidden Holmes: His Theory of Torts in History 139–40 (1995).

determine which among them involve sufficient evidence of negligence, while the proposed strict liability rule entails no such need and cost. It also fails to account for strict liability's superior deterrent effects that reduce the number of injuries and hence resulting claims. Even assuming some marginal filing-cost advantage of the negligence rule, it is doubtful that the savings would come close to negating the rule's disadvantages of great trial and settlement expense, and, most importantly, of regulatory deficiencies and resulting unpoliced device risk.[27]

20.3.3 *Compensation for Injured Patients*

Regarding payment of damages to injured patients rather than the government, the question, essentially, is whether patients would be better off under the conventional tort system of compensation than the proposed strict liability rule. The short answer is that under the conventional tort system the costs of the increased risk of harm far exceed the benefits of possible compensation. This would be so even if the tort system employed strict liability. Paying damages to patients would preserve subrogation reimbursement, shielding insurers from bearing total accident costs and resulting in their insureds incurring otherwise avoidable unreasonable risk of product-related accident, as well as higher insurance premiums to cover it.

Moreover, patients who suffer medical device injuries are already insured for their medical and other monetary losses from product-related injuries. Even if some patients need supplemental coverage, they surely would not willingly, let alone rationally, turn to tort liability to supply it. "Tort insurance" imposes exorbitant overhead costs – far greater than the cost for comparable coverage from public or private insurers – amounting to a dollar or more charge on every dollar recovered (before subrogation deduction).[28] Nor would risk-averse individuals, in need of insurance, willingly pay for taking the wildly variable chance of winning a lawsuit to cover pressing medical needs (for example, ICU stays for COVID-19 patients), with recovery depending not only on the fact of medical and other monetary loss (which alone suffices for true insurance) but also predominantly on the lucky alignment of such unlikely litigation contingencies as tortiously (as opposed to non-tortiously) caused injury, solvent tortfeasor, and net expected damages high enough for a competent plaintiff-lawyer to profit from taking the case.[29] Any suggestion that

[27] And, by paying damages to the government, the proposed rule also avoids the moral hazard problems of conventional strict liability rules that necessitate use of a highly expensive and factually complicated contributory negligence defense, which can diminish the strict rule's litigation cost and regulatory advantages over the negligence rule.

[28] See Polinsky & Shavell, supra note 5, at 1470.

[29] We emphasize "willingly pay" because, contrary to the conventional portrayal of the purported supplemental insurance value of product-related civil liability damages as free for, and freely chosen by, injured parties, it is neither. Insured patients (like all product consumers) pay a civil liability "premium" in the purchase price of the device (or other product) equal to the manufacturers' expected liability and litigation cost in the event of accident and suit – plus, implicitly, the price

patients might willingly buy tort insurance coverage of nonmonetary loss is refuted by evidence showing that despite the annual expenditure of trillions on premiums and taxes worldwide for public and private insurance, no insurer provides such coverage. The reason is simple: no one is willing to pay for it.[30] On top of all of that, tort liability imposes a grossly regressive "premium" tax for coverage of risk in the price of standardized products such as medical devices. While all patients (and other consumers) pay the same premium charge in the product price, tort recoveries greatly vary according to plaintiffs' relative wealth. This alone is sufficient to justify characterizing "tort insurance" "insurance fraud."

20.4 CONCLUSION

In closing, we note several possible refinements of the proposed system for correcting the market to further strengthen insurers' regulatory power. First, to increase operating efficiency, the system might make use of non-judicial administrative tariffs rather than judicially enforced strict manufacturer liability damage awards. Earmarking recoveries (or tariff levies) for deposit in Social Security rather than the Treasury might provide true insurance value without compromising the objective of eliminating subrogation and exposing insurers to the total monetary costs of product accidents. Finally, the proposed system could well be employed for all FDA-approved medical goods, pharmaceuticals as well as devices.

for their own expected legal fees and expenses. And "willingly pay," they do not. Product liability cannot be waived by contract, even for an appropriate reduction in product price.

30 See Polinsky & Shavell, supra note 5.